ANTIDIETS OF THE AVANT-GARDE

Antidiets of the Avant-Garde

FROM FUTURIST COOKING TO EAT ART

Cecilia Novero

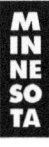 University of Minnesota Press
Minneapolis
London

An earlier version of chapter 2 was published as "Dada-Diets: Dysfunctional Physiologies of Devouring," *Seminar* 37, no. 1 (2001): 1–20; reprinted with permission of *Seminar: A Journal of Germanic Studies*.

Published by the University of Minnesota Press
111 Third Avenue South, Suite 290
Minneapolis, MN 55401-2520
http://www.upress.umn.edu

Library of Congress Cataloging-in-Publication Data
Novero, Cecilia.
    Antidiets of the avant-garde : from Futurist cooking to Eat Art / Cecilia Novero.
    p. cm.
Includes bibliographical references and index.
ISBN 978-0-8166-4601-2 (pbk.: alk. paper)—ISBN 978-0-8166-4600-5 (hc: alk. paper)
1. Food in art. 2. Arts, European—20th century. 3. Avant-garde (Aesthetics)—
Europe—History—20th century. I. Title.
    NX650.F64N69 2010
    704.9'496413—dc22
    2009050755

Printed in the United States of America on acid-free paper

The University of Minnesota is an equal-opportunity educator and employer.

17 16 15 14 13 12 11 10   10 9 8 7 6 5 4 3 2 1

CONTENTS

INTRODUCTION

Encounters of the Culinary and the Avant-Garde

Genealogy

This book arose initially out of a stupor provoked by Franz Kafka's enigmatic intricacy of unsuspecting metamorphoses and disturbing visions. Three of his short stories spurred my thinking about the connections or, as I would like to call them, *interferences* between the two fields investigated here: avant-garde studies and the culinary field.[1] The genealogy of this book does not underscore continuity and chronology — a causal series of connections — between the art considered and gastronomic discourse. Nor does it follow an itinerary beginning with immediately identifiable questions and ending with clear unequivocal answers. The following remarks suggest instead a number of constellated ideas that offer the reader some likely points of access to the heterogeneous avant-garde works studied here. The dispersed style of presentation should suggest that this book's themes could not be usefully separated into discrete, compartmentalized segments. Their very braiding and unbraiding at various points in time and in the arts is one of the book's concerns.

Similarly, the book does not aim to describe the evolution of such concepts as diets (or antidiets), incorporation, in/digestion, in/edibility from the avant-garde of the mid-twentieth century to the early 1980s and even today. Nor does it aim to write an alternative history of gastronomy from the perspective of either its avant-gardes or the artistic avant-garde or to show the development of these concepts as they manifest themselves in the avant-garde or in gastrosophy and gastronomy. Rather, I inquire into the antidiets and incorporation to uncover a network of complex temporalities informing both the classical avant-garde and the neo-avant-garde. This inquiry reveals temporal dynamics that counter the stigmatizing of the neo-avant-garde as a mere "failed" repetition of the avant-garde. Through this very analysis of temporality, in fact, the divisions and distinctions between the avant-garde and the neo-avant-garde are also questioned. Why should one consider the convergences or divergences of culinary discourse with avant-garde artistic production in the first place? What does a gastrosophical approach to the avant-garde tell us that we don't already know about the avant-garde, its historical relevance in the early twentieth century, and its return in the neo-avant-garde practices of the 1960s and 1970s? Is an alimentary perspective a productive constellation for rethinking the avant-garde, and if so, how and why?

In what follows I first attend to the "accident" rather than origin that spurred my thinking and generated the field of "avant-garde antidiets." Kafka's stories obliquely indicate some of those configurations — taken broadly to mean a set of practices of thinking as much as of writing and living — between art and food that I examine at length through works other than Kafka's own. I then delineate, in broad strokes, the emergence of the culinary field and that of the "gastro-avant-garde" field. The notion of the culinary field helps explain how textuality and writing have had an impact on both its normative and subversive qualities and also how precisely the different genres and areas of expansion of the culinary have effected differences in the normativity and literariness of the field in the cultures studied in the book, the German-speaking countries, France, and Italy. This introduction does not dwell on the constitutive differences among these countries' culinary discourses. I instead provide the reader — in a separate third section — with some art historical background for understanding how the avant-garde and the culinary field stand in a particular relation to each other and at what cultural–historical juncture that relation occurs. Accordingly, this third section devoted to the avant-garde introduces the theoretical issues at stake in the book. Analyses of works at the margins of those examined in the book are intended to prepare the reader for the subsequent chapters. The final section on the limitations of this book concludes the introduction.

Reading Kafka, Thinking Food, and Avant-Garde: A Starter

The initial impetus for *Antidiets of the Avant-Garde* came from Kafka's stories "Investigations of a Dog," "A Report to an Academy," and "A Hunger Artist."[2] In each, drinking and eating, but especially *thinking about eating,* even as abstaining from taking food, unfold as engines of writing before engaging more specifically the relations between art and knowledge and between producers and consumers of art. In "Investigations of a Dog," the thinking process manifests itself as a constant noise, the rumbling of knowledge that music instigates and that then also accompanies it in the text. Thinking becomes the other of music, an "other" that produces the text we are reading. The text itself spins and whirls with no simple beginning or end, without any apparent direction. The dog's nutritional — essential — questions remain unanswered, and the "Good Food" is not found. The dog's investigations are an example of a textual practice — writing — that reveals itself as a desiring force. The story does not address the mystery of food as an ontological problem. Kafka's story is not about food. It takes instead "thinking food" as the inescapable desiring energy that propels writing and artistic production.[3]

This textual, nonrepresentational relation between thinking food and writing — or artistic production more broadly — led me to identify a *performative* quality in food and eating as they manifest themselves in avant-garde manifestos, magazines, declarations, instructions, and so forth, as well as, surprisingly, in actual cookbooks (e.g., *The Futurist Cookbook*). This is a crucial point in the analyses of Dada in chapter 2. *Performative* here means an active rhetorical strategy that displaces food from its regular uses and turns it into words (e.g., names, insults), thereby destabilizing both the usual practical grammars of food and the grammars of language. Perhaps most significantly, the performativity of thinking food in a text or artwork both invokes and breaks with mimesis. It invokes a mimetic gesture toward food and eating as if they pertained to a separate realm of life, that is, of cultural practice and history. Yet this mimesis (often in the mode of mockery) destabilizes those very cultural realms, the sites of "life" that as the texts indicate are less the origin of the texts themselves than the effect of collective and cultural desires. Incorporation as an act of subject–object interaction and mutual metamorphosis (thus as constant production and operation) replaces "food" as theme or "thought" or object in the avant-garde. (I use "incorporation" interchangeably with "devouring," both of which are to be distinguished from assimilation.) The avant-garde texts themselves intervene in the production of the active desire of thinking food as a site where desire proliferates and changes.

For example, the mimetic impulse one may identify in Dada does not presuppose a representation of established patterns of capitalist consumption that the texts would allegedly imitate simply to then reject. Rather, the Dada antidiets through a *performative* textual repetition of apparently nonsensical forms of consumption, based in disgust and indigestibility, a repetition that is always excessive, *construct* bourgeois taste and its reproducibility as indigestible and insufferable. The Dada antidiets propose the indigestibility of representation itself. Thus in this book I do not claim, and in fact deny, any representational ambition on the part of the avant-garde. In taking the subject of food and eating as a "culinary field," I mean to highlight the discursive and textual basis of any interference between the avant-garde and the culinary. I call the interactions between the fields *interferences* because the avant-garde texts studied here enact practices of estrangement and deconstruction of the culinary, especially its gastrosophical–textual component. The deconstruction of gastrosophy/gastronomy in the avant-garde permits the "desiring" aspect in gastronomic texts to resurface from the normativity also typical of this discourse while aiding the artists and critics of the avant-garde to devour (literally in some instances) practices of normativizing art. A decomposed gastronomy interferes with the counteraesthetic discourse of the avant-garde, not to elevate gastronomy to the ranks of art but to dismantle the aesthetic premises of autonomous art and autonomous subjects in bourgeois capitalist society. The avant-garde and the neo-avant-garde contribute to the domain of the culinary insofar as this is one of the neo-avant-garde's internal counterdiscourses, one that functions as a centrifugal force field, like writing and thinking food operate in "Investigations of a Dog."

Kafka's stories were thus suggestive as I decided what issues, works, and artists to examine, namely, those in which thinking food, as a performative act, was central to conceptions and reconceptualizations of art and aesthetics. For example, "A Report to an Academy" raises the problem about the costs of edibility: What is the boundary between the human and the animal, between he or she who eats and that which is eaten? Whenever the operation of incorporation appears in avant-garde texts and performances, the issues of boundaries and otherness emerge. This is true especially in those avant-garde texts and performances that engage art producers and consumers — for example, Dada and the neo-avant-garde — as well as writing and reading as acts that demand an expanded bodily attention, beyond the more selective and perspectival sense of sight. The encounter with an unpresentable and unrepresentable otherness is the index of avant-garde acts of incorporation. The chance encounters with unexpected food described by the cultural critic Walter Benjamin, for example, bear similarities with the terrifying experience of awe — the sublime — that, for Benjamin, also returns in the tactile contact with the animal, a contact that again opens up an unstable and open threshold where transformation and fluctuation between beings and things bear the force of transformative thinking. Disgust and horror, as they relate to the body that interiorizes the abysses of fear and infinity, bring to the fore the question of the sublime in the avant-garde.

The main reason for including Benjamin in this book (in chapter 3) is his texts on food, which, like his theses on history, help break the artificial continuity of historical narration — and, in turn, the artificial continuity of the history of art and literature. To adumbrate the argument: Benjamin's stories present themselves as experiences of incorporation. For him, incorporation produces the threshold at which the now-time of history "takes place." As I show in detail in chapter 3, he conceives of the act of incorporation as a powerful and destructive reception — an opening — occurring in and through the body. Incorporation is an everyday act of disruption, of rupture, that can potentially expand the human sensorium and may even prepare the body for the work required by modern art and technology. Benjamin's "experiences" with food involve an intoxication that stems from profane illumination or, in other words, from the body's operations of metamorphosis. This metamorphosis ultimately may occur through an everyday act of eating rather than only, say, by ingesting drugs.[4] The way Benjamin relies on and uses psychoanalysis (Sigmund Freud) and surrealism in his reading of Charles Baudelaire's allegorical poems illustrates Benjamin's notion of incorporation, which — as I show — contributes to his broader views on criticism/reading.

Benjamin's theory of incorporation links up with his view of Dada montages and surrealist dream allegories.[5] He interprets some avant-garde work, from Paul Klee to Karl Kraus, from Dada to Adolf Loos and Kafka, as an act of destructive devouring. In his own writings on food, he does not advocate the idea of knowledge as assimilation. That is, he does not aim at transforming the object "eaten" into the identity of the self. Instead, he uses the concept of incorporation to mean a confrontation with otherness at a threshold of fear and surprise. The incorporation of something by a subject — whether that subject is a reader, a child, or a writer — produces avant-garde art inasmuch as avant-garde art is an act of incorporation. Both are acts of becoming other, and both generate "dialectical images" that, for Benjamin, wrest "tradition" from convention, the experience of time from historical time, and the artwork from art history.[6]

What matters most in Benjamin's food stories is that incorporation functions according to a disjunctive temporality that allows experience to occur. Experience (*Erfahrung*) is associated with traveling a distance, but experience also merges with remembering (*Erinnerung* [i.e., interiorization] but also *Eingedenken*). Incorporation as in *Einverleibung* (often translated as "absorption") conjoins distance and interiorization — that is, it corresponds to interiorizing a distance that is traveled, dialectically, between inside and outside, both within and without the subject.[7] The temporality in question lies in relays, sudden bursts of involuntary memory, a reversible and yet never redeemable temporality present in the individual and the collective. Food offers a shared discursive landscape that opens up at the crossroads of smelling, tasting, biting, and devouring, all of them acts that liberate remembering from structured memory. The inchoate, not-yet-worked-through experience of incorporation — one that forgets the mind in the body and resurfaces in the mind a posteriori as an effect of bodily acts (of metamorphosis) — becomes collective, "meaningful" experience when absorption transforms an intimate, disorienting subjective moment into everyday acts, decisions, thinking processes as moments of awakening. These everyday acts still bear the traces of and speak the language of dreams, as Benjamin writes in "Breakfast Room" ("Frühstück"), a short piece wherein the act of eating breakfast becomes the most radical translation of the dream work into the language of the awakened body.[8]

In addition, Benjamin's performative texts — which break into succinct allegories the history of Western culture, from the Bible via Homer to Marcel Proust — produce "unwritten" scripts for neo-avant-garde performances. The disruptive component of Benjamin's theory of incorporation identifies him as both a practitioner of the avant-garde and a forerunner of the neo-avant-garde. His texts bridge, I suggest, the avant-garde's historically oriented metaphoric and rhetorical use of food with the neo-avant-garde's more directly practical form of intervention in life praxis through Eat Art. Benjamin's theory of incorporation, with its understanding of transience and presence (now-time), provides the scripts, as it were, for the temporality of art in the sixties and seventies.

The most important of the three Kafka stories discussed here, "A Hunger Artist," presents an artist whose very art — profession — is self-starvation. The artist's art is to stage his or her own disappearance. In other words, the spectacle lies in this art's and the artist's self-erasure; its duration coincides with the vanishing of both art and artist from the public's sight; this art thereby negates entertainment. Not unlike Kafka's hunger artist, the Fluxus artist Ben Vautier shut himself up in a box and refused to eat for twenty-four hours. At the same time, this box was for all to see as a sign of absence, more specifically of art *as* absence (of the artist, of food, etc.). Note the role of writing here as well: a sign over the box states that Ben (Vautier is known by his first name) is in the box abstaining from food. Ben staged his happening as the dialectical other — at least at a first glance — of the Eat Art multiples on display and the banquets taking place in the neo-avant-garde artist Daniel Spoerri's Eat Art Gallery. In chapter 4 I deal at length with Spoerri and Eat Art — which was officially born when he started his restaurant in Düsseldorf in 1968 and opened the Gallery in the same building in 1970. Chapter 5 examines Ben's performance among many other food events and objects.

The hunger artist rejects food and does not eat; the Eat artist makes art that demands to be eaten and thereby to be actively subtracted from view in a participatory gesture that extends to the consumer: the consumer physically devours the art that he or she would otherwise look at and appreciate from a distance. Art now works from the inside out. Art is inside him or her and undergoes the metamorphosis that the consumer's metabolism allows while forcing the stomach — not just his or her eyes — to work. This food art leaves a bodily trace. At the same time it also hovers in the fleeting and changing memory of a taste or distaste, as a fragment of a past experience with a halo of duration, which may indeed resurface, uncannily and at random, beyond the institutional boundaries of any exhibition.

Kafka's hunger artist prefigures how important the dialectics between visibility and invisibility are in the neo-avant-garde of the sixties and seventies, especially Eat Art's insistence on food or eating performances that offered to the viewer/consumer the opportunity to engage an art of time that in time would leave behind only a trace of itself. Food art is "art in passing" and nonidentical art, also an art of condensed times, as Spoerri's trap-paintings and banquets show. "Hunger Artist," as well as "A Report to an Academy" and "Investigations of a Dog," seemed to link up any investigation of food in art with a temporal aspect. "Hunger Artist" focused my attention on actual "food artists" and thinking food in those texts and practices at the farthest remove from the representational art and literature on food.

One major suggestion of this book is that the antidiets, not just Spoerri's but also those of Futurism, Dada, and Benjamin, transformed some of the gastronomic principles of pleasure, taste, assimilation, and digestibility — as well as of history — and mobilized those principles to redefine art and the subject. The antidiets transformed these conceptual sites after these principles had become assimilated through bourgeois aesthetic discourse, through an increasingly disseminated mass culture, as well as through scientific and psychological notions of perception and attention.[9] The first chapter, like the last, is devoted to the more direct employment of food in art, namely, to the manifesto of Futurist cooking (1930), the *Futurist Cookbook,* and the Futurist restaurant the Holy Palate (both 1931). In contrast, in chapter 2 on Dada (particularly the Dadaist artists in Zurich) and chapter 3 on Benjamin's short texts on eating, the reader finds a rhetorical — and performative — use of incorporation. Throughout the book, I offer close readings of the texts and the art in question under the general rubric of the temporality that the particular concepts of incorporation and indigestion invite — a temporality that surfaces specifically from the unpleasant diets one encounters in these texts and in this art. In chapter 1 I pose one central question: How does the attention the Futurists devoted to food in the thirties help us reconceive this movement's chronology to which are attached notions of innovation and reaction?

It was late in their movement that the Futurists took up the subject of food. First, they needed to put to the test their own aesthetic agenda as a national and, more important, international avant-gardism. They needed to test whether their revolution in aesthetics could include a revolution of the stomach and the mouth. If Futurism had revolutionized "taste," why was the Italian national diet (pasta) still going strong? That Italians continued to consume pasta provided the Futurists with the goal of returning, now as a second-wave avant-garde, to rupture the ultimate boundaries of taste through a radical

Futurist cuisine. The Futurists applied to cooking the techniques of composition they had already used to compose their new art, music, theater, and poems at the beginning of the century. Through food they also reconsidered their own tradition of avant-gardism.

The second reason for the belatedness of food in the Futurists' work involves the intricate relation they developed with the fascist colonial state. The *Futurist Cookbook* was intended to actively shape the modern human being in accordance with modern (Futurist) lifestyles. The modern Italian state, however, for the Futurists as for the fascists, had come into being after the end of World War I, and more precisely with Benito Mussolini's antidemocratic takeover in 1922. The Futurists' version of nationalism, which was closer to the anarchic impulse present in the early phase of fascism, did not entirely square with the institutionalized politics of the fascist state. In their eyes, Italian culture had not changed under fascism, and therefore the project of modernity was still incomplete. With new diets in hand, the Futurists undertook as their "mission" to modernize Italian culture. While they developed ideological diets that were militaristic, chauvinistic, and racist, their program was also ironic and critical of the fascist bourgeoisie. The antipractical features of the culinary revolution, underscored by the Futurists themselves in the *Futurist Cookbook,* are self-reflexively ironic when it comes to the avant-garde's own agenda, its own myth about the revolutionary breadth and novelty of their art. Neo-avant-garde artists later appropriated this self-irony for their Eat Art, but they also had to work through, and leave behind, the missionizing colonial legacy — the territorializing impulse — inherent in Futurist cooking.

In sum, and to conclude this genealogy and adumbration, the culinary as incorporation is present in both the avant-garde and neo-avant-garde, and becomes the site for this art's internal investigations and experimentation with its own temporal project — its being in time and its construction of temporal imaginations that escape the historicist framework within which history continued to be conceived after 1945. Contrary to common wisdom, neo-avant-garde production from the sixties through the eighties did not appropriate the quest for *the new,* which was characteristic of the classical avant-garde. Instead, neo-avant-garde's Eat Art (for example) affirms itself as a *return* of the avant-garde — but also as a "turning" of it upside down. And so attention to food in avant-garde aesthetics underscores the salience of temporality, in the form of national history, memory, tradition, and change.

Tidbits of Gastrosophy

The Culinary Field

While incorporation and antidiets are the overarching concepts of Futurism and Eat Art, the culinary is the larger field in which incorporation is situated. Throughout I presuppose the crossing of the avant-garde and the culinary field, in which gastronomic texts played a crucial role since at least the nineteenth century. Thus far I have used the term *culinary field* without defining it. I borrow this terminology from Priscilla Parkhurst Ferguson's work on French food. In *Accounting for Taste,* she first differentiates between and then interconnects the areas that shape the culinary field into a full-fledged discourse, with its dynamics of power-knowledge and normative impulses of pleasure-control as well as its dimension of keeping at bay the psychic and social anguish linked to orality.[10] She writes:

> Comprehending producer and consumer, cook and diner, *cuisine* refers to the properly cultural construct that systematizes the culinary practices and transmutes the spontaneous culinary gesture into a stable cultural code. . . . As cooking makes food fit to eat, so cuisine, with its formal and symbolic ordering of culinary practices, turns that act of nourishment into an object fit for intellectual consumption and aesthetic appreciation. . . . this conception of culinarity continues to counter the ephemeral nature of food and to dominate the transitory culinary *gesture*.[11]

Here cuisine is shown to be more than a culinary code. It is a "panoply of narratives that sustain praxis" (*Accounting for Taste,* 8). Words sustain cuisine and allow it to exist in the present and reproduce in the future, to produce itself as history, not only as tradition but also as innovation. A culinary field emerges, then, when the *place* of cooking and consuming food is transformed into a space or when geography and agriculture metamorphose into cultural space, beyond the fixity of space, and circulate.

This circulation in writing — of published materials — allows cuisine to speak multiple languages, to move across fields as well as nations.

Because of its entwinement with the printed word, the culinary field, which spans disciplines as varied as economics and sociology, history and anthropology, the humanities and the sciences, could arise only in conjunction with the emergence of a public sphere. To put it simply, in Europe, one has become used to regarding eating as meaningful act and signifying practice since the French Revolution, when the bourgeois public sphere established itself, as did the "public" museum. At this juncture the popularity of public restaurants skyrocketed, and they soon replaced the inns, taverns, and street vendors that catered mostly to itinerant people and travelers.

Gastronomy: Pleasure and Normativity

Obviously, the world of cooking and eating — the alimentary world — has always been culturally important. Its role is acknowledged especially in ancient and premodern texts (in the work of Marcel Detienne and Jean-Paul Vernant, for example, and of Mikhail Bakhtin and Michel Jeanneret). Ancient recipe books and essays of dietetics as well as works of art (literature, theater, and music) all testify to the prominent symbolic and, indeed, cosmological function of food.[12] Food rituals also shaped living spaces in antiquity. In the homes of ancient Romans there was reserved the *xenion,* a place for food to be offered to guests. Both hospitality and the display of power were at work in such offerings. Royalty in later years celebrated their power with banquets, but the commoners, too, enjoyed their rare moments of plenitude through carnivalesque feasts in which town criers roamed the streets, announcing the quantities of animals slaughtered and the foodstuffs consumed.[13] One reason for the announcements was to turn the Christmas celebrations into a propitiatory sign. The criers' messages bound a fleeting moment of plenty to the hope for a prosperous and bountiful future (Montanari, 121).

The process of assimilation itself has functioned, since the Greeks, as a metaphor of knowledge, and eating has often marked a communion with the gods (see Detienne and Vernant). In Christianity the Eucharist is a moment of mystical union with the body of Christ, and for the Catholic and Orthodox as well as some Protestant churches the bread is literally Christ's body, so that the taking of Communion involves the literal eating of his flesh. Eating and food have hence constituted us not only physiologically but also culturally. Their signifying functions span the past, the present, and our future. That practices of food touch our everyday lives is nothing new. What is typically modern, however, is the expansion of the culinary discourse, the proliferation of the culinary as texts. The birth of the culinary field in the eighteenth century, during which gastronomic texts were important in relation to practices of eating, and then the consolidation of the field in the nineteenth century trained a spotlight on the subject of food. Gradually, with the expansion of this field, which already at the outset presented itself as spanning disciplines and areas of interests, food came to be the heterogeneous yet "focused" cultural product — the "discourse" — that Parkhurst Ferguson describes.

Gastrosophical writing was focused on the body that eats and also on the social aspects of the culinary world: on how communities of diners form and function, and on the construction of grammars for simple, less ostentatious cooking and for table manners.[14] The gastrosophical/gastronomical texts proposed norms and laws fit for the new hegemonic class, the bourgeoisie. For their normative aspirations, which also included the desire to integrate cuisine into the realms of the "high" arts, the texts sought inspiration in other established fields — in jurisprudence and philosophy, in economics and politics, in the world of *technē* and craft as well as of sublime art. Thus, for example, the German gastrosopher Karl Friedrich von Rumohr in *Geist der Kochkunst* (*Spirit of the Cooking Art*, 1822) invokes Montesquieu's *Esprit des lois* and the aesthetic culture of classicism. Rumohr was an art critic, in particular a scholar of Italian art, and occasionally a writer of fiction. Jean Anthelme Brillat-Savarin, the French author of *Physiologie du goût* (*The Physiology of Taste*, 1825), was, in Roland Barthes's words, "a polymorphous subject: jurist, diplomat, musician, man of fashion."[15]

Notwithstanding their normative aspects, which they share in a less-pronounced way with the recipe books and nutritional texts that have marked especially the German and Italian culinary field, the texts of the (French) gastrosophers display a "playful," *writerly* (Barthes) tone. The gastronomic genre, more markedly in France, is a way not only to control but also to produce new bodies. By bringing up the issue of pleasure and of bodily sensations in general, Alexandre Balthazar Laurent Grimod de la Reynière in *Almanach des gourmands* (1803–12), Brillat-Savarin in *Physiology of Taste,* and Antonin Carême in *L'art de la cuisine française au XIXe siècle* (1832) did indeed rework, even if unwittingly and against the texts' intentions, precisely those other stable discourses, such as jurisprudence, philosophy, politics, and the aesthetics they leaned on. The gastrosophers call for moderating desire, for measure, for balance. Pleasures — and taste — derive from control and exercise, the authors tell us. Thereby they aim to hold desire in check. Yet the writing of pleasure and the pleasure of storytelling that emerge so noticeably from the anecdotal and narrative style of these texts (particularly from Brillat-Savarin's "transcendental meditations," as the book is subtitled) build a stage on which desire plays a central role, both as the specific sixth sense described by Brillat-Savarin and as informing to some extent all human pleasures. For example, Brillat-Savarin envisages taste as a synergetic/synesthetic sense that keeps the body in touch with itself and the external world, facilitating such contact by rendering it pleasurable: "Taste is the sense which puts us in contact with savorous or sapid bodies, by means of the sensation which they cause in the organ destined to appreciate them."[16] Taste also creates a bodily memory, as it were, that can heal the losses of both body and soul: "It invites us, by arousing our pleasure, to repair the constant losses which we suffer through our physical existence" (*Physiology of Taste*, 35). In this context, appetite guarantees that the body finds restoration for its losses and sets in motion the soul as much as the body. Brillat-Savarin's text in particular, then, while it elucidates the principles of gastronomy and examines the social gourmandise of the age, thus fixing the readers' attention on the social settings of food (*Accounting for Taste*, 31–33), finally celebrates food as much as writing and both as universal operators of discourse (*Rustle of Language*, 269). In conclusion, an excessive remainder always appears to escape the normative drive of gastronomy.

The Temporality of Gastronomic Nations versus the Temporalities of the Avant-Garde

In the nineteenth century, the links between writing (publishing) and gastronomy had much to do with the need to redefine national identity — not only in France after the Revolution but also in other European polities that were taking the path to becoming nation-states. Gastronomic texts reflect attempts to define and stabilize culture. There is a need to fix and capture, to render available to this new hegemonic class its own fleeting daily practices, to perform bourgeois eating through the printed word over and over again, to make it homogeneous and universal. As Benedict Anderson might have it, the printed word here allows localisms and regionalisms to transmogrify into the French or German or Italian national community of bourgeois diners.

The European avant-garde also cuts across these national spaces, and in a dialogic manner, both bolstering and undermining the nationalist project. Through their antidiets, these artists engage the formation of national self-consciousness. The Futurists desperately tried to shape a modern Italian lifestyle against the widespread foreign and local perception of Italy as land of history and tradition. In contrast, the Dada artists, Benjamin, and the Eat artists of the neo-avant-garde constructed eating as willfully perverse and a subversive devouring of stable national and artistic identities and histories.

With regard to temporality, the philosophy of history that read the history of nations in terms of the progression of culture, Spirit, and national cuisine also produced anxiety about constant innovation and progress, anxiety evident in modern culinary discourse. Take, for example, Carême (1783–1833), the so-called founder of French cuisine, which he conceived as new and modern, supposedly in marked contrast to the *ancienne* cuisine of the seventeenth and eighteenth centuries. Carême's insistence on the novelty of his own culinary methods proves that gastronomy may be blind to its own philosophy and practice of history. Carême "seems to ignore the fact that many of his reforms are part of a more general historic movement. Because he has no real sense of history, he essentially sees all the cooking that preceded his own time as one confusing *ancienne cuisine* — a sort of dark age out of which his cooking emerges."[17] The assumption of a singular, indistinct, and barbaric past against which modern cuisine claims itself, and modernity more generally, as new *seemed* to be shared by the artistic avant-garde.

This book argues, by contrast, that the modern temporality informing gastronomy is displaced onto the field of avant-garde practice and that it is precisely this displacement that, counterintuitively, functions to halt and arrest, or at least suspend and complicate, the historicist element lingering in the avant-garde. To different degrees in the various cases, the avant-garde's culinary temporalities, while raising attention to a more-layered temporality at work within the avant-garde itself, also contest the claims of absolute innovation within gastronomic discourse while ironically appropriating that same discourse. The avant-garde's focus on eating as devouring — and, more aptly, incorporation — stresses the Now, both against the eternal in art and against the new as fashion. The now in devouring, not the here and now of the present but the Benjaminian "now-time" (*Jetztzeit*) of a bodily presence of mind, or in Jean-François Lyotard's words, the presence found in a mindless state of mind, the now as an "instant" of time that cannot be counted, well, this now works against the new. The now of incorporation is not singular but is ruptured by the temporality of nonsynchronicity in the experience of eating, both individual and collective, both present and past, but not homogeneously so. The neo-avant-garde Eat Art of the sixties and seventies incorporates the avant-garde. In doing so, it performs an archæological excavation of the leftover produced by the avant-garde work of devouring. The leftover emerges as polymorphous residue, which is new in the now(s) of this neo-avant-garde.

Desire imbues (French) gastrosophy, as Barthes noted. Desire as proliferation, unlike linear development, constitutes an escape from the norm in Deleuzian terms. For Gilles Deleuze, as for Lyotard, desire is a becoming that does not presuppose development, that is, desire does not presuppose the determined becoming of what one is supposed to be, a human being. The antidiets of the avant-garde and neo-avant-garde obstruct time flows and, consequently, also the idea of "human" developmental growth. They open abysses in the subject and in time. They are inedible even when, as in the nationalist Futurist diet, they intend to produce the perfect modern Italian. Even then, the meals and their theatrical settings are always already free energy, energy in excess of the "ideologically formative" intentions of the food served as much as in excess of the scripts and scenarios provided in both the manifesto of Futurist cooking and the *Futurist Cookbook*. The avant-garde movements considered in the present book ultimately appropriate incorporation as artistic means to rewrite the avant-garde.

The Avant-Garde: Antidiets and Incorporation

As sketched in the earlier genealogy section, devouring rather than just eating, incorporation rather than assimilation, pervades the avant-garde's concerns. In the first years of the twentieth century, avant-garde artists and critics from Pablo Picasso and Guillaume Apollinaire through the avant-garde of the sixties and seventies resort to the "culinary" to think about producing and consuming in the modern world. These actions (eating, cooking, and their metaphoric counterparts) bear more or less directly, more or less politically, on the avant-garde's immersion in and decomposition of this world that they ingest, bite into, and thereby construct anew in their works. The effect is a kind of active mimesis that varies depending on the artist. In Dada, one encounters a parodic mockery of functionalized capitalist production and consumption. Here, in the words of Deleuze and Félix Guattari, "desiring-production is used to short-circuit social production, and to interfere with the reproductive function of technical machines by introducing an element of dysfunction."[18]

Poverty and roughness, precisely the "rawness" smoothed out in the gastronomic discourse, render the avant-garde works/diets indigestible. In this context the demand to eat well means to shatter the habits of the senses, of taste as much as of seeing, and to solicit attention to the world, an attention that goes beyond its representability to the eye. To incorporate the modern world is to ingest it and be absorbed in it, losing one's own stable orientation or viewpoint as well as sense of taste. Taste demands a judgment that confirms the subject's harmonious use of the faculties, thereby rooting the subject in a stable identity. But early-twentieth-century onlookers of, for example, a cubist painting are compelled to react physically, bodily, from the inside out, as it were. They are compelled to learn how to taste differently — to break out of the given and known experience of taste and of recognizable flavors. At the same time, there is no giving up of "diet" altogether: what is required is a rethinking of the grammars of taste.[19] These avant-garde works draw viewers in and expel them. They elicit disgust, a fear of disintegration and of loss of center. Yet the confrontation with one's own disgust also generates a different, changed sensation that breaks down and breaks through the habitual contemplation of a painting. The strong affect of disgust and loss of orientation is not purely negative — a negation of taste — but generative of a new diet, a sort of diet "after/taste" (parallel to the idea of "postaesthetic art").[20] A tension between destruction and production (or construction) becomes manifest in the same manner that temporalities of before and after, causes and effects, are questioned.[21] In the remaining pages of this introduction I offer the example of an early avant-garde antidiet as symptomatic of the more explicit antidiets examined in this book. I turn in particular to Picasso's and Georges Braque's cubism to lay out some of the grounds at the bottom of the in/edibility of the avant-garde works that followed cubism and also distanced themselves from this pictorial style. The immediate aim of my discussion of cubism is to show that even this early avant-garde, which did not break away from the conventions of painting, already involved a counterdiet, namely, a translation of a visual aesthetic into countergastronomy.

In/Edible Cubism: Braque Devours Picasso

Theodor Adorno explicitly used the comestible as a derogatory metaphor of pleasure or enjoyment found in art; in short, he strongly rejected any association of art with the culinary. Yet even he refers to violent devouring as opposed to assimilation to illustrate his aesthetic theory. His invocation of the ugly and revolting as critical instantiations of art as well as his focus on art's need to devour something heterogeneous to become art may be recalled in this regard.[22] In "Art and the Arts" he writes:

> The clash between the work of art and the world of objects becomes productive, and the work authentic, only where this clash is allowed to happen and to objectify itself by its friction with the thing *it devours*. No work of art, not even the most subjective, can be completely identical with the subject that constitutes it and its substantial content. . . . This introduces an element of irreducible, qualitative plurality.[23]

Furthermore, when discussing the temporality of artworks, Adorno speaks of "an art that makes emphatic claims yet is prepared to *throw itself away*" (*Aesthetic Theory*, 178; my emphasis), like a food that gives itself up to being devoured and transformed. He speaks of "nonidentical elements that *grind away* at each other" (176), bringing to mind the image of grinding teeth at work on resistant material. In illustrating the dialectic between the parts and the whole (or the totality) of the work, he calls it a vortex that "consumes" the concept of meaning, or the "gaping divergence" that "tears meaning apart" (178). He contrasts these acts of incorporation beyond assimilation to a rather different devouring, that is, what produces proximity between the artwork and the world of practical affairs, the realm of life praxis. In this case, he condemns devouring as a "grasping" of the object and as an integration of it into the domain of the practical.[24] Here for Adorno devouring is tantamount to "assimilation" rather than incorporation and there-fore the opening of a threshold of confrontation. In the avant-garde, incorporation is a form of devouring that instead distances itself from assimilation.

More generally, the metaphor of devouring the inedible marks the first encounters with avant-garde works. In *Picasso and His Friends,* Fernande Olivier relates the "physical" revulsion Braque felt when fac-ing Picasso's first cubist attempts (possibly *Les demoiselles d'Avignon* in Picasso's studio at Le Bateau Lavoir in 1907):

> I remember a discussion about cubism which took place in Picasso's studio when, despite all Picasso's arguments . . . Braque refused to be convinced. "But in spite of your explanations," he answered finally, "you paint as if you wanted to force us *to eat rope and drink paraffin.*"[25]

First, in Braque's experience, Picasso's painting presents the viewer with raw materials, a rough, unfinished canvas (*étoupe enflammée* or oakum in flames) that is set on fire and ingested; second, the viewer's experience is transformed into the incorporation of an explosion, that is, a devouring—the opposite of assimilation—that burns the stable traits of subject (not a viewer any longer but a circus fire-eater) and object (not a painting but the leftover material for it). The moment of seeing clearly translates into a peculiar kind of synesthetic/syner-getic experience, which, contrary to the expectations that synesthesia naturally yields absolute pleasure, elicits actually a strong (dis)taste, unpleasure, and even pain. The (con)fusion of the senses is a response to cognitive dissonance, to a staggering of concepts typical of the expe-rience of the sublime.

Sublime and Countersublime

As Allen S. Weiss writes of Baudelaire's aesthetics of intoxication, "A technique of theatre-less theatre is suggested, one that effects a *countermemory, counterspectacle* and *countersymbolic.* The very body of the observer becomes theatre."[26] With Braque, the body is that of a circus fire-eater. For Baudelaire, drug-induced artificial par-adises produce the new "real" world that the subject must construct in the absence of referentiality. Weiss proposes that the "technique" of incorporation as it relates to intoxication emerges out of the abyss opened by the lack of referentiality. In Baudelaire, incorporation led to his artificial paradises. In Braque's case, and later in that of most avant-garde artists dealt with in this book, incorporation leads to an experience of devouring as "countersublime" or, as Weiss would have it, an interiorized sublime: "Temporality is constituted by a reflexivity closed in upon physiological rhythms and thresholds; [there] consciousness, subsumed by pure presence, eschews all transcendence; [there] the imagination exists in direct proportion to somatization; and [there], purged of language, the symbolic codes are abolished" (*Feast and Folly*, 25).

As an extreme example of the countersublime, Weiss names Antonin Artaud's work, which "manifests the ruins of synaesthesia" (70). Weiss speaks of "ruins" in reference to Artaud's synesthesia because the latter does not produce a harmonious total body. Instead, the body is a force field of undirected libidinal energies, beyond the organization that the organs (and various senses) provide. Applied to Braque and, in this book, more saliently to the Dada texts, the ruins of synesthesia manifest themselves as a dispersion of energy rather than a concentration of forces. Such dispersion does not constitute or confirm the unitary "efficient" (or healthy) subject. The subject of the avant-garde does not find its wholeness again. Hence the notion of countersublime can be associated with a broken synesthesia, both of which ensue from the interiorization or devouring of frictions and tensions that the body cannot resolve or synthesize. No harmonic merging of the senses occurs here. The avant-garde, then, oscillates between Baudelaire's testing of the physiological/sensorial limits of synesthesia (and correspondences) and Artaud's incorporation of the indigestible, which turns food into poison and bashes the ego.[27] These are the two poles in modernism as summarized by Weiss (the countersublime pole, in my view, being the avant-garde's culinary):

> The modernist conceptual trajectory of the aesthetics of intoxication epitomized by Baudelaire ends with Artaud: the implosion of the sublime engenders an anti-aesthetic that transforms all culinary effects into poison, and all transcendental forms into pain. This destiny of the interiorization of infinity was predicated, in some small part, on both a catharsis caused by violent intoxication and the rejection of food as poison. Such is an extraordinary purification that offers a foundation upon which rests part of the aesthetics, though certainly not the practice, of the gastronomic arts. (*Feast and Folly*, 72)

The sublime moment is expressed by a conceptual overcoming of the terror felt when facing a life-threatening situation. But one's own life is threatened also when the subject's imagination falters and has no readily available concept to help it grasp the magnitude of nature and its position therein. One's own finite nature is revealed as powerlessness against the infinite. It is at this point in the sublime experience that the intellectual faculty steps in and rescues the staggering imagination by providing the subject enthralled by terror with the concept of infinity. This overrides the sensation of powerlessness and substitutes in its place one of intellectual power and control. In Adorno's interpretation, the final domination of nature—the source of awe—first by the mind and then by reason (which, for Immanuel Kant, finally fosters moral law) closes off (in Hegelian terms, sublates) terror into the sublime.[28] The avant-garde that incorporates infinity suspends the final sublimation of terror through the use of mind and reason, which instead burns like a fire within the body. Accordingly, faced with Picasso's cubist painting, Braque has recourse to a synesthetic metaphor whereby the eyesight of the disoriented viewer seeks comfort by slipping over into another sense, the already synesthetic sense of taste—only that here an intoxicating, horrific dis-taste (*dégoût*) is found in place of taste and harmonious synesthesia. The inexact sensation of (dis)taste ultimately cannot provide the closure that the "missing" concept or adequate words of criticism would. Picasso's cubism was unspeakable for Apollinaire as well, who wrote in his journal on February 27, 1907, about Picasso: "Admirable language which no literature can address because our words are made in advance, alas!"[29] The lack of words indicates the ineffable nature of the experience of seeing: the words we know are insufficient to capture unknown visions and unknown experiences. The failure to make these recognizable to the eye and mind produces a vacuum in which the subject finds itself vulnerable, "open" to the "un(re)presentable," which erupts suddenly and which, as Braque's diet of fire and paraffin can only suggest, is transformative to the point of being potentially deadly.

Braque's disgust, which comes from the depths of his body, is a symptomatic moment of avant-garde antidiets. It is symptomatic in pointing us both to avant-garde's synesthesia as a series of slippages occurring in the body and, consequently, to a counterhistoricist and significantly anachronistic temporality, which for thinkers and practitioners in and of the avant-garde, like Benjamin, could be strongly critical of traditional subjectivity, bourgeois conventions, and the writing of canonical history.

Countersublime Temporalities in the Avant-Garde

Benjamin ascribed this anachronistic temporality to his notion of constellation in the "dialectical image," essential also in his "Theses on History" and the essay on surrealism. He defined his concept of "dialectics at a standstill" as "that in which the Then and Now come together into a constellation like a flash of lightning." The metaphor of constellation thus includes both the possibility of a "flash" of historical insight that could only "enter into legibility at a specific time" and a critique of historicism grounded in "the retrieval of the unfulfilled potential of the past."[30] For Benjamin, the nonlinear temporality of the image as dialectical contains in the present of its manifestation the afterlife (*Nachleben*) of what has been (*das Gewesene*) and the fermentation of the future. The dialectical image shares this mixed temporality with the food word in Benjamin's own antidiets, namely, his stories about eating. The latter through their dialectical temporality associate Benjamin with the avant-garde's own countersublime temporalities.

Georges Didi-Huberman clarifies that the temporality of the dialectical image is directly connected with Benjamin's conceptualization of the history of art less as history than as *symptomatic* reading of the emergence of history (or historicity) in the artworks. For Benjamin, the history of art then is a history of prophecies to be deciphered anew and differently in each epoch because in each epoch's actuality specific possibilities arise that allow one to see the prophecies of the art of the past. Benjamin adds that since a "brewing space of the future" (Benjamin's image) is alive in each work, the history of art is a constant starting anew: "Each new symptom leads us back to the origin. Each new possibility to read instances of afterlife, each new emergence of a far past throw everything into discussion again" (quoted in Didi-Huberman, 98).[31]

Benjamin's liberatory (and open) temporality in the dialectical image is and remains a violent lightning, as he writes in "Central Park." More to the point, in his paralipomena to the "Theses of History," Benjamin calls the dialectical image a fireball.[32] The disfiguring violence of this transformative experience of temporality is similar to the burning and threatening antidiet fed to Braque by Picasso and returns in distinct ways in most antidiets considered in this book. This burning lightning—the violence of which persists as trace—opens a passage and creates a threshold. For Benjamin, the threshold is a temporal space of conflict where unpredictable metamorphoses, processes of fermentation (the brewing of future possibilities), and hypertrophied swelling (the German for "threshold" elicits the term *swelling*) finally awaken the subject of and in history to the experience of multiple temporalities informing the now of production and consumption, in art and elsewhere. In the act of eating, the dialectical image is born as the actualization of both the subject and the food in the now-time of their reciprocal encounter. This is a time pregnant with possibilities, which include the destruction — or burning away — of the actual food and the metamorphosis of the subject (a burning away of self-identity). The act of eating thus opens up both the food and the subject who incorporates it to the multidimensional side of the subject in time and of time: past, present, and future refract each other in the eating experience and the open body, a body that is "shaken" and unstable.

As it will become clear through the analyses of the avant-garde works considered in *Antidiets of the Avant-Garde,* the slippage from temporal narrative or literary mastery of an unknown, unclassifiable experience (as of the past) to the bodily experience of devouring manifests itself, like for Braque, as a consuming and dangerous fire, which by burning away what is on its path (including the subject's identity) also allows for the potential resurgence of the image as an involuntary (new) trace, as ash, as aftertaste, even as a wound (or trauma). In Braque's case, ingestion does not come to rescue the subject from the "terror" that surrounds its incomprehensibility in the face of this "experience." First, Braque's recourse to synesthesia leads him on a slippery road rather than to an absolute sensation or to the sensation of the absolute. Second, in this form, synesthesia only reveals more deeply — from an internalized perspective — how deathly the experience of seeing is, now tantamount to (dis)tasting or disgust. If the act of looking at the cubist picture is transformed into being coaxed into eating burning flames and drinking paraffin, then one does not directly avoid the threat of death but finds a line of escape from it only through a deeper interiorization, an incorporation of the abyss that death, this burning instance, opens within. For Braque, cubism is a deadly dish, which does not confirm the viewer's position of mastery over a preexisting external reality. That reality is shattered, that is, shaken off and burnt away. It returns only as inflammation from within a body that is now open and vulnerable. Reality is nothing other than the fuel of an internal fire that ultimately devours the subject as much as its location — which is also the space of painting, the canvas. In effect, Braque himself will embrace or will be burnt by the flame of cubism.

Note that a few years after Picasso's *Demoiselles,* in a recipe the Dadaists draw up to make the glue for their collages, they write, "We boil proper notable people in paraffin and we blend them as well as possible."[33] Braque's initial aversion to Picasso's art has literally become diet, or at least a published recipe of and for a cannibalistic Dada avant-garde that mimes the cannibalistic/capitalist system of exchange value, based in money flows and commodity fetishism.[34] Money flows translate in Dada parlance with excremental liquids sold on the market as Dada art commodities, the ironically "organic works" of Dada nonassimilable dysfunctional bodies. In contrast, Braque (who then became one of the major representatives of cubism, at least in Apollinaire's eyes) strove for an internal harmony, for form, and underscored in his own cubist paintings and collages an awareness of the medium's limits. Yet the countersublime taste of Picasso's deadly diet left its mark — a burning trace or wound — on Braque, for whom, as for Picasso, no representation of reality was ever possible again, other than as *production of another reality,* namely, the event of painting. Braque thus writes: "The goal is not to reconstitute an anecdotal fact, but rather to constitute a pictorial event."[35] In dietetic terms that underscore a point of contact between eating — eating the world — and producing the world beyond lived experience (in Promethean fashion that is closer to Futurism and farther from the recipes of Dada's antiart), Braque comments: "I am against all morals, against discipline. To be a painter, it is necessary to have guts [*foi,* liver], the sacred fire. Just like eating: first comes the appetite, then the choice of the dish" (Braque, 14; my translation).

This life-threatening, unappetizing diet that is fed to the cubist, first an observer who is thereby turned into unwilling eater of poison and then a painter, or bulimic devourer who lives off an internalized fire, represents one moment in the avant-garde. This kind of antidiet exposes the avant-garde also as contradictory, multidirectional, and quite the opposite of either nonambivalent Promethean movements or purely nihilistic and "regressive" groupings.[36] The antidiet of cubism may be seen to look ahead to more radically oriented artists (operating in a vast area of fields beyond painting) and disparate avant-garde movements, including neo-avant-garde's Eat Art and the work of other food artists. In particular, as I wish to show in this book, the avant-garde antidiets bring to the fore the discrepant (burning) temporalities within each movement and between them; specifically they help illuminate, through their interference with the gastronomic temporality tensed between memory and innovation, the complex temporal relations between avant-garde and neo-avant-garde artworks.

Amorphous Space–Time: The *Informe*

Radically reworked (worked through), the antidiet launched by Braque's repulsive reaction to and, thereafter, incorporation of the indigestible in cubism returns in Georges Bataille's own response to the Kantian sublime, the *informe*. In an explicitly pathological (i.e., psychotic) manner, food as poison is also manifest in Artaud's radical *Theatre of Cruelty*. From there, the power of libidinal energy and "de-formation," as well as the operation of "lowering," debasing, rendering obscene (presenting the unpresentable but without a stage for the presentation), has generated many turns and returns in both art production and aesthetic (or counteraesthetic) theory.[37]

What is intriguing, however, in the cubist counterdiet and countersublime, which speaks to these variegated readings of art, is that a desiring and productive quality is at stake in avant-garde art, including Dada. The avant-garde is seen to operate both as negation and affirmation, for example, proposal, promise, or simply desire. (Affirmation here means life affirming rather than reified, affirmative art.) The *informe* qualities of this affirmative desire root it in raw and burning materials. Scholars have pointed out that an *informe,* that is, disjointed and dysfunctional, even death-driven desire or tendency, is at work in the avant-garde. Foster, for example, reads surrealism (not just Bataille's but also that of his antagonist André Breton) through the concept of the uncanny and of the death drive as formulated in Freud's "Beyond the Pleasure-Principle."[38] At the same time, Foster notes in Dada a critical parody that he calls "hypertrophic" and that I define, in chapter 2, as omnivorous and cannibalistic. In effect, Francis Picabia not only writes the "Manifeste Cannibale" but in this spirit publishes a literary Dada magazine, also titled *Cannibale.*[39]

Antidiets are at the center of the sublimations proposed in Futurist cooking, with its desire to free desire, which, however, falls prey first to anxiety and finally to sublimatory reterritorialization. Yet antidiets also ground the desublimatory (excremental and parodically regressive) antiart of Dada. This is not to say that antidiets (and the *informe*) are the common denominator to which we should conceptually reduce all avant-garde art. To the contrary, the ways in which the dynamics of incorporation operate — the *informe* is for Bataille an *operation,* and so I interpret incorporation in this book — produce the avant-garde as a plurality of libidinal flows. Some avant-garde artists attempt to transform and in fact direct desire toward the creation (and thus forming) of experiences yet unlived. The Futurists especially work assiduously to territorialize desire's flows. At other times other artists, or even the same ones, provoke desire to emerge as not-yet-imagined images of thought (Benjamin's *Denkbilder*), images that interrupt momentarily the course of time and productivity as measurable quantities. Food — gulped down, transforming and transformed, living on in its absence — may be seen as countering the commodity fetish. Finally, as Spoerri's Eat Art demonstrates, the neo-avant-garde, in this one manifestation at least, literally operates to *dé-collage* (to "unglue" but also to "take off") the historical avant-garde, which here takes off in different temporal constellations.

The Primeval Technological Antidiet of Futurism and Beyond: Mud Tossed with Gasoline

To be more concrete, let me once again return to the "disgusting" cubist diet and indicate how much one is dealing with an indeterminate space–time of the amorphous, if not always *informe,* when facing the avant-garde. There is another mythological, artificial, and foundational antidiet, a counterintuitive antidiet that, unexpectedly and retrospectively, may be read as the *motor* of Futurism and Futurist gastronomy.[40] This antidiet is counterintuitive because it seems to sharply contrast with the aestheticizing diet the Futurists propose with their cuisine. It is foundational because one finds a taste of it in the first manifesto of Futurism published in *Le Figaro* in 1909. From reading the manifesto it becomes apparent that Filippo Tommaso Marinetti fed on poisonous food, not unlike Braque. Because of this, it seems then that the repelling and archaic ingredients in this diet would stand in sharp contrast to the aesthetically edifying *Futurist Cookbook* of many years later. But artificiality and mythopoesis are juxtaposed in the Futurist diets and so their temporalities. Although the Futurists hold on to their autogenetic moment in 1909, every manifesto that follows also constitutes a new beginning, a further expansion of their diet. When they open the Holy Palate in 1931, the restaurant figures as the new theater for an expansive and ongoing Futurist revolution, which the restaurant, however, is paradoxically intended to both foster and contain and regulate.

The preface to the foundational Futurist manifesto includes an allegorical birth of the movement. The allegory also offers at once a fragment of an archetypal modern and mythical diet, which erupts out of a cataclysmic threat. The founder's first taste of this antidiet recodes as life's *jouissance* the newborn's first oral encounter with an ambivalent mother, both loving and threatening:

> "Let's break out of the horrible shell of wisdom and throw ourselves like pride-ripened fruit into the wide, contorted mouth of the wind! Let's give ourselves utterly to the Unknown, not in desperation but only to replenish the deep wells of the Absurd!" The words were scarcely out of my mouth when I spun my car around with the frenzy of a dog trying to bite its tail, and there, suddenly, were two cyclists coming towards me. . . . I stopped short and to my disgust rolled over into a ditch with my wheels in the air. . . .
>
> O maternal ditch, almost full of muddy water! Fair factory drain! I gulped down your nourishing sludge; and I remembered the blessed black breast of my Sudanese nurse. . . . When I came up — torn, filthy, and stinking — from under the capsized car, I felt the white-hot iron of joy deliciously pass through my heart! . . . And so, faces smeared with good factory muck — plastered with metallic waste, with senseless sweat, with celestial soot — we, bruised, our arms in slings, but unafraid, declared our high intentions to all the *living* of the earth.[41]

After this preface, Marinetti officially proclaims the first Futurist manifesto. A fast car inaugurates the race to Futurism, during which the subject throws itself in the mouth of death only to savor thereby the power of life. Once the car rolls into the ditch, Marinetti is in turn thrown to the ground, and avidly tastes the muddy water mixed with grease and gas, a fortifying concoction that in the throngs of trauma brings back memories from his nursing days in Egypt. Unlike the madeleine that unravels the past in Proust's memoirs, Marinetti's black milk of childhood returns as metamorphosed substance. He finds it in the modern-day fuel needed for his own metamorphosis into Futurist man. Here the diet of gasoline, grease, and mud, the mixing of (in his view) African primitive energy and modern technology, causes an ecstatic *jouissance* that translates, like the disgusting diet of inflamed rope and paraffin for Braque, into an appetite for life, into creative energy. While for Braque the disgusting is a threshold through which difference is incorporated and maintained, for Marinetti homology between the diet and the subject seems to be established. And this partly characterizes also the *Futurist Cookbook*'s recipes, which the Futurists present to the general public as revolutionary gastronomy.

With respect to gastronomy, the Futurists act truly in the spirit of gastrosophy. While they concretely try to feed Italians a modern diet of incongruent and dissonant food, prepared according to linguistic oxymora in addition to physical sensations, they rely on gastronomic "writing"—say, the French writing of a Brillat-Savarin—for their "crazy" "new" cookbook. Ultimately, their intentions (and thus their gastronomic grounding) hinder the character of absolute novelty to which they aspire, as was the case with gastronomy generally. The Futurists are anxious about reterritorializing the desire they want to and do indeed set free. For at least three reasons, however, this cookbook is not traditional. First, the dishes proposed are there for their "sensorial metaphoricity" (*Feast and Folly,* 23) with which, however, they ultimately clash: tastes and images don't match, or rather the flavors suggested in those images-recipes are revolting to the body. They are literally (or, to be more precise, physiologically) indigestible. Hence they are, in fact, countergastronomic. Second, the echoes of symbolism's (Baudelaire's) correspondences are still pervasive, here perhaps even more than in the Futurists' early poetry and manifestos. What distinguishes the "apocalyptic sublime," or the countersublime as illustrated by Weiss, is the transference of intoxication by drugs, as in Baudelaire, to intoxication by artificial (artistic) food in Futurism.[42] Most important, the Futurists adopt the synesthetic experience to rewrite gastronomy and to officially inscribe eating as *Gesamtkunstwerk* in the expanded field of avant-garde (counter)aesthetics. In this respect Futurist cooking differs from Dada's antidiets, which deconstruct eating, gastronomic grammars, and the eating body. As in Artaud, Dada's antidiets short-circuit synesthesia, which is still present but only as the catastrophe of the senses and also of concepts. The outcome of the Dadaist short-circuit is a schizo-body made of dissonances, a breakdown of all distinctions, hence *dégoût* or nausea (the countersublime).

Dada transforms the *Gesamtkunstwerk,* as wholeness and purity, into scattered leftovers. In an essay on Kurt Schwitters's *Merzbau,* Leah Dickerman notes a juncture between this Dada artist's preoccupation with bodily "fragments"—leftovers—and an important and yet unexplored Dada concern with memory. This will resonate later with Spoerri's own appropriation of Dada fragments. Schwitters's (aka Merz's) own monumental anti-*Gesamtwerk* is defined as "a pathological metastasis rather than growth," which as such is the opposite of the Futurist's "growth." Dickerman notes the assonances of the name "Merz" with the body's physicality. *Merz* inscribes the body with pain, echoed in the German *Schmerz*, and then, through its resonance with the French *merde* (shit), identifies the body with the scatological. These points delineate the focus of my own chapter on the coprophagous antidiets of Dada.[43] While in *Révue Dada*, bodily metaphoricity construes a contained body of indistinction and disgust, Spoerri's Eat Art in the sixties and seventies, since his early trap-paintings, deterritorializes in turn the Dadaist malfunctioning and sick, schizo-body/monument. Eat Art brings back a positivity that is not affirmative (in Herbert Marcuse's sense) in Dada. The tables of leftovers—his trap-paintings—are hoisted up vertically in defiance of gravity, which keeps us all with our feet on the ground.[44] Hence the "beautiful Dada excrement," mentioned in the *Révue Dada*, returns in Spoerri's trap-paintings, which both capture (glue) and free the avant-garde's fragmented and involuntary food memories.

Resistant Failures of the Avant-Garde

Mythopoeic antidiets of modern disgust open the threshold where the sublime becomes countersublime, where ecstasy turns into dysfunctionalism, art into countergastronomy, and food into antiart. Mud and gasoline, raw canvas and flames, however, nourish differently the distinctive bodies of Futurism and Dada, of Benjamin and Spoerri. Every return of antidiet effects a turn in the body/art produced. Yet avant-garde and neo-avant-garde antidiets constitute a dietetic (and aesthetic) undertow that pulls diet in countergastronomic directions. In every antidiet there is a resistance and thus also a hope as, in Benjamin's words, hope is only for the hopeless. What fails—and the avant-garde antidiets are already set up to fail taste and the bourgeois subject—is moved by resistance. The task of the avant-gardes that continue experimenting, testing their own and their societies' limits, is to look for that resistance, even civil/aesthetic disobedience, in what has been declared a historical failure. To echo Howard Zinn, how many struggles failed for change to occur? Each struggle constitutes a step on the way to change, even and perhaps precisely when it fails. Thus the future is a series of presents, and it is in each present — working through its "failed" pasts — that other futures (not the One Big Future) can be imagined. To rescue the power of the imagination(s) of other futures — not of the predictable futures but of the possible ones — in what might have failed (according to history's determination of victories) is not only what motivates Benjamin's rereading of history but also the neo-avant-garde's returns to and turns of the "failed" and resisting antidiets at the known risk of its failure and erasure. Thus, as Spoerri's trap-paintings reveal, the neo-avant-garde always already presents itself together with the traces of resistance, the leftovers of another imagination that might very well be considered failing instantly but still preserves its energy.

The avant-garde, read through its rumbling stomach, enters the world of art and cuisine through restaurants on the verge of breakdowns that are always potential breakthroughs and through (dirty) flying saucers (Spoerri's glued dirty cups and dishes). Jorge Luis Borges and Adolfo Bioy Casares report one fantastic and grandiose antecedent of the avant-garde's failed but resistant antidietetic experiments, with which I close this introduction.[45] Now these are experiments in failure, failure that is conceivable as the avant-garde's powerful minor war of position within majoritarian grammars that order language, the body, its pleasures, and society.

Here is a sample of the early flavors of the avant-garde, brought to us by a certain Ismael Querido, whose story may be taken to capture a micro history of the avant-garde itself. Probably inspired by Franz Praetorius's book *Les saveurs* (*Flavors*, 1891), Querido opened a legendary and peculiar restaurant, Les Cinq Saveurs. The consumer who ventured into this locale could choose from five tasting options listed in a menu: sugar, a cube of aloe, a piece of cotton, the zest of lemon, and a grain of salt. As Borges and Casares explain, initially the taster could choose the flavors in succession. Later, however, the maître allowed the flavors to be amalgamated. Ignoring the objections raised by indignant culinary experts, including Praetorius, Querido went even farther. He organized a weekly delivery of 1,200 rigorously identical pyramids of flavors — first grayish and then translucent and finally in the five primary colors (white, black, yellow, red, and blue). The authors continue:

> Querido made the dangerous mistake of playing at combinations; the fervent sustainers of orthodoxy accused him of having gone so far as to offer to the gourmands [*stet*] no less than one hundred and twenty mixed pyramids, recognizable through their one hundred and twenty different colors. These multiple mixings led him to his ruin. That very year he had to sell the locale to an ordinary chef who profaned this temple of flavors: Indeed, the chef cooked stuffed turkey for the Christmas's Eve celebrations. Praetorius concluded philosophically: "it is the end of the world." (Borges and Casares, 3; my translation)

Not only introducing experimental and unorthodox combinations that demanded the readiness of an indefatigable mouth and a bold stomach but also daring to contest, almost by excess, the laws (at the time) of gourmandise, Querido's avant-garde enterprise shone and collapsed. But it morphed into the subsequent ungrammatical diets of the avant-garde, with its own attempted revolutions of the senses, the constant testing of the body's limits, the dangerous investigations of the boundaries among the arts and the arts of life. Thus ends Querido's story and that of the avant-garde begins.

Impractical Directions for the Use and Abuse of This Unfinished Project

If there are any directions for use of this book, the first one is that I should like this work to be read as an open site. I ask many questions, especially in approaching the last chapters, for which I have no answers. While I contend that the crossings of the culinary and the avant-garde fields are important in rethinking the avant-garde, this is only one of the many perspectives — already elaborated and yet to come — that help us open up the histories with which we are already familiar.

Methodologically this book may be at risk of essentializing "incorporation" or the culinary, to write a grand history of the avant-garde through this other, so far unnoticed perspective. I hope that the fragmentation and dispersal of the avant-garde and neo-avant-garde, and my readings, which highlight different aspects within these movements, keep in check if not counter such an impression. In addition, my situating this book within an ongoing dialogue on the avant-garde and the culinary field hopes to deflect any essentializing. The fragmentation that ensues from analyzing the avant-garde through the culinary is due to the very discursivity that the culinary brings to the avant-garde. As practice, the culinary emphasizes action and effects over the observing subject, a practice the avant-garde cherished. This helps question the labels such as avant-garde versus neo-avant-garde, including their "use" in this book. For, ultimately, the avant-garde antidiets and the neo-avant-garde Eat Art, as they emerge from the study of incorporation, food, degradable materials, and so forth, defy their classification and imprisonment in chronologies. The chronological structure of this book is provisional, tentative, and, most important, ready to be put into question by way of the analyses it, perhaps ironically, carries out. It is hoped that despite the *dégoût* that exhales synesthetically from the following pages, the serious playfulness of the avant-garde antidiets will still stimulate our intellectual appetite for such art.

■ FUTURIST BANQUETS

Futurist Foods

No matter where we turn in our consumer society today, we are flooded with information about the body's physical and mental health. Radio and television programs, magazines and specialized books, cookery texts, advertisements and commercials all entice the public to purchase more and more information on how to consume less. We are caught in a paradox: to consume less (food) we consume more (information). Energy bars, vitamins and supplements, pictures of slender models and muscular athletes, self-help manuals and cookbooks on fast and practical ways of cooking aim at keeping us fit and healthy for a society on the go and not ready to accommodate bodies deemed unfit, weak, sickly, and simply ugly.

But this is not a new development. The Italian Futurist poets and artists of the 1930s called loudly for a new, modern cooking very much along the same lines. Their call, as they said proudly in the *Futurist Cookbook,* sounded "crazy." The diet they proposed had the same revolutionary and controversial public effects that their earlier literary and artistic manifestos had provoked at the beginning of the century. The first Futurist manifesto, published in France in *Le Figaro* in 1909, declared war on any kind of tradition, especially Italian cultural and historical traditions, which the Futurists believed were to blame for Italy's antimodernity. Accordingly, the main reason for the "craziness" of the Futurist culinary effort — which took place late in the movement's history, after World War I — was their attack on culinary traditions found not only in diet and social customs but also in broader questions of taste.

The impracticality of their proposed cuisine was another reason for the controversy over their call for modern foods, as the Futurists note in the *Futurist Cookbook*. The recipes and banquets they first imagined, and later published and staged, while aiming at efficiency and fitness, at closing the gap between a modern life and a modern body, were also based in a Futurist poetics and aesthetics in literature, the visual arts, dance, architecture, theater, and fashion. Ideas and artistic matter could, for the public, take new forms without too much ado, beyond the initial excitement or shock. But to use the public's own bodies as material to be subjected to radical transformation, as the Futurists did in their culinary revolution, provoked more than just curiosity. The audience of diners and critics, all consumers of Futurist food art, was invested personally, bodily, and thus it was *concerned*. Futurism showed here how an artistic revolution, involving taste, may truly affect the body.

At the moment of its inception in 1909, Italian Futurism had launched a program to bring the human spirit in line with the new modern environment by rejuvenating the senses. Nature had been radically transformed by the introduction of the machine and its diffusion in the industries. For the Futurists, a total revolution of the human body–mind included culinary culture. Cooking and eating habits — determined by class, culture, and nationality among other factors — were the most resistant to change. Traditional customs reproduced through known recipes led to an inclination to accept given tastes, adjusted to one's own personal likes and dislikes. To complete the total revolution of the senses and to forge a new modern Italian, as they had already set out to do with their aesthetic projects, the Futurists now felt they had to approach the long-established national bourgeois traditions of cooking.

This area of human intervention rethinks not only culture but also nature — albeit indirectly and unintentionally. Cooking undoes and reconstitutes nature through manipulating and transforming food. The Futurists appropriated cooking so as to take active charge of changes in body and in mind. Cooking has the potential to make these changes, but it proceeds gradually by introducing incremental innovations. Gastronomy, itself a revolutionary field as it emerged in the late eighteenth century, negotiated between innovation and normativity, between a view of bourgeois culture as changing (movement) and an institutionalization of bourgeois taste. The Futurists contested the reproduction of Italian popular bourgeois taste in current cookbooks and in cooking. Italy had not yet developed a full-throttle culinary discourse as France had since at least the French Revolution, with the plethora of writings and establishments concerned with food that characterized the modern age in that country.

In Italy, which became a nation-state almost a century after the French Revolution and which for some completed its Risorgimento only with World War I (or the Last War of Independence), modernization had just started when Futurism came on the stage, in the early twentieth century. The gastrosophical public sphere had different connotations than in France, and to some extent—not in diet but as cultural discourse—cuisine as a field did not yet exist, at least not in the same way. About 70 percent of the Italian population was rural, poor, and, in some regions, undernourished. Undernourishment was a major cause of death: it facilitated the epidemics of the influenza known as La Spagnola (the Spanish flu) between 1918 and 1920 and of tuberculosis until the fifties. Pellegrino Artusi, the nineteenth-century author of the most well-known Italian cookbook, compiled his recipes for the elites, notably the middle classes and the landowning aristocracy: these dishes, rich with fat and carbohydrates, are inconceivable today, as they were to the Futurists in the twenties.

Unlike Artusi, whose selection of foods was rooted not only in bourgeois traditions but also in the seasonal cycles, thus displaying affection for nature, the Futurists insisted on artifice, art, and science as aids in liberating the body from its limits and needs. A light fare—more attuned with the simplicity of the modern lifestyle invoked by Futurism—was available at highbrow restaurants in the midtwenties, such as the Savini in Milan.[1] Yet employees, businessmen, and students (those people, in short, who most made use of the restaurant) usually ate in taverns that offered conventional and monotonous menus of decent quality, where they could have their meals at reasonable prices. In sum, Italy—the country where Filippo Tommaso Marinetti launches his "crazy" cuisine, in itself a whole universe including a manifesto, a cookbook, a special language (thus a dictionary), recipes (which he called formulas), chefs, banquets, doctors, and critics writing about it—is a world in which food has not yet taken the "national," modern, and unifying function it had in France. And it is in the vein of modern French cuisine that Marinetti intends to enter and shape the Italian body and mind. With its strong categorical impulse toward innovation, the *Futurist Cookbook* quite literally followed in the footsteps of French gastronomic enterprises.

Cookbooks have long harbored the ambition to dictate practices. The growing publication of cookbooks and their wider distribution in the nineteenth century allowed for "public" discussion, as cooking moved from the private kitchen to the public domain, where different forms of writing—including the cookbooks themselves, criticism, gastrosophical essays, and so forth—played as essential a role as the food and its organization on the table. The Futurists situated themselves in the *modern* culinary tradition that tied "the new and the different-state-of-the-art to progress, an effort that inevitably entails categorical dismissal of one's predecessors."[2] They came to the culinary precisely to reflect on their "cultural–historical mission," their movement's temporality of progress and the implications of such temporality on the "destiny" of Futurism itself (and even, indirectly, fascism). By proclaiming with their new cuisine a new world in *their* making, the Futurists also announced—perhaps unwittingly—the end of their movement. Food consumed and transformed into energy, on the one hand, and an assiduous recording of all the documents, conversations, and inventions that are ephemeral, on the other: both moments are present in Futurism. These moments, I argue, highlight the contradiction that the Futurists as avant-garde were living in their second-wave phase and their attempt at reconciling with their "necessary" but important passing "task."[3]

The Futurists welcomed any invention, especially a free-range imagination in their combinations of foodstuffs. Their aim was to transform the spirit of Italians by way of food, as evinced in their polemical manifesto against pasta. They also sought a culinary revolution that was aesthetic. If food engaged the body most immediately, then the mind was affected by anything affecting the body. Hence the Futurists focused on the *kind* of food, that is, the aesthetic quality necessary to shape a healthy body and a healthy Futurist mind. They did not leave diet to popular customs, tradition, or even doctors. While believing in the fascist values according to which the Italian body had to be slender and combative, and could be endowed with both the beauty of a wild animal and the artificial speed of a steel machine, the Futurists, however, pointed to a conundrum in Italian (national) nutrition: how could Italians continue to eat traditionally? Futurists proposed to shape the new (modern) Italian body by rejecting pasta, the Italian staple. The new Italian spirit should no longer be imprisoned in the cubic and weighty physiology that had marked the Italian body and, in their view, had influenced Italian rhetoric. Through new ingredients and a new cuisine the body could be liberated from its inadequate "form," inadequate with respect to the totally new, modern, and fast-moving environment. Nature itself had, after all, already been modernized as, for example, the impact of electricity had shown with the growth of industries and traffic in cities that also had changed character. The Italian body had remained the exception too long.

On December 28, 1930, Marinetti and Luigi Colombo (better known as Fillìa) published the manifesto of Futurist cooking in the Italian newspaper *La Gazzetta del Popolo,* the people's gazette. The manifesto, which attacked pasta, marked the beginning of a long venture that, as in previous occasions, was accompanied by fierce public controversies. Gradually, the Futurist culinary adventure also included organizing numerous banquets (held in various Italian and foreign venues) and lectures. Marinetti and Fillìa's intended revolution of the senses led them to establish a Futurist restaurant. The blasphemous Tavern of the "Holy Palate" opened in Turin on March 8, 1931. Finally, as a record of their accomplishments, in 1932 Marinetti and Fillìa published the *Futurist Cookbook.* Conceived less as a cookbook than as a historical account of all that shaped Futurist gastrosophy, the text has an explicit ideological agenda.[4] The volume contains the complete documentation of the public meals the Futurists organized and the polemics that ensued after the manifesto's publication. It comprises the menus and recipes used in these banquets, as well as a dictionary of the new Futurist culinary terminology, and is prefaced by a Rabelaisian story, along the lines of Marinetti's youthful mythical writings such as *Mafarka le Futuriste* and *Le Roi Bombance.* In sum, the text is a "total work of art," like the restaurant itself, spanning different genres, offering a theory and practice of Futurist aesthetics. Through all the anthologized texts, the cookbook writes the movement's history of successes and gives an official story of its origins. It stands as a culinary account of Futurism's aesthetic revolution and of its ideological history.

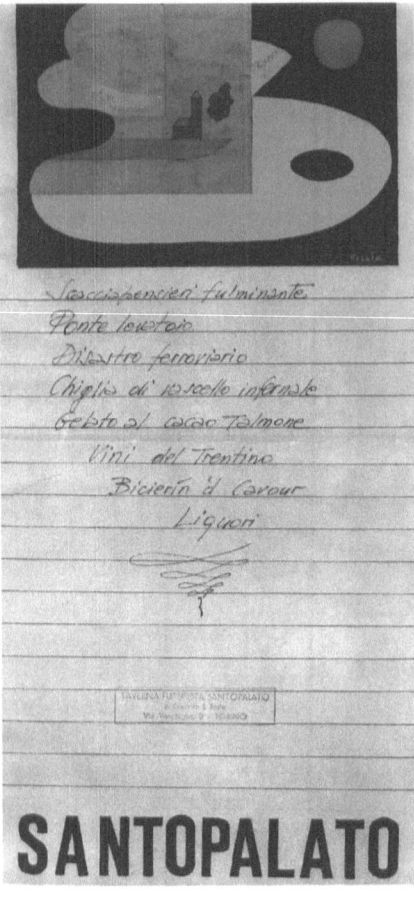

*Fillìa, "Futurist Menu for
Santopalato." On the menu:
scacciapensieri fulminante
[blazing jew's harp], ponte levatoio
[drawbridge], disastro ferroviario
[railway disaster], chiglia di
vascello infernale [keel of infernal
vessel], gelato al cacao Talmone
[Talmone chocolate ice cream],
vini del Trentino [wines from
Trentino], bicierín 'd Cavour
[Cavour's bicierin: a Piedmontese
drink made with hot chocolate
and coffee, served in a small glass],
liquori [spirits/liquor]. Private
collection, Milan.*

SANTOPALATO

Futurist cooking is also a project of return to the movement's beginnings before the war and before fascism. The strongly violent and
fascistic tendencies of the early stages of Futurism, and its most avant-
gardist art and poetry, are reproposed here as markers of an avant-
garde that, while needing to reestablish itself as revolutionary, also
does so ironically. Futurism paradoxically (oxymoronically) returns to
its origin, the origin of its aesthetic revolution, a revolution that—it
appears—has *not* produced what this avant-garde had set itself out to
accomplish, beyond the realm of the arts. In other words, the second-
wave artists, while testing this avant-garde's own project, also seem to
question, albeit ambiguously, the belief that any "revolution," includ-

ing the fascist/Futurist one, could ever be institutionalized, museified, and ossified.

Futurist cooking appears at a crucial point in Italian history and in the history of fascism. Hence the cookbook's polemical and ironic tone, as well as the constant reference to and rewriting of Futurism's history, takes on a specific political meaning. By advancing a Futurist cuisine that dispels boredom, weightiness, ugly cubic and static Italian bodies, the *Futurist Cookbook* shows its reservations about the politics of state fascism, even when it endorses the same fascist vitalist views: the cult of the body, the affirmation of biological life, and the view of existence as the survival of the fittest.

Benito Mussolini took office in 1922 with his infamous March on Rome. By the 1930s fascism had turned totalitarian. During its initial phase, fascism had caught the Italians nationalists' attention by virtue of its "revolutionary" ideology, that is, an antibourgeois, anti-decadent, and antiparliamentary (antidemocratic) doctrine. Marinetti had aligned himself with Mussolini in these early years, believing that Futurism had been the source of inspiration for fascism in its early stages. With its institutionalization, fascism settled on more traditional cultural values, which it still managed to reconcile with the task of modernizing Italian politics and the state. Mussolini was not keen on promoting revolutionary change, either economically or culturally. Thus Marinetti, who fundamentally believed in the initially radical agenda of fascism as extending to all realms of life, felt betrayed by the lack of consistency in fascism's pursuit of modernity as change, at a later stage. This transpires, for instance, in the following excerpt from the manifesto of Futurist cooking:

> Italian Futurism, father of numerous Futurisms and Avant-gardeisms abroad, will not remain a prisoner of those worldwide victories secured "in twenty years of great artistic and political battles frequently consecrated in blood," as Benito Mussolini put it. Italian Futurism will face unpopularity again with a programme for the total renewal of food and cooking. . . . Against practicality we Futurists therefore disdain the example and admonition of tradition in order to invent at any cost something new which everyone considers crazy. (*Futurist Cookbook*, 33–34)

The "impracticality" of Futurist cuisine so loudly proclaimed in the manifesto distances the Futurists from a strictly fascist, political agenda, even if distance is taken cautiously, only in contradictory and polemical ways.[5] Most importantly, distance does not erase the fundamentally chauvinistic values of second-wave Futurism; it only complicates its relation with institutionalized fascism.

The Futurists had welcomed World War I as the final and necessary Italian war against the Austrian invader. Their modernism, since the beginning, was both nationalist and international: ideologically nationalist, aesthetically international. The early Futurists had fiercely defended Italianism as the only valid modern religion, what they called the cult of the nation. Italianism would launch Italy into the sphere of developed modern states. Since their beginnings, they saw Futurist artists or, at least, Futurist politicians as heads of the new Italian modern state. As Futurists they would promote incessant change, be daring in all areas of life. The Futurists wanted, in quite utopian terms, to be creative, political artists. They did not consider art as a separate and superfluous realm of action.

The *Futurist Cookbook* transforms the Futurists' anxiety about the necessity to conquer modernity for a new Italy into a conflicted urge for a totalitarian revolution with the sacred end of Divine Italianism.[6] This urge was conflicted because Italianism also required a civilizing ideology, beyond nationalism. Furthermore, Futurism could not completely adhere to the sacrifice of the individual in the name of a national collectivity as represented in the totalitarian state. In short, totalitarianism for the Futurists remains more an end, an impossible ideal, even a desire. The recipes for the "definitive dinners" are typical in this sense: their theatrical setup and their wish to reproduce a definitive state of mind reveal an unresolved anxiety about signification, about the control of information. The anxiety of historiography then dominates the Futurist texts of the later period and reveals Futurism's biggest fear, the fear of being itself assimilated and erased as avant-garde within the totalitarian politics of institutionalized fascism.

In the *Futurist Cookbook* Marinetti and Fillìa continue the tradition of a bracing movement founded on the criticism of any "ossified" establishment. They again appropriate, without nostalgia, the revolutionary impulse of Futurist fascism or fascistic Futurism present in the original avant-garde. In this regard, the appropriation of cooking as the best way to deal directly with traditions — both the culinary *and* the Futurist tradition in this case — acquires an additional meaning. As the Futurists emphasize, the use of food in art is this avant-garde's way to impose its own ideological agenda, one based in change. Yet the *Futurist Cookbook* underscores the antipractical features of the culinary revolution, thus bringing some ironic self-reflexivity to this agenda. The diet they propose reveals both a serious and a self-defeating project. It produces and at the same time questions the avant-garde's own myth about itself as founder of traditions. The *Futurist Cookbook,* while aiming to establish itself and its goal in absolute avant-garde fashion, also discreetly shows the Futurists' doubts about their so seriously proclaimed intentions. The texts in the *Futurist Cookbook* relentlessly advance the call for progress and modernity while momentarily providing the reader (consumer/diner) with the ammunition to doubt the possibility of this (or any) avant-garde movement's success in relation to its revolutionizing intentions.

Modernity and Modernism on Stage

In matters of art and cuisine, the famous French art critic and poet Guillaume Apollinaire may have anticipated the Futurists. In his "Le cubisme culinaire," published in *Fantasio* on January 1, 1913, Apollinaire spoke of a new school of cooking that related "to the ancient culinary art exactly as cubism relates to ancient painting." He further noted that where "the novelties that appear in the arts and the letters astonish the public, but they do not nauseate it," this cubist cuisine might elicit such strong physical and sensory reactions. He asks: "What will the public say, however, when it will know of the existence of a new school of cooking that relates to the ancient culinary art the same way that dramatism relates to ancient poetry and cubism to ancient painting?"[7] With this question, Apollinaire is referring to *gastro-astronomisme,* which he had introduced in "L'ami Meritarte" in 1912 to define a cuisine that goes beyond gastronomic revolutions (the avant-garde in and of gastronomy) but demands instead a "dramatic" look at cooking and eating.[8] *Gastro-astronomisme* presupposes that food be—intentionally—used as drama so as to consciously have an impact on the viewer/diner's emotional and sensual perception of the world.

However, the concept that informs Apollinaire's *gastro-astronomisme* differs from the Futurist culinary principles. First, the French critic speaks exclusively of art, disregarding science and technology. Second, his cuisine has neither didactic nor political goals. Third, and

most important, Apollinaire's avant-garde discourse compares the culinary and artistic avant-garde (even in the case of *gastro-astronomisme*)
on the grounds of their intentionality. Ultimately, Apollinaire wishes
that his cuisine establish an absolute "aesthetic" relation between the
body and the world. *Gastro-astronomisme* expresses a quest for the
absolute — as one witnesses in Charles Baudelaire. Unlike Baudelaire,
however, this "expressionist" and "interior" cuisine mitigates and dissolves the disrupting effects of intoxication. More like expressionism,
it relies heavily on the productive imagination that emerges from interior sensations. In short, while doing away with referentiality, objectivity, and exactness, *gastro-astronomisme* is still rooted in synesthesia
and harmony. In contrast, the antidiets of the avant-garde, especially
Dada but also Futurism, do not partake, for their "un(re)presenta-
bility," of this harmonic impulse. The Futurists may be seen as still
attempting to reconstitute — anew — an aesthetic and synesthetic body.
Yet the Futurist culinary enterprise is not intended to rescue "taste"
and the "high" fine arts from a technologized world and the com-
mercialization of human sensations like Apollinaire's *gastro-astronomisme,* which Apollinaire nonetheless thought had anticipated the
Futurist culinary revolution.

The Futurists inherit Apollinaire's *gastro-astronomisme,* inasmuch
as it concerned itself with artistic form. Their culinary project, however,
looms larger than Apollinaire's stylistic approach to cuisine. Endowed
with the provocative aesthetic spirit of the avant-garde, Futurist food
is the Futurists' way to pursue also a civilizational renewal, that is,
the creation of a new human for a new modern world. This cooking — which does not disdain science and grounds itself entirely on the
culinary product as artificial creation against taste — intends to establish a relation of equivalence among cooking, eating, and meaning.
For example, the Futurists, in this like Apollinaire, solicit artists, doctors, cooks, and anyone interested in alimentary questions to contribute innovative culinary *formulas,* the Futurist word for recipes. While
this programmatic approach to art goes beyond the confines drawn for
it in classical aesthetics, and in this way is a typical avant-garde move,
the civilizational agenda of the *Futurist Cookbook* has its roots in premodern beliefs. Ultimately the formulas they propose are supposed to
function according to ancient "substantialist" nutritional beliefs. In
effect, the Futurists view eating as the bodily and spiritual assimilation of the quintessence of the food ingested. Foods are not neutral but
invested conceptually of specific magical powers of transformation.

ists want to intervene in modern civilization and wel-
taneous temporal dimensions, aerodynamic forms,
light spaces as expressions of modernity. Within this
becomes one way to take charge directly, with the force
of one's own will, of the "production" of the fittest body to inhabit this
new nature, that is, this artificially modified environment that allows
for multiplied and multifarious sensual experiences. Accordingly, eating foods conceived of as dynamic works of art transforms the consumer into a self-made Futurist work of art. The diner assimilates the
highly symbolic, spiritual, and magical qualities of these formulas and
in doing so assimilates his or her body to the world of steel, or the fleeting sensations and electrifying stimulations that these foods — as quintessential expressions of modern life — condense in themselves. The
Futurists' avant-garde approach to food is at once headed toward the
future and back into pregastronomic — that is, prebourgeois — beliefs
about the body and the world. In the *Futurist Cookbook,* the body
is an ancient material that needs artistic (artificial) reconstruction.
Paradoxically, then, the Futurists ground their affirmation of modernity in bypassing the history of *bourgeois* modernity. They radically
juxtapose ancient customs with future bodies and highly technological worlds. Their indebtedness to (or plundering of) ancient philosophies is not acknowledged, yet such influence is visible in the *Futurist
Cookbook.*

While Futurist cooking intends to prepare, in the present, the modern Italian for this imminent Futurist way of living, it also aims to
achieve optimism and thus intellectual stimulation through an efficient nutrition. Hence the manifesto launches its attack against pasta,
the Italian national dish. Pasta fills the stomach without energizing the
body, which remains weighty and shapeless. The misplaced idea that
healthy nourishment is less a matter of qualitative experience than of
quantity compels Italians to indulge in this antimodern alimentary
custom. Moving from the pseudoscientific register to the psychical
one, always invoking medicine in their support, Marinetti and Fillìa
also add that feeding on voluminous dishes of pasta induces "lassitude,
pessimism, nostalgic inactivity and neutralism" (37).

The supposedly scientific attack against pasta, "an absurd Italian
gastronomic religion" (ibid.), spurred the "unpopularity" of the Futurist diet, to which unpopularity these artists deeply aspired. It became
the Futurists' occasion to attack cultural traditions as "myths" while
founding a new Futurist mythical diet, an optimistic diet of the will,

through which Futurist aesthetics and ideology, now complete the inclusion of taste buds and corporeal reactions, could finally digested. As Marinetti and Fillìa underscore when writing about the manifesto of Futurist cooking in the *Futurist Cookbook*: "A violent controversy broke out in all the newspapers, with participants from every social category, from society ladies to cooks, literary men, astronomers, doctors, street urchins, nursemaids, soldiers, peasants, dockers. In Italy, whenever pasta was served in any restaurant, inn or home it was immediately interlaced with interminable discussions" (33). The controversy also documented in the text, in which amusing articles on pasta both pro and con are published, testifies to the definite entry into the public sphere of Futurist aesthetics.

No one could miss the fact that the proposed diet and then the staged banquets were nutritionally impractical, even when supposedly scientifically grounded. It was evident that the diets and the banquets were conceived literarily and were theatrically staged, as many reviewers remarked. The controversy itself, which also spread abroad, as articles in the *Herald Tribune* and the *Chicago Tribune,* among others, demonstrate, opened the doors to the aesthetic revolution that Apollinaire could not believe would capture the attention of many. He had assumed that the culinary innovations would affect few intellectual initiates. In contrast, the manifesto of Futurist cooking reached, at least rhetorically, a wider and "active" public, who wrote letters of dissent or approved of the attack on pasta enthusiastically. Because this public is also included in the *Futurist Cookbook,* the latter's ideological, civilizing elements that undeniably and strongly accompany the Futurist aesthetic program appear less authoritative and authoritarian, more discursive and even self-ironic. Irony is evident in the cookbook's multiple discursive registers. In addition, the cookbook is also contradictory in its scientific–aesthetic–psychic culinary proposal. As mentioned, the presence of irony plays down the fascist (if not nationalist) agenda that definitely informs the manifesto, the formulas, and the dinners. Nevertheless, the Futurists clearly selected the documents that went into the cookbook and circumscribed these materials with a strong ideological framework.

The Holy Palate Restaurant

After the manifesto of Futurist cooking appeared, the Futurists announced the opening of a restaurant in Turin. Fillìa and the architect

Nicolaj Diulgheroff took charge of its decoration. An article in *La Gazzetta del Popolo* on January 21, 1931, speaks of the practical and original translation from words into action of the principles that informed the Futurist culinary revolution. Till that time, the latter had been announced, studied, and debated only theoretically.

As the articles gathered in the *Futurist Cookbook* suggest, even if the announcement about a Futurist restaurant sounded unusual to most, it was received as part of the "active" tradition of Futurism. It seemed obvious to one journalist writing about this Futurist project that these artists' offensive against traditional cuisine had to be practiced — no matter how impractically — and tested on the "public" if the Futurist culinary revolution intended to leave its mark and truly change everyday habits. Only thus could a new "Italian Risorgimento," the article states, take place, in this case a gastronomic Risorgimento (65). In addition to meaning resurgence or rebirth, here, however, the term also refers to the historical period that started with the Independence campaigns in Italy in the nineteenth century and eventually led to unification under the king of Savoy. The journalist suggests that the agents of this Risorgimento will, this time, be experimental and daring artists. Hence the aesthetic culinary revolution is presented as rereading and rewriting Italian history. The latter is now literally in the hands of artists who will physically reshape, through edible foods, the Italian national body, the body-politics of Italy. The restaurant is the stage for this new Risorgimento, as evinced in the nationalist tone of the dinners proposed in the *Futurist Cookbook*.

If modernity had not been fully accomplished in the Italian state, now the Futurists took upon themselves the challenge to stage it in the restaurant, to give it the shape they desired. The Holy Palate tavern presented the public with an artificial and condensed — total — version of modernity that here took the form of an aluminum environment.[9] The total experience of modernity involved stimulating all senses at once, and consciousness, too. The banquets — both those that actually took place in the restaurant and those planned at different times and locations for special Futurist occasions — became modern "settings." The Futurists conceived of these banquets as modern situations in which, Futurist foods being served, the diner would experience the quintessence of modern life: its speed, its artificial "nature," its motors and noises, its multiple perspectives and transparency, to name just a few examples. The Futurist dishes were themselves synthetic (both synoptic and artificial) condensations of modern life, so that the diners who tasted them supposedly had the chance first to perceive in their bodies the accelerated rhythms of contemporary life and, then, express a strong physical reaction to them, one that the Futurists deemed entirely adequate to (in harmony with) the meal. The reaction was in fact already inscribed in, and thus prescribed with, the foods. Marinetti had defined modern life in his early work as dominated by contradictory and simultaneous dimensions.[10]

Along the same lines, the Holy Palate tavern's architectonic structure and its interior decoration were conceived in a Futuristic style that was intended to affect the diners emotionally and that also mirrored the intrinsic harmony between Futurist poetics and aesthetics and the Futurist diet. Diulgheroff and Fillìa relied on the "intelligence and fidelity to modernity inspiring those chefs who run the Restaurant" (*Futurist Cookbook,* 70). Similarly, the interior was intended "to give the place a metallic, shining, elastic, light and serene atmosphere; to give it the sense of how we live today, with our minds and bodies needing to find the correlative, the synthesis, and the artistic translation of the mechanical organization that prevails" (ibid.).

In the *Futurist Cookbook* the restaurant's architecture is described metaphorically as the skeleton of the Futurist diner. The analogy is with the foods that penetrate the interior—the stomach—of human beings and give shape to the body by actively sculpting it: "Dominant aluminum, the supple bone structure of a new body, completed by the rhythms of indirect lighting. Light is undoubtedly one of the fundamental realities of modern architecture and must be 'space,' must play a living role along with other forms of construction. Within the aluminum body, then, light served as an arterial system, indispensable to the surrounding organism in a state of activity" (71).

Consequently, the foods served in the restaurant, as the Futurist formulas reveal, are supposed to have the qualities of steel (or aluminum) or prepare the skeleton of the Futurist diner, just like aluminum sustains the restaurant's interior. They too are infused with the lightness of light that moves blood in one's veins. Light and steel are the two staple ingredients of most Futurist recipes, symbolically and rhetorically evoked in certain instances through organic materials, and concocted through actual metallic or artificial materials in others. Unfortunately, several of the Futurist recipes were Futurist in name only, both those proposed in Turin at the Holy Palate and in Milan at the Penna D'Oca where the first official Futurist banquet was held on November 15, 1930.[11] Examples of recipes in the *Futurist Cookbook* are Luciano Folgore's "dazzling appetizer" (*antipasto folgorante*, meaning also "incendiary" [148–49]) and the dishes known as "Mediterranean favorite zig, zug, zag" and "well-tempered little artichoke wheels" (32). Gastronomically speaking, these recipes were not so daring, as a reviewer remarked in 1930 (ibid.), and the Futurists became aware quite early on of the difficulties involved in translating a poetic vision into a gastronomic one (33).

Unlike for these recipes, the new architecture of the Holy Palate tavern and the new body of steel that the Futurists intended to shape with their diets came together for Marinetti, Fillìa, and Diulgheroff on the night of the restaurant's opening, March 8, 1931. The merging of actors and recipients, and inside and outside space, at the restaurant returns in the critics' description of the physical environment. Dr. Stradella, a staff journalist of the newspaper *La Stampa* who partook in the opening banquet, writes that the reader must imagine the Holy Palate as a "huge cube-shaped box grafted along one side on to another smaller one: the box is adorned with entirely luminous, semi-colourless columns and large metallic eyes, also luminous, embedded halfway up the wall; and this, finally, is covered with the purest aluminum from the ceiling to the floor" (76). The tavern's architecture resembling Chinese boxes best communicates the synergy of the Futurist enterprise that cuts across the divides between artistic genres and practices, comprehending all of them within a controlled synesthetic understanding of the aesthetic experience. It is controlled because the Futurists aim at eliciting specific states of mind and wish to do so according to *their* book. So the Futurists' edible works are total works of art, and the restaurant itself is a total and synthetic space. The poetic intensity of the foods lies in their synthetic nature, where the word *synthetic* means "summary" and condensation, in addition to "artificial."

Take, for example, a recipe like "chickenfiat," which was executed at the restaurant's opening. (The name *Pollo Fiat* clearly referred to the major Italian car manufacturer Fiat, but also possibly to the Latin *fiat* as in the fascist statement, quoted by Walter Benjamin in relation to the Futurists' perilous aestheticization of life, "Fiat ars — pereat mundus.")[12] According to a journalist and participant in the opening banquet, the version of the dish he ate included real steel: "One takes a good-sized chicken and cooks it in two stages: first boiled, then roasted. A capacious cavity is dug out of the shoulder of the bird, within which one places a handful of little ballbearings made of mild steel. On to the rear part of the bird one sews in three slices a raw cockscomb. The sculpture thus prepared goes in the oven for about ten minutes. When the flesh has fully absorbed the flavor of the mild steel balls, the chicken is served with a garnish of whipped cream" (*Futurist Cookbook,* 78). Another diner at a subsequent banquet held in Novara refused, in a sign of protest, to evaluate this dish in his review (85). With chickenfiat, the Futurists moved from poetic metaphor to its sensual application. The presence of steel in this dish is not surprising but an important variation of those game dishes that also preserve in their preparation the bullets that killed the prey. Yet while in the traditional dish a reference is made to the world of "hunters," chickenfiat uses car ball bearings ("cuscinetti a sfera") to transform the natural prey into the medium through which to transfer speed from the machine (car) to Futurist diners who themselves acquire the quality of a car: their bodies now roll on the steel balls inside them while they are also inside the Futurist restaurant, itself decorated with steel. Steel is thus both the container and the contained. It forms the outside and the inside of the Futurist diner.

The synthesis between modern lifestyle, modern architecture, and Futurist food was intended to shape the modernist Futurist sensibility of those who entered the Holy Palate and there consumed, as agents, this restaged modernity. The restaurant becomes the sacred space where the fusion between the individual and the external modern world occurs both structurally, as reflected in the restaurant's architecture, and theatrically. The restaurant in effect was an extreme version of the Futurist genre of the dynamic theater, a theater without a fourth wall (the wall between players and audience) where actors and spectators interacted. In the theatrical space of this tavern, cooks, artists, consumers all met to stage a modernity that was approaching Italy, but was not yet experienced as the country's dominant feature.

The parallel between the table and the theater was common already in the nineteenth century and has been ever since.[13] The Futurist restaurant, however, differed from this tradition insofar as the theatrical space that functioned as its reference and the meals that functioned as its stage were not the familiar architecture and decor found in the regular bourgeois theaters—or restaurants—of the twenties in either France or Italy. Rather, the Futurists' reference points were the happenings and events, the poetry and the "rumori" (noises) of the open modern world that these artists had already captured in their music, paintings, costumes, and fashion. Antonio Sant'Elia, who signed the manifesto of Futurist architecture published in *Lacerba* on August 1, 1914, had insisted already then on both the synthetic and the ephemeral aspects of Futurist architecture that return in the Holy Palate tavern: "That, just as the ancients drew inspiration for their art from the elements of nature, we—who are materially and spiritually artificial—must find that inspiration in the elements of the utterly new mechanical world *we have created,* and of which architecture must be the most beautiful expression, the most complete synthesis, the most efficacious integration."[14] To this he added:

> We have lost our predilection for the monumental, the heavy, the static, and we have enriched our sensibility with *a taste for the light, the practical, the ephemeral and the swift.* We no longer feel ourselves to be the men of the cathedrals, the palaces and the podiums. We are the men of the great hotels, the railway stations, the immense streets, colossal ports, covered markets, luminous arcades, straight roads and beneficial demolitions. We must invent and rebuild the Futurist city like an immense and tumultuous shipyard, agile, mobile and dynamic in every detail; and the Futurist house must be like a gigantic machine. . . . From an architecture conceived in this way no formal or linear habit can grow, since the fundamental characteristics of Futurist architecture will be its impermanence and transience. THINGS WILL ENDURE LESS THAN US. EVERY GENERATION MUST BUILD ITS OWN CITY. This constant renewal of the architectonic environment will contribute to the victory of Futurism which has already been affirmed by WORDS-IN-FREEDOM, PLASTIC DYNAMISM, MUSIC WITHOUT QUADRATURE AND THE ART OF NOISES, and for which we fight without respite against traditionalist cowardice." (*Futurist Manifestos,* 170, 172)

But the theater—to be understood as the Futurist Variety Theatre—in its juxtaposition with the restaurant, in fact disturbed another more important public space, namely, the museum of art.

According to the tradition of overlap between theatrical spaces and events and the restaurant, the *Futurist Cookbook* informs the reader that if Futurist architects designed the restaurant, it was actual chefs (cavalier Bulgheroni especially, who was the most active Futurist cook in these years) who prepared the artists' recipes. The diners consumed these artists' ideas (rendered edible by the chefs) and, during the banquet, were also graced with the presence of the artists themselves who took pride in, besides responsibility for, their creations: "Even

Academician Marinetti will take part in the opening and answer any criticisms. This is certainly a useful new idea. Until now in a restaurant the poor consumer has never found anyone who would answer for a nasty meal. At the Holy Palate we'll have a member of the Academy. And he'll respond in rhyme" (68). Again, the participation of both producers and consumers at the banquets completes the idea of a restaurant as a site of exchange, which for Futurism is also the original birthplace of a much-debated new sensibility that needed testing both intellectually, that is, rhetorically, and physically, namely, in each of its facets: as a concept and a material, and in its reception. In this restaurant, the mouth and the palate are "holy" means of communication and creation shared between artists and consumers, critics included. So too does the restaurant's space allow the individual to experience synthetically the outside world as it's created. The diner is in fact constructing it in both body and language while eating the Futurist meal and living in the ephemeral theatrical modern architecture described above by Sant'Elia.

The foods reproduce the synthetism of the Futurist simultaneous poems, both in their reactualization of less common combinations of ingredients and in their linguistic creation of new terms that indicate the procedures for realizing the dishes. While naming dishes is typical in culinary history, it is less common to witness the coinage of new terms for practices of cooking that, furthermore, for Marinetti were inspired by Futurist aesthetic concepts (such as the coperfume and cotactile, etc.).[15] Marinetti theorized and produced his synthetic poems with the so-called words in liberty, or else words that destroyed syntax and were purely "expressive," like the body in a state of excitement: as he writes, here gestures and fragments of words substitute for prose and structured sentences. In addition, as evident in the analogies also used to construct the Futurist restaurant, in the foods, and in the diners' states of mind, analogy is the red thread of Futurist aesthetics. Marinetti had expressed in his earlier manifestos that analogies are the best rhetorical way to "embrace the life of matter." They are invaluable for their sensual and spontaneous logic always stimulating new flows of images.[16] In the case of Futurist cooking, this translates into the "simultaneous mouthfuls" that Marinetti mentions in the manifesto of Futurist cooking. There he invites the "creation of simultaneous and changing *canapés* which contain ten, twenty flavors to be tasted in a few seconds. In Futurist cooking these *canapés* have by analogy the same amplifying function that images have in literature. A given taste of something can sum up an entire area of life, the history of an amorous passion or an entire voyage to the Far East" (*Futurist Cookbook*, 40).

The restaurant itself is made to function according to the Futurist poetic principles of synthesis, synesthesia, and analogical correspondences. As far as its space is concerned, the restaurant is conceived as a "multimedial" space of experience in which all senses are conjured up "ritualistically," hence the name Holy Palate. In the restaurant, as especially the definitive dinners in the *Futurist Cookbook* show, food comes to the table according to a carefully studied plan. Yet the banquet itself is an ephemeral performance. Fillìa stresses: "Our initiative and actions in opening the 'Holy Palate' have only the artistic, creative and energizing aims of a culinary theory of ours" (66). The artistic–poetic creativity informing the Futurist culinary theory demands that the restaurant transgress the canonical — in early Futurist language, "academic" — classification of disciplines and relative institutions that separates the art world from the life world. This divide is represented, for instance, by the separation between the museum, exclusively devoted to the arts, and the common restaurant, a space traditionally devoted to the transient social — that is, nonaesthetic — pleasure taken in the physical consumption of perishable, nonartistic materials. In contrast to this separation of spheres, the Futurist restaurant is conceived as the antimuseum par excellence, the only sacred place where Futurist art can be shown and consumed, without being preserved.[17]

The Holy Palate tavern reverses the function of the museum, the latter taken as a site for the artist's inspiration (the muses) moved by the museum's preservation of classical artworks and, through them, of the idea of beauty. The Futurists use the restaurant as their modern antimuseum or, more precisely, as the source of a modern artistic (theatrical) inspiration. The latter is the inspiration of optimism that, in the prefatory story introducing the *Futurist Cookbook*, is derived from the edible sculptures created by a group of Futurist artists and friends for this purpose and, specifically, to rescue a suicidal friend from death. The Holy Palate is an architectonic space devoted entirely to production and consumption as bodily artistic performances aimed at spurring the diners to embrace modernity. The physical consumption of artworks characterizes this "holy" antimuseum. It is not the work of art that is preserved and then "adored" in its static, atemporal integrity in this antimuseum. Rather, an artistic experience is born from a material act of consumption: eating, which leaves its traces on the consumer's body — or rather translates food into energy. The consumer's experience is artistic rather than purely aesthetic because, in the act of consuming Futurist foods, reception becomes metamorphosis through the body's total involvement. Participation substitutes for individual disinterested judgment. So the critics, to fulfill their critical task, that is, to be able to judge the enterprise aesthetically, must eat and acquiesce to the risk of becoming Futurist while assimilating this diet physically. The act of collaboration in creating the Futurist artwork as total performance also precludes the fall of this material consumption into a commodity fetishism determined by capitalist economy and the logic of exchange. Nonetheless, the diet is moved by a powerful ideological agenda.

Recipes and Recipients

The official and nonofficial diners at the restaurant, for instance, doctors and Futurist fans, also included journalists and critics. The Futurist artists despised art critics: these so-called interpreters of "good taste" were seen as in fact minions of aesthetic conventions and institutions.[18] Yet the *Futurist Cookbook* prominently includes among its texts the reviews and articles published in national and international papers about the proposed Futurist cooking and the banquets that took place. The journalists' and critics' documentation endows the Futurist enterprise with an air of urgency. Their presence at the banquets, situating the debate entirely within the public sphere, contributes to the final affirmation of Futurist cooking and Futurist art as discourse, as Marinetti and Fillìa intended.

However, the publication of the *Futurist Cookbook* also testifies to the Futurists' awareness of the limited temporal framework, thus the actual limitations, of their culinary revolution. Marinetti and Fillìa's awareness of its temporary impact may be inferred from the fact that the cookbook, containing various materials and articles, was already published in 1932, just a year after the restaurant opened in Turin. The speed with which the publication came into being suggests that the artists involved in Futurist cooking did not foresee that their actions would be up and running for a long time. They wanted thus to make sure there was a record of their efforts. In a January 21, 1931, interview Fillìa hopes that the restaurant will be successful, but then adds that while business success is important, the focus of the entire enterprise is putting theory into action, that is, testing Futurist theory (*Futurist Cookbook,* 54).

But why would the Futurists, who despised history as much as they despised critics and museums, and who welcomed their own supersession, finally compile a historical document to record ephemeral banquets? Why would they want the *Futurist Cookbook* to capture the memory of their fleeting actions in the very same way that the repugnant museum preserves a work of art? While the museum—for the Futurists—hypocritically capitalizes on the exchange value of an artwork that it pretends to put on display for its immortality, the Futurists put together a literary documentation of the ephemeral that may be read as ironic about its own durability and aesthetic value. Some "definitive dinners" point to this irony textually, and the historicity of the debates around pasta and xenomania indicate it contextually. The *Futurist Cookbook* is the Futurists' own writing of their tradition, their own museification of the ephemeral. Yet the documentation that gathers a great variety of writings plays down the monumentalization of the enterprise itself. The documentation's ironic dimension lies not least in the Futurists' choice of a nonacademic genre, the cookbook, for their monumentalization. This genre also enables the Futurists to capture well their ironic avant-garde approach to fascist nationalist and imperialist politics.

The consignment to a cookbook of the Futurists's final—and most important, because most basic—revolution of sensibility undermines history, capitalist accumulation, and commodity fetishism alike. It also plays down Futurism's own accomplishments in the face of the temporality of modernity and the art critics' self-importance. Their words are temporalized and made less definite, more bound to the moment than the critics may wish them to be.[19] Their "aesthetic" judgment is thus less central, less permanent. Consequently, art criticism is no longer viewed as the epicenter of aesthetic discourse. Yet the critics' words, highly represented in the *Futurist Cookbook,* allow that Futurist ephemeral *artworks* come into being.

As recipients of Futurist foods, and thus as the object/subject of the Futurists' artistic–ideological experiments, the critics not only comment on the Futurist culinary revolution, their words become Futurist works of art. The Futurists had intended that the consumers

(among whom the critics) become Futurist at the moment of ingestion of Futurist food. They demonstrate this by collecting the critics'
words in the *Futurist Cookbook*. Incorporating the critics as actors in
the cookbook testifies, in some cases, to the power of Futurist poetics
even against the critics' own opinion.

The critics who wanted to "have" an opinion in effect had to eat,
to taste with their mouths, and to participate in the Futurist theatrical banquets. They could not judge them based on just looking at the
art or listening to it. Criticism — despite its "judgment" — is made com-
plicit in actualizing Futurist cooking, or total aesthetics, in its existence as effective discourse. In this instance, one could detect a totalitarian impulse in the avant-garde at large, beyond Futurism itself. It
lies in coercing the public — independently from its value judgment,
distance, or identification — into assisting with the production of the
work. Coercion hence is coextensive with the public's participation. In
the case of Futurist banquets and foods, however, the works are consumed and destroyed actively and spontaneously by the public, thus
also undermining the clear distinction between active producer and
passive consumer, and possibly inducing an act of criticism toward
common and conventional consumption.

The creative, instinctual, and, in particular, improvisational features of Futurist actions are maintained in these otherwise carefully
staged banquets thanks to the spontaneous addition to the dinner programs of unexpected dishes that the diners and critics, as they let us
know, could not decipher. (In some instances they did not even know
what the dishes really were.) One consequence of the improvisational
nature of these dishes is the silence the food occasionally seemed to
provoke in critics who found themselves almost deprived of "technical skills" and thus at a loss in terms of their reactions and "position"
with respect to the particular work (of art). As a result, critics were
unable to produce *their* work of art — the article on Futurism — or at
least to complete it authoritatively. One critic wrote: "We thought we
tasted hints of Bologna mortadella sausage, mayonnaise and the sort
of Turin caramel known as pasta Gianduia; but 24 hours after eating
it, after a careful examination of our consciences, we don't believe we
can say for sure" (*Futurist Cookbook*, 78). To be sure, the critic, who
still believes he or she could assess this kind of artwork from a normative perspective, wanting to fix once and for all the art objects' aesthetic value, is defeated by time. Time is the stage where ephemeral

yet powerful desires and intuitions come into being and are experienced. The critic who looks for "presence" in these meals is disappointed, as is the pasta lover who, according to the Futurists, finds "presence" when he or she fills the present — the void — with it.

Instead, in the Futurist restaurant, eating is part and parcel of the performance being created. As such, it is paired with the consumption of music, verse, and painting. If each one of these arts demands the attention of at least one sense, all senses come together in the acts of cooking and eating. These total sensations that the Futurists intend to capture in their foods are supposedly transferred to the reception of other arts, investing the latter, too, more fully. This also works in reverse: each specific sense normally used for one or the other art is added to the experience of eating, as in the case of "aerofoods."

On its opening night the Holy Palate boasted some of its most emblematic synesthetic recipes. The aerofoods are described as tactile, but they also involve sounds and scents. A journalist writes of one particular dish:

> It consists of four parts: on a plate are served a quarter of a fennel bulb, an olive, a candied fruit and a tactile device. The diner eats the olive, then the candied fruit, then the fennel. Contemporaneously, he delicately passes the tips of the index and middle fingers of his left hand over the rectangular device, made of a swatch of red damask, a little square of black velvet and a tiny piece of sandpaper. From some carefully hidden melodious source comes the sound of part of a Wagnerian opera, and, simultaneously, the nimblest and most graceful of the waiters sprays the air with perfume. Astonishing results: test them and see. (77)

Like a Wagnerian opera, the aerofood is theatrical in the temporal structure that determines it: it unfolds in time, but it also defines the use that must be made of that time. It is operatic (or synesthetic) because of the senses involved, yet it does not possess opera's "excessive" melodrama. Rather, it elicits intuitively (or analogically) the tastes of all the dishes that may make use of these ingredients. It does so through an abstract composition of minimal ingredients while allowing one to focus on each individual detail. Each ingredient, though, is not taken in isolation: its taste is reinterpreted and recontextualized. The diner now focuses on it through the filter of the accompanying sensations that ensue from touching whatever material is paired with it and from smelling unrelated perfumes. This dish, more than others, suggests that Futurist food is not about satisfying hunger or filling a void.[20] It is about composing new sensorial texts for the body called into action in all its senses. The body's action is what energizes it. In much the same way that modern architecture combines natural and artificial materials in new buildings, here ingredients are tasted for the first time in different sensorial "environments" that reveal other previously unimagined qualities and produce astonishing sensations, as the critic writes. The banquet thus is conceived less as a representation than as a theatrical performance or an act of production.

The aero qualities of foods — their analogy with the lightness of being, their incorporation of noise and movement, among other things — were to be understood as appropriate to the dynamic life of the Futurist individual, the winged, speedy creature in airplanes. Actual aerobanquets took place in Chiavari and Bologna in 1931. The diners were served Futurist dishes named after a plane's take-off and landing. A critic in Chiavari amended that the dishes were "too poetic to be appreciated by the needs of the stomach" (91). In Bologna the diners ate in a setting made to look like an airplane, including engine noises. In contrast to the critic in Chiavari, the critic here admired the synthetic tables and the theatrical setting. He mentioned the props made with edible ingredients, such as the potatoes used in place of flowery decorations. This Futuristic, clearly artificial setting transformed the diners into "experimental" passengers, true actors of and in their own Futurist experience.

In sum, the Holy Palate stages the simultaneity of multiple sensations in its space, defying the unity of space–time crucial to classical drama, and views the theater as an arena for all the arts to come together: "The tavern will not be a simple, ordinary restaurant but will take on the character of an arts centre holding competitions and organizing Futurist poetry evenings, art exhibitions and fashion shows instead of the usual post-prandial coffee evenings or dances" (67). Marinetti and Fillìa emphasize, along the same lines, that "discussions about Futurist cooking were not limited only to the gastronomic sphere, because our desire for renewal has always been expressed clearly in favour of all branches and all activities of art and life" (79). Not simply a museum, or an art gallery or a restaurant, this tavern is a multimedial space for experience, except for the surreptitiously coerced critics. Everyone participates in the creation, and success, of the manifestation; it is led by some, but grasped in its entirety only through the shared endeavor of cooks, artists, and diners, everyone shaping the final work of art. To a certain extent, even the critical critics are, in this sense, represented in the *Futurist Cookbook*. This is an early example of performance art, one that involves the choice of nonconventional (anti-institutional) spaces for consumption and the presentation of the artwork as work in progress.

For the Futurists, artistic experience is based in production and consumption as one activity that generates a sensually multilayered aesthetic experience in which no single sense dominates another. The hierarchical syntax that privileges one sense — and meaning, in particular, as *the* ultimate sense — is dismantled in favor of a productive confusion of the senses, which is nevertheless always accurate and specific. In the dictionary of Futurist gastronomic terms included in the *Futurist Cookbook,* for example, synesthesia is indicated by the terms *conprofumo* (with perfume), *contattile* (with touch), *conrumore* (with noise), *conmusica* (with music), and *conluce* (with light). Each term is described as standing for the sensory affinity between one material, which is "perceived" through one sense, and another material experienced through another sense. So, for example, the *contattile* is the word indicating "the tactile affinity between a given material and the taste of another. Example: the *contattile* of the banana puree with velvet or a woman's flesh" (172). In the restaurant's multimedial space, where the banquets are total performances (in an operatic sense), every art is experienced through another seemingly unrelated sense.

Cooking and eating always involve more than one sense simultaneously. The restaurant as a laboratory of creation and consumption is the ideal space for the encounter and study, the discussion and reception of artworks expressly conceived to augment their synesthetic nature. The restaurant is the theater where the Futurists test the limits of Futurist aesthetics, that is, its effects. In the Holy Palate tavern, the Futurists consume their own works; they surpass themselves and continue their experimentation with the body so as to mold the imagination and, in their parlance, generate modern states of mind. The desire to shape the consumers by feeding them Futurist ideological and aesthetic food has two effects: it pushes the Futurists to invent the restaurant as a stage of collaboration, where the consumers participate in the Futurists' completion of their edible artworks, and the Futurists try to superimpose an ideological agenda on the banquets and recipes with the aim of controlling — structurally or architectonically — the effects of such collaboration. This is most evident in the persuasive coercion of the critics, which can only occur through their participation. Yet absolute ideological control fails both in the tavern and in the ideologically constructed "definitive dinners," where a performative element in these texts exceeds their agenda. But first: what is this ideology exactly?

Futurist Cooking and Chauvinist Dinners: Aestheticization of Politics?

To answer the question about ideology, I now turn to the attack on pasta in the manifesto of Futurist cooking and the second-wave Futurists' antinationalist (antipopulist) nationalism.

Pasta, Nationalism, and Fascism

The attack on pasta as an Italian religion is part and parcel of the total renewal the Futurist modernist artists seek. The Futurists' aversion to pasta originates in their nationalist concern for a not-yet-attained modern Italian identity. To be more specific, when the Futurists of the second wave discuss pasta they grapple with the open question of Italian modernity. This includes subtle references to World War I, which the interventionist Futurists had called the "Great War." The tradition of pasta as essentially Italian is disavowed, and pasta is said to descend from the northern and barbarian Ostrogoths, in Libero Glauco Silvano's article included in the *Futurist Cookbook* (50). In Marco Ramperti's treatise, pasta then enslaves Italians in the foreigners' eyes: "The danger and disgrace of this myth of 'maccheroni': this *macaroni* as they call it abroad which has made us the butt of indecorous metaphors beyond the Alps. . . . And it's an offensive image, derisory, grotesque, and ugly" (45). Pasta fills the stomach without nourishing it, in the same way that Italian rhetoric fills the mouth with meaningless words: "Swallowed down the way it is, spaghetti poisons us and weighs us down. We suddenly feel as leaden as false coins. Something jams us up, down below, like a log. We have no more easy syllables or ready images. Our thoughts wind round each other, get mixed up and tangled like the vermicelli we have taken in. Words get knotted into a sticky ball in the same way" (45). This sticky ball, or rather its consequences, expresses the Futurists' anxiety about Italians being identified as barbaric by foreign people. Most of all, pasta becomes in their eyes the declaration of *passéist* affection (a sticky attachment to) a nonmodernist nationalism. Modern Italians must free themselves of these stereotypes that they themselves reproduce and help keep in place by feeding on an archaeological ruinous memory of a great past, instead of the recent welcome destruction of the Great War that brought closure to the formation of the modern Italian nation. The "defenders of pasta are" — accordingly — "shackled by its ball and chained like convicted lifers or carry its ruins in their stomachs like archaeologists" (37).

The Futurists abhor the image of Italy as embodying an ancient cultural past. In their view, World War I completed the glories of the nineteenth-century Italian Risorgimento with the constitution of a unified Italian state now free to be a modern nation-state. For the Futurists, World War I marked the country's entrance into modern European history, as they write in the manifesto against xenomania, included in the *Futurist Cookbook*. This manifesto concludes: "Always remember this Italian masterpiece, which is even greater than the Divine Comedy: the battle of Vittorio Veneto. In the name of this masterpiece, symbolized by the wreckage of the Austro-Hungarian Empire which our armored divisions had to overpower on the road to Tarvisio, we, at the first alert, will shoot anti-Italian xenomanes" (62). The chauvinistic violence that surfaces here was typical of the Futurist manifestos, antedating World War I. Unlike then, when nationalism was a certain project for the future, now it is a project that needs redefinition because it is part of history, albeit a near history. A certain anxiety emerges about the Futurists' self-definition with respect to their own Italianist agenda and the present state of nationalism in fascist Italy.

The Futurists' focus on national history, like their stress on the movement's history, reveals the debt of the Futurists' texts to the strong legacy of Risorgimento. The appropriation of "Italocentrism" allows the Futurists to both partake in the fascist nationalist ideal, or rather to take positions in line with party politics, and envision a different way for Italy to enter modern history. Just as the Futurists face the dilemma of their institutionalization in relation to their avant-garde history, their Italocentrism questions their relation to Italian history. They invent a modern Italy that does not square with the fascist neoclassical and imperial ideal.

Even the most fascistic piece included in the *Futurist Cookbook*, the manifesto against xenomania in which they rail against those who fancy only what is foreign, has less to do with xenophobia than with defining a proper Italian nationalism. The problem is one of self-definition first, and then of imperialism. This disturbing manifesto notes at its outset that the words *xenomania* and *xenomanes* are "unfortunately becoming more necessary every day . . . despite the Imperial strength of Fascism" (58). Let us be clear: Futurism does not dissent from an imperialist politics. The Futurists seem to imply in the cookbook, however, that not even fascist nationalist propaganda sufficed to evoke enough affection for Italy as a nation. The Futurists seek to develop a sense of national pride, to raise national consciousness, where fascist nationalist politics, in their view, has failed.

Futurist cooking and eating are the realm of action, beyond fascist politics, where Futurist rhetoric and aesthetics may be translated. The Futurists' actions take place as and in the rhetorical–theatrical banquets. Through the body, the Futurists believe they can accomplish their nationalist, Italocentric agenda better than the fascists can through politics alone. The body — like a text — demands constant reading. The need for permanent construction and change of the body assures the Futurists, who now take the body to be their main object and principle, that they can find here a central and continuous cultural role in the production of modernity.

Hence the attack on pasta is unexpectedly, and subtly, also an attack on a present fascist culture and fascist state politics that testify to Italy's incomplete modernization and disappointed nationalist vision, according to the *Futurist Cookbook*: "Apart from celebrated and legendary exceptions, until now men have fed themselves like ants, rats, cats or oxen. Now with the Futurists the first human way of eating is born. We mean the ART of self-nourishment. Like all the arts, it eschews plagiarism and demands creative originality" (21). The Futurists are claiming their stronger and more powerful will to change and transform culture over any strictly political revolution. Their total aesthetic renewal will accomplish more directly, through the art of perfecting the body machine, what the *fascists* had not completed or even accomplished with their destruction of the democratic institutions. They had not affected the cultural tastes of the Italian body. Artists are the ultimate agents of transformation, rather than politicians, who settle for their own and their agenda's stability.

While fascism must complete the nationalist project politically, the Futurists must make sure to complete the fascist *"revolution"* culturally. Thus the Futurists keep alert and reconstruct the memory of World War I's major victory—Vittorio Veneto—as a work of art to be admired (a monument!) rather than a provocative modern artwork to be discussed. War as art must be contemplated and monumentalized. The victory of Vittorio Veneto ironically demands a kind of aesthetic reception informed by the classical aesthetics of the beautiful, rather than by the Futurist aesthetics of destruction. The Futurists' claim that war or indeed destruction was and is a work of art assures them a political role in the fascist organization and conception of modern Italy, according to which the liberal bourgeoisie must be destroyed and so its culture. The Futurists show that modernity must be constructed—and can be constructed—beautifully, and this entails appreciating the aesthetics of destruction. The aestheticization of destruction (as object and technique of art) serves the fascist avant-garde agenda especially in a country long dominated by the idea of its own everlasting cultural beauty. Bourgeois Italy views itself as beautiful. Italy represents and is represented as the beautiful, for example, in the eyes of traveling foreigners. In the Futurists' view, this official natural beauty of Italy must be violently shattered, along with the representation of the beautiful. Only then can a new modern image of Italy be produced. The task of the Futurist avant-garde is to destroy both organic natural beauty and the organic work of art that reproduces it indefinitely through representation. This task is the production of the destruction of representation.

Yet this work of destruction is reconciled with a traditional concept of aesthetic reception, or contemplation. Destruction of the old, of nature and of the organic, and the work of production of the modern that ensues from destruction (or war) appears at once to tear the veil of beauty and to require a displacement of organicity and "harmony" onto the inorganic artwork (the battle of Vittorio Veneto, war in general, devouring). Only through this reconstructed artificial organicity can a new modern Italian be posited and affirmed, one ideologically sound and with a solidly grounded identity, albeit a mobile one.

Some of the definitive dinners speak clearly to this desire of assimilation and strong identity. Take, for example, the *Heroic Winter Dinner.* Permeated by the nationalistic, interventionist fervor that animated the Futurists during the Great War and that fed their support of the colonial politics of fascism, this staging of a meal glorifies war as a manly field of action. While the text of this meal performs the production of a destructive sensibility, it also ends up fetishizing its value, its aim.

The recipes to be served to the soldiers getting ready for war contain ingredients that should overcome their melancholy and fear of death. The fear and anguish felt by the soldier about to fight in the war and thus facing probable death are first materialized in the object to be eaten and then overcome through the action of eating. The fear of death is displaced onto a gastronomic pleasure, a material and non-sentimental way to reconcile oneself with death through life:

> A group of soldiers who at three o'clock on a January afternoon will have to get into a lorry to enter the line of fire at four, or go up in an airplane to bomb cities or counter-attack enemy flights, would seek in vain the perfect preparation for these in the grieving kiss of a mother, of a wife, of children or in re-reading passionate letters.
>
> A dreamy walk is equally inappropriate. So is the reading of an amusing book. Instead these fighters sit down round a table, where they are served a "Drum Roll of Colonial Fish" and some "Raw Meat Torn by Trumpet Blasts." (102)

The affection of a mother, wife, or children does not encourage action; it is a memory from the past and a sign of origin, rather than destination. Instead, the aggressive act of devouring, enhanced by the symbolic quality of the Futurist dishes, becomes a courage-enhancing ritual act that prepares the soldier for combat. Eating is here considered from the perspective of a struggle for life. The recipes connect eating and war via analogies. They microscopically contain the battle against the enemy, as well as the fighter's victory that they communicate, putatively, to the soldier.

The recipe for the "Drum Roll of Colonial Fish" (*Pesce coloniale al rullo di tamburo*) calls for mullet, *cefalo* in Italian. The word may be interpreted as a reference to the head. The fish is first cooked with colonial produce, such as bananas and pineapples, and eaten to a continuous drum roll, which evokes associations with the drums of the colonized indigenous people (resisting?) and the call to war known from ancient times. The Colonial Head is cut off and devoured. The second course, "Raw Meat Torn by Trumpet Blasts," metaphorically brings the experience of the trenches to the table:

> Cut a perfect cube of beef. Pass an electric current through it, and then marinate it for twenty four hours in a mixture of rum, cognac and white

vermouth. Remove it from the mixture and serve on a bed of red pepper, black pepper and snow. Each mouthful is to be chewed carefully for one minute, and each mouthful is divided from the next by vehement blasts on the trumpet blown by the eater himself.

When it is time for the *Peralzarsi*, the soldiers are served plates of ripe persimmons, pomegranates and blood oranges. While these disappear into their mouths, some very sweet perfumes of roses, jasmine, honeysuckle and acacia flowers will be sprayed around the room, the nostalgic and decadent sweetness of which will be roughly rejected by the soldiers who rush like lightning to put their gas masks on.

The moment they are about to leave they swallow the Throat-Explosion, a solid liquid consisting of a pellet of Parmesan cheese steeped in Marsala. (102)

The raw meat electrocuted and then torn by the trumpet blasts marks the possible future of the soldiers, who are also referred to as "cannon fodder" (lit. *carne da macello,* meat to be butchered). The snow, spotted with black and red peppers, forms a Futurist bird's-eye view (or indeed the view from the beloved airplane) that reproduces a winter landscape of black trenches, black corpses, and blood spilled on white snow. The trumpet blasts interrupting the succession of bites evoke the sudden assaults on the soldier's life. Thus the body that while eating asserts life is here simultaneously assaulted by sudden death, the noise of which, however, the soldier himself (his consuming body) brings about. In this meal, he becomes the master of death (his or his enemy's) by blowing the trumpet. The trumpet is both the instrument of his death and the weapon that he may use to kill the enemy. Note the assonance between *tromba* and *bomba* (trumpet and bomb). The foods eaten are all associable with either the soldier's identity or some instrument of death. The dessert is a fruit plate containing, among other things, persimmons, *cachi* in Italian. The fruit is written just like the Italian transliteration of the English khaki, colonial and military uniform. Finally, the assonance between pomegranates and grenades (*melograni* and *granate*) changes this fruit into a weapon. In contrast to this painting of war and its effects, the sweetness of the other life, the life of affect and love omitted from the meal, is evoked through the use of volatile perfumes. These are chosen specifically to provoke nausea and force the soldiers to leave the nostalgic scene and pursue, optimistically, their military goal or, as the painterly meal described commands, death. By the end of the meal the soldiers have reached the "definitive" and conclusive state of mind necessary for combat. This achievement is signaled by their rejection of the perfumes. First the khaki, then the gas mask, and finally the pellet they ingest as a sign of pending death complete the cycle of this "heroic winter meal." The winter marks, somewhat traditionally, the path to death.

Heroic Winter Dinner represents a mini war-scenario in which the soldier metaphorically anticipates his death by devouring, consuming life. Before being "lived," war is heroically experienced as an act of devouring. In this act, the soldier is figuratively in control of both his life and his enemy's. The meal stages a living-theater of war in which the soldier becomes the agent of his life, a life that flows into death: his act of eating is here both a figurative and literal act of consuming life, of the products that most sustain it, as well as the act of "killing time." Devouring is the moment in which life and death are experienced simultaneously. The soldier experiences death as gastronomic — sensual — will for life and overcomes his crisis (and fear) through an act of devouring that puts him in control. Yet a textual reading of the meal (as I have just performed) also paints quite literally the bloody aspects of war. In this sense, the painterly-text does not shrink from presenting war's gruesome aspects, as the violence of devouring. Yet this dish intends to achieve optimism and does so by glorifying death in a fascist manner. But unlike the fascists, this "definitive dinner" performs the destructive energy of war rather than present the consumer with just an organic, complete picture of war's glories. Here aestheticization is less about disavowing conflict than about fetishizing its production in the aesthetic realm.

Assimilating the Other: Maps and Landscapes of White Male Desire

At first glance, the contemplation of war as beautiful seemingly has nothing in common with incorporation and devouring as destructive acts of reception, most typical of the avant-garde. In the *Futurist Cookbook* the ingestion of destructive/dissonant warlike foods seems to generate a modern individual whose organic beauty is artificially constructed rather than supposedly "naturally" given. This modern eater of Futurist meals is produced as beautiful nonorganic work by a voluntary act of destruction. The latter is itself a work of art that contains the beauty of the new, which in turn emerges from the ashes of the old. As a product of this destructive construction, the modern eater perceives himself or herself as second nature, as technological product, attuned to the artificial modern world. His or her body and senses have reached a new organic harmonious relation to the external world, this time attained not through imitation of a pregiven beautiful but through an act of voluntary production. In effect, focusing on the difference between contemplation (aestheticization) and incorporation (devouring and destructive methods) will be Benjamin's approach to the avant-garde's material poetics and aesthetics. Benjamin calls this aesthetics — that conflates destruction with organicity — the Futurist/fascist aestheticization of politics. Benjamin, however, does not account for the fact that production is clearly displayed as part of the work here. The *Futurist Cookbook* claims that art is a work of production based on destruction. It also aestheticizes or recomposes the fractures that such destruction produces within a necessary, postorganic organicity and harmony, this time called "artificial optimism." Classical nature and organic aesthetic forms of beauty appear in the cookbook as embodied in forms of otherness that are redefined, assimilated, and transformed violently both in cooking and through devouring.

The cookbook's opening story is an account of how a group of Futurist artists rescues a friend and colleague from falling into depression and committing suicide after he has lost his love. They rush to his villa — very much described in the style of aestheticism whose best-known exponent was Gabriele D'Annunzio — and prepare for him a gargantuan meal that not only halts his suicidal intentions but also instills optimism in his veins. The Futurists, inspired by their erotic desire, build female food sculptures in this story. These edible women offer the momentary illusion, and attendant pleasure, that desire can be fulfilled. They replace the unique woman that the protagonist, Giulio Onesti, has lost. More importantly, though, these edible sculptures of male desire present themselves as the only solution to a fetishization of love and the love object; the Futurists' target is evidently aestheticism. The edible women not only substitute for the actual lost object, glorified by aestheticism, but also satisfy Giulio more deeply and more successfully than another "real" woman who, he tells his friends, is soon coming to visit and with whom he already fears he will fall in love. Giulio mentions her arrival and describes her as looking just like the former lost love.

These edible Futurist sculptures, in which little womanly feet are set in motion and curvy bodies rotate in the air, demystify the notions

of the eternal feminine (now turned into an edible feminine) and of a
natural woman. They present love as a hypocritical romanticizing of
the ardent and devouring desire to possess the other. In this roman-
tic/aestheticist constellation dominated by love for real women, who
are accordingly considered unique in their natural being, loss and
fear are dominant sentiments. Love in the decadent bourgeois world,
as Giulio demonstrates for us, does not bring joy, and women are in
fact responsible for the depressive state of mind in which a man like
Giulio—up to this point still a traditional artist—finds himself. His
Futurist friends intervene to make him see that in consumerist society,
dominated by commodity fetishism, value is exchange. The belief in
authentic true love for one love object is of no use. Only the artificial,
intense moment of gratification one finds in the consumption of the
reproducible fetish counts. Gratification happens when one artificially
constructs and then devours the fetish object of one's own desire. All
desire is to be found in synthesis in erotic desire, which the Futurists intend to liberate by feeding it with their "Futurist" edible female
sculptures. The Futurist fetishes, in the hands of the artists, are the
true sources of inspiration of a will to life that defies nostalgia and
melancholy.[21] The story initiates Giulio into Futurist mythopoesis. As
the introduction in the *Futurist Cookbook,* it also highlights the mission of Futurist cooking: give voice to a devouring desire by feeding
it with ad hoc objects, artistic, artificial foods, which stimulate desire
and optimism.

But are women a desiring subject in the story? Is woman conceived
here as partaking first of the act of creation and of devouring of herself,
reproduced in the shape of an edible sculpture or object? In addition to
the lost love and a first woman, a second woman is expected to arrive
on the scene. This woman's power is threatening to Giulio's identity, optimism, and creativity, and must be diminished by constructing edible replicas that cannot themselves devour (him) in return. The
second woman then arrives only to witness her power's defeat by the
completed Futurists' masterpieces. She becomes a passive recipient,
a spectator, of her own transformation into a commodity fetish. Her
function is to propel the vital energy of eroticism. So, her fetishized
body parts are reconstructions of machines in motion. Furthermore,
she inspires the artists to produce their work only through her absence.
Her physical presence, once she arrives, is excessive, superfluous. The
works are then almost completed, and she can only be an admiring

witness to the creation of herself by the male artificers. She does not desire, she does not despise, and she does not devour the edible feminine sculptures. She does not annihilate the power of these images as Giulio does in his act of eating, which becomes an act of empowering one at another's expense.

Instead, she is made into an accomplice of the male's desire. When she finally arrives at the house, her "feminine and aggressive" voice precedes her. She is a traditional beauty who neither attracts nor "distracts" the artists. Her beauty — based, as usual, on her curves and illuminated by her green eyes — parallels, but does not compete with, the artists' masterpiece titled *The Curves of the World and Their Secrets*. In the description of her, we read, her mouth is missing. Her voice introduced her as aggressive; nevertheless, in praising the Futurists, she says: "I'm dazzled! Your genius frightens me!" and then, in a stupor before their great accomplishment, she asks them to explain the thoughts possessing the artists at work. While awaiting the artists' answer — that is, in expectation from the men's mouth — she receives the appellation of "sculptress of life." Silently, she sculpts her body into the cushions and rugs, as would a "delicate wild beast" (*Futurist Cookbook*, 28). She becomes sculptress in their eyes either when she is absent or when her "aggressive voice" changes into an attentive ear ready to absorb the Futurists' poetic of desire that then will inform the *Futurist Cookbook*. The rest of the cookbook is the actual continuation of the story. It offers recipes for optimism in which desire is pursued through creating edible art. The edible sculptures are a monumental version of the cookbook's recipes, some of which were also written by Futurist women.

Several of these recipes take women's body parts, especially the breast, to express both the liberation of male erotic desire and the artist's mastery over the desired object. Take, for example, the recipe called "Strawberry Breasts": "A pink plate with two erect feminine breasts made of ricotta dyed pink with Campari with nipples of candied strawberries. More fresh strawberries under the covering of ricotta making it possible to bite into an ideal multiplication of imaginary breasts" (156). These imaginary breasts are the nourishing breasts of maternal milk that restore Giulio to life. The breast re-created to please and satisfy can now be internalized as the good, ideal breast, over which the subject has total control, for he has deprived the maternal of its symbolic authority. The male subject has opposed to the real breast of childhood memories, the authoritarian one. He creates this one and devours it at his convenience.

The wish to master nature's creative power that is expressed through the mastery over the threatening breast is also quite explicit in "Italian Breasts in the Sunshine," a sculpted dessert, which is contextualized as an imaginary Italian landscape:[22] "Form two firm half spheres of almond paste. Place a fresh strawberry on the center of each of them. Then pour some zabaglione onto the plate and some dollops of whipped cream. The whole may be sprinkled with strong pepper and garnished with sweet red peppers" (161).[23] The Italian breasts are explicitly exhibited in the sun, which is the male generating force in Marinetti's symbolic world as well as in the Futurist writer Enif Robert's epistolary novel (cosigned by Marinetti; see *Other Modernism,* 111), *Un ventre di donna* (*A Woman's Belly*). The sun embodies the creative power of the demiurge–sculptor of geography, whose work – the sculpted edible breasts – guarantees both the survival of his desire and the satisfaction of a gastronomic pleasure: he can imprison the eternal feminine in the stomach. Like *Un ventre di donna,* the formula "Italian Breasts" is written by a woman. Graziella Parati comments on the symbolic use of the sun in Marinetti's texts: "The overpowering futurist 'sun' becomes the agent of Marinetti's violence over a woman's body, an act of rape over the acquiescent Enif" (66–67). Parati shows how violence and the war mold nature, in the form of landscape, and woman. Marinetti's war novel *The Steel Alcove* (an excerpt is included in the *Futurist Cookbook*) further testifies to the feminization of landscape by the palingenetic desire of man at war.

The cookbook presents cooking and eating as arts of desire and desirable arts, or so we are told. The quality of edible art is to energize and give an edible – thus pleasurable but especially controllable – form to the "painful superacute tension of the most frenetic lusts," lusts that, the introductory story tells us, may turn into a suicidal nostalgia for a lost past if they are not conquered in the name of an artificial optimism that can shape modern life:

> Kneeling before it, he began like a lover to adore it with his lips, tongue and teeth. . . . At three in the morning, with a terrible writhing of his loins, he bit into the dense heart-of-hearts of pleasure. Sculptors and sculptress slept.

At dawn he devoured the mammillary spheres of all mothers' milk. . . . A flood of vain tears followed. Endless. It seemed only to deepen the sleep of the sculptors and sculptress of life. Perhaps to refresh himself Giulio went out bare-headed into the park criss-crossed by the reverberating sounds of thunder. He felt at the same time unencumbered, liberated, empty and bursting. Enjoying and enjoyed. Possessor and possessed. Unique and complete. (*Futurist Cookbook,* 29)

In a mythopoetic act of self-generation, Giulio devours this statue made just for him. But where does the sculpting of an edible feminine — rather than, again, an eternal feminine — as the governing principle of the cookbook leave us? Futurist cooking and the Futurist banquets aim to affect the same metamorphosis of spiritual and ideological landscape undergone by Giulio in the story. The diner who feeds on his liberated desire, embodied in gratifying edible art, will feel unique and complete, enjoying and enjoyed, as Giulio does.

The feminine statue, called *The Curves of the World and Their Secrets,* is an ideal landscape, a symbolic territory demarcated only by the male subject's boundaries. Most of the edible sculptures aim for a Futurist optimism based on velocity and movement, which are here projected onto the pleasurable erotic shapes of these sculptures. The enthusiasm for life is manifest in Onesti's statue called "Passion of the Blondes," which entices its maker to express his love for life by tongue-kissing it "like a child" (26). Optimism is expressed as the oral ecstasy of velocity: optimism as oral and fast becomes a Futurist state of mind. The ecstasy of velocity, condensed with oral pleasure, appears in Enrico Prampolini and Fillìa's "Slender Speed": "A swirling lasso of pastry, synthesis of every car's longing curves in the distance, and Lightness of Flight which offered the watching mouths twenty-nine silvered lady's ankles mixed with wheel hubs and propeller blades, all made of soft leavened dough" (26). The rapidity of erotic satisfaction transfers onto the car, and the car's velocity devouring the surrounding landscape involves fetishizing the woman's body, turning the classically erotic "ankle" into the image of fast-moving modern erotic desire. Edible sculptures reshape nature. To the Futurists nature is an ever-changing object shaped and reshaped by human culture (*natura naturans* versus *natura naturata*). Reconfiguring nature into an edible landscape summarizes the idea that Futurist art is applicable to every object/subject. The relation between the artist and the world is one of incorporation, in which the subject who eats devours the object—subject turned object—and reshapes it according to his will, and only thus is he empowered.

The edible quality of Futurist art as architecture of the soul makes its appearance in the *Architectural Dinner* in which Marinetti and Fillìa stress the stomach's assimilatory functions. Able to transform and adapt the object eaten, the stomach creates a harmonic relation between individuals and their surroundings. Marinetti and Fillìa speak of the Futurist artists as cooks who shape their environment and then eat it with pleasure. Umberto Boccioni believed that human beings re-create nature over and over again through incorporation: the incorporation of the realm of nature within the cosmogonic and creative potential of humankind. Nature is not to be reproduced or contemplated as *natura naturata* but assimilated and reshaped by human intervention. Marinetti and Fillìa write in "Architectural Dinner for Sant'Elia": "To dine they used their hands like children and alternately built and ate, towers, skyscrapers, battleship guns, airport slipways, belvederes, sports stadiums, military pontoons, elevated railways one after the other [list of ingredients]. . . . The Futurists, the better to construct the Futurist house perfected it with their teeth each one sitting on inedible cylinders of compressed pasta" (121). The Futurist landscape is built and eaten in an autoregenerative process. The only inedible, static, and weighty material is pasta, dismissed as not a food at all.

The edible creation of a Futurist urban landscape is extended to the reappropriation in Futurist, Italianist terms of the Italian landscape in *Synthesis of Italy Dinner.* This is a performative act of power in which the new nation conquers other states. This meal performs Italian unification and liberation against the definition of Italy by others. Because the dishes are meant to be eaten, they are assumed to transform Italians into the agents of their own landscape and state: "Italy has always been in the past a gourmet food for foreigners. Today we, too, can taste her, though it is impossible if we want to savor all the flavors and perfumes of her orchards, meadows and gardens, to order on a single occasion all the various foods. Therefore I suggest this meal which is a synthesis-of-Italy" (127). Futurist paintings by Fortunato Depero, Giacomo Balla, and Prampolini constitute this landscape, which is neither the inspiring natural landscape reproduced by many classical painters nor nature itself. It is the beauty of a city that rises (like Boccioni's painting *La città che sale,* 1910) with the aid of powerful cranes endowed with the energy of wild horses. The dishes served both condense and reproduce through various ingredients the Italian territory from the Alps, via the plains, to the south, but these are re-created artificially, by taking inspiration from the painters' views on and of Italy.

If these painters have produced other images of Italy that have subtracted the country from the tradition of landscape painting and from the archaeological, ethnographic gaze of the foreign tourists, the Futurist artists–cooks go a step farther. Against this foreign act of "appropriation," and cultural definition, the Italian Futurists recommend to their Italian diners a dish named "Colonial Instinct": "A colossal mullet stuffed with dates, bananas, orange slices, crabs, oysters and carobs is presented floating in a liter of Marsala. A violent perfume of carnations, broom and acacia is sprayed into the air" (128). Italy is no longer a static object to be painted, a traditional food to be eaten, but an imperial state that conquers, eats, and concocts its own dishes. After having unified Italy—this time gastronomically—and having reinvented its delicacies to assuage the modern Italian palate, the dinner is completed with a colonial dish that incorporates foreign (colonial) ingredients in a total recipe now assimilated to the unified Italian territory of which it is the last appendix. The national specificity of the ingredients in this recipe is not mentioned, and a name for the dish that may acknowledge the provenance of the foreign ingredients does not appear. The other is a blank slate inscribed here in the new Futurist Italian landscape. The Italian diners participate in an act of colonization with the artist–cooks and through an act of cooking and eating assert Italy's national identity and its civilizing mission.

The colonizing and civilizing mission is completed when the other loses his power to the Western white man. The other is embodied by the much-envied strong black man's "primitive," "brutal" instinctive desire that the Futurists had claimed for themselves, for example, in "Futurist Painting: Technical Manifesto." Here they intend to artificially re-create it in and for the modern Italian, most explicitly with foods. In *Dinner—White Desire* the civilizing rhetoric discloses the Futurists' own anxiety toward the black African or African American male: "Ten Negroes, each holding a lily in his hand, gather round a table in a city by the sea, overwhelmed by an indefinable emotion that makes them long to conquer the countries of Europe with a mixture of spiritual yearning and erotic desire" (136). The desire to conquer Europe is gradually substituted for by the cathartic quality of the white foods served and eaten, which purify the black desire for conquest and turn it into a white desire by sublimation: "The Negroes' state of mind is affected as it were unconsciously by the paleness and whiteness of all the foods. . . . The sensibilities of the Negroes feed on the white flavor color odor of the food, while from the ceiling an incandescent globe of milky glass descends towards the table and a smell of jasmine fills the room" (136). The black man is disavowed as desiring subject. His powerful—and potentially destructive anticolonial desire—is exorcized and held in check when the white male Futurist first constructs him as his own desired other but soon reveals him as in fact desiring white man's "cultural" identity, the whole Western civilization. His desire only then becomes acceptable and even noble because ultimately domesticated, deprived of its aggressive force toward the West. This colonial meal liberates the Futurist aggressive optimism about the Futurist Italian male's power to create and mold the other according to one's own taste, which is always the better taste for whiteness.

The "incandescent globe of milky glass" displaces (as interiorization of the desire to be white by the Negroes) the Futurists' anxiety about the "desiring qualities of the black male"—and thus about his potential political agency that constructs him as competitor and even victor. The Futurist "Western diner," throughout the Futurist meals, always rejects catharsis in favor of action. In contrast, the black man's aggressive desire is smoothed out, anesthetized, in this "anti-Futurist"—traditionally cathartic meal—strategically invented to conquer the other. More often, however, the Futurists' envy for the beauty and potency of the other manifests itself in the form of an exotic territorialization brought about in the actions contemplated for completing meals.

In the "geographic dinner," the colonial instinct translates into a microcolonial act of occupation through which only the diner is able to get his (or her) food. To order a dish one must touch a living menu, namely, the waitress's body, which is wrapped up in a map of Africa:

1. A room in a restaurant decorated with aluminum and chromium tubing. The round windows disclose mysterious distant views of colonial landscapes.

2. The diners, seated round a metal table, its horizontal plane in linoleum, consult large atlases, while invisible gramophones play loud Negro music.

3. Once the meal has begun the *listavivande*-waitress enters the room, followed at a distance by the waiters: she is a shapely young woman dressed in a long white tunic on which a complete geographical map of Africa has been drawn in color; it enfolds her entire body.

4. The guests must choose the dish they want not according to its composition but by indicating on the geographical map the city or region that proves most seductive to their touristy imagination and spirit of adventure.

5. Example: if a guest points his finger at the *listavivande*-waitress's left breast, where CAIRO is written, one of the waiters will silently disappear and return immediately with the dish that corresponds to that city. In this case: "Love on the Nile," pyramids of stoned dates immersed in palm wine. Around the largest pyramid, juicy little cubes of cinnamon-flavoured mozzarella stuffed with roasted coffee beans and pistachios . . .

And so it goes on, varying the geographical maps and the *listavivande*-waitresses for every dinner party and never letting anyone know the dishes in advance. In this way a gastronomic orientation inspired by continents, regions and cities will prevail. (129; my emphasis)

The taste for dominion/domination is expressed through the Promethean re-creation (the creative force of the genius) of nature, here appearing as both "woman" and "geography." The Futurist diner uses woman and Africa as the original fetishes. Africa becomes a woman, albeit not necessarily a "black" woman, who in turn is embodied by the synecdoche of her breast. The breast is recast immediately as a city, behind which hides the dish that the diner orders and ultimately eats. Through a series of fetishes arranged in a more and more manageable — and edible — order, the threatening power of woman and Africa is disavowed, and the fear of "castration" or "occupation" inverted into a pleasurable moment of conquest through which the diner rewrites the map of Africa.

The woman-Africa is the "menu" that the white diner "re-orders" and assembles through an act of reading/consumption. The white male's act of reading woman is portrayed literally as his final appropriation of her creative act of "life-giving." Woman is robbed of her reproductive power as indicated by juxtaposing the term *lista-vivande* with the "map of Africa," both inscribed on her body. *Lista-vivande* is the Italian composite word for the foreign term "menu." It is synonymous with another Italian expression for the menu: *carta*. The latter means more generally "paper," as well as "geographic maps." Hence the map of Africa *is* physically the *lista-vivande,* which, in addition, is female and woman because — as the meaning of the word *vivande* indicates—she is both the carrier of life and the caretaker (in the Futurist imagination). The menu is presented as a list of things needed for living, all embodied in the woman.

In addition, the word *vivande*—a term used in ordinary Italian to indicate that food is the sustenance of life (*Lebensmittel* in German)—can also graphically be associated with the Latin gerund/gerundive *vivenda* of which it is a playful perversion/inversion. The word *vivenda* could stand for a passive impersonal form of "duty," in this case something like "that which is to be lived" or "what must be lived." The diner takes pleasure in touching and marking this woman–Africa with his finger. His territorializing gesture both enlivens and rewrites this body that "must be lived" and experienced, or else possessed. Pleasure captured in the recipe is a *graphia,* a sign of writing on the woman's body. She is concealed behind the map (*carta*) of the dark African continent. The woman–Africa impersonates the foods that keep the diner alive: she erotically triggers his appetite for life, his desire while also pointing to the necessity of her being touched, possessed, and finally devoured qua food. At the same time, the dark, "mysterious distances of the colonial landscapes" are forced into a readable, approachable *graphia,* a geo-graphic representation, a *legenda* (both "map" and "to be read") of Africa. Writing is then in turn inscribed on the woman's live body off of which the reader/geo-*grapher* nourishes his desire for conquest.

This desire has to become the modus vivendi of the Italian citizen who, as Marinetti stresses in the manifesto against xenomania, must avoid the trap of an excessive "love" for everything foreign. Unlike the xenomaniac, who is seduced by foreigners "simply because they don't speak the Italian language and come from distant countries" (59), the diner signs, puts his hands on the other's body-map in an authorial act of writing. The graphic twist forced on the word's root to live, *la lista-vivande,* bears the trace of the violent original inscription of the other's nonreducible will to life. The inscription imprisons the other's life within the writing of an all-encompassing, totalizing self (and the self's economy of pleasure), whose boundaries are here ethnically and sexually established.

The regenerative, architectural effort to shape nature into a modern landscape, which accompanies the parallel effort to regenerate a virile modern man through an act of destructive (for the other)/constructive (for the new regenerated self) incorporation, is the prevalent feature of this meal. Through erotic desire, nature can be shaped to suit the desiring man who, by incorporating the random object of his acknowledged desire, wins over the object and becomes an agent, a subject. The meal describes this process of identity formation at the expense of an object that is first fetishized and then cannibalized.

Yet the *Futurist Cookbook* also contains sections that are extremely fragmentary, nonreconciliatory, and, above all, open-ended. Among them are the reviews of the banquets, the descriptions of aeromeals, and the recipes for special anticonformist banquets to be staged in specific traditional settings. Thus while the cookbook fractures the ideological agenda of Futurist cooking, the Futurist meal still commodifies and aestheticizes the destructive function of avant-garde art and makes fascism more palatable to the masses, its violence apparently more innocuous. The dinners described above accomplish this new organic aestheticizing and commodifying function of Futurist/fascist art by granting the consumer the satisfaction to experience while eating the artistic power of destruction typical of the avant-garde. Consumers devour and destroy avant-garde art while, the Futurists tell us, assimilating the civilizational, nationalist, misogynist, and racist messages embedded in these recipes. Their acts of eating implicate them in the creation of a Futurist edible art that is nonorganic and avant-gardist but also chauvinistic.

The question is whether the ephemeral aspect of this art — that gives itself up to destruction while it so emphatically proclaims itself optimistic, Futurist, and nationalist — plays a role in scaling down through ridicule (at least in part) the programmatic agenda of the definitive banquets, rather than just making them, and fascist ideology, enjoyable. If the state of mind these banquets intend to promote is less the one established by each dinner's setting than irony or disbelief itself, the dinners could function as both advancing an apparently serious and practical ideological agenda and presenting it as at least politically impractical. The avant-garde aesthetic structure of the recipes and dinners, in addition to their production as transient objects made to be enjoyed while being destroyed, interferes with the self-importance of the fascist political agenda and seems to play with the air of tradition that Futurism itself had taken in its own eyes as much as in the eyes of critics.

Let me return, in this regard, to the pasta polemics. Should we read it as pure aestheticization of politics, following Benjamin's comments

about Marinetti's second-wave Futurist production? Or does the provocative and polemical element in the manifesto insinuate a mild
political dissent from fascism's own cultural and nationalist agenda?
While pasta should be abolished from Futurist cooking, in the attempt
to shape the Italian body into a perfect war machine (according to the
militaristic fashion most consonant with fascism), the *Futurist Cookbook* does not provide any practical instruction on obtaining such a
body, nor does, even, the manifesto. As I have shown, even *Heroic
Winter Dinner* is composed according to poetic principles of analogy
between the text and the body. While the recipe presupposes the act
of reading and eating as homologous forms of physical and intellectual understanding, both promoting the desire to act, the cookbook,
which contains discrepant views and reactions of critics and consumers, posits the identity of the two as an aesthetic and political construction. This construction leads to a complex subjectivity rather than an
immediate fascist identity.

The antipasta diet suggested throughout the *Futurist Cookbook* is
antipractical. This is all the more true for the most chauvinistic definitive dinners. The term *definitive* means both determining and conclusive. Even Futurist cuisine's alleged lightness is such only according to artistic principles. As some of the critics' reviews informing the
cookbook iterate, the dishes themselves were not always digestible.
At other times, they were clearly even too light to be ingested at all
and only involved the senses synesthetically, without considering the
stomach at all. The Futurist diet is artistically fantastic and fully literary. The cookbook seems interested in stating and reaching its nationalist goals only insofar as these still constitute a provocation and thus
can guarantee some sort of national uproar that, in turn, guarantees
Futurism its renewed avant-garde status. Through the return to an
aesthetic agenda originally informed, in the early years of Futurism,
by strongly violent fascistic tones, politics's aestheticization (or the
enjoyment of fascism) reveals itself to be a complicated mechanism.
That agenda, to be true, is practiced in the production of ephemeral works. Through the Futurists' adoption of the aesthetics of the
ephemeral, it is rather fascist politics that is exposed as being stuck
in a rigid interpretation of the avant-garde. The Futurists' staging of
their own avant-garde's theatricality—hence the avant-garde's need
to be mobile, flexible, and self-destructive, too (as far as its products

or their presence are concerned)—appears as the only chance they have to beat the movement's museification and to distinguish themselves from an ossified fascism.

Cooking and Digesting Futurism: The Return of the Avant-Garde

The theatricality of Futurist cooking emerges most clearly in the definitive dinners. These are an important component of the *Futurist Cookbook.* To my knowledge, they were never staged in the 1930s. Formally at least, they read as fairly conventional accounts bearing a strong ideological goal. They respect syntax, for instance. However, at second glance, as in the case of the *Geographic Dinner* and *Dinner—White Desire,* the texts are also extremely performative. As theatrical recipes to be followed minutely, they do not respect the rules of classical mimesis, and although they sound like narrative fictions, they do not represent, they perform.

The Textual Performances of the Definitive Dinners

All texts in the *Futurist Cookbook* are synthetic dramatic versions of the various manifestos. The textual dinners perform the impracticality announced in the manifesto of Futurist cooking, and in so doing the dinners paradoxically subvert the manifesto's impractical program. What these textual dinners—scripts of performances—show is that desire at the source and at the end of the productive–consuming process always already exceeds control and intentionality. Because desire is "excessive," control reappears in the texts but to no avail. For the Futurists the texts demand control precisely because it is impossible to obtain. In other words, the definitive dinners disclose the fact that the state of mind that they physically intend to provoke is less a *state* of mind than a *process,* namely, the process and performance of desire's arousal itself.

The *Wedding Banquet* offers a good example of, first, the literary and, second, the performative nature of food in the *Futurist Cookbook.* Food in this banquet represents the fusion of object and image that the "Technical Manifesto of Futurist Literature" sets as its goal. The *Wedding Banquet* shifts from a descriptive text, identifiable with a theatrical script, to the Futurist verbal rendition — inscription in the text — of this script's intended theatrical effects. The dessert is crucial to show the intersection between the dinner's textual level and the performative one. More specifically, in the *Wedding Banquet*, a theatrical "long freeze" substitutes for the ice cream or "gelato" that in Italian literally stands for the past participle of the verb "to freeze." On stage, a theatrical freeze translates the meal's ice cream. The stage directions read: "A long freeze seems to paralyze the diners, substituting for the usual ice-cream which as it happens is bad for stomachs which have become so heated in the acrobatic juggling of happiness, alarming mushrooms and dynamic partridges" (*Futurist Cookbook*, 113). The metaphoric dessert appears less damaging than the real *passé-ist* food. Yet the diners' freeze follows a participant's comment about the decomposing stage of the food being served during the banquet: "Among all these partridges, the fattest, that one there, gave me a ten kilometer chase. . . . Now it's finally stopped, or rather it still seems to be alive, actually I think it is still moving. — 'It's moving because it's crawling with worms,' shouts a wag" (113). This comment about worms "freezes" the diners who now, being *gelati* themselves, being themselves ice creams, do not *need* to eat it. The freeze provides the gestural, theatrical end to the meal/performance. The text about this meal is not a representation. Rather, it performs the performance that the meal is, only it performs it on the page, not on stage. The *Wedding Banquet* demonstrates that the *Futurist Cookbook* functions as a theatrical script for a self-decomposing Futurist aesthetic and ideological conduct. In effect, these dinners are not definitive: the states of mind the Futurists want to achieve to aesthetically and ideologically prepare the Italians of the future are theatrical effects generated, first, by the text-as-practice and, second, in the course of theatrical mini-actions. The text demands these actions as both its premise and its goal, and thereby renders itself superfluous, that is, excessive (a supplement). The text *is* that performance already. Here desire is at once liberated and controlled, but control is revealed to be impossible.

The definitive dinners' playful and complex textuality interferes with the goal of rhetorical persuasion. The question remains whether both the joking playfulness of the curious banquets and the complex synesthesia of these texts in fact make more palatable the chauvinistic and militaristic agenda they endorse and propagate. A specific form of irony or playfulness ensues from the texts' performative unfolding.

This is the final state of mind that the texts provoke, a state of incredulity. While not eliminating the totalitarian, controlling impulse — and modernizing mission — of Futurist cooking, such paradoxical playfulness plunges the fascistic dimensions of the dinners into the tradition of early Futurism's facetiousness and rhetorical provocation, which is thus turned against fascism itself. In short, by flaunting impracticality, as announced in the manifesto of Futurist cooking, both the banquets and the definitive dinners appear to overshoot their practical target, their ideological agenda.

Impracticality has two implications: (1) the artists' ideological agenda made itself useless, in the form proposed, to the strictly political "fascist" program that took itself seriously, and (2) any "ideological" cultural program that proclaims theatrical *change* to be its core, albeit within the major boundaries of a total ideology of modernity, cannot also take itself to be definitive. It must rather see itself as in continuous progression. While unmistakably chauvinistic, these late Futurist *texts* — especially the definitive dinners that propound again the poetics of the long Futurist tradition in a different context — are also embedded in the Futurists' reconsideration of both their own aesthetic tradition and their attack on the bourgeoisie. Applied to the fascist situation, early Futurist aesthetics is more dissonant than homologous with the ideological agenda. Paradoxically, then, the most fascist texts — that is, these definitive dinners — sound the least credible and usable, precisely because of their returning "Futurism." They almost involuntarily return from the past of the avant-garde to disturb its "rootedness" in a present too tightly defined.

Autophagy, or the Limited Power of Irony

In their original 1909 manifesto, published in *Le Figaro*, the Futurists had maintained that their ideology was necessary and important. In reading the *Futurist Cookbook*, we may add that to be definitive, the Futurist/fascist ideology always needs to be redefined, adjusted to new situations. Since their very beginning the Futurists had declared: "The oldest of us is thirty: so we have at least a decade for finishing our work. When we are forty, other younger and stronger men will probably throw us in the wastebasket like useless manuscripts — we want it to happen!"[24] Thus it is ironic — for the Futurists themselves, above all — that in 1931, roughly twenty years after their founding, they still represent the Italian avant-garde (although one that fascism almost disregarded). Some new artists, such as Fillìa himself, had joined their circle; the shocking effects of their actions had waned somewhat; and new movements, such as Novecento, had challenged their domination over the cultural scene. Nothing radical had outmoded the Futurists, however, and their polemical tone continued to be their distinctive feature, which guaranteed them some popular attention.

The irony of the *Futurist Cookbook* lies in its being a gesture of artistic *autophagy* (self-cannibalism). The Futurists themselves now finally consume their own works of art to continue their Futurist activity. They eat the works that launched them as the avant-garde movement of the twentieth century. Thus their early manifestos are at once assimilated and changed by becoming edible quite literally. As perishable products they never remain the same, even when they come from the past that, of course, was the most reviled notion for the Futurists. If one links the emergence of Futurist cooking with the Futurists' need to deal with their own long history, one could argue that the theatrical use of food allowed the Futurists to comment on the dilemmas of a second-wave avant-garde. More than any other avant-garde movement, Futurism, by encompassing most realms of production, not only reconceptualized art's temporality in modernity but also developed an idea of history, if not exactly a systematic philosophy of history.

Accordingly, the second-wave Futurists appropriated Baudelaire's injunction to be absolutely modern and took it to be their task to forge this modernity. While the Futurists prepared the modern individual for an absolute modernity that seemed possible only in the future, in effect, they conflated the future with their present. Their diets state that the future is in every *now*. The future is in the way one eats one's present. When the present and presence along with it are already devoured by a fast-moving future that is not only here and now but also immediately behind us, then there is no superseding of modernity. The Futurist meals partake of modernity as an absolute time *within* which transience, in the guise of ephemeral materials, lives. Thus, while hating tradition and the past, Futurism could only continue its work by endorsing its own destructive tradition and displacing it onto Futurist materials. The Futurist materials are absolutely modern when transient, and they are transient only if they are devoured — thus assimilated and reconstructed — in Futurist ways, which in turn affect *futuristically* the stomach that assimilates them.

Thus Futurism could appropriate the transience of the kitchen phi-losophy only after it had developed a tradition of its own, which, to be Futurist, also required it to surpass itself or its products, although not its ideology. This process of overcoming still remained within the framework of a modernity intended as absolute, even if always incom-plete. Read from this angle, the banquets' fragmentary and theatrical aspects, their evanescence and playfulness, are all traits that guaran-tee success to the total modern project. In this light, the avant-garde project does not interfere with the movement's totalitarian impulse, which, in the case of Futurism, took fascist "revolutionary" hues against institutionalized state fascism. Yet the restaurant (as anticapi-talist museum), the banquets, and the textual definitive dinners exceed the practical politics of a fascist regime in which the principle of total identity (*Gleichschaltung*) reigns. It is a principle of presence and the present, according to which in effect fascism, in contrast to Futurism, appropriates the past (the glorious victories from the past) as *anterior* necessity of the present. If the Futurists did look back at the national victory of Vittorio Veneto, which they wanted to monumentalize as a work of art, they nevertheless considered it the past that put an end to the past. Vittorio Veneto is worthy of return only insofar as it stands for a war declared against the premodern past of Italy. In mentioning in the *Futurist Cookbook* the glories of the past (of Italian explorers or scientists, for example), the nationalist Futurists underscore each event as a disjunction or an exception, a break with Italian traditions.

During the second wave, the Futurists are both this tradition and its break, both history and its exception. In effect, by constituting a break with tradition, they continue their own tradition. They reconcile this aporia (which will become the aporia of the avant-garde after World War II) less by interrupting their tradition of break than by applying Futurist aesthetics as a break within Futurism itself (which involved a break within institutionalized fascism). This application then hap-pened to be in an area they had not yet explored: the culinary realm. First, working with food does not allow the edible Futurist products to endure and thus become tradition themselves. In effect, in cooking up Futurist aesthetic principles, the very same principles are given up to incorporation, assimilation, and, ultimately, their own transformation. Second, Futurist aesthetics now becomes Futurist cuisine and attacks the most traditional pillar of taste, the bourgeoisie's culinary customs, including a by-now-established self-assured fascist ruling class.

An avant-garde temporality of the ephemeral does not necessarily guarantee a nontotalitarian, nonassimilatory project, a project of
multiplicity and differentiation. Not even when the avant-garde, so it
seems, makes itself evanescent by producing ephemeral products that
could not thereby enter the museum. In the Futurist case, though,
the culinary revolution does complicate the evaluation of second-
wave Futurist art as aligned with the fascist idea of history. The manifesto against xenomania calls for contemplation and absorption at a
time — during fascism — when the political class enemy was brutally
silenced and annihilated. The exaggerated manifesto sounds affirmative (in Herbert Marcuse's sense) and aestheticizing. Yet the theatricality and excessive elements of desire, present in the Holy Palate, the
banquets, and the textual dinners, throw the diner and reader into
situations of conflict, disarray, and wild energy, typical of the early
Futurist actions. Although the Futurists believe that the reception of
Futurist texts and paintings is definitive and defined, and thus use
their art to perform and in the act produce specific states of mind in
their banquets and proposed dinners, the fact that, in the 1930s, their
diet is ultimately again introduced as a challenge to a resilient bourgeois taste shows that the Futurists' aesthetic success could not be
taken for granted. Hence constant adaptation, change, and intervention appear to the Futurists of the second wave as an absolute must.

While the context of modernity within which optimism must be
affirmed is a given for the Futurists, the process of approaching it is
always tentative, never definitive and concluded, hence the open-end-
edness of these ideologically closed texts/banquets. Such indispensable
fracture within the texts — the fracture between the liberation of desire
and its immediate fascistic control — demonstrates that the Futurists
use diet to deal with their own presence as necessarily insufficient with
respect to the temporality of the modern. With the appropriation of
food — in terms of the willful construction of a modern diet — even the
Futurist/fascistic absolute project of modernity faces its own aporias.
Evident in the Futurists' impractical diet, these aporias do not question the idea of an absolute and necessary modernity, yet they display a
mild Dada nihilism toward the relevance of their own role in fulfilling
modernity, an ironic cynicism that makes itself manifest in producing
and consuming temporary edible art.

The tension or even contrast in these texts between an openly
declared racist, imperialist, and misogynist agenda and an intertextual

(synesthetic) structure may produce distance or laughter in a critical reader. These reactions, however, are not sufficient to dispel fascist readings or, in other words, the possible critical enjoyment of reading a fascist, excessive text. The *Futurist Cookbook* then requires a theatrical or readerly reception that always highlights that tension in the texts.

For the disturbing fascist elements to emerge strongly, it was necessary to concoct less provocative or pleasurable meals, meals deeply embedded in the reflections about aesthetic pleasure as well as an aesthetic of disturbance. The neo-avant-garde inherits the breaking legacy of Futurism's erupting energy and the fascistic totalizing tendencies of the classical avant-garde's projects, all somewhat implicated in the paradigm of an absolute modern temporality. The antimeals of the neo-avant-garde are all informed, albeit in different ways, by a historical dimension according to which the new avant-garde's reflection about history/tradition is fundamental to a renewed project about the utopias and dystopias of modernity. Futurism's impasse becomes the most important lesson for the Eat artists since the sixties. Despite itself, and because of its own philosophy of history, Futurism had recourse to its own tradition, which it had rendered ephemeral precisely to fight against the ossification of the movement itself. This impasse had partly rescued Futurism, almost unwillingly, and had slightly but importantly separated its path from institutional fascism. The aporia of the avant-garde's tradition, or in other words the anachronism of the avant-garde, becomes an important factor in the neo-avant-garde artists' attempt to rescue the avant-garde from its implication in the temporality of modernity.

While some Futurist banquets were recently restaged (e.g., on March 12, 1993, at the Getty Museum in Malibu, California), and their recipes republished, their fascistic elements have been erased from their staging. This obliteration of fascism opened up the possibility of a much-needed rediscovery of the innovative features of even second-wave Futurism, at least in Europe.[25] The Futurists opened the way to considering food in art as one powerful way for art to think actively, playfully, and importantly on the everyday of consumer societies and the role of art in these societies. It is still necessary, however, to situate this Futurism's ideological intervention — for the good and the bad, for its subtle critique of fascism and for its chauvinistic imprint — within the cultural politics of fascism. The "other" modernism that the

Futurists, as fascists, represent is the modern legacy that faced the postwar avant-garde. The Eat artists (discussed in chapters 4 and 5) do not just blindly reproduce the historical avant-garde's shock techniques in an effort to break the conventionality of art. Instead, whenever food is involved in their art, the neo-avant-garde shows a need to embrace the avant-garde's impulse to change and forge the future while questioning the politics and the aesthetics behind the desire for utopia. An initial doubt at the "success" of an aesthetics fully devoted to producing a Futurist humanity is already perceivable, although only slightly, in the return of a Futurist aesthetics in the ephemeral products of second-wave Futurist cooking.

22 ANTIMEALS OF ANTIART

Dada-Diets

THE USE OF INCORPORATION and digestion in selected Dada texts and manifestos was a rhetorical approach to food detectable in the texts written by the forerunners of the surrealists. This group of Dada artists and poets, primarily associated with Zurich and Paris but also with Berlin and Cologne, includes Tristan Tzara, Walter Serner, Francis Picabia, Arthur Cravan, Paul Eluard, Louis Aragon, André Breton, Philippe Soupault, Georges Ribemont-Dessaignes, Max Ernst, Hans Arp, and Raoul Hausmann. *Revue Dada,* published in Zurich between 1917 and 1922, gathered those texts that seem among the most fragmentary and dispersed and, hence, also those that would least suggest any specific rhetoric of the body. Yet such rhetoric is indeed present.[1] These texts — which read as absurdist, nihilistic, destructive, and cynical (or *kynical,* as Peter Sloterdijk put it) — differ from the virulent and explicit political and social critique of the Club Dada in Berlin, most famous for its photomontages, caricatures, and speeches. Take, for example, the photomontages by Hausmann and Hannah Höch or George Grosz's caricatures and Richard Huelsenbeck's "First Dada Speech in Germany" (1918). Direct engagement with exploitation, poverty, and revolution was evident, and so was the immediate political appropriation of motifs such as hunger and bourgeois binging. But preoccupations with the stomach and its physiological operations as cultural are prominent throughout Dada, and they are worth exploring also where they seem to be absent.[2]

Dada's alimentary metaphors construe an alternative modern subjectivity, a subjectivity played against the equation functionalism equals modernity, which was especially proposed in the German nutritional texts.[3] Considering that Dada emerged in opposition to World

War I, the traditional subject that the Dada antidiets combat was the "hardened ego" of an ideal soldier machine. To this personality, which was very much present in F. T. Marinetti who tried to sustain it up to a point also through the Futurist militaristic and chauvinistic diets, the Dada poets and artists opposed their *kynical* reason, namely, a Bakhtinian carnivalesque open subject or, in Sloterdijk's words, a "bashed ego."[4] The Dada artists conceive a modern subject whose dysfunctionalism mimetically parodies the disorder of modern society. This is a technique of schizo-dissolution into "organs without a body," a pathological state well recorded in later years by Antonin Artaud. In several instances this French poet registered his painful madness as disintegration of the body's wholeness. In Mexico, after a difficult journey on the way to the land of the Tarahumaras, Artaud wrote that he felt like a "heap of poorly assembled organs."[5] Dada plays out schizo-dissolution, and various other rehearsed pathologies, for example, "glossolalia" or babble, against the dynamics of consumer capitalism and the flows of liquid commodities. Yet it does so from its location inside such an economy.[6] Dada's preventive act of commodification — a strategy of reification against reification — is the body's own dissolution in indigestion first and liquid excremental flows second.

Futurist poetry does not free itself of the idea of correspondence between "sentence" (albeit a dynamic one) and reality (reconceived as dynamic, too); thus the Futurist words of food or food in words are still a way to directly connect the dynamic body with dynamic states of mind, through which the world ought to be shaped.[7] (As seen, a doubt lingers that such analogies in effect may be insufficient to control an indeed unrestrainable desire.) In contrast, the Dada artists and poets observe a lack of correspondences, correspondences constantly reiterated as real and natural in the world of exchange value. Dada performs these correspondences over and over again in an act of destabilization that demonstrates their illusory and laughable character, even logic. The Dada poets show how this "philosophical" logic is in fact part of the modern Western being's absurd hubris. If philosophical systems try to capture the complexity of an increasingly ungraspable reality (splintered in fluxes of energies and microscopic particles, as scientific theories of the times started to prove), the Dadaists play at transferring such philosophical and scientific systems directly onto human physiology. Then they ironically and mockingly re-present the latter as intrinsically chaotic, disorderly, and full of excrement.

Correspondences per se become carnivalesque, excessive with respect to any referent, the body and the ego included.

According to Dada, this disorder is always already present in a pathological human physiology that, in the war and postwar age, is at once repressed by the most technological and functional means of production, and instrumentalized by a consumerism that capitalizes on commodity fetishism. Thus the Dada artists constantly mimic and reproduce the society in which they live to expose its vain cultural emptiness. Dada knows itself to be enmeshed with this emerging (disgusting) society as well as its distorting mirror, as Theo van Doesburg's statement in "Was Ist Dada?" demonstrates: "Dada is the most immediate expression of our shapeless time, and wants to be such expression. . . . Dada has born of its head both the stiffness and the pace of this age. Dada is definitely civilizing, but it is able to view historically also the limits of its own appearance in time, it relativizes itself in its time."[8] Civilizing in this context means to call attention to civilization's blindness and pitfalls. As it were, it is an act of civilizing beyond civilization, or, with Friedrich Nietzsche, beyond good and evil.

Dada attacks modernity and Western civilization, and tries to break through the *Schein* (appearance) of modernity. It aims to expose the direct relation between the hollow human being who must consume and annihilate the external world to survive, and the hypocritical ethical and cultural system based on an economy of exploitation and destruction that civilization denies. Dada's own historical function, as the Dadaists see it, is to speed the decline of this sick system. The Dadaist develops a model of dysfunctional consumption and devouring that disrupts the modern concept of efficient consumption.

The critical authors and artists — also when writing "food" — disobey the ideological programs sponsored in every sector of modern life (including in nutritional science, but also in popular cookbooks). They oppose to such modern models their own counterideologies, countersystems of language and manners, which literally translate as counterdiets. For example, the era's cookbooks were born of a society driven to rebuild itself after World War I to once again attain fitness and health by applying modern principles of efficiency and work. Preoccupied with modernity, these cookbooks attempted to reconcile nutritional and economic precepts with an ideology of taste and a modern lifestyle. Their authors' dilemma was how to sell efficiency in the kitchen while preserving the sociology and politics of class and gender.[9] In contrast, the digestive metaphors appearing in the Dada texts construe coherent countersystems of consumption, even when these metaphors seem to be purely absurd provocations devoid of any specific context. Many Dada poems, manifestos, or advertisements contain uncanny recipes, unsettling in part because of their unexpected context. For example, *Dada au grand air* (*Der Sängerkrieg in Tirol*) has on its cover an ink drawing by Ernst, "Die Leimbereitung aus Knochen" ("Bone-Glue Preparation"), followed immediately by a list of aphoristically brief news. The news then gradually morphs into recipes:[10]

> A friend from New York tells us that he knows of a literary pickpocket. His name is Funiguy, a notorious moralist, also called musical bouillabaisse with travel impressions.
>
> ——————
>
> Tzara sends to Breton: a box of souvenirs preserved in ostrich-milk and in Prince Rupert's drop. Enclosed are instructions for transforming the box in bee powder. . . .
>
> ——————
>
> We boil proper notable people in paraffin and we blend them as well as possible . . .[11]
>
> ——————
>
> Tzara sends to Soupault: 4 whales in a soft sponge, two needles for the poisoning of trees, a comb with 12 teeth perfected, a live and agitated lama and an apple cooked with corpse ham. To Mic greetings of his open heart.
>
> ——————
>
> Arp sends to Eluard: a turban of entrails and of 4-room love. To Benjamin Peret: some boiled minerals some flags of ants' nests.[12]

The gifts or greeting-card messages listed above are particularly odd because form and content clash. The exchange of gifts and the pieces of information that form the cover "article" are a recipe for the Dada collages (as in the title of Ernst's drawing), and in effect, qua recipe, this text becomes the Dadaist collage. Because the genre of news is ostensibly recognizable, the format provokes the readers' disorientation, since neither the message nor the function of the recipe is ever transparent. The collage elements point up the organic but disorderly aspect of art, and embody the Dadaist antiaesthetic and ethical task to short-circuit the logic of seemingly efficient systems of communication. Thus they enact a semiotic indigestion of scattered words, for the collage of words, images, and matter disrupts the logic of communication. This is also in accordance with Tzara's 1918 proclamation in *Dada 3*:

We have disorganized the inclined Whimperer in ourselves. Any filtration of this nature is bottled diarrhea. To encourage this art means to digest it. We need works that are strong, straight and precise and which will never be comprehensible. Logic is a complication. Logic is always false. . . . Married to logic, art would live in incest, swallowing up, gulping down its own tail, this is its own body, and fornicating with itself. Its temperament would become a nightmare, tarry with protestantism, a monument, a heap of grayish and heavy entrails. (*Réimpression,* 1: 56; my translation)

The Dada artists and poets also exhibit the disorder and confusion of the bourgeois diet in matters of life and culture. The bourgeois diet is based on its reproducibility: in the specific case of food through practical recipes aimed at producing nutritious and tasty meals. The recipes, however, once they are taken out of their culinary context, prove no more than collages themselves. They are a series of words, lists of ingredients, and they mix organic and inorganic matter. The reader can see the recipe's meaning only if and when the meal's end goal is agreed on and known: the recipe's practical, functional side is to produce through a nutritious meal an organic and beautiful human being, as perfect as the meal, which itself can also be reproduced like the recipes.

In contrast, the Dada artist highlights that the recipe by itself reproduces the dysfunctional, disorderly, and meaningless, rather disgusting and confused, human physiology. Without the "illusionary," "ideal" organic image, actually deriving from the end of the recipe (a perfect human body, a perfect total dish), the recipe is just another *Salat,* weltanschauung, or, also in Serner's phrase, another mix of words.[13] The Dada artist exposes both life and art as always already an organic/inorganic confusion, a purposeless mix of indistinct things, concepts, and acts.[14]

The motifs condensed in Tzara's collage are an example of a poetics of disgust and "indistinction" with which the Dadaists attack taste. Thus they frame art as the modern physiological product of a dysfunctional body with which they contrast art as sublime and taste as dissociated from physiology. Borrowing from Allen Weiss in another context, here too one encounters the "countersublime": "The sublime is interiorized, entailing the confusion of the senses, the wreck of the body, the dissipation of thought. . . . The implosion of the sublime engenders an anti-aesthetic that transforms all culinary effects into poison, all transcendental forms into pain" (*Feast and Folly,* 72). The Dada poets' and artists' appropriation of art as physiology—and its disguised historization—also demolishes the digestive function as a model of economic efficiency. In contrast to the selective process of digestion, the Dadaists conceive of both art and life, for them an inseparable unit, from the perspective of the dissolution of boundaries, a perspective that gives rise to the notion of indistinction. Indistinction and disgust are one and the same principle applied at two different levels in the Dada works: semiotic and physiological, the level of the recipe and that of the food. The metaphors of food in these texts confuse the two levels and aim to rework the meaning, or rather the functioning, of both language and body by changing the culinary language of taste into a physiological and childlike (regressive) language that evokes disgust. The Dadaists thus invent a poetics entirely grounded in disgust and nausea, whose roots are in the physical reactions that the physiological processes mentioned in the texts may provoke in the domesticated bourgeois adult, especially when they appear to be fully abstracted from their physiological—read medical—context.

Ernst's allegorical ink drawing "Die Leimbereitung aus Knochen" is itself reappropriated and theoretically incorporated in Tzara's suggestion about boiling the bourgeois into paraffin. *Dada au grand air* epitomizes both the Dadaist semiotic techniques and the social criticism deriving from them. Ernst's drawing is the exact representation of his view about "collage," which in turn informs Tzara's illustration of his own theory of physiological indistinction—physiological collage—as he describes disgust in his 1918 manifesto already mentioned (*Réimpression,* 1: 55–56). In the gift-exchange quoted above, Tzara's points are hinted at in the concepts lying behind the word "paraffin" and in the overall genre of the recipe, which he appropriates here. Indeed, paraffin is the signifier for the Dada theory of *allophagous* devouring and indigestion, of constipation and diarrhea, countering, on the one hand, bourgeois taste and, on the other, capital accumulation and flow.

In Ernst's drawing, the paraffin's laxative qualities, the recipe's cannibalistic traits, and the attack against the bourgeoisie, the use of all this for aesthetic purposes, in short, are here condensed in one example of Dada poetics. The drawing of the bone-glue preparation shows a woman lying on a surgical bed, wrapped in bandages. Tubes connect her limbs and her head with some alchemical apparatus. Ernst literally

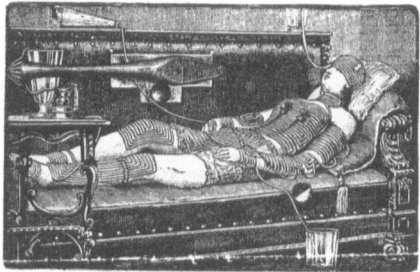

DADA
ꓘOЯIꓕИI
AUGRANDAI R
ꓷƎIЯꓘЯƎᎴИÄS ЯƎꓷ

TARRENZ B. IMST 16 SEPTEMBRE 1886—1921 1 FR. 2 MK.
EN DEPOT AU SANS PAREIL 37 AVENUE KLÉBER PARIS

MAX ERNST: Die Leimbereitung aus Knochen
La préparation de la colle d' os

"Die Leimbereitung aus Knochen," in Dada au grand air — Der Sängerkrieg in Tirol *(Paris, 1921). Courtesy of the International Dada Archive, University of Iowa, Iowa City.*

transfigures, that is, gives shape (figure, image) to, the alchemical process marking any visual experience and any transformation of matter, as it also occurs through the stomach. He associates glue (*colle* in French) with collage. Elsewhere, Ernst speaks of collage as "*placing in marine whiskey.* It is something like the alchemy of the visual image. The miracle of absolute transfiguration of beings and objects with or without modification of their physical anatomical aspect" (*Réimpression, 2:* 134). The creation process of collage is already indicated in the word used for it. In a collage one glues together heterogeneous bits of reality, one abstracts them from reality or nature and creates a new clearly artificial context out of their fragmented nature. This new context transfigures their given meaning without necessarily interfering with their anatomical nature. Ernst's drawing is a recipe/collage of a word and a meaning put together according to the "alchemical vision" of the artist who translates the word and its meaning into a picture. The collage's meaning is like the anagram of its making. The collage as "bone-glue preparation" rematerializes the word by linking it to the actual process of producing glue: a process for which there is a recipe and one in which bones, as pieces of life, are turned into ingredients. Ernst emphasizes here the surgical and indirectly material aspect of art, in addition to its indebtedness to human language.

Furthermore, the "recipe" aspect of the text that accompanies Ernst's drawing adds yet another effect—a cultural critique—to this act of semiotic deconstruction. Tzara's announcement about how to cook—in paraffin—"proper" ladies and gentlemen may again be interpreted as a statement of Dada poetics, one that underscores Dada's emphasis on the physiological order as the means and the aim of the Dadaist revolution. The term *paraffin* derives from the Latin *parum*, "little," and *affinis*. Thus paraffin is a material that has a small affinity for other bodies. It is a "colorless tasteless inodorous oily and waxy substance got by distillation from petroleum and shale and used for making candles etc. . . . (paraffin liquid, odorless tasteless mild laxative)."[15] Tzara's use of the term echoes the use of parallel terms such as *oily, waxy, tasteless, laxative,* which recur frequently in other Dada texts by Ribemont-Dessaignes ("Au Public," originally published in the review *Littérature*, 13, 1920; now in Huelsenbeck, *Almanach Dada*, 252), Hans Richter (in Riha, 34), or by Tzara ("Seven Dada Manifestos," in Motherwell, 75–98).[16] Behind the choice of these terms lurks a philosophy, or rather an antidiet. According to Ernst, collages, like glue, are in effect made of life, human bones, and they are a distillate (marine whiskey) of reality that needs to be captured through the hands of an alchemist, namely, the constructor rather than the believer. Tzara, for his part, boils the bourgeois in a waxy and laxative substance to create his "distillate" of Dada art. Boiled bourgeois in paraffin condenses the recipe for Dada's cannibalistic poetics of disgust and indistinction that informs these poets' will to devour the bourgeois word (the linguistic order on which ethics and aesthetics have been historically based) and then discard it. *Katpepsis* or laxative effects are the favorite form of Dadaist catharsis against the bacteria of bourgeois culture. Diarrhea is also the Dada artists' way to infect and kill the sick bourgeois body, which they have condemned to death. Particularly crucial is the association of the tasteless laxative qualities of this oily substance (one that does not stick but flows) with candles, and thus light. The Dadaists paradoxically are enlightened and enlighten about cannibalistic impulses and the disgusting nature of the civilized culture of recipes and gourmands.[17]

Paraffin's "affinity for other bodies" is thus especially important because the Dadaists, who always stress the difference between themselves and the bourgeois, also read their own life and art as excrement, anal products—hence refuse, what has been separated—of human pathologies. In this respect, the Dada artists cook the bourgeois word, add it to their omnivorous diet, and with the aid of paraffin expel the bourgeois word as their beautiful excrement (10, 21).[18]

Thus in the Dada kitchen (as "Galerie Dada" was defined in retrospect by the Dadaists themselves [Motherwell, 33]) one cooks with paraffin and produces tasteless oily food out of the supposedly nutritional words of bourgeois culture.[19] The result is a diet, which is a collage and produces a collage: no difference is drawn here between the producer and the product, life and art. Hence Tzara can define the Dadaist subjectivity in *New York Dada* thus: "Dada is a new type, a mixture of man, naphthalene, sponge, animal made of ebonite and beefsteak, prepared with soap for cleansing the brain" (Motherwell, 216). Tzara's description of the Dada subject sounds very much like that of the Dadaist work. Indeed the word *Dada* refers to both Dada art and Dada artist. No distinction is made between the subject and the object of the Dada work. The disorder of words reproduces the disorder of foods and the disorder of the human physiology. The Dadaist subject itself is this collage, a disorderly physiology of multiple needs.

Through the motifs of disgust, indistinction, and dysfunctional physiologies, the Dadaist disrupts and reconstrues language by erasing the principle of taste as the principle of aesthetic, ethical, and social distinction. Taste is reinscribed from the Dadaist's physiological perspective, as based in the mouth.[20] Corporeality is the framework for Dada's semiotic and cultural antidiets, which these artists ground in the senses and especially in the deformation or remapping of taste. Dada "taste" in effect loses both the pleasurable and functional aspects ascribed to taste by Jean Anthelme Brillat-Savarin, author of the founding book of "Gastrosophie," *La physiologie du goût*. For Brillat-Savarin the will to live is condensed in the functional reason of taste. The physiological ability to taste invites humans to eat in order to repair the loss of energy necessary for the conservation of every individual. For Dada, the will to live is situated less in the reproductive instincts, also sustained by taste, than in the bowels. The Dada artists and poets locate their antitaste in the intestines, a disgusting space of indistinction as multiplicity of forces and elements that alternate with each other are confused or juxtaposed.

Dégoût: Tasteless Indistinction

Instead of functionalism, taste, and pleasure, the Dada artists and poets proclaim "Dadaist disgust" (Tzara, 1918 manifesto) and "dysfunctional physiologies." The unavoidable and thus typical contradiction of the avant-garde movements is between affirming and criticizing modernity. In the Dada text, modernity becomes the age that best epitomizes the fetishistic drives of human beings constantly caught between consumption and projection (dejection).[21] For example, in "Pamphlet gegen die Weimarische Lebensauffassung," Hausmann speaks of the German Spirit as sold on the market and of intellectuals who contribute to construct education as surplus value (*Literarische Dokumentation*, 37). Serner's manifesto exposes art and culture, as well as organized thought, as fetishes of the human pathology. Like Serner, Tzara speaks of moral and philosophical systems in terms of chocolate or the choice between cake and cherries. These are sublimated objects that in the end only help humans to fill their emptiness, their empty stomachs, and indeed mouths (through both the food in question and language).

The critique of modernity and civilization from the perspective of physiology was not new. Because Nietzsche had a strong influence on many intellectuals, the association of *Kultur* and illness was very much in vogue in Germany both before and after World War I. The Dada artists, for their time, however, are unique in applying physiological concepts directly to their texts. They take the use of physiology even farther than Nietzsche in that they show physiology to be pathological in itself, what then returns full blown in Georges Bataille, Salvador Dalí, and Luis Buñuel especially, namely, in the element of perversion that haunts surrealism.[22] The Dadaist attack on the German Spirit and on modern consumerist society is expressed through the physiological metaphors of indigestion, excessive and indistinct devouring, and expulsion or excrement. More specifically, the Dadaist discourse of food occurs *most evidently* at the linguistic level, at the metalevel of language. The Dada artists are not interested in the *topic* of food; they do not elaborate on food as either a theme or a means of social critique. Instead, through a language of metaphors reduced to scattered food-words (insults), the Dada poets try to invent a semiotics that emphasizes the ability of words to duplicate bodily symptoms — the body as illness. These words — they seem to say — are immediately incorporated into the body, not just into the mind, because the reader despite everything invests them with a semantic context or meaning. Reading these words provokes a physical reaction to the desire — or rather disgust — that these ordinary words sensually evoke.

In his essay on Brillat-Savarin, Roland Barthes presents the food-word as the best representative of language's desiring qualities, because the food-word sensually elicits the desire for the food, the absence of which is only more evident in the presence of the substitute word (*Rustle of Language*, 250–52). This kind of desiring consumption that informs language is especially typical of Serner's caustic texts. He frames his "Last Loosening Manifesto" within the context of a meal that the reader, in his view, must enjoy to be able to enjoy this text on the art of becoming con-artists (i.e., the art of succeeding in a bourgeois world).[23] Reading his instructions is tantamount to a dual bodily activity: on the one hand, the eye has to move and gather Serner's scribbles into signs, words, and meanings; on the other, the ensuing text is also a call to activity as pleasure, the pleasure of engaging in some action (*Unternehmungslust*), such as eating. Furthermore, reading is also spurred by an activity: the consumption of words is induced in Serner by consuming food. Finally, the "state of exceptional desire for action," as he writes, is immediately reinvested by yet another form of consumption, the erotic one that takes place in another *Lokal*. The text's effect is of a movement from physical consumption through digestive and active interpretation to sensual consumption, so that every stage and kind of activity has its grounds in a physiological "need" (see "Last Loosening Manifesto").

Whether allegorically or through an allegedly physiological desire, both Tzara and Serner associate art production and art products (artworks) with bodily cycles of consumption that they deprive of any embellishment. Instead they exhibit these in their brutal nakedness. The roughness and rudimental (regressive, primeval) mechanisms of *this* civilization's cultural instinct rather than intellectual refinement manifest themselves even more strongly in how innocuous food-words at some times are transformed into insults and at other times in the

Dada antidiets. Dadaist texts thus often refer to food: for example, *pommes frites* recur frequently. Phrases such as "you are all pears" are childish insults, and recipes appear as loose and simple inventories of words. The texts may contain several lists of ingredients and foods that one or the other artists like or dislike, without ever specifying which, as well as poems bearing food-titles.[24] Among the words of food and the references to physiological functions that return in the eight issues of *Dada* are *taste, disgust, saliva, to devour, cannibalism, vomit, deterioration, corpse, excrement, stench, bitter, fat, digestion, preserve, cheese, camembert, vol au vent, pancakes, chocolate, alcohol, meat, powder and pills, bread, milk, tripe, ragout, radish, trout, salad, pommes frites, strudel, onions, brains, artichokes, bones, fish soup, ham, brioche, tartine, eggs, pears, apples,* and *pumpkin.* Most of these food-words are devoid of the connotations of pleasure normally ascribed to them by Western culinary traditions. Instead they are equated with words of disgust. Taken out of context, they sound most often like insults.

Accordingly, foodstuffs are "stupid": they have no meaning when they do not come from a context and do not flow into one, when they do not shape one. In this respect, scattered food-words shooting out individually from vaudevillian texts preempt the possibility of building up a meaningful system, yet, precisely because of their asystemic use, they best represent Serner's notion of weltanschauung. They literally operate — in their signifying nature as words — the most internal annihilation of philosophy. Tzara already demolished philosophy with the aid of food in his 1918 manifesto, where he wrote: "Philosophy is the question: From what side one should start to contemplate life, god, and the idea as well as the other phenomena. Everything that one contemplates is false. The relative result is to me of no more importance than the choice between cake or cherries after a meal" (*Réimpression,* 1: 55). Philosophy is a whimsical choice, a preference between two equivalent desserts. Food is also the same as this empty philosophy, a system that, while supposedly grounded in universal values, is actually based on spontaneous likes and dislikes, as well as interests. All desserts are declared to be superfluous sameness, the sameness and superfluity of bourgeois "class" (distinction and class). Only the individual "bumbum bumbum bumbum" — Tzara writes — provides foods and words, as well as food-words, with their flavors and meanings. But the Dada poets and writers show that these words are easily reduced to free-signifiers by being relieved of their semantic functions. Food-words and the system of distinction in which they are rooted and that they reproduce become just like any other word or system; they lose their distinctive meaning and thus their difference and their flavor. At the same time, the Dadaist juxtaposition (or substitution) of eating and defecating attempts to erase by writing directly on the body the meanings that the bourgeois use of language has associated with these actions.

Tzara invokes disgust to level out and erase the values ascribed to these embarrassing physiological functions.[25] By claiming disgust (*dégoût*) rather than taste as the unique signifier of their Dada semiosis, one based on the constant shift of the signified, Dada writes a physiology in which to eat, to defecate, to vomit, to speak are synonymous.[26] Hence Tzara also writes: "Active Simplicity. / The impossibility to distinguish among degrees of clarity: to lick the twilight and to float in the big mouth full with honey and excrement" (*Réimpression*, 1: 55). For Dada, the human body acts before it is written. There is no sequence or logical order of functions. As the analysis of the metaphors of food demonstrates, Dada rejects alimentary semiotics. *Pommes frites* and pears, excrement and vomit, are used as substitutes for the same things. Any food is replaceable by another, and food-words are not organized according to the discriminatory signifier of taste. Food itself represents an immense and indistinct category, which reproposes the body as a disorder. This Dada body escapes functionalization (diet) and also *decor,* a sense of well-being (gastronomy). This body thus created by the absence of an alimentary syntax is like a puzzle where every piece is identical to the next. Because the Dadaist writers also aim to crack the functioning body of the modern subject as it is being created by the scientific discourse of health and nutrition, as well as consumerist and capitalist ideology, then their physiology of disgust focuses on the fixation on one stage of the full cycle of incorporation, assimilation, and excretion. Such a fixation intends to interrupt the cycle, prevent it from being complete, from reaching meaning.

By metaphorizing the eating and digestive processes, the experience of eating is atrophied and replaced by a random feeding and secretion (indigestion and diarrhea) of words held together by an alimentary dictionary without alimentary syntax: while the Dadaist recipes are devoid of foods, the manifestos and poems are full of them.[27] Yet these food-words are either "all the same" — disgusting (and disgusting also because they are identical, incomprehensible, too extensive, too purely physical symptoms) — or completely alien, separated, hence indigestible.

The Dadaist food-word is indigestible *for* the bourgeois. It functions as the leftover (and the rubbish, the bad-consciousness) of the process leading up to pleasure — the digestive cycle of consummation/consumption. This attack against pleasure as bourgeois pleasure, one that occurs at the linguistic level and not at the political level, gradually shifts ground and becomes an attack against the concept of taste and hence the aesthetic experience and art (as separate and specific). Hence we can read in *Bulletin Dada*: "Everyone with good taste is rotten" (*Réimpression*, 1: 110).

More generally, it is an attack against the ideology of aesthetics. Dada devours and is devoured in the market and represents this cannibalistic cycle of dependence by using the alimentary categories. The same logic of classification is then questioned through a critique of taste and the distinctions between subject and object, eater and eaten, the tasteful and the disgusting.

First Tzara and Serner, then the surrealist painter Dalí, present life as being caught in a big mouth. For Tzara, in this gaping mouth one cannot and should not discern between honey and excrement (*Réimpression*, 1: 55), while for Serner the entire globe becomes a "blob of filth." In Tzara's manifesto, in the section "Dadaist Disgust," Tzara also writes: "Every product of disgust susceptible of becoming a negation of the family is Dada" (56). The family stands both for a social institution, that is, the established order and hierarchy of sexual relations, and for "family" in linguistic terms, namely, as class or category. Against categories and nomenclatures, Tzara opposes the word LIFE, in capital letters, in short, his vitalism. The products of the "category" that taste names disgust (*dégoût*) are all those things that constitute the changing and unstable movements of LIFE and that thus can hardly enter a class. They are the antithesis of taste. For Tzara, this "flux" (later appropriated by Fluxus) is Dada and Dada is life. Life has been deserted as disgusting by the Spirit (philosophy, the intellect) and by high art. Against both, LIFE and Dada (later described as antiart) mean the full immersion in the "contradictions, the grotesque and the inconsequent," those last few words with which Tzara closes his manifesto. On the cover of *Dadaphone* this immersion is further qualified as "Lady! Hands in canonical shit" (*Réimpression,* 1: 111). These words resonate with Bataille's later invocations of and hymns to the "Big Toe," the solar anus, and the *informe.*

The Abject Excrement of Indistinction

The antidiet that Dada proposes with its "Dadaist disgust" rewrites a semiotic system (of linguistic signs and body symptoms) based on the principle of lack of differentiation, lack of distinctions, and thus lack of absolute meaning in logic as in "physio-logy." Dadaist disgust, as Julia Kristeva would argue, is clearly a poetics of the abject, originating in the abject rather than in the act of abjection. Kristeva construes a theory of modernism based on abjection, the modernist texts enacting at the linguistic level the abjection of the semiotic language spoken by the mother's engulfing body. The mother is for Kristeva the ultimate signifier of the abject. Kristeva claims that the modernist poetics of abjection is enacted because the abject always returns in the modern times. Dada dietetic principles are immersed *in* the abject. Dada's texts call for the return of disgust, the destruction of boundaries, and thus the erasure of the symbolic, the language of the father, the absolute signifier and its culture. For Dada language is and remains baby prattle reminiscent of the semiotic language preceding the symbolic language. The Dada point of departure and indeed arrival is to inhabit the space–time of the abject.

"Dadaist Disgust" as proclaimed by Tzara is thus "active spontaneity" and "indifference." This indifference seems to imply less a concept of insensitivity and unconcern than one of in-distinction, in-differentiation, the opposite of "taste" as the faculty of distinction, as shown above. Taste has its antonym in the term *disgust* or, in French—the language of the 1918 manifesto—*dégoût.* One could argue that Tzara privileges this term over *Ekel* (nausea)—later chosen by Jean-Paul Sartre for his novel—because the Dada manifestos have the task to speak the abject, the disgusting, rather than to operate abjection, distinction. The Dadaist does not stop where nausea manifests itself. The idea of indifferentiation emerges quite clearly in the metaphors of "dysfunctional physiology" as represented by diarrhea, vomit, and indigestion in which there are no objects and no subjects but only flux, mixed abject words.[28]

Indifferentiation does not distinguish between Dada's own excremental products and disgusting bourgeois words. From the perception of Dada both the body of society and the human body are sick — and these bodies are disgusting. However, in Tzara's 1918 manifesto, Dada welcomes disgust and aims to disgust others, to work as *"microbes typographiques"* (typographic microbes) that will infect and kill this societal and physiological organism in which Dada also includes itself. The culture of the bourgeoisie is so taken by sweetness — its own disgustingly sweet, too sweet ethical codes — that it does not even perceive its own disgusting qualities and favors the sweetness of honey over the bitter reality of excrement. The bourgeois distinguishes, discriminates between the self and the other, and represses the presence of an abject other within the self.

The bourgeois has two options: fearing disgust, he or she can abhor Dada art as disgusting. In this case, the bourgeois simply remains blind to the decaying condition of the social body and thus his or her own body. Or the bourgeois can partake of the Dadaist game, either as a spectator or as a consumer, and be forced to eat Dada's beautiful excrement. The bourgeois stomach, however, is unaccustomed to disgust. Hausmann thus predicts a lethal indigestion for anyone who indulges in Dada: "Wer Dada *isst* stirbt daran, wenn nicht Dada *ist*" ("whoever eats dada, and is not dada, dies of it," quoted in Riha, 8; my emphasis). Then, according to Serner, Dada texts, the "bad" and "fake" copies of the bourgeois commodities and works of art, are reproposed to the bourgeois who cannot resist the fetishistic need for consumption and attempts to repossess his or her own anal products. Like Serner, Picabia writes in his "Manifeste Cannibale," in *Dadaphone 7,*

> Honor is bought and sold just like . . . one's own bottom. The bottom
> represents life like french fries and you all with your seriousness stink
> worse than cow dung DADA is just like your hopes: nothing
> like your heavens: nothing
> like your idols: nothing
> like your political men: nothing
> like your heroes: nothing
> like your artists: nothing
> like your religions: nothing
> Whistle, cry, break my jaws — and then what? I will always tell you that
> you are stupid bucks. In three months my friends and I, we will sell you
> our own paintings for a few francs. (*Réimpression,* 1: 113)

Dada proclaims disgust as its poetics. Thus these writers' incoherence and contradictory statements are not defining, and this allows the Dadaists to devour the bourgeois word (their abject) — reduced to just another food, just like *pommes frites*. In contrast, Picabia tells us, the bourgeois is hypocritical when he or she believes that bourgeois values

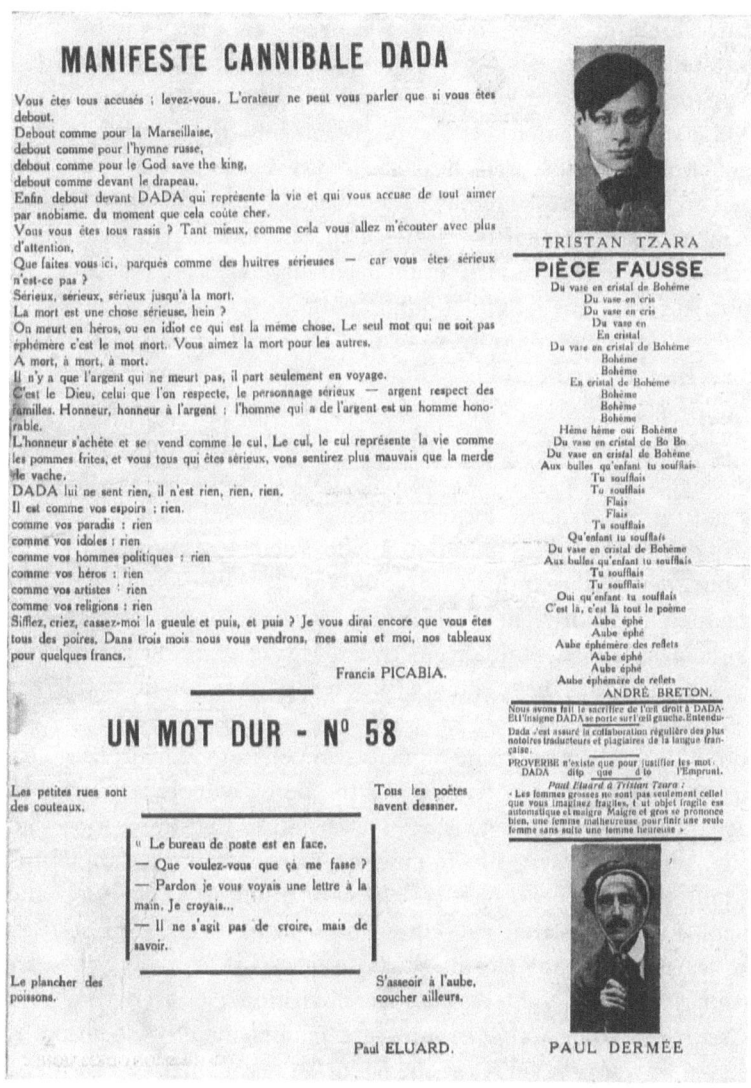

"*Manifeste Cannibale Dada*," in Dadaphone 7 *(Paris, 1920): 2. Courtesy of the International Dada Archive, University of Iowa, Iowa City.*

are stable, that his or her worldviews are coherent. Picabia informs his bourgeois audience that although they consider Dada disgusting, they indeed continue to pay to see it or own it. He adds that the collector, the museums, that very same audience will buy Dada's works once the market will have set a price for them.

Unlike Dada, the bourgeois, limited by taste, is caught in a perverse and incestuous cycle, with no way out, or so Tzara writes in his 1918 manifesto: the bourgeois does not necessarily perceive Dada as disgusting, or, if he or she does, he or she still follows the market's laws, the values set by the market. The bourgeois buys these artists' works without noticing that thereby he or she is duped because the works purchased are his or her own remasticated words, now turned into Dada's excrement. As the Dadaists put it, Dada can devour its own abject-object—the disgusting and moralizing bourgeois word—because as products of the same malfunctioning, pathological physiologies, both the bourgeois and Dada partake of the same indistinct abject. Hausmann writes in "Synthetisches Cino der Malerei" ("Synthetic Cinema of Painting"): "Human being is simultaneous, a monster of self and other, now, before, after and at the same time" (quoted in Riha, 30).

Doesburg associates a view of nature as corpse and corrupt (and thus nature as our own decaying image) with the Dadaist struggle against decomposition as pollution. In the crucial text "Was Ist Dada?" Doesburg defines the "Indifferenzpunkt" (point of indifference): "Nothing changes radically. The world always remains the same. Dada sublates the acknowledged duality between Matter and Spirit, Man and Woman and creates the 'point of indifference,' that is, a point that lies beyond the human concept of space–time" (*Literarische Dokumentation*, 49). At the same time he feels compelled to explain this with a theory of decay and corruption of the body, namely, a whimsical theory of disgust: "Dada does not see in nature that apparition that inspires adoration as we like to imagine; rather [Dada sees in nature] that foul smelling corpse that corrupts our intellectual pleasures and immediately allows that everything be transformed into a state of putrefaction: From the cleaning lady to the artist (in reality they are one thing), everyone fights against decomposition, against nature" (49). What appears to be a claim against the endorsement of pollution by Dada—that wants to get rid of the pollution of the infected Spirit and body of culture—transforms itself into the unveiling of the natural state of decomposition of the human being, of the cadaver-like nature of every organic life. Thus Dada looks for the *Indifferenzpunkt* where nature is shown to be a corpse, where the meaningful and the meaningless are the same thing. Yet the Dada artists do not erase completely the line between putrefaction or decomposition (*Verwesung*), on the one hand, and purity or, in some texts, "whiteness," on the other. In effect, their semiotic concern is definition or, as Richard Sheppard put it, balance without harmony but in cacophony and contradiction. They are especially at pains to rethink the categories in which to place the polluted and the pure.[29]

Everyone fights against one's own pathological body and sublimates one's own horror of death, the emptiness of which is the Signifier of Serner's "Last Loosening Manifesto."[30] Logic as a system — a beautiful system — tries to erase death by making it its other, the debased corpse that is "not life." The Dadaists, in order not to operate distinctions themselves, also fight against *Schmutz*, dirt, but equate dirt with the products of culture, high culture, and civilization. The Dadaists set out to show that these high products are the excrement of a sick body, both the human body and the modern society that civilization has produced. Yet these artists — and this is the circular and cannibalistic semiotic system they construe against logic and dialectical thought — cannot limit their critique to a reversal of the beautiful and the disgusting, and thus embrace the disgusting, the excrement, illnesses, and the corpse all together, which are at the core of life as flux. Thus one reads in "Monsieur Aa l'Antiphilosophie": "It is white and beautiful, this excrement because we are all angels stones certify to it our ink is white and we write on our white paper our illnesses are those of aquatic animals" (*Réimpression,* 1: 120). What is on the margins (as Kristeva defines the abject), the corpse, the decayed, the decomposed, the dejected, is beautiful because it is excrement and in particular "Dadaist excrement."

Dada's point of indifference as associated with the Dadaist poetics of disgust aims to separate taste as moral and political principle of distinction from tasting as the bodily experience of difference, experience that does not need order and that, in fact, incurs in indigestion and excess, on the one hand, and uncontrollable bouts of laughter, on the other: rather than just words, "a mouth's words." In his manifesto on feeble love and bitter love, Tzara claims that words only express the reasons and tastes of any particular mouth, rather than some immaterial, distant, and intellectual/spiritual entity, the Word.

Taste, as the privileged signifier according to which "order" (aesthetic

Letzte Lockerung manifest

1.
Um einen Feuerball rast eine Kotkugel, auf der Damenseidenstrümpfe verkauft und Gauguins geschätzt werden. Ein fürwahr überaus betrüblicher Aspekt, der aber immerhin ein wenig unterschiedlich ist: Seidenstrümpfe können be—griffen werden, Gauguins nicht. (Bernheim als prestigieuser Biologe zu imaginieren.) Die tausend Kleingehirn-Rastas embêtantester Observanz, welche erigierten Bourgeois-Zeigefingern Feuilletonspalten servieren (o pastoses Gepinkel!), um Geldflüsse zu lockern, haben dieserhalb Verwahrlosungen angerichtet, die noch heute manche Dame zu kurz kommen lassen. (Man reflektiere drei Minuten über die Psychose schlecht behandelter Optik; klinisches Symptom, primär: Unterschätzung der Seidenstrümpfe; sekundär: Verdauungsbeschwerden.)

2.
Was dürfte das erste Gehirn, das auf den Globus geriet, getan haben? Vermutlich erstaunte es über seine Anwesenheit und wusste mit sich und dem schmutzigen Vehikel unter seinen Füssen nichts anzufangen. Inzwischen hat man sich an das Gehirn gewöhnt, indem man es so unwichtig nimmt, dass man es nicht einmal ignoriert, aus sich einen Rasta gemacht (zu unterst: schwärzlicher Pole; zu oberst: etwa Senatspräsident) und aus der mit Unrecht so beliebten Natur eine Kulisse für ein wahrhaftig sehr starkes Stück. Dieser zweifellos nicht sonderlich heroische Ausweg aus einem immer noch nicht weidlich genug gewürdigten Dilemma ist zwar vollends reizlos geworden, seit er so völlig absehbar ist (wie infantil ist eine Personenwage!), aber eben deshalb sehr geeignet, gewisse Prozeduren vorzunehmen.

3.
Auch einem Lokomotivführer fällt es jährlich wenigstens einmal ein, dass seine Beziehungen zur Lokomotive durchaus nicht zwingend sind und dass er von seinem Ehgespons nicht viel mehr weiss als nach jener warmen Nacht im Bois. (Hätte ich La Villette genannt oder die Theresienwiese, so wären beide Beziehungen gänzlich illusorisch, Fingerzeig für Habilitanten: „Ueber topographische Anatomie, psychischen Luftwechsel und Verwandtes".) Im Hotel Ronceroy oder in Picadilly kommt es hingegen bereits vor, dass es verteufelt unklar wird, warum man jetzt gerade auf seine Hand glotzt und tiriliert, sich kratzen hört und seinen Speichel liebt. Diesem scheinbar so friedlichen Exempel ist die Möglichkeit, dass das penetrante Gefühl der Langeweile zu einem Gedanken über ihre Ursache sich emporturnt, am dicksten. Solch ein lieblicher Moment arrangiert den Desperado (o was für ein Süsser!), der als Prophet, Künstler, Anarchist, Staatsmann etc., kurz als Rasta Unfug treibt.

4.
Napoleon, ein doch wirklich tüchtiger Junge, behauptete unverantwortlicher Weise, der wahre Beruf des Menschen sei, den Acker zu bestellen. Wieso? Fiel ein Pflug vom Himmel? Aber etwas hat der homo doch mitbekommen, supponiere ich mir eine liebesunterernährte Damenstimme. Nun, jedenfalls nicht das Ackern; und Kräuter und Früchte sind schliesslich auch schon damals dagewesen. (Bitte hier bei den deutschen Biogeneten nachzulesen, warum ich Unrecht habe. Es wird jedoch sehr langweilen. Deshalb habe ich recht.) Letzthin also: auch Napoleon, der ansonsten sehr erfreulich frische Hemmungslosigkeiten äusserte, war streckenweise Stimmungsathlet. Schade. Sehr schade.

5.
Alles ist nämlich rastaquéresk, meine lieben Leute. Jeder ist (mehr oder weniger) ein überaus luftiges Gebilde, dieu merci. (Nur nebenbei: meine Gunst dem Tüchtigen, der mir nachweist, dass etwas letztlich nicht willkürlich als Norm herumspritzt!) Anders würde übrigens ein epidemisches Krepieren anheben. Diagnose: rabiate Langeweile; oder: panische Resignation; oder: transzendentales Ressentiment etc. (Kann, beliebig fortgesetzt, zum Register sämtlicher unbegabter Zustände erhoben werden!) Der jeweilige landläufige Etat der bewohnten Erdoberfläche ist deshalb lediglich das folgerichtige Resultat einer unerträglich gewordenen Langeweile. Langeweile: nur als harmlosestes Wort! Jeder suche sich die ihm schmackhafteste Vokabel für seine Minderwertigkeit! (Herziges Sujet für ein scharfes Pfänderspiel!!)

6.
Es ist allgemein bekannt, dass ein Hund keine Hängematte ist; weniger, dass ohne diese zarte Hypothese Matern die Schmierfaust herunterfiele; und überhaupt nicht, dass Interjektionen am treffendsten sind: Weltanschauungen sind Vokabelmischungen...

"Letzte Lockerung Manifest" in Dada 4–5 *(1919): 15 (Zurich, international edition). Courtesy of the International Dada Archive, University of Iowa, Iowa City.*

and ethical) is affirmed, is replaced by the disgusting. The disgusting
is associated with indifference in the sense of in-distinction. For the
Dadaist to "wage his battle of dadaist disgust," however, there must
exist an abject other against which war is declared. This other is the
hierarchy of taste itself and the society that requires and has established the culture of taste. In the battle, Dada first sets out to identify this other, this order and these categories, and then to devour it.
Devouring is an act of destruction and dejection that makes everything abject, both counterparts. Then, according to Picabia, the Dadaist does not feel repulsion when facing excrement because survival
means to deepen one's own hands in canonical shit. This is the only
possibility to live beyond false morals, as stated on the cover of *Dadaphone 7* (*Réimpression*, 111). In contrast, the Dadaist is nauseated by
chocolate's sweetness, a motif that will return in the neo-avant-garde
art dealing with food, especially in Dieter Roth's works. Sweet and
enticing dishes provoke the Dadaist's disgust, or at least a negative
reaction; in *Dada 4–5*, Serner defines bourgeois thought in terms of
crêpes and *gnoles*, which numb the brain (*Réimpression*, 1: 89; French
translation). Life, as excretory activity, and nature, as an ongoing process of putrefaction, are not in themselves nauseous to the kynical
Dadaist; on the contrary, it is civilization and culture as two deceiving
means that provoke abjection or Dadaist nausea. One solution to overcome abjection is to strive for that *Indifferenzpunkt* whereby taste
as an intellectual ability to distinguish is abandoned and replaced by
the Dadaist reliance on the physiological act of separation (*Ausscheidung*) that transforms bourgeois sweetness into the Dadaist stomach's
production of excrement. The Dadaist artist approaches this point of
indifference by calling his work a refuse, too, so that no distinction is
made among all human products, artistic or not.

Art is not distinct from the corrupt body of nature, whose power
turns everything into decomposed corpses in the end. Cravan, a forerunner of the Dadaists, often quoted in their texts, initially declared
his disgust at painting (at "canonical shit"), and then called painting
life. Writing about the Salon des Independents held in Paris in 1914,
he calls the paintings exhibited "rotten" and then adds: "Painting is
walking, running, drinking, eating and fulfilling your natural functions. You can say I am disgusting, but that is just what it is" (Motherwell, 12). What is disgust is his unwillingness to distinguish between

honey and excrement (as does Tzara), art and physiology.[31] The same occurs in a slightly more subtle way in Erik Satie's description of his diet of white foodstuffs, in "The Day of a Musician": "I eat only white foods: eggs, sugar, minced bones, the fat from dead animals, veal, salt, coconuts, chicken cooked in white water, the mould from fruit, rice, turnips, camphor sausages, pates, cheese (white), cotton salad and certain fishes (without the skin)" (Motherwell, 18). The idea of a white diet, and thus of a system, and more specifically one organized around a very particular pictorial principle, is undermined by the principle itself. First, the principle does not have anything to do with nutritional notions, it stems from the painter's palette. Second, the color itself — white — annihilates every distinction within the dietetic (and color) system and exposes the diet as devoid of order. Hence Satie's diet is disorderly, overabundant, and in effect approximates a (poetic) bulimic binge.

Dada's position with regard to "organic waste" raises several crucial points. It allows Tzara and Serner as well as others (Hausmann, Doesburg, and Cravan) to establish a nonstatic syntax in which signs change meaning depending on their reciprocal and constantly shifting position. Yet the theory of spontaneity (Tzara) or "point of indifference" (Hausmann) also acknowledges Dada's intervention as an act of distinction and separation, one, however, that coincides with and is performed as digestion, a physiological process that is hailed against art and aesthetics. At the same time, spontaneity and indifference theorize confusion — an act of indigestion — in which the only conceivable beginnings and ends are, according to Tzara, in the "big mouth." Distinction and confusion coexist as physiological approaches to the modern, consumerist Western world: the mouth takes in this world in its variety — human beings are, after all, omnivorous — and the stomach processes; it interprets and selects the world, transforms it without, however, "judging" and organizing its matter, and even the abjected fecal matter remains indistinct and primal.

Indigestion: The Diet of the Allophagous Dadaist

For Tzara, only the order of the body can actually do justice to life in the multiplicity of the earthly chaos. The body's true order, however, functions according to its own multiple needs, as Hausmann makes clear in his "Pamphlet against Weimar." In short, it does not reflect an absolute unitarian logic:

In this great climate, in this dull destruction one cannot be a righteous kind of conventional artist. Then, en avant DADA!

Let us take on the inconvenience of a free, independent gesture! Let us set aside the stupidity of good taste. . . . And art, in all of this? Attention, it becomes active. Away with AESTHETICS; I no longer know any rules, neither of truth, nor of beauty, I follow a new direction, one which is prescribed to me by the order of my body. (Hausmann, quoted in Riha, 5)

Accordingly, human beings live thanks to an act of constant consumption that is itself inefficient and reveals the limits of an empty physiology caught between the dialectics of emptiness and the need for fulfillment. To eat then appears from this perspective to be a reason for the body and a need. Food takes on a functional role, that is, the preservation of life. Yet without success, the body dies.

The Dada artists and poets, Serner in particular, show that this function to preserve life — as it manifests itself in the dysfunctional human physiology — is the only reason at stake. Not only can human beings devour everything, but they also can overeat and suffer from indigestion. Eating does not fulfill a need then but in fact, by never satisfying the body, easily calls for excessive indulging and thus is always excessive with respect to its functional purpose. Eating, against the reason of the body, is an act of indigestion, and, paradoxically, its real function is excess: it enlightens humans about their dysfunctional being, their mortality (temporality), and, possibly, the irreverent pleasures of life beyond purpose.

The Dada poet unveils the fact that the carefully conceived organized social diets on which modernity is based in effect are no more than salad. Modernity is even more a disorder than the Dadaist natural omnivorous diet. As stated in *Dada 2,* the latter in fact is based on the "order of the cosmos" (*Réimpression,* 1: 48). The bourgeois diet, in aesthetic and cultural terms as well as in the nutritionists' texts of the same period, focuses on the perfectibility of the digestive system and its energy intake and consumption, not only its functionalism but also its beauty (as determined by bourgeois taste or even the Futurists' visions). Dada's theory of indigestion in contrast suggests that their "work" is constituted by the act of devouring in a "cosmogonic" way.

From within the category of indifferentiation that brings about indigestion and hence disgust, pleasure is still present. It is taken in the act of ingesting the world, indistinctly, like the Rabelaisian giants. Digestion and well-being are no preoccupation for the Dada artist. Consider Eluard's "Patisserie Dada" (1920), a list of a series of daily events, or rather Dadaist acts: regular statements, observations, comments, that is, various kinds of utterances, with potentially different "truth-value." Eluard then concludes his "prose-poem" thus: "We ingest all this, whether we digest it or not, we could not care less" (*Literarische Dokumentation,* 79). Digestion, an efficient system taken as a potential modern economic model, functionalizes eating that, interpreted through this lens, erases pleasure, for it negates the enjoyment of the dessert ("La Patisserie" to which Eluard refers). Dessert is superfluous, excessive with respect to the purposes of nutrition. Aron's comments on the meaning of *patisserie* in France at the time of "La Belle Epoque" show the bourgeois attempt to mitigate pleasure through aestheticization as well as engineering of baking.[32] In contrast to the early-nineteenth-century patisserie, Eluard is semiotically destroying both the concepts of taste and function: his pastry shop does not specialize in construction or on perfection, that is, the two defining skills of the confectionary art as described by Aron. Above all, there is no trace of artistic initiation. The art (*technē*) of the baker is recalled, yet the poem is not about it. In effect, the text's title, "La Patisserie," makes reference to a specific genre of food and of words. Eluard, however, does not distinguish among the words he uses. His alternative — avant-garde — bakery produces something inedible, or rather indigestible: it constipates, halts the digestion of the bourgeois stomach like Serner's interjections.[33] This because the bourgeois stomach, "selectively interpretive," searches for the circulation of meaning as well as of commodities, all of which it consumes.

In effect, Serner shows that constipation was *the* illness, both physical and mental, of consumer society, in short, a metonymy of this society, in which the capitalist bourgeois, having indulged in conspicuous accumulation of surplus value, could not enjoy excess any longer and thus must run to the *Kurort,* a health resort, to liberate his or her intestines and free the circulation of anal products. Serner — who lived in Karlsbad, a famous health resort at the beginning of the twentieth century — picks up on this real-life bourgeois anxiety about digestion (palpable also in the nutritionists' texts) and interprets it as the symptom of the decline of this wealthy society that in his view is condemned to both consume and accumulate. Note that both the Dada writers — who ingest the bourgeois word in order to discard it — and the bourgeois who stuff themselves are obsessed with the issue of cleansing, purification. But the bourgeois and the avant-garde artist use rituals of

ation with different purposes: the Dada artists intend to pro-
uuce a pure refuse and purge themselves of the hypocritical bourgeois word. Their excrement — in their writings — is the word finally
materialized and shown in its indigestible, real guise. In contrast, the
bourgeois is anxious about not interrupting the flow or else circulation
of fetishized commodities, which these artists equate with the consumers' anal products. Hence, whereas the avant-garde artists worry
about producing an art of white refuse that will constipate the bourgeois compulsion to consume and accumulate, and whereas they worry
also about purifying their stomachs — albeit excrementally — from the
assimilation of bourgeois values, the bourgeois worries about liberating his or her stomach to be able to keep consuming and discarding
and to be able to repossess, that is, reconquer the products rejected.

Serner indeed shows that the cure from constipation is intended
for the bourgeois to facilitate circulation and thus to ameliorate the
"assimilating quality" of the bourgeois digestive apparatus. In contrast,
as Tzara announces more explicitly in his 1918 manifesto, "detoxifica-
tion" is for Dada a "destructive, negative work" that breaks and stops
circulation or digestion.

Counterposed to the fecal work of art is performative language,
itself a symbolic excretory act of *Sprechen* (uttering). *Sprechen* is also
opposed to the "word said," as the signifier is opposed to the signified.
No meaning and no nutrition are being retained, and the speech-act
is associated with a hemorrhage or *Durchfall,* which is the liberating
product of an upset stomach. Diarrhea (lit. "flow through"; in German
"fall through," or *Durch-fall)* characterizes at once the Dada creations
as organic flux, spontaneity, and intensity, and the moral principles,
the compensatory offspring of the constipated body of the bourgeois.
The act of "flowing through" metaphorizes the fluidity of the free-
floating signifier that the Dada writer sets against the critics' aesthetic
judgment or else the notion of universality of taste.[34]

In contrast, in "Last Loosening Manifesto" Serner writes: "sweated
out of people's pores . . . [and] symphonies are groaned out" (Green,
156, and *Réimpression,* 1: 89). From this perspective, language as well
as art are yet another metaphor for the human body and the body's
lacking connections with the external world. For instance, according
to Nietzsche, sounds and signs only transcribe images with their origin in the body. Similarly, Serner considers language a nerve stimulus
put into sound; for this Dada writer, language exists in the speech-act

as bodily performance, as *Geste* (gesture). To the poisoning bourgeois word that threatens to constipate the Dadaist body, Dada responds with an organic flux of words as gestures. The disgusting and/or non-sensical food-words pronounced by the Dadaists function as antibodies (and, more aptly, "antiverba") in reverse: a liquid "flow-through" of words that in this way not only do not nourish (and thus reproduce) the consumer's body (and the consumed but never quite assimilated message) but are in fact thrown back at the audience as their own product, now transformed into a disgusting, beautiful Dada excrement. Dada makes indigestion and disgust into its banners. Dada's aesthetic and creative stance is one of absolute devouring. As Hausmann suggests, the Dadaist incorporates to destroy, deject, or vomit the "spiritual, nourishing word" of classic culture with its *Bildungsideal.* Indigestion as aiming at constipation and/or diarrhea—the symptoms of a malfunctioning, dysfunctional circulation of nourishment—is Dada's strategy of consuming against bourgeois consumption.

The Mouth in the Belly: Dysfunctional Physiologies

Tzara exhibits the physiological nature of language and the thoughts words articulate in the already mentioned manifesto on feeble love and bitter love. There he writes: "Must we cease to believe in words? Since when have they expressed the opposite of what the organ emitting them thinks and wants? * (Thinks wants desires to think). Here is the great secret: *The thought is made in the mouth*" (Motherwell, 87). As discussed previously, Tzara conceives of the Dada subject and object as one, and thus of life and art as the same. He writes in his manifesto of mr. aa. the antiphilosopher: "Myself: mixture, kitchen, theatre" (85). In *Dada 4–5* he contrasts his view of words, that is, language as secretions of the mouth, with the pretension of philosophy and logic. As he writes in his "Proclamation without Pretension," the systems of knowledge to which one grows accustomed are to him "mere calculations, a hypodrome of immortal guarantees," or "a pretension warmed by the/TIMIDITY of the urinary basin, the *hysteria/* born in THE STUDIO" (*Réimpression*, 2: 168, French page). Tzara's accusation—that culture is a pretense to run from death, the ultimate destination of life, for life is pathological human physiology—echoes Nietzsche's critique of Western civilization. In Nietzsche's view, civilization is caught in the mechanisms of reactive forces, in particular of ressentiment: "A certain fleeing before life and the world in which we

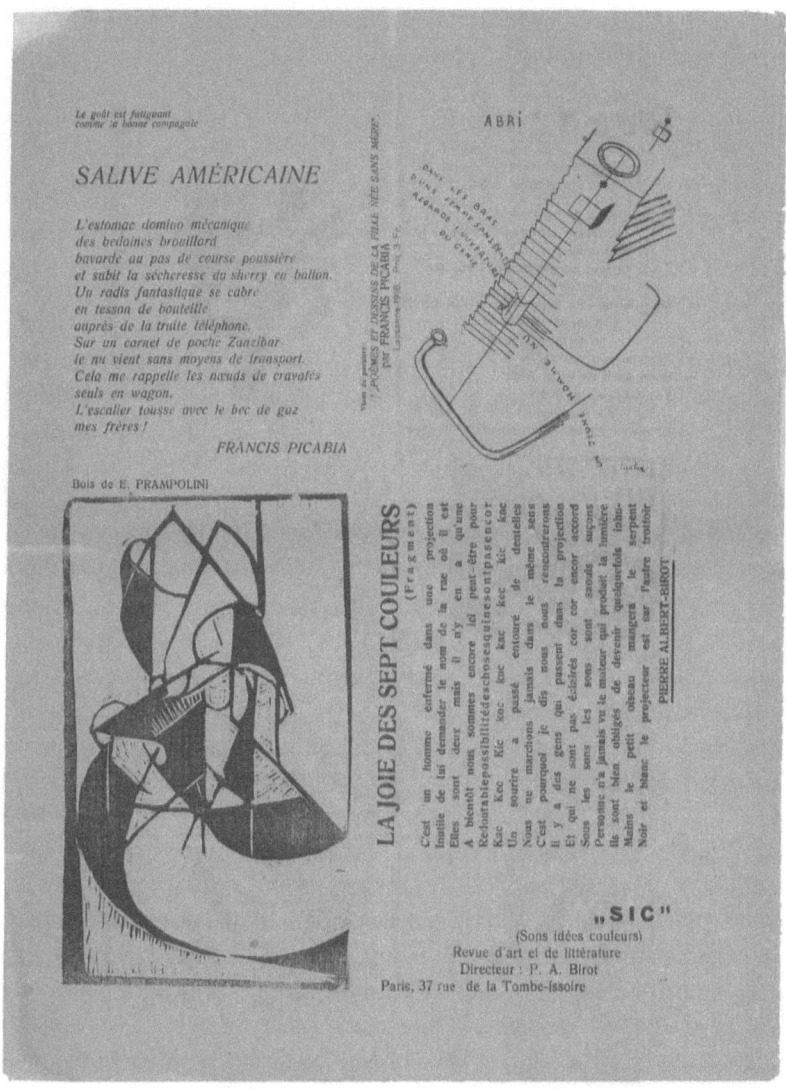

"Salive Américaine," in Dada 3 *(1918): 5 (Zurich, French edition). Courtesy of the International Dada Archive, University of Iowa, Iowa City.*

live, a fear and reaction to the body's activity, its constitutive role in the production of language, values, morals, truth or knowledge."[35]

For the Dada writers, especially Picabia, Serner, and Tzara, language is an expression of the body. The speech-act *is* a bodily gesture, and poetry literally becomes salivation, thus taking place in the mouth

as is evinced also from Picabia's poem tellingly titled "Salive Américaine" ("American Saliva," in *Dada 3*):

> The stomach, mechanical domino
> some tripes fog
> loquacious running step dust
> and suddenly the dryness of the sherry in a balloon.
> An imaginary radish rears
> in a fragment of a broken bottle
> next to the trout telephone. (*Réimpression*, 1: 58)

Tzara argues that thoughts happen in the mouth: they come into
being when they are uttered. Picabia's poem is made of words linked
together in the mouth that pronounces them one after the other or
even simultaneously, like the foodstuffs the stomach takes in one after
the other, which it mixes and only then selects. The poem mimics this
collage of "foods and things" and does so from the perspective of the
stomach, which acts like the listener's ear or the reader's eye. They
too take in the words uttered by the poet's mouth or written by the
poet's hand. At the same time, Picabia's salivation process also accompanies the expulsion of words from the poet's mouth. Salivation dissolves the difference between the stomach receiving and the mouth
spitting out, thus establishing equivalence between the excretory and
incorporating moments of the mouth and the stomach. Saliva is indistinguishable from gastric juice. For Picabia, poetry — a vocalization of
words — also occurs in salivation. He maintains that human language
is thereby processed just like foods.

The mechanical, physiological reality behind this poem, which situates itself halfway between the mouth and the stomach (and in both),
may be dirty, confusing like the stomach's fogs, and bitter like dry
sherry, the tripes, or dust: saliva is *amer*; bitter and *salive* is both *sal*,
dirty, and "live," a sign, a product of the living body-machine, the
mechanical domino that is finally the stomach.[36] "Salive Américaine"
describes poetry and the poet as existing in the body that ingests to
produce words that the mouth utters and that become thoughts only
after having undergone a digestive process in reverse, from the bowels to the mouth.[37]

As shown above, for both Serner and Tzara, language, in a written
text, functions as and becomes a metaphor for the body. In life it is one

of its expressions. The speech-act *is* a bodily gesture, a *Geste,* and language for the Dada poets is the "flow-through" that has its bodily correlative in diarrhea, on the one hand (the anus), and in laughter, on the other (the mouth). The Dadaist body moves through the speech-act laughing vehemently to impose its own order. The mouth, Tzara comments, occupies a central position between the body's order and an (anti)aesthetic of destructive (disgusting) incorporation. Tzara writes and sings the deformities of art and aesthetic visions when their physical, corrupt nature is disavowed, yet he does so through the wordy insult that metaphorically already embodies a bodily discharge. Consider the manifesto of mr. aa. the antiphilosopher:

> Take a good look at me!
> I am an idiot, I am a clown, I am a faker.
> Take a good look at me!
> I am ugly, my face has no expression, I am little.
> I am like all of you.
> But ask yourselves, before looking at me, if the iris by which you send out arrows of *liquid sentiment,* is not *fly shit,* if the *eyes of your belly* are not sections of *tumors* that will some day peer from some part of your body in the form of a *gonorrheal discharge.*
> You see with your navel — why do you hide from it the absurd spectacle that we present? And farther down, *sex organs of women, with teeth, all-swallowing* — the poetry of eternity, love, pure love of course *— rare steaks and oil painting. All those who look and understand, easily fit in between poetry and love, between the beefsteak and the painting. They will be digested. They will be digested. . . .* Call your family on the telephone and piss in the hole reserved for *musical gastronomic* and sacred stupidities.
> DADA proposes 2 solutions:
> NO MORE LOOKS!
> NO MORE WORDS!
> Stop looking!
> Stop talking! (Motherwell, 84)[38]

Tzara first construes himself as a work of art to be looked at, then he declares himself to be exactly like his audience, and finally he takes away any meaning from the aesthetic and ethical judgment based on "looking." The eye is no privileged organ; instead, the central organ becomes the belly, the eye of which is the navel. The female genitalia, moreover, are depicted with teeth and resemble the interior mouth corresponding to the interior eye: all the sites of the refined senses, out of which an exterior pleasurable contact between the subject and the object surfaces, develop into an internal organization of the body, which the blind aesthetic eye does not acknowledge.

Tzara envisions a model of interaction between subject and object, creator and work of art, based on swallowing, digesting, and discharging. The belly's poetics is to take in and transform, to "grind": no loving tastes but a tearing one another apart, a reciprocal devouring.[39] Tzara equates the poetry of eternity and love with the gaze on an oil painting: these conceal anxiety about devouring and swallowing, an anxiety that "musical gastronomic stupidities" actually sublimate. Tzara attacks the artists and critics who produce in order to be understood. Their production is in fact a reproduction (a passive art) of the cannibalistic, consumerist system. Tzara's manifesto proclaims an indigestible art against canonical art that is easy to digest. Dadaist art follows the belly's rhythms, and its words are just products of the mouth, namely, insults as symptoms of the mouth. The Dadaist writers do not place themselves between rare steaks and oil paintings. Rather, they make clear that all there is are rare steaks. Life and art are nothing but a great process of consumption and digestion. Dada art then sets out to interrupt this process. It makes it overflow, or it constipates it with insult/anal products that are different only because "pure" products of the Dadaist belly. In Picabia's words: "Our head / has two needs / like the belly" (*Literarische Dokumentation,* 144).

According to Ribemont-Dessaignes, in *Dadaphone 7,* the Dadaist, in this case himself, has the advantage of knowing that there is no way of knowing the difference between life and art, the organic and the eternal: "What is beautiful, what is unsightly ('laid' — lurid)? . . . I don't know. What am I? Don't know, don't know, don't know. Don't know" ("Artichauts," *Réimpression,* 1: 112).[40] Ribemont-Dessaignes recommends that the artist look closely at the cosmos, at eternity. He seems to imply that only by equating stars and stomach will art be made: "To watch the stars or the entrails of a stomach with opera-glasses is a truly artistic occupation" (1: 112). Not only is the cosmos equated with the entrails, but in the haruspices' old fashion, the entrails reflect the laws of the cosmos in another language and reveal a strategy of reading life that most clearly goes through the interpretive mechanisms of the grinding stomach. He then concludes: "Dada has a dowry to eat, but Dada is difficult to deflower" (1: 112). Dada then becomes the stomach

VÉLODROME AUX OIGNONS

le mariage 1/3 est aussi un résultat de la vie maritime comme la fin de phrase voilà et mat le fleur remue la queue on lui met des ventouses de lampes électriques il croit à l'inviolabilité des négations valables pour un mois il est donc très gentil et extrêmement sympathique

le téléphone nous reste fidèle comme un chien nickel dit le dadaïste il baille baille les rideaux avalent la lumière des rues Aa envoie express tout cela pour l'exposition des colonies le monde normal le mien phosphate le tribunal est un raid conjugal entre la poudrière la manivelle la manifestation et les bagages des grains de migraine savon lunaire et hors-d'œuvre avantage ont adopté un fils nouveau vierge et l'ont caché dans le piano garage

Il y a encore le cancer de la lampe rouge du corridor

et la mâchoire enguirlandée d'ongles attend le nain le train et le lapin monsieur Aa attend le courrier l'applaudissement civil de l'attentat criminel et perpétuel

Tristan TZARA

La queue du diable est une bicyclette

la morsure équatoriale dans le roc bleui

accable la nuit senteur intime de berceaux ammoniaque

la fleur est un réverbère poupée écoute le mercure qui monte

qui montre le moulin à vent accroché au viaduc

avant-hier n'est pas la céramique des chrysanthèmes qui tourne la tête
et le froid

l'heure a sonné dans ta bouche

encore un ange brisé qui tombe comme un excrément de vautour

étend l'accolade sur le désert fané

lambeaux d'oreilles rongées lèpre fer

Tristan TZARA

ARTICHAUTS

Dada n'ayant plus que quelques années ou quelques mois ou quelques jours à vivre, cherche un notaire pour lui confier ses dernières volontés.

Les mathématiques Dada n'ont pas encore été cultivées. Jusqu'à présent l'étude du nombre a rendu complètement idiot. L'idiotie est le saturnisme du mathématicien.

Il y a aussi quelque chose qu'on ne connait pas : c'est le dadaïsme dada. Mais Dada a des mamelles jusqu'aux orteils.

Dada doute de tout. On dit : cela aussi est un principe. Non, le doute n'est pas in principio. Mais quand cela serait si Dada croit au doute, cela prouverait qu'il n'a pas de principe.

Quand Dada verra que les cochons châtrés commencent à avoir la voix jaguar, il fera comme l'iode, il se sublimera. Et il revivra dans l'air respiré par les cochons châtrés et dans leur bauge. Et les cervelas que l'on servira au repas familial seront malgré tout possédés par Dada.

Dada, o Dada, quelle figure ? Si triste ? Si gaie ? Regarde-toi dans la glace. Non non, ne te regarde pas.

Qu'est-ce que c'est beau ? Qu'est-ce que c'est laid ? Qu'est-ce que c'est grand, fort, faible ? Qu'est-ce que c'est Carpentier, Renan, Foch ? Connais pas. Qu'est-ce que c'est moi ? Connais pas. Connais pas, connais pas, connais pas.

Regarder les astres ou l'intérieur de l'estomac avec une demie-jumelle de théâtre c'est une occupation artistique. Et la seule occupation des hommes. Et pleurent, ils pleurent comme si l'oignon entrait dans la composition du verre.

Il est intéressant de noter à quels partis appartiennent les sourires d'alliances offerts à Dada. Politique et mariage, Dada a une grosse dot à manger. Mais Dada est difficile à déflorer : la vierge est étroite.

Georges RIBEMONT-DESSAIGNES

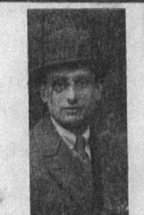

Philippe SOUPAULT

"Vélodrome aux oignons" and "Artichauts," in Dadaphone 7 *(Paris, 1920)): 2. Courtesy of the International Dada Archive, University of Iowa, Iowa City.*

and the cosmos, and as such Dada devours, takes in without being either "seduced, penetrated," or devoured itself. Aesthetic theories of taste allow pleasure only within the dimension of the digestibility of the product absorbed, namely, its assimilation. Pleasure is a form of well-being that confers a harmony to the human being who feels "in consonance" with the environment. In contrast, the Dadaist writer calls for a diet of excrement and launches a strategy of indigestion and diarrhea that accounts for devouring beyond taste and/or abjection (nausea).

Conclusion

In Dada, the body and its physiology constitute a metaphoric (dialectically mimetic) model for appropriating and interpreting reality, a physiology at once unitarian and individualist, contradictory and pluralistic, alive in the present, decomposed in the past, absent from the future yet always reproducing despite its pathological condition. The Dada artist contrasts his model of dysfunctional physiology and the contemporary "devouring body" with the nineteenth-century "gastronomic" model of the unified, assimilating, and reconciled body. The Dadaist body is fragmented, its physiology disorderly: it suffices to consider Tzara's pathological, deformed body, where the eyes are in the belly, the navel is an eye, the iris is full of excrement, and the body is itself ultimately a tumorous organism producing "gonorrheal discharge." Digestion — or rather indigestion — are used and exhibited in Dada's writings as the fetishes into which the bourgeois attention to and literal metonymization of the stomach have made them. More interestingly, the Dadaists use the performatively metaphorical gastroenteric apparatus and its multiple actions of ingestion, indigestion, expulsion to offer a distorted anthropomorphic caricature of the fetishistic and commodifying system of interpretation promoted by a functionalist modern society. With the physiological/digestive metaphor, the Dada poets and artists displace the seductive fetishistic instincts of humankind (exploited by consumer society) onto the bourgeois body being dissected, exhibited in segments, limbs, separate malfunctioning parts: as Nietzsche established (and as Francesco Meriano reiterated in his poem "Walk," quoted in *Réimpression,* 1: 10) the bourgeois stomach stinks, and the Dada artist exposes it as the site of death, decomposition, and pollution, in short, a producer of filth.[41]

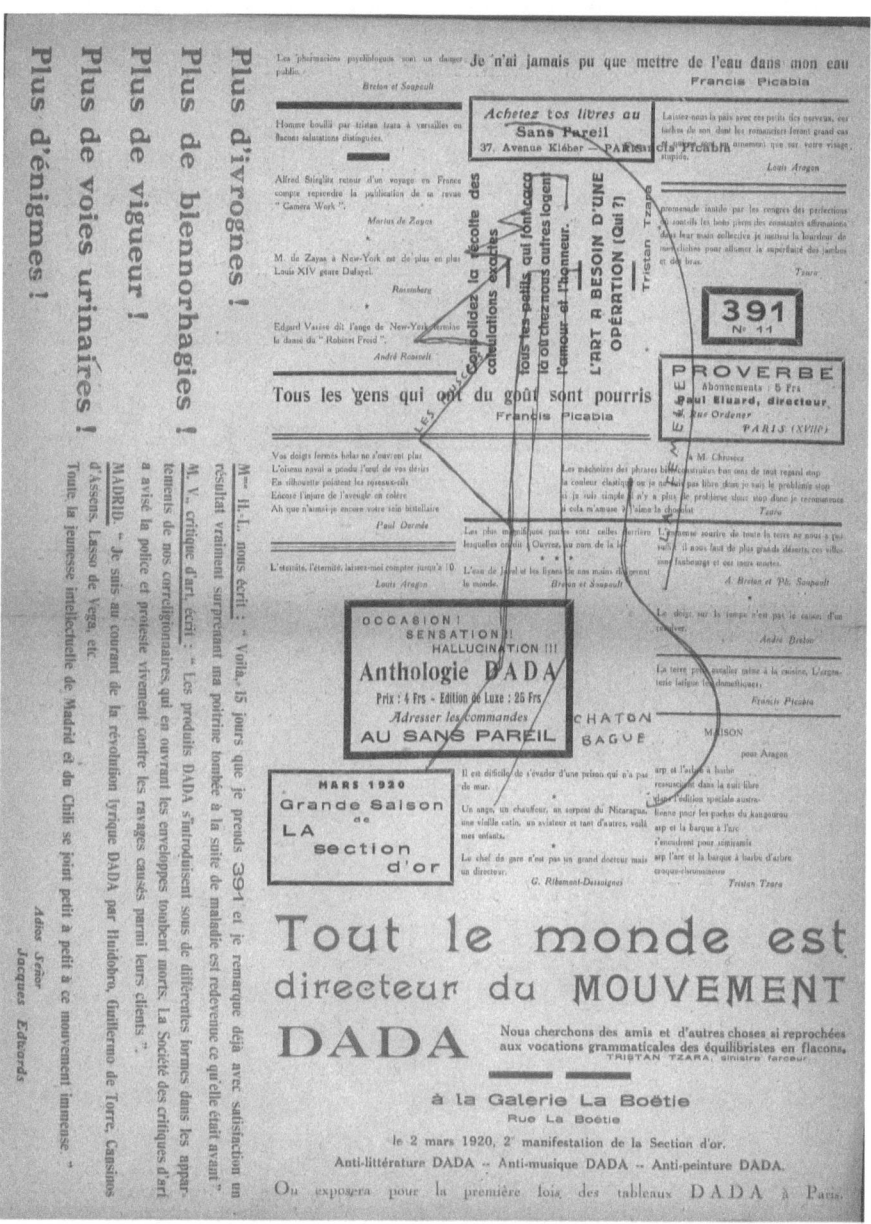

"Tous les gens qui ont du goût sont pourris," Dada 6 *(1920): back cover (Paris, "Bulletin Dada"). Courtesy of the International Dada Archive, University of Iowa, Iowa City.*

The avant-garde artists have recourse to this gastronomic–semiotic order as the crossroads between physiology and the semiotic. In other words, they consider alimentary discourse for its semiotic organization of the body. Unlike for the nineteenth-century gastrosophers, however, for whom gastronomy was the science that could reconcile the body and its pleasures with the systems of signification and meaning, the Dada artists and poets use gastronomy's semiotic order only to disrupt at once the linguistic system and the physiological organization of the body that derives from it. For Dada, the body becomes physical evidence of an increasingly pathological way of life, most typical of modernity.

When Tzara writes, "We pass for poets because we attack language which is the worst of conventions" (Motherwell, 204), he is not only equating language as sign-system with a convention but also criticizing the fact that according to the class-cultural (as well as semiotic) systems of difference, poets have the privilege to control the domain of language. The Dadaists then exploit the systematic discourse of gastronomy (food, body, pleasure) to disrupt the micro grammar of its conventions that aim at establishing and then fixing the order connecting language and culture. In attacking this semiotic and cultural order, the Dadaists break down and expose the seeming objectivity and neutrality of not only concepts of modern subjectivity but also functionalism and efficiency in general.

Food, or rather the consumption of food, and digestion translate into textual mechanisms, metaphors, that once extrapolated from their realm show the pathological element of human physiology. To the Dada artists and poets, consumption, food, organic dissolution and decomposition are the fundamental pathological features of the human being, which modernity has brought to the fore. The Dadaists' attack is less against the pathology of humankind than against the hypocrisy of civilization that denies and sublimates pathology into *Kultur*. The Dadaist scatological texts echo Nietzsche's criticism of Western civilization while wittingly and provocatively immersing themselves in the doomed societal and cultural body. So these texts endorse pathology—especially the pathology revealed in the human need to consume food—to dismantle the set of moral and aesthetic values that are supposedly detached from material life and physiology. The Dada writers embrace consumption paradoxically and in carnivalesque fashion, to criticize but also play with its commodified form.

They turn consumption — and with it all the physiological human acts that make up the digestive cycle — against the bourgeois sublimated erasure (censorship) of physiology from their system of culture. The conspicuous presence of scatological imagery as well as indigestion and disorderly physiologies in Dada's texts show these poets imagining a subject construed as the deformed mirror image of the perfect modern man, and of the tactful and tasteful bourgeois.

Dada's metaphors of food initially disorient their readers, distracting them from a straightforward social critique of modern society. These metaphors function in the text, or rather in the relation between the reader and the text, like the signified they evoke in its relation to the world of actual consumption. The references to indigestion, excess, vomit, and diarrhea block, obstruct, or, in other words, render inefficient the principles shoring up consumer society and the capitalist system. Against the accumulation of capital, and the capitalist's anxiety about loss or constipation, Dada's texts propose a countersystem, that is, a counter–modern physiology.

Dada and Walter Benjamin

Benjamin's use of food-words and, more generally, his theory of incorporation — which the next chapter analyzes in detail — bear strong affinities with Dada's antipoetics of disgust. Benjamin's notions of pleasure and desire remain embedded, however, in the belief in the communicative structure of the language of both food and prose. The flaneur/diner's body finds an in-depth new unity in the "illuminating" (and disruptive) incorporating act.

The Dadaist writers attack the poetic (contemplative) economy of communication altogether and abandon the notion of taste — and distinction along with interpretation — for that of *dégoût* (disgust). Yet, for both Benjamin and Dada, the alimentary processes constitute a repository of powerful images for construing alternative languages that at least temporarily escape or defeat instrumentalization and prefixed codified linguistic systems.

Against the modern bourgeois manipulation of pleasure, Dada's agrammatical foods reduce any food-word to just a word among others, in fact, to an empty signifier that only momentarily and jokingly makes brief contact with its referent from within the ordinary system of language. The Dada writers operate an absolute abstraction from

the actual context of food and eating practice, of which their apparently absurd recipes and incomprehensible menus are empty remind-
ers, that is, traces. Dada's approach to food produces an absolute met-
aphorization of food into word and of word into free-signifier. This
entails an atrophy of the eating experience as pleasurable, which is
replaced by a random feeding on words. Words come together as in an
alimentary dictionary reminiscent of an alimentary syntax here subtracted from the reader who is left with the reduced pleasure of read-
ing/eating the text.

In his essay on surrealism (1929), Benjamin writes: "And it is as
magical experiments with words, not as artistic dabbling, that we must
understand the passionate phonetic and graphical transformational
games that have run through the whole literature of the avant-garde
for the past fifteen years, whether it is called Futurism, Dadaism, or
Surrealism."[42] The revolutionary use of words constitutes the poetic
(magical and transformative) politics of the avant-garde. Dada's food-
words and their atrophy represent a first step for Benjamin: with their
disgusting, disorderly, and unbound flowing and moving about in the
Dada texts, they release cultural antibodies that constitute for Benjamin a first necessary interruption of the cycle of commodification
of objects and language. Unlike Dada's anarchist criticism, however,
Benjamin is fond of the magic of words, which he views as profoundly
able to communicate meaning. In many texts Benjamin acknowledges
that Dada attacks instrumental language and returns to writing its lost
power—he refers to the strong presence of words and their vertical-
ity in the collages, advertisements, and billboards. Unlike Benjamin,
however, the Dada writers are less interested in the effects of liberating the power imprisoned by the commodity than in accomplishing the
revolutionary integration between body and image, of which Benjamin and the surrealists were also fond.

Dada, the surrealists, and also Benjamin's avant-garde projects and
impossible diets situate themselves within circular signifying systems
and established economies of capitalist exchange. Their perspective
is that of "within," which explains the extended presence of textual
references in the circular patterns of consumption and incorporation
in their works.[43] The "within" perspective breaks through contemplation and distance, and fights power from the inside. It leaves the artists, however, with the problem of how to reappropriate for political

action the images set forth by their disruptive actions with their works. Dada's own circular pattern of disruption of the already circular digestive system (consumption) aims to short-circuit it through "indigestion" and excessive consumption, that is, through deformation and caricature, through a kind of mimesis gone crazy. Dada acts in the direction of *indistinction* and self-dissolution. Dada's theory of disgust as "distaste" asserts reproducibility as a powerful mechanism of production as well as critique. However, Dada's antidiets do not involve pleasure, despite the fact that they liberate repressed desire. For his part, Benjamin attempts to overcome the impasse of disgust that arises in the attempt to interrupt the digestive and efficient systems of language and culture. Thus Benjamin's own critical work aims to go beyond Dada's intended dysfunctional communication, as well as beyond the surrealists'. The latter managed to see the potential hidden in the object and in obsolescent commodities, which Dada instead disregarded. Thus the surrealists directly inspired Benjamin because they reinvented the object for experience. The surrealists find new worlds for art (where the Futurists construct them). They open up these worlds in simple acts. For Breton, for instance, reading and dreaming are art. For Benjamin, this also extends to politics so that in turn political action is or can be art (poetry). In effect, in Benjamin's opinion, politics is constituted by a reservoir of poetic images, an idea that returns later in Herbert Marcuse. Artists reach their creative task — in a Marxian sense — when their art is their work, and vice versa. However, Benjamin remarks, when poetry limits itself to be a substitute of politics, in an unchanged capitalistic society art is not productive. Instead, it is tendentious art, that is, a deficient form of art. Film technology accomplishes Benjamin's *physis,* or the fusion of art and artist (in a sense also proclaimed by Dada). In effect, in cinematic production the actor, the director, and the camera all work from within modes of production that for Benjamin are the closest to the interruption of contemplation, the laboratory of "cooking" that precedes and completes tasting and, more generally, consumption. As for Benjamin's interpretation of the cooking art and eating experience, the film art and its reception allow an identification in and recuperation of the alienation present in the process of production. The "cinematic" subject actively partakes of production and consumption of the self as well as of the product, the product as the artist. Here, according to Benjamin, art overcomes its state as metaphor of politics and becomes poetic politics.

However, Benjamin is ultimately no artist, no politician, and no filmmaker. He writes articles and essays, and he works for the radio. Does he view himself as surrealist or Dadaist? How does he pursue the "interruption" of his "career" (as he demands of the surrealist artists), and how do his "interruptions" put forth their own critical images?

3 WALTER BENJAMIN'S GASTRO-CONSTELLATIONS

THERE ARE NO EASY WAYS around Walter Benjamin's writings. Yet the intricacy of his thought opens up multiple points of entry into his corpus, which, as the critic Gerhard Richter argues, never advances concepts readily available for everyday use.[1] A seemingly ordinary trope of the everyday, the operation of incorporation, as in devouring and eating — taken rather widely — provides a filter for reading Benjamin's tangential contact with the avant-garde, especially the surrealists. Through incorporation, I argue, Benjamin proposes a critical, theoretical, but nonsystematic activity that first moves beyond the disciplinary boundaries between specialized academic work and cultural/political journalism, hence between the separation of word (*Schrift* especially) from action. Second, as an activity, incorporation functions as swiftly and sharply as the act of *cutting* itself, a term etymologically related to *critique*. Here incorporation is for Benjamin tantamount to the *cutting* practiced in the cubist collages, Dada montages, and surrealist allegorical works. Third, Benjamin, in juxtaposing reading and eating, suggests that criticism leave behind the idealist historicist — teleological and empathic — approach to history and embrace the allegorist's dissecting and broken gaze.

The *critical* operation that Benjamin associates with the "physical" qualities of incorporation establishes the connection between Benjamin and the avant-garde. Incorporation is for him fully distinct from assimilation or empathy.[2] Yet critics have seldom analyzed Benjamin's use of incorporation in conjunction with the coeval avant-garde's similar applications of the term. This chapter explores those mechanisms underscored by Benjamin's unfamiliar uses of incorporation, which he associates with the avant-garde's own devouring *Kunst* (techniques, technologies, and tricks), an art that interrupts and disrupts received ideas and that constitutes a nonorganic, temporal intervention in a reality presented in the avant-garde as de(con)structed. In Benjamin's texts, incorporation privileges those aspects most immediately associated with destruction but finally aims at overturning destruction into construction (versus creation).

Incorporation takes the function of a primal bodily technology of art and life. Benjamin thinks of incorporation as a profane, more expansive everyday version of drug intoxication. Intoxicating devouring occurred first during Benjamin's hashish eating experiments, starting in 1927, and then in those *Denkbilder* (*Thought-Images*) titled "Eating/Food" ("Essen"), written around 1930.[3] In the latter, Benjamin proposes incorporation as a base kind of intoxication able to revert to a material apperception the idealist (fusionist) instances of intoxication he ascribed to surrealism, which nonetheless he took to be one of the most successful examples of the avant-garde.[4]

Benjamin uses incorporation strategically: it is a textual mechanism not unlike his notion of allegory. Incorporation also serves, in other fragments, for example, in *Einbahnstrasse* (*One-Way Street*), as an act of quotation from avant-garde techniques of montage and collage. In this case, incorporation/quotation aims at *consuming* conventional language, that is, an instrumentalized and naturalized (mythical) use (or abuse) of language, in each text's process of unfolding. For Benjamin, textual incorporation or quoting in turn becomes—in his own writings—criticism, a dialectical forgery. Benjamin further associates such quoting to indigestibility.

Benjamin conceives of incorporation as a dialectical operation leading to a sensory epistemology, grounded in a heightened primeval (early) perception as opposed to both instrumental reason and abstract aesthetic taste. As a "primitive" materialist dialectical operation, incorporation first impinges on aesthetic illusions and political/historical ideologies of continuity, stability, and progress. Second, incorporation is indistinguishable from a deep immersion (*Versenkung*) in the productive abysses or restlessness (André Breton's term) of the mind's thinking processes, as the latter are rooted in the stomach's metabolism. Readers of Sigmund Freud, both Benjamin and Breton believe that this restlessness originates in the innards of human sensibility. For Benjamin, restlessness is the appropriate state of mind for transformative processes inherent in incorporation, from the teeth's tearing and grinding of matter, via the "collage" of food and saliva, the disintegration of nature in the bowels, to nature's transubstantiation into energy and nature's mortification into excreta ready to "fertilize" new grounds and become new life (the brewing of the future, as Benjamin refers to it). Restlessness also marks the temporal dialectic that Benjamin sets up between natural time as decay and historical time. In his "Food Fair" article (1928), the allegory of Saturn, the devourer of his children and the god of time, juxtaposes the image of the cannibal (Cronos) with that of the god Chronos (time). Saturn is an ambiguous figure that Benjamin uses to exhibit the dialectical turns in history and to expose the other repressed sides of history's own mythologizing.[5]

The restless process of metamorphosis visible in nature becomes even more evident in the ways food changes from nature to culture. Likewise for Benjamin, ideas migrate through history, and in history they take up different forms, becoming different phenomena. Similarly, the surrealist writers and artists use notions of incorporation and transformation to capture the passing of history. Breton takes the persistence of the marvelous through its transformation as one such case of historical restlessness.[6] Fittingly, Breton sees the marvelous — in which the human imagination perseveres — as manifest in allegorical fragments that bear witness to time passing. Thus, for surrealism, the marvelous may be uncovered — a posteriori — in the romantic ruins first and in the modern mannequins later. The former are on the threshold between natural and human history: in Hal Foster's interpretation, ruins show how "cultural progress is captured by natural entropy" (*Compulsive Beauty*, 21). In the mannequins, the animate is confused with the inanimate; the artificial body condenses mimetically capitalist reification. For Breton, however, the marvelous may above all be detected in those poets' works that are pervaded by a welcome "unhealthy atmosphere" that shatters all illusions of an acquired happiness.[7] As allegories of a restless imagination, still inclined toward some happiness that needs liberating from within the commodified world of modernity, which imprisoned its promise, these allegories "coincide with an eclipse of the taste I am made to endure, I whose notion of taste is the image of a big spot," Breton writes.[8] The surrealist objects as allegories or "phrases," as Breton calls his first automatic surrealist experiments, are clearly objects not for aesthetic appreciation but for reading as multilayered "texts."[9] And they are in fact closer to restless states of mind and restless perception, the truthful distortions that make up dreams.

For his part, Benjamin employs bodily incorporation as a brute corporeal *technē* that disturbs or breaks through semblance, that is, a surface — a world of commodities and phantasmagoria.

> The nineteenth century a spacetime <Zeitraum> (a dreamtime <Zeittraum>) in which the individual consciousness more and more secures itself in reflecting, while the collective consciousness sinks into ever deeper sleep. But just as the sleeper — in this respect like the madman — sets out on the macrocosmic journey through his own body, and the noises and feelings of his insides, such as blood pressure, intestinal churn, heartbeat, and muscle sensation (which for the waking and salubrious individual converge in a steady surge of health) generate, in the extravagantly heightened inner awareness of the sleeper, illusion or dream imagery which translates and accounts for them, so likewise for the dreaming collective, which, through the arcades, communes with its own insides. We must follow in its wake so as to expound the nineteenth century — in fashion and advertising, in buildings and politics — as the outcome of dream visions.[10]

The sleeping body of the collective in capitalist society goes on producing dreams as always already distorted images (thus allegory) of its own profound bowel movements, or profound anthropological needs. Through incorporation, the repressed desires of the body collectives of history manifest themselves in antiaesthetic allegorical form (e.g., in the "edible" soft art nouveau as surrealist dream-kitsch). Allegory always refers to something else, something already gone, something other that constitutes allegory as deformation in its own passing; allegory is the leftover of the food that has nourished the body. Benjamin thus focuses on the transformative deformations of nature that occur first in cooking, second in eating through the mouth, and third in dissecting with the stomach. Dream work is itself an act of distorting translation that generates dream as allegory. Bodily incorporation, like allegorical dream work, opens up a corporeal imagination that operates through acts of radical metabolic translation. This imagination exists beyond the constraints of reason and historical consciousness. For Benjamin, the avant-garde brings to fruition this morphic translation in its "scriptic" works; likewise, the theorist must engage in allegorical, materialist criticism (devour his texts): a deep penetration and dialectical transformation of the allegorical world that totality has deserted and in which thus totality appears negatively, for example, in and as ephemeral distorted phenomena. Like avant-garde artworks, allegorical criticism violently disfigures, consumes, burns, and severs contextual ties, when reading "everything," from art and literature to everyday objects and spaces. Reading, as Benjamin announces, is incorporation and thus occurs within and beyond the readable. Reading is in effect an act of interruption of reading whenever the latter is intended as interpretation (hermeneutics).

Thus, for Benjamin, reading/criticism, reconsidered from an avant-garde viewpoint, becomes the privileged site for his surrealist intervention in the production of culture. This production demands an "incorporative" approach, a materialist and dialectical operation.[11] Benjamin's short essays, reviews, pamphlets, autobiographical notations resonate with the critical constructs—never *re*constructive or representational texts—of Dada, Bertolt Brecht, and Karl Kraus, namely, with those protagonists of the avant-garde whose work Benjamin engaged directly in his writings and in person.[12] Both Benjamin and the avant-garde, in particular Dada and surrealism, view incorporation as a potential counterassimilatory function able to bring about a break in the structures of human experience, whether one speaks of the experience of art or that of time (history). Benjamin sees in this function the possibility humans have to infringe on individual and collectively ingrained forms of bourgeois consciousness and identity, hence to transform the subjugation to conditioned forms of thinking and action into the freedom of a newly conceived bodily mind.[13]

Benjamin's texts on food and incorporation also resonate with his more introspective and analytic investigations of language and experience. In this latter case, his food aphorisms echo the language of dreams and remembering first dissected by Freud and then deployed by surrealism. Unlike surrealism, however, Benjamin always stresses the moment of awakening, or the profane illuminations emerging from unusual eating experiences. These writings highlight a corporeal awareness needed to transfer the distorting power of dreams and the unconscious to the discipline required for a revolutionary will.[14] This awareness of the body and its desires as both historically rooted (not determined), which he calls bodily presence of mind, is neither pure origin nor simple effect.[15] It is both at once: the precondition for "just" action, for example, for a disruptive (revolutionary) action with regard to the status quo, and an effect of bodily "innervation," for example, an excitement of body–mind as a current of electric impulses running through the nerves.[16]

Like the surrealists, Benjamin detects the allegorical language of dreams and its potential of rupture in forceful, even if forgotten, works from different epochs, present or past, that eerily echo the cast-off desires of one's own age. Similarly, Breton and, before him, Guillaume Apollinaire find the crucial core of surrealist sensibility in a variety of works from different ages such as Gothic and romantic literature, once the work's content and context are torn off.[17] In his Second Manifesto, Breton observes that despite the official attempts at historicizing romanticism and reducing it to a specific epoch of French culture, a hundred years previously, "to be a hundred is for it to be still in the flower of its youth." He then concludes: "We say that what has been wrongly called its heroic period can no longer honestly be considered as anything but the first cry of a newborn child which is only beginning to make its desires known through us" ("Second Manifesto," 153). The desire of another century makes itself heard in a new guise but with the same intensity in a different time. Benjamin also returns to the newborn child as a figure of the avant-garde. The newborn expresses Benjamin's fantasies of a counterhistorical time, or a history that must be imagined as against the grain, as always "emergent" (*das Entspringende*) or primordial (*Ursprung*).[18] Incorporation functions in Benjamin as a primitive technology through which the modern subject experiences again, albeit in a different way, the newborn child's cry. Caught in the throngs of devouring, the subject becomes disoriented because it loses sight of the quotidian.

Benjamin sets incorporation against assimilation (passive consumption and comfort). Where the former is process oriented, the latter is product oriented. Assimilation centers on the effect of incorporation. In contrast, incorporation (*Einverleibung*), which is an appropriative act, is nonetheless one that, as Benjamin's food stories demonstrate, disowns the subject by dislocating it from its self-identity to a threshold of not-knowledge as other knowledge. For Benjamin, incorporation is endowed with the force to dialectically change consumption (and generally reception) from a state of passivity and conventionality into a constructive nonorganic production (of otherness). The disorienting qualities of devouring epitomize for Benjamin the essential features of experience (*Erfahrung*). As Benjamin illustrates in some of his "Eating/Food" aphorisms ("Fresh Figs" and "Pranzo Caprese" in particular, but also "Café-Crème"), the word *experience* entails the idea of passage and crossroads. Devouring like waking—the threshold between dream and active life—are two profane areas of possible experience.

For Benjamin, the body and the mind work in similar ways and interact at some submerged level.[19] What incorporation does within the body (how it works with the substance given, the kinds of operations it sets in motion in the processes of transformation), the mind also accomplishes in the intellectual space. Incorporation and dream work, and dream work and consciousness, are different but parallel systems that communicate through acts of radical translation of seemingly irrelevant, forgotten elements—traces—within the body and between the body and the mind. The result is knowledge as noncognitive apprehension of phenomena, a knowledge that does not possess objects.

Both Benjamin and Breton believe that dreaming entails in itself its dialectical turning point, for dreams may provoke awakening. On this view, Benjamin crosses paths with nonorganic Dada collage and montage, and with surrealist allegorical artworks, uncanny objects, and outmoded spaces, above all, for the enigmatic structure and functions Benjamin ascribes to dreaming as dream work. He then recognizes the dream work in the avant-garde. More than Breton (but less than Salvador Dalí), Benjamin stresses the materiality at the base of dream work. In his view it operates along the lines of a bodily allegorical activity—that of incorporation—which then resurfaces in the mind. The first technology of incorporation, as related to the body and its language, is the repressed basis of the second technology, for example, the mind and instrumental language.

Through scattered references to Benjamin's more notorious essays, to some surrealist manifestos as well as other works of the avant-garde, and through a few close readings of selected *Denkbilder* in which food and incorporation are an issue, the chapter proposes a modest grid on which Benjamin might have established the above-mentioned connections.

Metabolic Operations: Dream Work and Other Acts of Radical Translations

The short chapter "Breakfast Room" (*Frühstück*) in *One-Way Street* offers a cryptic illustration of how body and mind, incorporation and dream work, function according to "transgressive" laws. Working and reworking fragments of conscious life, they transgress the rules of memory, consciousness, logic, and thus conventional perception.

> A popular tradition warns against recounting dreams the next morning on an empty stomach. In this state, though awake, one remains under the spell of the dream. . . . He who shuns contact with the day, whether for fear of his fellow men or for the sake of inward composure, is unwilling to eat and disdains his breakfast. He thus avoids a rupture between the nocturnal and the daytime worlds — a precaution justified only by the combustion of dream in a concentrated morning's work, if not in prayer. . . . For only from the far bank, from broad daylight, may dream be assessed from the superior vantage of memory [*Erinnerung*]. This further side of dream is attainable only through a cleansing analogous to washing, yet totally different. By way of the stomach. The fasting man tells his dream as if he were talking in his sleep. (*One-Way Street*, 1: 444–45)

Eating breakfast is tantamount to taking in a fragment of the external reality as food, after the long night spent in dream work. Breakfast is the best parallel work of *translation*, a kind of radical transformation of the dream work into the day's work; in the latter, consciousness, while breaking away from the dream, absorbs its activity and lets the dream work speak from within as its other language. In the waking state the incorporation of food operates on this external object, that is, food, just like at night the dream works with the day's memories. The distortion of mnemonic traces in dreams — through allegorical operations such as condensation and displacement — tricks consciousness, thus allowing the language of the unconscious to speak through it in its own *other* language; the same happens with the incorporation of food, which tears food apart, decomposes it, and transforms it in and through the body, hence nourishing the body through an allegorical bodily language.

Transferred to the sociocultural world, cooking operates the "magical," in this case to be read as allegorical and distorting, transformations with regard to nature. In "Decline of the German Cooking Art" (1923), Benjamin observes:

> Because mankind augments everything that is natural and is immensely superior as a "Creature" (although not as an individual) to the manifestations of nature, then also its alimentation should equally be superior to the animal "diet" (*Nahrung*). Mankind needs the essences and quintessences of natural matter (*Naturstoffe*) to survive, but not in the reduced form of food supplements that are believed to contain these essences and quintessences

in their chemical formulas. Instead mankind needs to find them in the products of cooking, products which could prove to be no less rational, belonging as they do to another area much closer to human life, an area still unknown to us.[20]

The disturbing reference to the superiority of humans (because of their divine task of naming nature, for example, of their linguistic communicative faculty) is mitigated by the critique of a degeneration of the human to petty individual interests and instrumental reason. The human is intended as the humanity of humans, as Benjamin also explains in yet another passage of *One-Way Street*.[21] The instrumental use of cooking manifests itself in the latter's reduction to chemical products, which are there to satisfy a physical need. These modern accomplishments paradoxically reduce the alchemical and radical language of cooking—as translation—to a modern equivalent of animal diet. Unlike the Futurists, who welcome this modern chemical diet, for it leaves the need of cooking behind and transforms it thus into a realm of experimentation for aesthetic/ideological purposes, in this article Benjamin first observes the perversions of German cooking (which could easily be referred to the degeneration, in his view, of the German avant-garde into the representational Neue Sachlichkeit).[22] Then, he imagines a panorama of reversals where this perverted nature takes revenge against its abuse and perverts social/historical perversion, as it were, offering thereby a glimpse of hope. Lastly, however, Benjamin, in an act of total rejection of the present state of German culture and art, takes refuge in exalting the *Suprême,* that is, a conflation of a French recipe and of supreme French avant-garde art. Benjamin never hesitated to state that he found a more fertile environment for his own thinking in France than in Germany.[23] The French *Suprême,* counterposed to the hell of the German kitchen, identifies cooking/ art as radical translation (without a fixed original) that lets speak that "area still unknown to us" through "other" products. The latter break the spell of repetition of the same, that is, of recognition and pure comfort that Benjamin sees ensuing from the German fare.

First then, in the profane historical world, nature is already distorted. As Benjamin writes in "Decline of the German Cooking Art," nature in modern times devours with a vengeance: like Paul Klee's "Angelus Novus," the rapacious angel that "preferred to free men by taking from them, rather than make them happy by giving to them"

(*Selected Writings*, 2: 456). Benjamin also cites from August Strind-berg's *Ghost-Sonata* where the German kitchen is run by female vampire-cooks:

> What has become of them [the products of cooking] in Germany? Here *Schmalhans* is the king of the kitchen, and *Ressentiment* is the name of his female cook. Cooking has only one purpose for her: to allow the use of lesser substances, which, unmixed, everyone would reject. The noble augmenta-tion of a substance is here degenerated into a bad practice that borders on poisoning. Strindberg has voiced in his dramas his presentiment about this, as well as other specifically female kinds of vice. It is unmistakably clear in the female cook of the "Ghost Sonata." (GS, 6: 922; my translation)

These figures of ressentiment — the indigestion of the German stom-ach, as Friedrich Nietzsche called the German Spirit — are demonic perversions that can do justice to the perverse injustices of human soci-ety. These demonic figures complement Benjamin's cannibals (e.g., his man-eaters, lion tamers, images from children's books, children them-selves, and the satirist, in the figure of Kraus). He describes the canni-bals as inhuman when referencing first William Shakespeare's Timon and then the writer Kraus, in Benjamin's view a satirist-cannibal him-self. The inhuman is the only creature "befitting the world as your kind have fashioned it, something worthy of it. . . . Neither [Timon nor Kraus] wants or has anything in common with men" (*Selected Writings*, 2: 449). In tandem, cannibals and vampire-cooks speed up bourgeois progress — unmasked by Benjamin as natural decay — and directly contribute to the end of modern bourgeois history. In their perverse act of devouring and self-devouring these creatures are res-cuing the human species from what the bourgeoisie calls progress but which Benjamin discloses — through his allegorical images — as catas-trophe. He maintains: when phenomena, in this case cooking/art, fall into "their enshrinement as 'heritage.' . . . There is a tradition that is catastrophe."[24] Tradition translates as the repetition of the same, the hell of the status quo that, for Benjamin, following Strindberg (*To Damascus*) again, is here and now, in the deadly products of German *Kultur* (*Arcades Project*, 473, N 9a, 1).

The demonic kitchen produces everyday fare that paradoxically carries the same features of that art that captures the diner/viewer through empathy and comfort. It shuns consciously the popular "thrills," the shocks, and "traumatic energy" that Benjamin describes as the most valuable element of the circus, the carnival, and fairs.

He also sees these powers in the Dada montages and Dada's magical language, and, finally, in the uncanny dreamlike surrealist allegorical art and poetry. All of the latter are in fact the qualities of the French *Suprême,* which Antonin Carême classified in the group of sauces he called *Veloutés.*[25] For Carême, sauces are a source of variations and infinite possibilities in the kitchen. In contrast, for Benjamin,

> The contemporary German dishes are prepared in such a fashion that the total taste (all encompassing) does not hover and float over the peaks of taste of the single substances (that which generally provokes a *powerful surprise* for the *recognition* of a known taste in this Elysium). Instead the total taste lies under the basis of the single pyramids of taste, and that is in "porridge," "purée," and "gravy" (here the tasting of a single flavor is accompanied by a *feeling of relief,* the same one we would feel upon *encountering a familiar rascal in hell*)." (GS, 6: 922; my translation and emphasis)

These monotonous dishes elicit the comfort of routine and repetition, which approaches the comfort of death. Benjamin's allegorical illustration depicts cooking and tasting in Germany as the modern, lonely individual's embrace with deathly cooks. According to Benjamin's description, German cooking/art serves the conservative nature of the death drive. For Benjamin, the German dishes are tantamount to the bourgeoisie's illusory and fetishistic hope to find comfort in the disavowal of this class's historical crisis. The hell of the German kitchen, however, is a treacherous cooking that, by impairing action and life through repeating the repressed, already presents *this* life, the present, as condemnation to hell. To us, readers, the hellish characters in the German kitchen are the surrealist visage things put on in the moment of crisis, as Benjamin writes elsewhere. They show in his depiction the grinning death mask of history that reveals the "Now" as the final moment of rupture—namely, the moment of a "traumatic" recognizability that bursts, with its truth, the hell of repetition as comfort.

In contrast, Benjamin finds in the French *Suprême* the *"powerful surprise* for the *re-cognition* of a known taste in [the gastronomic] Elysium." As in a surrealist *trouvaille,* in this dish, each individual ingredient, albeit familiar, is found again as if for the first time. Woven together in a complex, not immediately identifiable texture of flavors, the *Suprême* displaces something familiar with its return as surprising. The new emerges in its contrasting effect against a background, or total taste, which varies at each combination, like the colors of a kaleidoscope.[26] Individual flavors and the general taste, he notes, function rhythmically and contrastively, the former, however, still emerging from the general taste, as its internal other, which the individual flavors then refocus. The *Suprême* thus surprises one into cognition through an act of uncanny recognition:

> Observation regarding the physiology of the cooking art: The ground or *conditio sine qua non* of every pleasing taste is the appreciation [*Herausschmecken*, also discrimination] of one or more definite substances selected from a mixture. Thus the real mixture must be composed in such a way that only the peaks of taste of each one or more substances, which must absolutely be tasted distinctly, equally [*gleichsam*] dominate above the threshold of total taste. French cuisine sought to accomplish this kind of selective tasting, concentrated on the taste's finest pinnacle, with its *Suprême*. (ibid.)

Benjamin describes tasting the *Suprême* as an ecstatic aesthetic yet profane experience. Here disjunction and interruption of a given repeated taste block the easy recognition of an external reality. The feelings of relief and comfort Benjamin mentions in relation to the ordinary German food/art are contrasted with the shocking recognition of a transformed trace in the *Suprême*. This one, among the mother sauces identified by Carême, presents experience as "lived similarity," as Benjamin wrote elsewhere: "What is decisive here is not the causal connections established over the course of time, but the similarities that have been lived" (*Selected Writings*, 2: 553, fragment from 1931–32). The tongue — rather than the eye — composes and recomposes fleeting and changing constellations of emerging and vanishing figures, against, as it were, the nightly sky of total taste.

The art of the French *Suprême* compels a radical judgment or critique that also fragments and disturbs semblance, and that mimetically reproduces the composition of the dish itself. The *Suprême* functions like a collage or even montage.[27] The *Suprême*'s flavors produce a "grid-like" surface of tastes.[28] Here the separate ingredients arise in rhythmic and spatial disorder, following no hierarchical principle of composition but rather the urgency of a forgotten, involuntary trace. Like the art of cooking, the *Suprême* translates that area "still unknown to us" that cooking — and avant-garde art — reproduces as temporal collective *frottages* or allegorical palimpsests beyond representation.[29]

As Benjamin compares technologies of translation at work in incorporation and dreaming, he also sets up a parallel between the culinary world and the artistic world, the making and appreciation of nature into food or art. The parallel is important: unlike the language of chemistry—mentioned in "Decline of the German Cooking Art"—as positivist reduction of nature to formulas, for Benjamin, the language of gastronomy is grounded in the magic inherent in the human ability to translate and radically metamorphose nature, first in the stomach and then culturally.[30] This is most evident in two passages in the *Arcades Project,* as well as in most fragments of the "Eating" thought-figures. After I examine these two passages, in which external space is rerendered through reading food as the labyrinthine space and time of the flaneur, I conclude the section with Benjamin's own journey through the diner's body as the radical translation of Odysseus's epic travel out of myth and into the paradigm of Western knowledge.

In the first passage from the *Arcades Project,* Benjamin associates a diner's reading of the grandiose menu of the famous restaurant Les Trois Frères Provençaux with the flaneur's wandering of Paris streets:

> The menu at *Les Trois Frères Provençaux*: "Thirty-six pages for food, four pages for drink—but very long pages, in small folio, with closely packed text and numerous annotations in fine print." The booklet is bound in velvet. Twenty hors d'oeuvres and thirty-three soups. "Forty-six beef dishes, among which are seven different beefsteaks and eight filets." "Thirty-four preparations of game, forty-seven dishes of vegetables, and seventy-one varieties of compote." Julius Rodenberg, *Paris bei Sonnenschein und Lampenlicht* (Leipzig, 1867), pp. 43–44. *Flanerie* through the bill of fare. [In German the term used by Benjamin is "Flanerie des Essens."] (423, M3, 10)

Like the menu, the city is a labyrinth of names or, in Baudelaire's terms, a "forest of symbols" that have lost their "referent." In this case, the reader incorporates first the names of the dishes, then the food they name, through an act of wandering that, as Benjamin also remarks in *Berlin Childhood,* involves losing one's own way. This act of forgetting allows involuntary memory to emerge as uncanny knowledge, precisely the knowledge of the repressed that is hidden in names—as in food—and their lost history. The flaneur wanders both in space and in time, on the surface and in depth, in the exterior and in the interior. Benjamin writes: "The street conducts the *flaneur* into a vanished time. For him, every street is precipitous. It leads downward—if not to the mythical Mothers, then into a past that can be all the more spellbinding because it is not his own, not private."[31] The associations between a temporal *flanerie* that leads to the depths of a city and the

reading of a menu reproduced in a tourist guide to the same city connect unintentionally the surface (the present) with its depth (the past
as "has been"). The reader who peruses the menu, or else this list of
names — a menu that itself is a microcosmic version of the macrocosm
of the city — absorbs first through reading, then through eating, the
unwritten and forgotten history of this space: this space is captured
by the names and the topography they generate. Another space–time,
a *Zeitraum* that is most intricately a *Leibraum,* emerges in the act of
eating, as the effect of involuntary wandering. Through incorporation
this other space–time produces in turn a physical self-loosening that
parallels both the flaneur's dissolution of external space and the eater/
reader's further dismantling of the menu.

The surrealists illustrate the spatial–temporal alteration of historical surface as well. They have recourse to the nonlinear temporality
that governs the threshold between the unconscious and consciousness.[32] For Benjamin, however, the surrealists stop short at the visions
produced by their acts of intoxicating *flanerie* and fall prey to spir-
itualism. Benjamin is interested in developing a materialist surrealist
criticism: he is interested in the implications of surrealist perception
and *flanerie* for a critical, historical awareness, which teases out the
dialectical historical connections emerging from the *vases communicantes* between the entrails and the mind.

Accordingly, in his essay on surrealism, he critiques a passage in
Breton's *Nadja.* He argues that after having raised the promise of
liberation by pointing to objective chance relations among (1) Sacco
and Vanzetti, (2) looting, and (3) the *Boulevard Bonne Nouvelle* (good
news), the novel, however, fails to translate these objective connections into a historical network of signs that too are lying in the actual
spaces of history in wait of redressing.[33] For Benjamin, Breton leaves
to fate, that is, to a *voyante* (importantly named Madame Sacco!), the
crucial task to bind the future to an action in the present. In the novel,
Breton gives Madame Sacco, a reader of signs, the last word: she *sees*
in Nadja's mad wanderings a bad omen for surrealism's future (in
the person of Paul Eluard), which then allows itself to be consumed
in this foreboding. In contrast, Benjamin seems to suggest, the surrealists should have read *this* woman, the voyante, as a historical protagonist, namely, as the "wife of Fuller's victim," a casualty of history
herself. One can assume that, had they been able to constellate her
own and her husband's victimhood — a cipher of the destructiveness

of history—with her (chance) address on *rue des Usines* (factory road), the surrealists would have indeed broken the chain of historical misdeeds and injustice (*Selected Writings, 2*: 209). The "other" history emerging in the constellation of Madame Sacco and rue des Usines could intimate the dialectical, bursting truth of an impending proletarian revolution. Thus they could have become subjects of the revolution rather than witnesses of time's and the future's consumption. Reading should be an act of convulsive bodily absorption that dismembers and distorts, hence an act of incorporation of history. It should consume historical contexts and contents first, then words, and even "Names" (proper names). History's crimes would be uncovered, and, if not redeemed, its victims and the desires they carry would be the ones "tapping on the windowpanes of the future, rather than 'spiritualist premonitions'" (ibid.).

In the second passage from the *Arcades Project,* Benjamin associates the power of names with the power of an almost unconscious, involuntary historical memory. The latter proliferates in space (and in language) against the most evident topographic displacements in the city:

> But no less important than the life of the city's layout is here the unconquerable power in the names of streets, squares, and theatres, a power which persists in the face of all topographic displacement. . . . Even the better-known eating establishments are, in their way, assured of their small municipal immortality—to say nothing of the great literary immortality attaching to the Rocher de Cancall, the Véfour, the Trois Frères Provençaux. For hardly has a name made its way in the field of gastronomy, hardly has a Vatel or Riche achieved its fame, than all of Paris, including the suburbs, is teeming with Petits Vatels and Petits Riches. Such is the movement of the streets, the movement of names, which often enough run at cross-purposes to one another. (516, P1, 1)

The names of the better-known eating establishments stubbornly insert themselves here and there as temporal ciphers in the present, thus constructing a random and uncontrollable topography atop the city's spatial layout. In these few brief sentences, Benjamin offers his theory of art and history. The account of the theaters' and eating establishments' history speaks of the persistence of the "truth-content" of art in the phenomena of this world, phenomena that, subject to decay, migrate from epoch to epoch, from form to form, and return elsewhere transformed. Likewise, the names of restaurants proliferate across the city, only to pop up in unexpected spaces, as physical copies of an original that they disseminate and conjure up: they are miniature versions, quotations out of place. The singularity of time and space surfaces as the effect of reproducibility, that is, of an act of quotation or citing that always distorts. Benjamin tests it on restaurants, but it is also mirrored at a micro level in the food names and dishes that are respectively reprinted and reproduced in these reproducible establishments. Incorporation opens up spaces of singularity and difference within multiplication and reproduction in time and in space. In this space the magic of foodstuffs and their names emerges, especially in the act of reading as rewriting, that is: incorporation. The thought-figures in "Eating/Food" are a reading of the knowing subject's history. Each in a different way offers a picture of eating and devouring that rewrites some fundamental instance in this history: from the Bible (in "Fresh Figs") to the *Odyssey* (in "Pranzo Caprese"), from fairy tales (in "Mulberry Omelet") to modernism (and Marcel Proust's "madeleine" in "Café-Crème").

"Pranzo Caprese"

The story "Pranzo Caprese" tells of a journey that involves contamination with a dangerous mythical world and with the subject's corporeal nature. In this text the narrator encounters a mother who is said to have been a cocotte:

> She had been the famous "town-cocotte" of Capri, now the sixty-year-old mother of the little Gennaro, whom she beat in her drunkenness. . . . I came to look for the friend who had rented from her. . . . She was standing on the kitchen threshold, wearing a discolored [inharmonious] skirt and a blouse where one could have looked for stains in vain since dirt on her clothes was so perfect and uniform. "Voi cercate la signora. È partita con la piccola." (*Selected Writings*, 2: 362; translation slightly modified)

After this first chance encounter, the mother/"prostitute" invites the reluctant guest to taste her primal—and at first sight uninviting—soup: "From an exhalation of garlic, beans, mutton fat, tomatoes, onions, oil, her domineering [peremptory, but also irresistible] hand made its appearance, from which I took the tin spoon" (362). The mother and the loose woman are united in one figure representing Benjamin's concept of the threshold. Later in the text Benjamin explicitly calls the cocotte a whore. Both mothers and loose women in different ways have open bodies. In "Pranzo Caprese" the mother and the loose woman are juxtaposed and distinct also by way of temporality: the past of the woman, as famous town cocotte, and her present, as mother, cross in the sharing of the soup.

Inviting the traveler to a taste from her cauldron, she initiates his crossing of the threshold between myth and history. The text shows its allegorical quality of a physical and textual experience of passage as new birth. This is indeed the birth of a reading subject that in the act of consumption constructs his experience of passage as that of a novel Odysseus. The mother/cocotte is not only on her home's threshold when she offers food to the visitor but is also conflated with a sorcerer like Circe:

> But this was just the start: it was followed by a flood of inviting words uttered in her shrill, high-pitched voice, accompanied by rhythmic movements of her imperious head, which decades previously must have had a provocative power. I would have had to be an accomplished gentleman to decline her offer, and I was not even able to express myself in Italian. I understood this much: it was an invitation to take a break and have lunch with her. (362)

The narrator, accepting her "gift" (not unlike Derrida's *pharmakon*), takes a "break," thus traveling to the other time of myth. She speaks a language of rhythmic gestures and shrill words the narrator cannot comprehend, a language of the body. The story illustrates a trip to the point of emergence of Western rationality, or subjectivity, specifically, to the epical journey of Odysseus, in order to write it anew. More aptly, in this story myth and history confront each other from within the mythical false totality of capitalism (the present), thus disrupting linear historical accounts (from myth to history). Instead, fragments of an ancestral world resurface in the present of the subject on a threshold. "Pranzo Caprese" focuses on reading the *Odyssey* as productive misreading, that is, on the appropriation of language as breaking through and rewriting the mythical.

Benjamin's New Odysseus

In "Pranzo Caprese," the narrator accepts the mother/cocotte's soup, thus agreeing to submit to the ritual of passage in reverse, crossing the threshold, where this mother/cocotte also figuratively stands and in which mythology and civilization merge.[34] The account of the modern Odysseus's oral encounter with the prostitute (a contemporary reproduction of Homer's oral epos) appears as subtle inversion of the "sublime" trajectory of the civilizing process. Benjamin's modern Odysseus thus walks "against the grain": walking uphill he is faced with a primitive, "dirty" world, the whore/witch's "home," and with her primordial soup. Rather than objectify and abject this world — as the discourse of civilization would have him do — he instead incorporates it within himself. Beatrice's hand — the hand that led Dante to the world of knowledge — is now the prostitute's hand, beckoning him into an inferno of sensual knowledge that transforms him. Only through incorporating the abject, and the ensuing transformation, can he be "enriched" (*bereichter*). After this contamination and loosening of the self, he rereads the *Odyssey,* through an act of physical re-membering caused by eating.

Through eating he confronts otherness — an act of incorporation of the other and of openness to the other. While eating, this modern Odysseus becomes aware of the repression of materiality, re-*members* it, and lives again — in retrospect — the process of alienation that changed the body and materiality into the other of the subject.[35] This other is expressed in nature, matter, and — one could argue — the subaltern, represented by Odysseus's comrades transformed into swine, all allegorically condensed in the mother/cocotte's primordial soup. While eating, the narrator of "Pranzo Caprese" experiences with both lust and fear the resurgence of the magical power repressed in the other language of food:

> Now, you probably think that tasting this must have made me sick and that my stomach could not but reject at once this sort of porridge. But how little you know of the magic of foods, and how little I knew for my own part, until that moment. The tasting itself was nothing, it was only the decisive, and trivial transition between two stages: first, the smell of the food and then the moment of being grasped, refilled, from top to bottom, being squeezed and rubbed by this food as by the hands of this old whore and being massaged with her juice — whether that of the food or that of the whore I could not say. (*Selected Writings,* 2: 362; translation slightly modified)

When the narrator leaves behind taste to immerse himself fully in this soup — a collage of inchoate ingredients — it grabs him as in an erotic embrace. Eating becomes a form of sexual intercourse — in which the partners don't taste each other. This embrace transforms the soup into a powerful active agent and the consumer into the active recipient of another knowledge. This knowledge includes happiness:[36] "Having paid my homage to the lady's hospitality, and also to the witch's demand, I could now go on up the mountain, enriched with Odysseus's knowledge as he saw his comrades being transformed into swine" (*Selected Writings*, 2: 362; translation slightly modified). Intellectual growth must imbricate itself with seduction and embrace a dangerous material approach to the world discovered as the subject's internal fracture or difference. This is evinced by the fact that the narrator in "Pranzo Caprese" — after eating — misreads and rewrites the *Odyssey*.

The narrator remembers Odysseus's epic adventure, especially his comrades' metamorphoses into swine after they have given in to temptation. Odysseus gained his strength by resisting the seduction of myth to which he opposed cunning and thus by giving up the senses and the body. His knowledge was grounded in an experience of distance, that is, in sight as sublimation of the senses. (While Circe transforms his comrades into swine, he is on his ship; only after Hermes provides him with the means to defeat the sorceress will he face her, and drink her wine; finally, when passing by the Sirens, whom he can see and hear in the distance, his body is tied to the ship's mast.) In contrast, Benjamin's new Odysseus engages his full body; he drinks — with terror — the conjurer's gift. Knowledge — after Odysseus — involves an act of sensual transformation, a literal "swelling" out of proportion and "form," which Benjamin describes as the subject's conflicting experience of dissolution on the threshold.[37] The new Odysseus in Benjamin's story interrupts his journey (takes a break), follows the senses, and thus descends into the realm of contamination: the oral world of the mother/cocotte, which in "Fresh Figs" (below) he calls the "primeval forest of devouring." This Odysseus's epos lies in *his own* transformation into swine.

Benjamin distinguishes knowledge as pure contemplation (Odysseus's act of seeing) from knowledge as an acceptance of the transformation ensuing from seduction. Experiencing knowledge, as the act of eating demonstrates, Benjamin implies, involves the danger of a loss of self that may lead to reification in Western consumerism. This is why "taste" (or the faculty of distinction that marks bourgeois aesthetics, including gastronomy) is per se unimportant to the narrator. Rather, as he writes, taste marks the transition between smelling — as the faculty of a still active, autonomous subject situated in the external world—and eating. Eating inaugurates the confusion of boundaries between the eater and the eaten. Taste is relevant if redefined in terms of a threshold itself, when it stands for the transitional space where the subject metamorphoses. (The text "Borscht" reiterates this, too.) Benjamin calls this tension the magic of food, the ability to generate a metamorphic encounter. Abandoning the conventions of bourgeois taste, Benjamin's narrator experiences eating as the magical dialectic of material experience, with which the subject dissipates the semblance of autonomy and identity.

Yet the narrator also retains the distance of the former Odysseus's gaze, thanks to which the modern Odysseus can this time *observe* not another (a subordinate's) transformation but his own "metamorphosis." He indeed experiences it as a retrospective act of self-observation, as in the dissociative hallucinations during intoxication, which he details in his reports on hashish. Endowed with a split-self, this *Nachgeborener* can struggle with the mythical forces (the prostitute as the mythical fetish of modernity, as the embodiment of reification, and the mother as the archaic) and with Odysseus himself, on their own grounds. He eats the soup; he changes but does not repeat Odysseus's epic adventure, which then too undergoes transformation (rewriting).

Body and gaze are both engaged at once in "Pranzo Caprese": Odysseus and his comrades, the subject and his other (the woman, the public body, and the past) remain intertwined. The modern Odysseus, in effect, starts from the point of arrival of the mythical one. Only because of where (when) he is, because of his location in the now of history as *Nachträglichkeit* (belatedness, deferred action), can he then begin to journey into the origins. Thus he can critique the course history has taken by finding the loss of the body in retrospect, a loss that advances its demand aggressively and materially in the present body, challenging vision and a pure abstract gaze. He throws the repressed past in the face of the present (as does Klee's *Angelus Novus,* in Benjamin's view).

The experience of eating as sensual/sexual devouring inflects the reading of the *Odyssey.* The epos returns in Benjamin's text, but this time it includes the question about how Odysseus's journey would have turned out had it also been told simultaneously from his comrades' metamorphic experience. The text indirectly asks about the meaning of the comrades' fate and especially about the impact of their

transformation on the construction of another history and another aesthetic — sensuous, perhaps mimetic — experience. By adopting at once
the split perspective of an overseer and of the "reified" subaltern (the
masses, and women, for example, as the privileged consumers of the
seductive experience found also in modern myths), Benjamin does not
condemn the masses to a state of irredeemable oblivion and false consciousness. Rather, reification and alienation, possibly implied in the
transformation generated by the acceptance of the prostitute's invitation to eat (the call of modernity to consume), engender the consumption, or devouring, of the received ideas of civilization, of prostitution,
of modern identity itself. Incorporation can be an active process of
consumption that opens the relation of subject and object to a threshold beyond pure seduction or pure contamination and that rethinks
the liminal space between myth and reason, sleep and the waking
state. On the thresholds of these dangerous encounters different infra-
states of consciousness (and humanity) are enabled to emerge.[38]

The transformation produces a different temporal experience of
history, as in the modified reading of Odysseus's journey. To read the
Odyssey in modern times does not mean to identify with Odysseus
and his destiny. Rather, reading is a critical, incorporative, and transformative act. When the reader absorbs what befalls the characters
and affects their behaviors, their ways and relations, then, reading
is productive and formative. The act of sudden reading — or devouring — of the founding epos of Western civilization, as conjured up by
this witch's soup, tears it away from "the causal connections established in time" ("Experience," 2: 553) and places it in a material and
temporal constellation that "actualizes" it. The unusual circumstances
and foreign food, language, and place in which the narrator eats disclose eating — an everyday occurrence — as a potential act of profane
communion with the object as other. Similarly, the *Odyssey* appears
in an alien context as erupting from the body's recesses. Eating the
soup comes as a break, an interruption. After this transformative culinary encounter, his walk has no predetermined destination. The act of
devouring does not involve either an act of repetition of the same — an
identification with Odysseus — or the regression to an idyllic or premodern world, a maternal pre-oedipal realm dominated by purely
irrational forces. Rather, the text shows immersion — here through an
act of incorporation — as a fundamental precondition for the subject's

acquisition of a material, dialectical expansion of bodily boundaries and mental horizons. As he writes in "Fresh Figs," this expansion — in effect, a testing of the human boundaries and thus of human experience — occurs by moving away from the straightforward paths (appetite) and into the ambivalent forest of devouring, leading ultimately to a new sobriety of decision and action.

A Detour through "Fresh Figs"

As the German critic Sigrid Weigel maintains, the feminine character often embodies the ambivalence of the commodity in modernist texts. Benjamin did use the figure of the prostitute as incarnate of the Parisian arcades, that is, the prehistory of modernity. Mostly, however, as Weigel demonstrates, the feminine becomes the allegory of this passage because in its openness and ambivalence the feminine embodies the repressed language of the other.[39] If in her interpretation allegory is "another language," in modernity this other language transforms and coincides with the language of the other, hence with the feminine, which in turn takes the form of mother/prostitute. According to the anthropologist Mary Douglas, the polluted, being connected with the open, the boundary zones of the body, is once again most easily embodied by the mother/prostitute. And, for Douglas, the polluted is "matter out of place."[40] In "Pranzo Caprese" the witch's clothes and her soup are both irresistible and dirty in the visitor's eyes, the scene further reminding the reader of the witches' sabbath (e.g., the night of Walpurgis and the witches' kitchen in Goethe's *Faust I*).

The mythical — engulfing, dangerous — mother returns in "Fresh Figs," where, again following Goethe, Benjamin mentions a descent into the "original forest of devouring," also echoing Baudelaire's forest of symbols, and its lost language. "Pranzo Caprese" and "Fresh Figs" are journeys of self-loss and finding anew, involving defilement and purification, and an immersion in the lost world of m/others. Not by chance do these eating encounters take place in the "porous" spaces of Italy, in an archaic, brutal but also magical/mythical landscape, according to the German traveler who is here caught between idleness and intoxication. The narrator eats his soup in Capri and his figs in Secondigliano (near Naples). Benjamin spent some time in 1924 in Capri in the company of Asja Lacis.[41] Many centuries before Benjamin, Odysseus's vessel navigated off the coast of this island in his wanderings across the Mediterranean (hence the reference to Odysseus, a mythical hero, in "Pranzo Caprese").

"Fresh Figs" tackles more directly the question of language and writing as these relate to a body that voraciously eats and, while it eats, also redefines its relation to language. The story introduces the reader to Benjamin's concept of profane illumination, which here is also associated with intoxication. Yet the story demonstrates how the subject, through incorporation, also breaks through his own intoxication or spell. Benjamin speaks of taking a walk in an intoxicated landscape (he uses the term *verrauscht*) to which he adds that his desire for the figs he buys from a vendor is determined by dissipation, waste, excess (*Verschwendung*).⁴² In the story, intoxication is a sensuous material experience. As in "Pranzo Caprese," the bodily experience that ensues from the act of devouring provokes intoxication, which in turn provokes other sensations: gluttony, voracity, greed, powerlessness, nausea, power, destructiveness, and pleasure. These are all depicted as dissonant feelings:

> No one who has never eaten a food to excess has ever really experienced it, or fully exposed himself to it. Unless you do this, you at best enjoy it [*Genuss*], but never come to lust [*Gier*, greed] after it, or make the acquaintance of that diversion from the straight and narrow road of the appetite which leads to the primeval forest of greed [*Frasses*, devouring]. . . . How did I first learn all this? It happened just before I had to make a very difficult decision. A letter had to be posted or torn up. . . . So I left with figs stuffed in my trouser pockets and in my jacket, figs in both of my outstretched hands, and figs in my mouth. I couldn't stop eating them and was forced to get rid of the mass of plump fruits as quickly as possible. But that could not be described as eating; it was more like a bath, so powerful was the smell of the air through which I carried my burden. And then, after satiety and revulsion — the final bends in the path — had been surmounted, came the ultimate mountain peak of taste. A vista over an unsuspected landscape of the palate spread out before my eyes — an insipid, undifferentiated, greenish flood of greed that could distinguish nothing but the stringy, fibrous waves of the flesh of the open fruit, the utter transformation of enjoyment into habit, of habit into vice. A hatred for those figs welled up inside me; I was desperate to finish with them, to liberate myself, to rid myself of all this overripe, bursting fruit. I ate it to destroy it. Biting had rediscovered its most ancient purpose. ("Eating/Food," 2: 358–59)

The devourer of figs is materialistically inspired by this temporary dissonant experience. In other words, his intoxication transforms — through his senses — in a form of bodily will that generates decision and action unexpectedly and beyond rational will: "When I pulled the last fig from the depths of my pocket, the letter was stuck to it. Its fate was sealed; it, too, had to succumb to the great purification. I took it and tore it into a thousand pieces" (359).

Devouring provokes a whole series of actions that lead to a new relation to writing (i.e., the letter). Most importantly, devouring is framed within the symbolic rituals of contamination and purification. Juxtaposed, these rituals also help break the "psychotic" confusion of subject and object. The ritual of contamination is interrupted by the appearance of the letter/the word: the letter purifies the object (fig) by paradoxically taking its place and itself becoming the object of sacrifice. In this story, as in "Pranzo Caprese," the subject must surrender his boundaries to the object, "expose himself to it" to counter oblivion. Only thus may this modern subject gain substance: by engaging in a battle, by taking up the struggle, by making himself into a *"Feige"* (fig and coward in German) and then establishing a different — reelaborated, material — distance.

"Pranzo Caprese" stops at this awareness, depicted in the illuminating new act of material misreading of the *Odyssey*. "Fresh Figs" extends this material interpretation to the use of written language that appears in the text as the letter. In the story, the subject devours and destroys the figs with voracity and even hatred. The narrator's body is inscribed by this material experience. Subsequently, he (the subject) is compelled to find a different language of communication. While the material experience appears to be destructive and annihilating in relation to the fig object, in reality it has a constructive effect. It affects the subject and turns his voracity against written language: the letter, in Julia Kristeva's idiom, could be identified with the realm of the symbolic or the language of the father. Benjamin's fig devouring opens up a space from within the acquired language of self-identity for bodily interferences and disturbances that emerge from another "swampy world," as he writes in his Franz Kafka essay. This bodily remembrance induces the subject to tear up the letter and write a different text, the story we read. This text stems from and describes the acquisition — through self-dissolution and contamination — of his new "heterogeneous" subjectivity. Benjamin shows that to have access to knowledge, the modern subject has to come to terms with his own body and its "boundless" desire. The narrator abandons the paths of appetite and taste that have accompanied the civilizing process and follows the treacherous paths of voracity and greed to find the original forest of devouring. The experience of devouring is a journey, like the one taking place in "Pranzo Caprese." It halts the civilizing process and contaminates epistemology and aesthetics with the human sensory apparatus, a contamination that then paradoxically purifies the subject and that is revealed to lie in a sensuous material form of remembering and rereading.

The cycle of stories "Eating/Food" is built in such a way that for every confrontation with nausea another narrative relates a less fearful and threatening encounter with food. Nausea implies here a confrontation with one's boundaries and rejection rituals, thus with one's cultural imprint, taboos, and repressions. Food in these other experiences is linked to remembering, to the magical world of food and words, as for example in "Borscht," analyzed at the end of this chapter. Ultimately, Benjamin's accounts speak of the experience of eating as the subject's most fragile personal and collective memory.

The many references to language—its faltering, its rejection, or its necessity—invite reconsidering its constitution and tradition. In particular and most evidently, Benjamin points to the sacrifice of the body in language. For Benjamin, during eating the body and language are frozen, superimposed as in cinematic montage, and the subject gains a glimpse of knowledge in the face of their abysses. In Jacques Lacan's idiom, then, the oedipal language of the father, or the symbolic language, is violently opened up to the internal rhythms of other languages (the repressed allegorical language of the other, the feminine, the mother, the prostitute, the abject). This is why the "Eating/Food" cycle, which opens with a deep immersion in the subject's prehistory ("Fresh Figs") concludes with a fairy tale. "Mulberry Omelette" is about eating as storytelling, that is, as the material orality of culture. For Benjamin, fairy tales embody the power of language, and through this language one manages to break free of fate and myth. One detects a dialectical swinging in Benjamin's food stories: from immersion in a swampy world of creatures that inhabit the modern subject as his forgotten realm to the resistance against falling into this realm of oblivion and its seductions. This dialectics then manifests itself here in the exercise of a bodily presence of mind.[43] Here it suffices to mention that in Benjamin's encounters with food one encounters anew the Kafka described by Benjamin in his essay, specifically

Kafka's alienated body (as the beast within). One also observes the important moment of awakening or, in other words, that attentiveness beyond a practical goal or destination which Benjamin on Kafka (in reference to Judaism) calls "study" and qualifies as animal asceticism. In "Some Motifs on Baudelaire," rather than renunciation, asceticism becomes the counterpoint of ardor. In the food stories, asceticism is the illumination but also the contamination that arrests devouring at its peak, namely, when it can become self-devouring or melancholy; asceticism is, in short, the reversal and interruption of the course taken by the subject as by history; it is a language spoken beyond language from the inside of the body. It is beyond the law, beyond established orders. Not a fall into silence but, as Benjamin interprets Kafka, an escape into song or animal language, into a direction unaccounted for and, for Benjamin, a way to arrest the systems of abstract knowledge and rationality, namely, the path leading from known pasts to a predicted future.[44]

Incorporation as Reading

Benjamin's own system of *vases communicantes* between the body asleep and awake, night-work and day-work, returns more explicitly in a direct analogy Benjamin draws between reading and eating. "Reading Novels" is included in Benjamin's series of *Thought-Figures,* tellingly titled "Little Tricks of the Trade," or, in German, *Kleine Kunst-Stücke* (*Selected Writings,* 2: 728). The words *Frühstück* (the "Breakfast Room" in question above) and *Kunst-Stück* resonate with each other and supplement each other. As shown before, breakfast is for Benjamin the first bodily act of translation — and preservation through radical change — of the night's work into the day's activity. Taken literally, *Frühstück* (a composite word formed by the adverb "early" and the substantive "piece") could be read to indicate an early form of first technology, which is then highlighted by the term *Kunst-Stück,* the title of the general chapter. *Kunst* signifies *technē,* art, and trick, and, according to Benjamin's title, more specifically small (*klein*) examples of these terms. A montage of *Früh-stück* and *Kunst-stück* only underscores better that the body itself functions as a first operator of change, precisely through its *technē* of absorbing and transforming, its faculty to "trick," on which art and technology rest.

In a few short theoretical reflections Benjamin grounds reading in incorporation; in the realm of letters, reading functions as and serves the principles that he ascribes to incorporation in the realm of the body, for example, absorbing, disintegrating, intercutting, transforming. In reading as in the act of eating breakfast, one comes to embrace the dialectical mechanisms, such as involuntary memories and forgetting. According to these dialectics, mind and body are interconnected in generating material knowledge. So the little tricks of the trade — or technologies of art and culture — suggest that reading always involves instances of penetration, destruction, and construction, not unlike the active language that speaks through dreams. In this light, reading is a process of signification also rooted in bodily acts of disintegration of the word (and sentence, etc.) into its constituents, for example, the letters, as occurring in sight (the eye as it connects with the external object). Letters shape new figures in words that generate nonsensory ideas through imagination, resting on sight, itself an inversion of reality. (Benjamin speaks of these relations as mimetic, where mimesis for him is nonsensuous similarity, namely, constellated clusters of mediated relations between things/actions that differ from each other.) Dreams, both as tricks and as "work," are thus unconscious manifestations of small (allegorical) art/artificial fragments (*früh-Stücke*), which Benjamin's own surrealistic texts — the fragments in *Thought-Figures* but also in *One-Way Street* — intend to capture.[45]

Breton's apotheosis of dream work as artwork, as proposed in his 1924 manifesto, is transferred in Benjamin's writing to those unconscious activities through which the awakened speaks. Both Benjamin and the avant-garde envision an Archimedean mental and bodily force in everyday, even mundane twofold acts of destruction and construction, such as one finds in dreaming but also eating and reading. This force overcomes the seeming contradiction between destruction and construction, and propels the subject beyond the instrumental uses of reason it has been trained to make. The body that dreams and eats is the body infused with insuppressible desire for change. Politically, bodily transformations and the desire for change, frustrated in the hell of consumer capitalism, where exchange value disavows difference (work) and causes the return of the same (money), translate as an immanent and radical desire for justice.[46] The latter, like incorporation, is manifest in the interruption of continuity and stability and marks the emergence (the leap, *Ursprung*) of a temporal difference, interference, and/or intermittence that comes from the realms of the forgotten past. Incorporation as active and destructive but also metabolic reception of the world, whether through eating or through dreaming, always shatters the world's semblance of continuity. In contrast, consciousness, aided by voluntary memory (as Benjamin remarks of Proust and Breton), contributes to preserve its apparent totality, alongside the subject's own illusion of stable identity.[47] Incorporation interrupts linear time, brings about involuntary memory, and thus situates the eater into a collective countertime of repressed desires, which he stirs up. New historical and collective constellations of the leftover — the unconscious fragments that reemerge as allegorical phenomena of history in the arts (literature as architecture) — become available for alternative narrative constructions of time and subjectivity, which Benjamin sets out to read (politically).

Contrary to common wisdom, then, Benjamin explains the act of reading novels on the basis of disruptive incorporation, rather than assimilation of experience or knowledge. Why do we read? he asks. Because incorporation provides bliss, even when one incorporates commercial novels lacking in nourishing qualities. Those theories of reading that speak of assimilation and nourishment focus on the intentions and the rewards of reading. For Benjamin, underscoring incorporation as voluptuousness, as orgasmic pleasure of absorption in the body, is invoking pleasure — one that is beyond consciousness and rationality. Incorporation helps Benjamin dissolve reading as capitalization. By focusing on each action involved in eating, Benjamin underscores the interruption of the teleology of the digestive process (thus the relevance that involuntary memory and dream work have in his considerations of eating as of reading).

From within the same framework, Benjamin in the fragment "Theory of Distraction" (1935–36) suggests the possibility of a nexus between how incorporation (*Einverleibung*) — both in eating and in reading — may be linked to yet another kind of interruption: distraction, a connection he thinks might be clarified if studied in relation to film (*Selected Writings*, 3: 141). Although he does not pursue this idea, he hints at the fact that the relationship might be found through the connection between distraction — *Zerstreuung*, an act of scattering — and destruction, *Zerstörung*, a word that is not distant in sound from *Zerstreuung*.[48] Reading as incorporation would interrupt and destroy the "natural" and logical connections of common language, as it suspends identity in an act of self-scattering as self-loosening.[49]

As Benjamin explains, one does not *substitute* oneself for the novel's heroes to experience their lives. Growth through reading lies in devouring, first a destructive and then a constructive gesture, rather than in assimilating content (and reproducing identity) itself. The reader is an ally of the cannibal actors who devour every role they play, as Benjamin mentions in his Kraus essay: they do not become the roles; rather, they embody their differences.[50] While the actor moves on stage, the reader/critic incorporates what befalls the heroes into himself or herself, through the vivid narration of events. The latter take "the enticing form in which a nourishing meal is presented at the table" (*Selected Writings,* 2: 728). This semblance and staging of events (phenomena) entice one to eat and/or read more than does the promise of finding nourishment. In reading/eating, nourishment is indeed found in the experience of otherness. Benjamin writes: "There are many nourishing foodstuffs that are inedible when raw" (729).

Reading/eating offers the opportunity to familiarize oneself with the absolute otherness of death. Death is "lived" both in the experience of reading to the end the life stories of the novel's characters and through the narrated death of the characters when it so happens.[51] Novels—prose—depict death as communicable but not assimilable into life other than through its own difference. In an earlier fragment of "Reading Novels," he speaks of a gastronomic arrangement of prose; in other versions he succinctly states that the novel's muse is the kitchen fairy, who "raises the world from its raw state in order to produce something edible" (729). Yet it must be noted that "edible" does not mean digestible. Rather, it is what gives itself up to incorporation (reading) for an annihilation that finds in the edible its crucial point of indigestibility (its own expressionlessness).[52] For Benjamin, reading as incorporation tears asunder the enticing, ornamental, and necessary part of art that Baudelaire called the circumstantial (transient and contextual, I may add) element of beauty, or the "appetite-whetting coating of the divine cake." In Baudelaire's metaphor, the cake is the eternal that, without its icing, would otherwise be "indigestible, tasteless, unadapted and inappropriate to human nature."[53] Benjamin, who in his incipit to *Berlin Childhood* condenses notions of history into an allegorical cake monument reminiscent of both Baudelaire and Proust, insists on this act of incorporation of the cake.

Café-Crême: Reading Proust

"Pranzo Caprese" offers a misreading of the classical epos of Western civilization. Incorporation brings back materiality into the subject that while consuming is able to produce a new body and a new text. "Café-Crême," also included in "Eating/Food," is Benjamin's dialectical reading of Proust's modernist memoirs *À la recherche du temps perdu*:

> And what don't you have along with your coffee! The entire morning, the morning of this day, and sometimes also the missed mornings of life. If you had sat at this table as a child, countless ships would have sailed across the frozen sea of the marble table-top. You would have known what the Sea of Marmara looks like. With your gaze fixed on an iceberg or a sail you would have swallowed one mouthful for your father and one for your uncle and one for your brother, until slowly the cream would have come floating up to the thick rim of your cup, a huge promontory on which your lips rested. How feeble your sense of revulsion has become! How quickly and hygienically you behave now! You drink; you don't crumble up your bread, or dunk it. You sleepily reach out to the breadbasket for a madeleine, break it in two, and do not even notice how sad it makes you not to be able to share it. ("Eating/Food," 2: 359–60)

Benjamin's story focuses on the loss rather than on regaining the past as in Proust's work, namely, Proust's quest to retrieve the past intact. "Café-Crême" juxtaposes a fictitious and imagined past with the contemporary atrophy of the senses in the adult's mechanical approach to the famous Proustian madeleine. The story's title is dialectical. The dialectics unfold in the text, in which coffee—or the lost morning, interpreted as the lost future the past might have promised—is juxtaposed to an imaginary childhood and ice cream (*crème*), interpreted as the past that could have bred a different future, different from the adult sipping his coffee in the Parisian bistro. These two temporalities occupy simultaneously the space of this text. In the difference between the imagined child and the numb adult, the text reveals the sad affair of a modernity gone awry and caught in pedantic habit.

As the text exposes the gap between the adult and the child, between coffee and cream, it also presents itself as the actualization of the stories the child might have invented, had he or she been "there." "Café-Crême" unfolds these stories by being itself there for the reader. "There" could refer both to time—there in the nineteenth century, as in the *Arcades Project* or in *Berlin Childhood*—and to place, in

Paris, where the story takes place (but also there as "text").[54] The text inserts itself in the gap between the past the child embodies and the present the adult embodies, offering another historical (or ahistoricist) account. It constitutes a dialectical temporal encounter that juxtaposes childhood, the imagination, and a past to adulthood, the loss of imagination, that is, loss of childhood, and the present. The text does not recuperate the past for the narrator but invents a narrator, a subject (child), which activates that slumbering imagination in the now. Through dialectic juxtaposition, "Café-Crême" literally creates that imaginary childhood-space for a new adult and subject, that is, the reader born after this story.

The reader/adult is told that breaking the madeleine in two is now done by force of habit: this adult "you" does not know how the madeleine could "speak" and how indeed it spoke in the (literary) past, namely, by opening up a world of submerged childhood experiences in Proust's *Recherche*. Proust's madeleine instead appears here as a hard cookie unable to speak, a literary artifact of the past. Yet the narrator breaks through the adult's numbness. While this text speaks of the loss of that madeleine, at the same time it revives the old cookie's magic. Indeed, the text stresses the madeleine's absence (or erasure) while putting it to a different use in the café — depicted here as a public space — of concave, distorting mirrors. Hence Benjamin's story is less about recuperating the lost past than about imagining how the past's dream of the future might have produced a different present. Redemption is always already behind us in Benjamin's view, but its promise lingers on in some "forgotten" object. "Café-Crême" is about becoming aware that a promise of happiness is always in the childhood of different ages, hence that childhood itself is the possibility to reinvent and see another future in the old or obsolescent. As Benjamin writes in the *Arcades Project,* the child can remember the new once again, contrary to the adult (855, M°, 20). "Café-Crême" suggests that one recapture this promise by situating oneself in the present and interrupting the past–future continuum as already written, thus as invariable history.

> You have to have it [coffee] in a bistro where, among all the mirrors, the *petit déjeuner* is itself a concave mirror in which a minute image of this city is reflected. At no other meal are the tempi so varied, from the mechanical gesture with which the clerk sitting at the bar downs his café au lait, to the contemplative relish with which a traveler slowly empties his cup in the interval between two trains. ("Eating/Food," 2: 359)

The present appears in the text as the multifarious rhythmical tempi of the people gathered in the bistro and as interval in and suspension of homogeneous time. This is a space of refracting mirrors, where outside and inside overlap without conflating their differences, as in superimposed images, and where individuals perceive themselves awkwardly. In the mirrors of Parisian cafés, Benjamin writes in the *Arcades Project*, "before any man catches sight of her [the *Parisienne*], she already sees herself ten times reflected. But the man, too, sees his own physiognomy flash by. He gains his image more quickly here than elsewhere and also sees himself more quickly merged with this, his image" (537, R 1, 3). Benjamin comes up with his own "mirror-stage" theory of subject-becoming à la Lacan. The identification with the mirror image is in his words a flashing by, a temporary identification that these mirrors refract infinitely, in a multiplication that questions the stability of that identification. The self's unitary image is shaken even further by the imaginary child's own projected landscapes — also possibly contained in the world-city Paris. Above all, however, Benjamin writes in one *Denkbild* devoted to Paris as the mirror city par excellence that the entire world (as in street and restaurant names) is reflected in this city, which itself has engendered and is refracted in a full spectrum of literary texts. Rows of mirrors reflecting one another are the match (*Gegenstück*) of the infinite acts of remembering, remembering into which Proust's pen fragmented his own life.[55]

"Café-Crème" subtly prepares the reader — and the adult in the story itself — to find the hidden element of play that survives in habit. Play lies in an indeterminate space–time that is embodied, in this story, by the figure of a traveler sipping coffee between two trains.[56] The traveler stands for the other of that adult who sips his coffee without pleasure and awareness. The traveler's present is now the "temporary" station between one point in space–time and another. He personifies the juxtaposition of childhood and adulthood, of the past and the past's future. The traveler, like the child, appears as both a close foreigner and a foreign relative. Child and traveler are the specular "other" images of the alienated grownup. In their enjoyment of food as the enjoyment of an expanding time of the imagination, they mark the possibility of fulfillment.[57] The chance to recover one's own being in time is through the child's image or else the child's imagination that expands the self's spatial and temporal confines. The traveler's anticipation of the future captures the child's vision.

Child and traveler offer to the adult reader (the coffee drinker) a displaced mirror image of himself: they become the possibility for him to shift position. The interchangeability or ambivalence of positions is enhanced by the author's use of "you" in "Café-Crême." The effect is that readers of the story find themselves constantly oscillating between identifying with or distancing themselves from the narrator as well as the "domesticated" adult in the story. Are the readers the numb adult? Or is it the narrator who has now awakened from his numbness? The ambivalence of "you" in the end compels readers to question their own standing in the present and with regard to their and their age's childhood (the age of cafés). The mirrors reinforce the function of "you" in the text. They break the readers' identificatory processes through multiplications and magnifications. The adult is one of many images as is, suddenly, the reader, who, drawn into the text by the "you," sees himself reflected in the other images.

Proust's madeleine tries to bridge the gap between literary representation and sensation. The multivolume novel *Recherche* expresses Proust's attempt to capture a sensation through representation, that is, the word *madeleine*.[58] In contrast, Benjamin's "Café-Crême" situates itself within the gap between sensation and words, as well as between the past and the present, namely, the act of remembering an imaginary childhood and the adult life. It specifically invokes the transformation of the nineteenth-century dream of a modern future into a hard madeleine. (One could think here of art nouveau, and Antoni Gaudí, both mentioned by Benjamin: this architecture is viewed as the solidification of dreams.)[59] Hence the reader's task is to eat this hardened cookie with the imagination in order to break through it. In this story the promise of the future lies in exposing the gap, in the dialectical juxtaposition of dream (images) and alienation, which Benjamin calls "café-crème."

In "Pranzo Caprese," eating beyond taste initiated a subversive act of reading of the *Odyssey*. This meant the emergence in the present moment of other temporalities and other subjectivities. In "Café-Crême," a modern reader grasps the present through a suspension of homogeneous time. In this multitemporal space of refracting mirrors, Benjamin both acknowledges and displaces Proust's own quest to regain time, or the modernist longing and nostalgia to resuscitate as pure and untouched what is lost within the temporal framework provided by involuntary memory. Involuntary memory, for Benjamin, involves distortion through distance and rhythmical, syncopated temporality (tempi). As Benjamin's new Odysseus travels a different — parallel — route than the epical hero's, the multiple subject positions (the narrator, the you, the child, the traveler, and the reader) opened up by "Pranzo Caprese" engage dialogically Proust's monologue.

Proust's narrative seemingly tries to recompose obsessively the lost past through a textual mechanism of displacement. It strives to suture the wounds provoked by its being broken off from the present. In contrast, "Café-Crème" condenses imaginary, alternative spaces that manifest themselves in contrasting images. The text collages them with one another dialectically (café and crème, ice and cream, ice cream and hard cookie) so as to block the incessant flow of images found in the Proustian narrative. Benjamin's dialectical mirror images return to us in a composite word, a dialectical name, itself a frozen image or allegory of the hardened madeleine.

In sum, Benjamin transfers Proust's isolated (private) modernist experience to the bistro's public space, not only bringing the imagination of the past to bear on the present but also appropriating the madeleine as a trace, a concrete remainder of modern subjectivity that Benjamin includes in his avant-garde montage of clashing tempi. His montage — alluded to in the dash or gap that separates and unites "café" and "crème" — is a text of and about the now-time. The present is the now in which the traveler of Benjamin's story lives; he who, as the narrator tells us, "is suspended between two trains."

Indigestible Language: Quotes and Names

In writing, incorporation translates as the shattering power of quotation. For example, Benjamin reads Hugo von Hoffmannsthal's texts as mnemonic, involuntary forgery or a kind of subliminal quotation that makes his stories indigestible:

> They [Hoffmannsthal's works] present us with all the materials of their originary images [*Urbilder*], and they do so in their most condensed and most highly sublimated forms; but they have not been truly assimilated. We may perhaps put it best by saying that they are nourishing, but not really edible. To call them edible would mean they were digestible, and very little of what Hoffmannsthal wrote is digestible. — His genius could be summed up in a single phrase as a genius for quoting; and this comes very close to defining what we meant by forging. The great forger who has little or

nothing to do with forgery as a purely commercial activity cites the origi-
nary image. . . . For in fact the forger cites the work in that other sense: he
conjures it up. (*Selected Writings*, 2: 421–22)

The critic's task is to devour to the point of indigestibility. On Benjamin's view when the words of another, or *other* words, are conjured
up in one's own text, they speak their own temporal difference. Their
magic is revealed at the exact moment of their return or reproduction
because they are extracted from their habitual location and thus are
defamiliarized. In this way they speak uncannily beyond and against
an author's intentions and any definite spatial or temporal location.

Thus for Benjamin, quotations counterintuitively defy the repetition Roland Barthes ascribes to *encratic* language. Where Barthes sets
up a radical opposition between the magical bliss of the "New" word
and the statutory language of repetition, Benjamin maintains that
radical quotation undermines the stability of meaning and the intentionality of linguistic communication, opening up the new as blissful.
Bliss is present, repressed thus distorted, in the commodified word,
which awaits devouring, first in quotation, then in reading.[60] Quotations — of his own texts and of others' works — transform Benjamin's
own pieces. For example, his thought-figures, among others, become
Kunst-Stücke, those very same "tricks of the trade" that in his view
also define the avant-garde's collages, montages, and surrealist allegorical paintings, from the most enigmatic yet still figurative works
(René Magritte's, Max Ernst's, Klee's, and Dalí's) to the most fragmentary and least representational (e.g., Joan Miró's). Like the dialectical tensions in the avant-garde works — between fragment and whole,
between allegory and meaning — Benjamin's antinomian textual constructs demonstrate that any text entertains nontransparent and complex relations, beyond intention and representation, with the time of
its production as well as the times that precede and follow it. The
critic/reader has the task to bring this temporal incongruity of artistic
production to the fore, an aspect that the textual analogy between eating and reading, as *mise-en-abyme* of each other, highlights.

For his part, Barthes accounts for the reasons behind the presence
of food in realist novels and also associates food with temporality. He
writes that in "citing, naming, *noticing* food," the novel offers "the hallucinatory tail of 'reality': astonishment that in 1791 one could eat 'a
salad of oranges and rum,' as one does in restaurants today: the onset

of historical intelligibility and the persistence of the thing (orange, rum) in *being there"* (46). The ordinary name of a dish that we associate with a reality we are familiar with is defamiliarized by its transfer outside our time and by the dislocation of our time into another. Not unlike Barthes's interpretation, Benjamin's thought-figures quote food through various foreign, magical names that as tastes might not be that familiar. They thus disavow the pleasure of pure representation. As Barthes put it, the pleasure experienced solely by the greedy reader who may indeed enjoy these foods extends beyond it. Hence the text's *jouissance* — in Benjamin's own words, the voluptuousness of incorporation — derives from the "undoing of an initial nominalization, a rubbing against the limits of language" (Barthes), which Benjamin finds in a devouring of intoxicating proportion. In effect, prior to his engagement with profane food itself, Benjamin kept detailed protocols of his drug experiments.

In these reports on hashish eating, no mentioned name corresponds to a given external reality, and the dimensions of consciousness are redefined. While under the influence of the drug, Benjamin experiences an opening up of the name into an image-action whereby an ordinary word or a seemingly insignificant name disclose an unsuspected power and effect on the subject. He writes, for example: "The Open Sesame of this name, which was supposed to contain all the riches of the earth in its interior, had opened up" (*Selected Writings*, 2: 392). In this specific account, an insignificant code name, *Braunschweiger*, which the narrator had seemingly picked at random to run bank transactions long-distance, discloses to the narrator the grounds of his own unexpected historicity at the end of the hashish experience. The improbable but finally obvious meaning of the word — in German it stands for the inhabitants of the town named *Braunschweig*, but it can also mean "brown and silent man" — awakens the subject's consciousness to a profound self-knowledge. In the throngs of intoxication, the narrator is suddenly asked to decide about an investment. Afraid that he will forget the code name, he struggles with the drug's dissociating effects. The final illumination about the narrator's identity is the product of "objective chance." It happens as the direct effect of his psychic dissociation, which then produces the narrator's situation as a series of allegorical visions. Having realized that drinking coffee — as he is about to do — would enhance the effects of the hashish eaten, thus making him forget rather than remember the code, the narrator holds the cup in a "rigid grip like an emblem, a sacred stone or bone." The allegorical vision of the everyday, the cup of coffee, with its brown undrunk liquid, metonymically embraces the narrator who then recognizes his own hand as "a brown, Ethiopian hand." He realizes who he is (*an other* from the self) when his alienating and alienated gaze falls on his hand as the hand of another. The shocking revelation is that he now inhabits the arbitrarily chosen name: he is the *Braunschweiger,* not the inhabitant of that small provincial German town but the "brown" and "silent" man that the name suggests from within this other displaced location. The revelation of this identity as other (in Marseilles) and of the other intimate meaning of *Braunschweiger* beyond its conventional use is important: the narrator does not go to the post office and lets go of the potential gain that, the reader knows, he would in fact have had, had he gone ahead with the investment (392). In the pangs of intoxication, which transforms the eater of hashish into an allegorist, the name is eaten, its concealed power of transformation released, so that this German Jew in Marseilles, if the narrator were indeed to be Benjamin, now sees himself as the brown, silent immigrant worker in the port town, which Benjamin elsewhere described as the gigantic maw of an amphibious *Minotaure*: "*Marseilles* — the yellow-studded maw of a seal with salt water running out between the teeth. When this gullet opens to catch the *black and brown proletarian bodies thrown to it by ship's companies* according to their timetables, it exhales a stink of oil, urine, and printer's ink" (*Reflections,* 131).

In his hashish accounts Benjamin stresses the recurrent coinage of neologisms arising from the "blizzard-like" production of images independently of any attention. He underscores the speed of the images' appearing and vanishing, and associates them directly with "the exotic, indecipherable images of the kind we know from Surrealist paintings" ("Eating/Food," 2: 329). Benjamin thus explicitly connects his name-emblems with surrealism. His allegorical words (as picture puzzles, his definition of script) are produced automatically, during the trance, and transcribed in letters rather than in visual representational images. On two occasions at least, names unfold into text when the subject is prey to a *lionish* hunger (676). The hallucinated images-texts are immediately and quickly consumed by the same hunger that devours, like a lion, the hashish eater. As visions, however, they do not undergo the same physical consumption of food. Benjamin's hallucinations are eminently grounded in language, not symbolic language but a new bodily alchemical language of names. Thus, while a countersublime, as innate apocalyptic sublime, may still be the result of "food-intoxication," for example, in the case of "Pranzo Caprese" and "Fresh Figs," the emerging magical word-images in his hashish accounts accentuate the alienation and gaps within the subject. A countersublime is produced that is "counter" also because it explodes from within any unified source of creative intuition (*Feast and Folly*, 25).

In one drug experiment related by Benjamin, the subject hallucinates gigantic cakes that he does not feel compelled to eat, only to look at. He instinctively names them *Augenbrot* (eye bread).[61] Subsequently he unfolds this name into a micro theory about the decline of the confectionary art. Because cakes have lost their perfection and ornamental quality, people want to take satisfaction in consuming them by mouth rather than aesthetically, that is, through visual contemplation. Although for a moment Benjamin seems to mourn the loss of contemplation, the visionary cakes in fact do not call for it. The cakes are so humongous that only small portions of them are visible at one time so that the total visual field is disturbed and vision breaks down. In effect, while Benjamin seems to set up an opposition between aesthetic — contemplative — pleasure, through the hallucinated food meant for the eyes, and the less imaginative act of the physical consumption of cakes, these "images" ultimately are less visual representations than phrases, in Breton's language. Not only do they appear here in and as a text but they also bear the graphic quality of "picture puzzles," the magical sentences children produce in play. In these games, as in the hashish experiments, the magical figural quality of names consumes the image.[62] The emblematic *Augenbrot* (a substantial *Augenblick*) hardly lends itself to a sudden visual "grasping"; instead, it emphasizes its montage character. The *Augenbrot* demands a temporal textual unfolding and its dissolution in the radical (critical) act of reading — also intended as interruption — which incorporation is. As is the case with the term *Braunschweiger,* Benjamin's found coinages, in the course of intoxication, challenge contemplation with their critico-allegorical status as rebus.[63]

In yet another report of hashish eating, Benjamin first peruses a menu in disorderly and undecisive fashion (as he maintains in politeness toward the dishes that he does not wish to refuse). Finally, he decides on one dish that seems to capture his ravenous condition: *paté de Lyon.* In this state of "lionish" hunger, he translates the name of the dish as Lion paste, not without some humor. The name brings to the fore the difference and distance between the gigantic devouring of an enhanced imagination and the reality of the food on the plate: no lion meat is served, just a pink, tender, edible substitute. While Benjamin justifies hunger in the hashish accounts, and elsewhere, as the physical consequence of intoxication, and while hunger may appear as the tie that binds the eater under the influence of hashish to "reality" and physical space, it is instead the corporeal engine of Benjamin's visionary acts of production as misreading and renaming of the real — for example, food. Like "missing eating," to miss reading and to miss understanding (misread and misunderstand) are the only guarantee for a knowledge that goes beyond classification and the rationality of knowledge. This is the devouring hunger of desire, which consumes the subject and his location in the world, also through language. The transformations undergone by ordinary names and initiated within the subject by these names both during intoxication and in his thought-figures, during Benjamin's profane but foreign eating encounters, are reminiscent of the welling up, at the time just before falling asleep, of the revelatory and inextricable "phrases" of automatism, suspended between consciousness and dream. At the same time they carry the productive critical quality — the force of dialectical illumination — of Dalí's paranoiac–critical objects. (Following Knut Hamsun in his novel *Hunger,* Breton also supports the hypothesis that these "phrases" may be the effects of hunger.)[64]

This painter's paranoiac–critical method was developed in accordance with Breton's own critique of earlier automatism.[65] The paranoiac–critical method was intended to bridge the gap between the passive and the active, the subjective and the objective elements in the production of surrealist dream-obsessive objects and texts.[66] Dalí, who wanted to escape the psychoanalyzable representations taking hold more and more across the art world, critiqued the translation of dreams into ordinary logical language. He also believed, however, that "they [dreams] still continue to offer an uninterpretable residue and also an authentic and very vast margin of enigma" (Finkelstein, 266). Benjamin, for his part, speaks of translations within the various apparati (stomach-mind) of the body. These translations allow critical insight and creative production to occur simultaneously (the hallucinated *Augenbrot* alongside his theory about the decline of patisserie). For Benjamin, critique reaches beyond logic and beyond assigned — semantic — contexts but also extends beyond pure irrationality. Benjamin grounds his critical method in a language generated by a bodily will that surfaces in the act of incorporation. The profane illuminations Benjamin experiences in his hashish eating — and in eating itself — not only affect the subject but also draw new connections between the subject and the collective world he inhabits: whether the proletarian mariners of Marseille or the art of confectionery, the textual culture of Western civilization (the Bible, Homer, and Proust) or the spaces of history such as Berlin, Moscow, and Naples.

Benjamin and Dalí radically differ in how they think of their critical activities' effects. Both arrive at eating, consuming, devouring, and cannibalizing as interstitial and fundamental operations between mind and body, art and life. While Dalí invokes fusion with the object, which he conceives as in the shape of one's own desire, Benjamin rejects fusion — assimilation — and wholeness. In contrast, he imagines the act of incorporation as struggle, and the subject–object relation (name-word) as a battlefield, which ultimately leads to an empowered, nonidentical, and other *reason* compelling the subject to engage in bodily minded will, decision, and action. This, however, does not exclude that Benjamin upholds the antihumanistic humanity of cannibalism, a cannibalistic art.

The stimulated body is the medium of an allegorical — for example, figural, *writerly* — production and, possibly, in Benjamin's suggestion, also of its translation into "revolutionary experience" first and into action later, as he writes in his essay on surrealism. The body's own disruptive dialectics are thus what breaks with the "inadequate, undialectical conception of the nature of intoxication," which is better understood through those other "minor" narcotics Benjamin finds in everyday foreign food as both familiar (everyday) and impenetrable (foreign) (*Selected Writings,* 2: 210, 216).

Benjamin's Porous Avant-Garde Food

For Benjamin, Kafka was the writer of dialectical fairy tales, stories in which the world of swampy creatures metamorphoses itself and oblivion into the labors of study (learning), wakefulness, and attentiveness. For Benjamin, too, Baudelaire dissociated true historical experience in two antithetical moments: that of an anterior time or prehistory murmuring from the distance, and that found in allegories of an objectified time. Time reified appears as the engulfment of history or as human time encroached by natural history (e.g., a geologizing of history that in Baudelaire's verses figures as snowy and icy landscapes of empty time). Benjamin's own writing on food — like Kafka's parables — is also framed within the dialectics of "learning." His texts are dialectical in their combination (either within each text or in juxtaposing one with the other) of the same antithetical moments Benjamin identified in Kafka's and in Baudelaire's work: contamination and purification in the former, the auratic *correspondance* and the allegorical spleen (melancholy about time) in the latter. In Benjamin's "Eating/Food" cycle, "Fresh Figs"—which as seen is a journey through a primeval forest that ends with the act of tearing a letter/writing — finds its *Vollendung* (completion and consumption) in the magical qualities of storytelling (or oral communication) that appear in the cycle's last story, "Mulberry Omelet." Likewise, the witch's soup of "Pranzo Caprese" is absorbed and changed, but not assimilated, in the vulgar yet divine borscht in the eponymous text. Each story is a conglomerate of heterogeneous and conflicting components, some straight "citations" or "quotes" from other texts. "Borscht," for instance, may be read through the filter of yet another text, Benjamin's "Naples." This magical red beet soup condenses the "porosity" Benjamin identified in the southern and, for him, archaic Italian city. The Russian soup transposes the archaic onto the postcapitalist "rural metropolis" of postrevolutionary Moscow to which "Borscht"—the story—also alludes, yet again, intertextually. Both the soup and the text "Borscht" incorporate (quote) Benjamin on Naples and on Moscow (Benjamin wrote an essay on the Russian city and a diary of his stay there in 1926–27).

These dialectical constellations are at work, as I have shown within "Café-Crème" alone: there a hardened madeleine finds its obverse mirror in an imagined remembering of a childhood displaced "elsewhere," which is further identified with the seeping quality of a child's soft (ice) cream juxtaposed to the adult's coffee (hence the story's title). "Borscht," like "Café-Crème," contains a veiled dialectics within itself, which surfaces more evidently if the text is read side by side with "Pranzo Caprese" and "Naples." Furthermore, Lacis truly functions here as the "street" (name) that connects the north and the south, the archaic and the revolutionary. She was indeed Benjamin's companion in both Capri (1924) and Moscow.[67]

According to these textual collages of heterogeneous spaces and times, this soup's magic is at once the same and "other" of the peasant witch's cauldron that Benjamin had tasted in Capri. There contamination by ways of the soup — the primeval brew of life, linked to the mother — and the consequent metamorphosis of the modern Odysseus into swine had generated the experience of an open threshold; here, in "Borscht," a similar "ancestral" and peasant "red" soup — with a touch of white and soft sour cream with the quality of snowflakes — brings the body that eats closer to the heavenly meal, manna:

> First it places a mask of steam on your tongue. Your eyes water and your nostrils drip with borscht long before your tongue captures the spoon. Your eyes have already drunk for a long time from the red "overflow" of this dish, long before your intestines have pricked up their ears and your blood has become a wave which cleanses your body with that perfumed foam. Now they are blind for all that which is not borscht or its reverberation in the eyes of the dinner guests. And you think, it must be sour cream which gives the soup this viscid glaze. Perhaps. But I have eaten it in the Moscow winter and all I know is one thing: snow is in this soup, molten red flakes, the meal of clouds that is akin to Manna, which also once came down from up above." (*Selected Writings*, 2: 361–62; translation slightly modified)

In a series of displacements, from sour cream to the Russian snowflakes, which too fall from the sky like the divine bread given to the Israelites, that is, manna, this earthly soup changes into heavenly. At the same time the paradisial becomes sensually perceivable through the glowing red of borscht.

Both the earthly and the temporal and the heavenly and the eternal mingle manifestly in Moscow's open streets, which Benjamin describes elsewhere as scattered with dirty or melting snow, itself a "true" (impure) manna. On these streets, the "sacred" force of the city's human life and labor is opposed to nature's rigidity. This life animates and empowers nature, for example, the ancestral Russian forest transforms into the glowing logs — the light of fire — in the common woodstoves of the city dwellers, a fire that in Benjamin's essay on Moscow is depicted as oxymoronic force — a dialectical image that refers to art's migratory forms and captures the soul of the beautiful wooden crafts sold on the streets.[68] Unlike Baudelaire's melancholic man prey to the ticking of the seconds, where "minute by minute, Time swallows me, / as the snow immense swallows a body become motionless" (*Illuminations*, 184; translation slightly modified), in "Moscow" time is swallowed by the human activities of the city's inhabitants.[69] Heaven and snow, like manna itself, mix with the earth, the street, the vulgar (vernacular) popular language (and food, i.e., borscht), in short, with the gestures of the Russian/Neapolitan crowds and their myriad activities. It is not a coincidence that manna, while descending from the sky as divine bread, was found on the ground, covered in morning dew, like a mushroom of intoxicating and energizing power, by the Jews on their exodus. The power of this manna-borscht is then that of the divine word, which, for Benjamin, gives itself up as a profane food in the fleeting time of social life. As in "Pranzo Caprese," borscht penetrates the subject who is thus opened to the new transitional — unbound — and indecipherable reality, the new materialist poetry or poetic materiality of ever-transforming Moscow, in Benjamin's experience.

The emergence of a people's art that would cross high and low, divine and profane, had already been the subject of Vladimir Mayakovski in his 1915 poem "Cloud in Trousers" in which this poet raged against hypocritical bourgeois art, interrogated God, and chanted profound love by invoking words — Names — such as "swine" (or else profanities) and borscht. While Mayakovski does not figure among the avant-garde figures Benjamin studied, the critic was familiar with LEF and Pavel Michailovich Tretiyakov (both mentioned in "The Author as Producer"), with Soviet cinema and theater and with the political controversies within surrealism with regard to communism. Furthermore, Benjamin's visit to Moscow in 1926 and Mayakovski's journeys to Paris, where he also met Louis Aragon, indicate the likelihood that Benjamin knew his work, or at least of his work.[70]

In the second part of Mayakovski's long epic in the vernacular (in *volgare*), the lyrical "I" attacks those poets and literati (i.e., the non-cubo-futurists) who believe that the creative process consists in inspiration, in singing, in "boiling down, strumming with rhymes, some sort of concoctions from loves and nightingales" (Mayakovski, 35).[71] The revolutionary poet's rage is directed against the salon's refined poetry in the prologue of "Cloud in Trousers," against both the fiction of "creation" and the beating drums of fashionable styles. In contrast, Mayakovski proposes a metamorphic lyrical "I," which speaks through various voices and from many positions, from "raging on raw meat" to being "irreproachably tender, not a man but a cloud in trousers."[72] This modern young poet takes it upon himself to give a raw material voice to the cries of pain and joy, of anger and hunger, the pangs and the abysses of the city streets to which traditional poets had not yet offered their services. The "tongueless" street, the people and the rhythms of an incessant bursting life, are embodied here, on the verge of their revolution, with their polyphonic vernacular still blocked in their throat. The city itself becomes an uncanny organism with a language that growls—a language that for the modern poet is hard labor to produce: out of this organism's gullet a shout stands erect, in its throat are wedged taxis, and bony cabs bristle. Mayakovski writes: "Krupps and Krupplets paint / a bristling of menacing brows on the city, / but in the mouth / corpselets of dead words putrefy; / and only two thrive and grow fat: 'swine,' / and another besides, / apparently—'borscht'" (ibid.). These are the new yet archaic "words of mouth," the only sacred words. They are sacred because profane, popular, and dirty. The revolutionary poet can use only such words to produce his *anti*poetry, which is less poetry of inspiration than a nervous physical gesture, an insult, a scream, and an action: "the minutest living speck / is worth more than I'll do or did! . . . / I spit on the fact / that neither Homer nor Ovid / invented characters like us, / pock-marked with soot" (ibid.). Here the prerevolutionary city is the site of a new world's emergence, a place imbued with *antipoetic* possibilities, expressed by the rising people. In Mayakovski's recourse to the body's low language—the carnivalesque, open, and polyphonic language described by Bakhtin—lies a powerful ambivalence, or a dialectical moment of reversal:[73] the modern poet can "purify" his or her mouth of the false language of bourgeois poetry precisely in uttering the unspeakable.[74] Likewise, Benjamin's modern/archaic Odysseus, the eater of fresh figs, the reader of Proust, and the traveler to postrevolutionary Russia must taste the seemingly "inedible" to experience another knowledge and another "modern"—or "contramodern"—time.[75]

But how can "borscht" for Benjamin become the material yet magical precipitate of a dialectical image?[76]

A quick look at the "red beet" used for borscht may be of help. It descends from a "wild forebear whose green tops doubtless nourished our own *prehistoric forebears.*"[77] In the Christian era the root, "the versatile plant *Beta vulgaris* started to become appreciated. . . . However, the first mention of a *swollen* root seems to have been in a botanical work of the 1550s."[78] Several features of borscht could have inspired

Benjamin to take it as "the dialectical" soup of postcapitalist and post-revolutionary Russia, namely, that Mayakovskian world—which as I show also borders with the porous city of Naples—located not beyond but aside modernity. Among the features are the ancient—almost pre-historical—times from which red beets descend; the frequency of red beets in popular cooking; the "redness" and the kaleidoscopic combi-nation of ingredients that one finds in several borscht recipes; and the paradoxical uprootedness or transrootedness (the diasporic nature) of the root (the beet), which as borscht itself has crossed many lands and returns in many dishes. Finally, the synthetic and condensed reality of this word/soup mirage, including the red beet's "swollen" nature and the full sound of the foreign name ("Borscht"), exemplifies Benjamin's *Schriftbild* (picture puzzle) and, socially, the world-historical experi-ment of the reality he encountered in the new Russia, "the complete interpenetration of technological and primitive modes of life" ("Mos-cow," 2: 32).

In the *Schriftbild* "Borscht" the instances of rhythmical juxtaposi-tions—from low to high, inside to outside, from one sense to the other, from the ancestral to the revolutionary—are less obvious perhaps than the text's auratic dimension, a dimension, however, that is present only to be estranged. In other words, the potentially auratic phenom-enon of eating borscht—"the wave which cleanses your body with that perfumed foam"—is immediately interrupted, displaced, rendered impossible by the intertextual, dialectically metamorphic quality of the experience condensed in the *Schriftbild* (including the text's mixed metaphors). Less the auratic prehistory of a lost paradise, or the "ante-rior times" of a distant and absolute past, than a distant or displaced, always already *other* past emerges as one live component in the mutat-ing present of this city-organism. The present of Moscow incorporates this prehistory, without succeeding to it or sublating it but in the act of opening itself up to prehistory's afterlife. The present thus incorpo-rates surprisingly new hybrid and heterogeneous landscapes of bor-dering, interpenetrating, but irreducible differences. "In the suburban streets leading off the broad avenues, peasant huts alternate with Art Nouveau villas or with the sober façades of eight-story blocks. Snow lies deep and if all of a sudden silence falls, one can believe oneself in a village in midwinter, deep in the Russian interior" ("Moscow," 2: 42). Nostalgia—which also comes with the snow, "its starry luster by night and its flowerlike crystals by day" (42)—is, however, immediately shot through and interrupted by the warmth of the food tasted in the city's glacial temperature: "When you have finally found a restaurant, no matter what is put on the table—vodka (which is here spiced with herbs), cakes, or a cup of tea—warmth makes the passing time itself an intoxication. It flows into the weary guest like honey" (44–45). Food brings on the intoxicating power of life—the passing of time is experienced as this intoxication—which the severe cold threatens but also covets in anticipation of its dialectical reversal. Mealtimes, Benjamin writes, are moments of expectation and fulfillment, the vertical coordinate that sensuously defines each moment of the laborious weekdays (44–45). The melancholic man's spleen dissolves in this warmth: "And doesn't the warm flow soften the pieces of meat, so that it lies inside you like a ploughed field from which you can easily dig up the weed Sadness by the root?" (362).

Alternatively, nostalgia is interrupted by the surprising artificial and artistic edible reproductions of snow and springtime in the pastry works of fairy-tale cooks, in the author's own words. One indemnifies oneself against the bitter cold, he writes, in the act of tasting counter-mimetic structures of spun sugar, sweet icicles, and the candy-icing flower beds on cakes. Thus the nostalgic aura attached not only to the sublime snowy and starry landscape of this city but also to the rigid white winter morphs into edible installations or montages of seasons (icy flowers, blooming spring in the heart of winter) that in nature are antithetical and sequentially ordered: "Most intimately of all, snow and flowers are united in candy icing: there at last the marzipan flora seems to have fulfilled entirely Moscow's winter desire: to bloom out of the whiteness" (34). Moscow constructs itself anew—its other crafted redness from its natural redness, its other artistic whiteness from its natural whiteness—dialectically, pushing nature beyond its "limits" and mutating its laws into laws of human production.

As borscht overtakes the subject with its magic—the magical power of a dialectical image—in the same way the swarming life of Moscow takes over its streets and the body of the traveler-eater. But, in yet another textual and geopolitical displacement, Moscow's public life (or life in the open) is also juxtaposed to the basket sellers' trading in Capri and to the open streets and houses in Naples: "All this sprawls on the open street, as if it were not twenty five degrees below zero but high Neapolitan summer" (25). Natural seasons are retimed, north and south exchange places, and sacred (high, manna) and profane (low, borscht) reveal their imbrication also in the sensual devotional icons of the Mother of God, "with open belly; clouds come from it instead of entrails" (a "feminized" reproduction of Mayakovski's poem). Furthermore and not irrelevantly, these icons are sold next to the portraits of the defunct Vladimir Lenin (who died in 1924, when Benjamin was in Capri).

So, how does Benjamin write of Naples? Benjamin defined this southern city by its "porosity," a porosity one finds indeed in borscht — the Name, the soup, and the text, all flowing into each other, without end, explanation, or clarification, in a collage of oxymora, mixed metaphors, and nonharmonious synesthesia. Here I turn to that south as the converse mirror of Moscow.

The city is layered both vertically and in-depth, tenement blocks point to the sky, while "at the base of the cliff itself, where it touches the shore, caves have been hewn. As in the hermit pictures of the *Trecento*, a door is seen here and there in the rock. If it is open one can see into large cellars, which are at the same time sleeping places and storehouses" (165). Benjamin locates porosity in yet other interchangeable functions of dwelling:

> As porous as this stone is the architecture. Building and action interpenetrate in the courtyards, arcades, and stairways. In everything they preserve the scope to become a theater of new, unforeseen constellations. The stamp of the definitive is avoided. No situation appears intended forever, no figure asserts its "thus and not otherwise." . . . In such corners one can scarcely discern where building is still in progress and where dilapidation has already set in. For nothing is concluded. Porosity results not only from the indolence of the Southern artisan, but also, above all, from the passion for improvisation, which demands that space and opportunity be at any price preserved. (166–67)

Porosity means above all a temporal perception that is not definitive and unilateral, a perception that — as in dreams — is open to constant transformations and indefinite temporalities. Most importantly, the notion of porosity as illustrated above helps Benjamin to reinforce his view about progress as decay and about natural decay as the emergence of progress. A work in progress displays its "deconstruction" (*Abbau*), as it were, as a necessary part of its construction, its temporal nature, and its incompleteness. Similarly, in these Neapolitan spaces inhabited by the passing of time, porosity implies a life that puts itself on stage or, rather, that makes itself the public stage of human time, that is, of history and change, as life's opportunity. A particular notion of historical change and action emerges:

> Buildings are used as a popular stage. They are all divided into innumerable, simultaneously animated theaters. Balcony, courtyard, window, gateway, staircase, roof are at the same time stage and boxes. Even the most wretched pauper is sovereign in the dim, dual awareness of participating, in all his destitution, in one of the pictures of Neapolitan street life that will never return and of enjoying in all his poverty the leisure to follow the great panorama. (167)

The fourth wall in the theater of life vanishes, actors and viewers can interchange positions. No History, with capital "H," is put on stage, only little stories of poverty in which one becomes aware of one's own position as both a witness of history and as an actor in it. And this awareness of being part of a never-returning "picture" of history is associated with human *action* through Benjamin's interpretation of Brecht's epic theater: "In the center of its experiments [of the epic theater] stands the human being in our crisis. . . . What emerges from this approach is that events are alterable not at their climactic points . . . but solely in their normal, routine processes, through reason and practice" (585).[79]

Naples's theatrical porosity—the city as theatrical "square" of history (*Schauplatz*)—is then also reminiscent of the variety show, the theater much beloved by the avant-garde (think of Futurism, but also Dada and surrealism); porosity finally presents itself most clearly in the temporary art of street chalk-painting, and, by association, it again surfaces in the equally temporary art of eating:

> In a few moments the picture is erased by feet. Not the least example of such virtuosity is the art of eating macaroni with the hands. This is demonstrated to foreigners for remuneration. . . . So everything joyful is mobile: music, toys, ice cream circulate through the streets. . . . Irresistibly the festival penetrates each and every working day. Porosity is the inexhaustible law of the life of this city, reappearing everywhere. A grain of Sunday is hidden in each weekday, and how much weekday in this Sunday! (168)

Although Benjamin does not associate Naples—and the carnival this city is to him—with modernity, his gaze on it is the surrealist materialist historian's. Accordingly, he finds in Naples the physiognomic traits of a social body—as he will later find in the Parisian arcades—that is deeply rooted in time as passing and in the historicity of that passing.

In this constellation, eating spaghetti is a material art of time, the spectacle of which, in Naples, involves monetary exchange. Spaghetti eating is on display; it is about using one's own hands like the virtuosi of the temporal art of song who, from the bourgeois opera stages, moved to the street as theater of life. On this stage — the squares — they act just like the chalk painters who draw rapidly, leaving behind only self-erasing traces. Not unlike Dada's willful turn to children's games as art, or like much performance art of the sixties and seventies, for Benjamin these street virtuosi engage in everyday activities and actions shared by everyone. Anyone and everyone is a participant (like in the epic theater) and in history. Everyone also participates in a market economy, however, where everything circulates, just like the money of the paying customers/and viewers. Yet the art proposed by these virtuosi, while indicating a substratum of familiarity and collective grounds, also exposes these physical sculptors of time — and their audience of participants, also eventually spaghetti eaters — to some "foreignness": it thus hints at alienation in marketability.

This dialectical view of the city with its shifting spaces and ambivalences presents Naples as both mythical and cunning. Thus Benjamin underscores the transitory and multiple temporalities of the forms life takes in this city, not unlike life in Moscow, which, he stresses, is just as porous in its openness — doors are never closed in communal spaces (30–31) — and which is characterized by "unconditional readiness to mobilization." In postrevolutionary Moscow, "shops turn into restaurants and a few weeks later into offices. This astonishing experimentation — it is here called *remonte* — affects not only Moscow. It is Russian. In this ruling passion, there is as much naïve desire for improvement as there is boundless curiosity and playfulness" (29).[80] The festive days, like Sundays, always already presuppose and are immersed in the daily activities — the human actions — of history. Porosity is then a key term for depicting these archaic and contramodern cities, a term that indirectly affects the soup/text "Borscht." Through porosity the metamorphic spatial–temporal dimensions of Benjamin's city and food constellations are made clear.

Naples's porosity captures the historical physiognomic expression of a prehistorical — metamorphic rather than phantasmagoric — southern capitalism that could be compared to the prehistoric capitalism of the nineteenth-century Parisian arcades. Unlike in the Paris arcades, Naples's prehistorical porosity brings to the surface the intestinal churns and metabolic transformations of the slumbering body. These occur in an active and awakened (aware) body, the body of a lived asynchronous history; the same is true of Moscow's postcapitalist "belly" that—in the example of the borscht's eater—"pricks up its ears." In other words, the stomach's rumbling in Benjamin's quote in the introduction to this chapter is heard and listened to by all in Moscow as in Naples. This stomach's digestive operations, without shame and innocently, take place in public, on the street, namely, on the stage of history. History is a collective happening. In the dialectical constellation north–south, that is, Moscow–Naples, to which porosity gives shape, the late stage of capitalism is bypassed or blasted on the threshold opened by both primeval capitalism and the postcapitalism of the rural metropolis, that is, of borscht-manna.

At the same time, the Russian experiment is a laboratory of space–time and does not stand for the absolute end of history, the *Finis* that inaugurates the reign of chaos in Benjamin's "Food Fair" review (see *Selected Writings*, 2: 139). In contrast, the soup, as Benjamin writes, "gradually pervades you entirely, while with other foods a sudden cry of 'Enough!' abruptly causes a shudder to pass through your entire body" (362). Against saturation, the soup allows one to experience the porosity of Moscow, the space–time of openness and innocence beyond historicist notions of progress, historical tasks, and absolute knowledge. Progress is thereby reconceived again and again as the process of learning how to walk, which, as Benjamin remarks, is exactly what the foreign visitor in Moscow must do: "At first there is nothing to see but snow, the dirty snow that has already installed itself, and the clean slowly moving up behind. The instant you arrive, the childhood stage begins. On the thick sheet of ice of the streets, walking has to be relearned" (23).[81]

Conclusion. Epic Incorporation: From Storytelling to the Epic Theater

The incompleteness of the historical project—as of the experience of eating borscht—shares the features of storytelling. Benjamin writes that in storytelling the anonymity of the narrator and the subjectivity of the narration go hand in hand; the mystery of life and death is incorporated in a story without explanation; and epic remembrance (*Erinnerung*) guides the network of multiple, endless, and varied accounts

told by the storyteller.[82] In accordance with this idea, Benjamin concludes the thought-figures on "Eating/Food" with a fairy tale — titled
"Mulberry Omelet" — in which a cook summoned by a king transforms
his cooking art into the narrative art. This artisan in the end cooks up
a story about the impossibility of reproducing a lost taste (or meaning), that of a dish the king remembers from his childhood. Hence not
the cook's food but his final story about loss satisfies the king's mnemonic appetite. Benjamin applies this principle to his own food stories, which he cites in the opening of "Mulberry Omelet": "I shall tell
the following story for all those who would like to try figs or Falernian
wine, borscht, or a peasant meal in Capri" (*Selected Writings, 2*: 363).
In short, he tells his readers that the texts they just read can only teach
ways to experience the food described rather than *the content* of the
experience of tasting it. Experience can't be repeated or reproduced.

As a written form of storytelling, "Mulberry Omelet" is devoted to
orality in all its aspects. It is a classical oral tale: Once upon a time
there was a king. So the story starts. The king believes he will find happiness (the gratification of his desire) only if he is able to taste again the
very same omelet he once had as a child while escaping with his father
during a war. An old little mother (*Mütterchen*) cooked the omelet for
both of them, thus providing respite, shelter, and energy while they
were on the run. Presented with the challenge, the cook tells the king:
"Of course I know the secret of the mulberry omelet. . . . Despite all
my efforts my omelet would not taste right to you. For how could I
spice it with all the tastes you enjoyed on that occasion: the dangers of
battle, the vigilance pursued, the warmth of the hearth and the sweetness of rest, the strange surroundings and the dark future" (363). At
these words, the king remains silent, then dismisses the cook "richly
laden with gifts" (364). The king spares the cook's life because the latter's failure in cooking provides the king with nourishing words that
do not substitute for the food of the past, always already lost, but are
a new, different "medium." The cook's words stand for an absence,
the same as Benjamin's food stories, which stand for the absent food
they mention. They do not provide the reader with the meaning of life,
the knowledge of food, or the possibility of identifying with the experiences narrated. They only convey perhaps that knowledge is about
knowing to learn.

The king's story also underscores the issue of the irretrievabil-
ity of the origin of pleasure and meaning. The child first forgets the

Mütterchen who rescued his and his father's life and then, when as an adult he initiates a search for her, she and what she stands for, that is, his happiness, are gone. The cook's story both illuminates and breaks the fetishistic fantasy of the king's aggressive demand to find yet another object that would disavow the loss of this mother/material pleasure. The cook in fact seems to satisfy the king by feeding him his own words, or else by replacing the oral pleasure of eating with an oral narrative about an irretrievable (and incomplete) meaning. The king takes satisfaction in words — an art that communicates because of its distance from an original source. The cook's retirement — which concludes the series of stories — signifies the retreat of a production and consumption of meaning confined to reproducing fetishistic forms of pleasure and the life of the culinary art (in the life of the cook) beyond the obsessive demands of the return of the same.

   Like the cook's words, the borscht in the eponymous story equally avoids procuring immediate satisfaction while enhancing desire: it intoxicates with warmth, expanding one's bodily confines. In "Moscow Diary" Benjamin speaks likewise of the difference between some painting and certain photography (he does not refer here to Eugene Atget's or August Sander's photographs.) Benjamin mentions his liking for the early cubism of Paul Cézanne.[83] As he states, one cannot project oneself into these paintings and thus empathize with the fragmented space; rather, space hits the viewers from a great variety of viewpoints, leaving them exposed to the intoxicating experience of self-liquidation or decentering, thus, in Benjamin's words, to windows opened on a possible recognition as the remembering of a distant other past. As shown in this chapter, eating and storytelling — like Cézanne's paintings — are not the expression or source of a pure auratic experience. Rather, they situate the subject on a threshold of intoxication that reveals the auratic experience as dissonance, dissolution, and consumption of both the subject and aura. One's own stable location in time and space is therein dissolved. In its place a nonsynchronous aura appears that in its emergence (and liquidation) provokes spleen together with its immediate devouring.

   Benjamin does not write a cultural critique or sociology of food, not even when he seems to suggest this in "Decline of the German Cooking Art" (in *One-Way Street*) and "Food Fair." Instead, incorporation (as technology, tricks, and art, *Frühstück* as *Kunststück*) coincides with reading as physical operation on and through the body, an operation that is disruptive, even disturbing, yet always magical/alchemical. For Benjamin, physical reading (reading physically) is necessary, for it translates the potential of dream-thoughts into the language of decision and action. At the core of Benjamin's operation of incorporation is a shattering moment of profane illumination — found in profane intoxication — which breaks through passive and reified consumption (contemplation) to awaken in the subject the dissonant noncognitive knowledge Benjamin labels "ascetic animal." With this knowledge Benjamin hopes to counter assimilation (identity) and empathic models of reading or reception. Laughter and humor are also a counterforce during intoxication. Both break the engulfing spell of enchantment (and mysticism) — whether provoked by profound sadness or narcissistic empowerment — which Benjamin views as the dangerous mythical moments also present in intoxication (the moments to which the surrealists succumbed) (216). In this light, incorporation strategically posits the body as open medium between inside and outside, as a primitive internal technology for producing sensorial critical activity. Incorporation would then seem to correspond to a bodily expression of Brecht's techniques of "estrangement" (*Verfremdung*) and dialectical turnaround (*Umfunktionierung*), according to Benjamin's interpretation. Like the epic theater, thus incorporation retranslates "the methods of montage — so crucial in radio and film — *from a technological process to a human one*. It is enough to point out that the principle of Epic Theater, like that of montage, is based on *interruption*" (584–85). The primitive body-technology of incorporation and the medium of cooking are for Benjamin the first physiological, creaturely potential (at once individual and collective) to transform and change (e.g., to translate and to innervate) those desires rooted in the body for an expanded life in modern times. In conclusion, for Benjamin, the body that incorporates is the first instrument of an epic (re)production of reality, the first stage where dialectics expresses its force and is practiced. The avant-garde "body" then performs dialectics publicly and politically on the stages of collective history.[84]

◀⬛ DANIEL SPOERRI'S *GASTRONOPTIKUM*

D A N I E L   S P O E R R I inaugurated Eat Art in Düsseldorf with the Spoerri Restaurant (1968) and the Eat Art Gallery (1970).[1] Eat Art does not illustrate but actualizes the flows of energy and multiple temporalities passing from the singular eating body to the collective body. Years before Spoerri invented Eat Art, he had produced the trap-painting that already expressed these ideas. Trap-paintings are collages made of planks or tables on which Spoerri glued dishes, silverware, glasses, and leftovers of an actual meal. The trapped objects and their bases were then hoisted vertically, like paintings.

While Spoerri's trap-paintings used food to mark, initially, a temporality of chance and personal action, they gradually came to stand for constantly unfolding variations and self-reproducing desires. Together with his Restaurant Galleries and the later banquets, the trap-paintings as a first expression of Eat Art reorganize the temporality of art history and history. In Spoerri's works history returns, yet it is remade anew, through the stomach. In short, the gastronomic and physiological worlds of consumption provided Spoerri, and others who occasionally participated in the Eat Art project (among others, Joseph Beuys, Dieter Roth, Arman, and Robert Filliou), with a direct means to visualize and stage the returns and turns of art, especially the avant-garde. The proliferating yet dialectical and self-reflexive productions of Eat Art constitute its novel character and point to a critical relation between the neo-avant-garde and the avant-garde.

Spoerri, a Romanian whose Jewish father was a victim of the Nazis, grew up in the German-speaking area of Switzerland. Since his youth, Spoerri and consequently his art have had a nomadic character. He has been a dancer, a choreographer, a poet, an editor, an artist, and a cook. Like his late-1960s European colleagues — that is, the French

New Realists, Arte Povera, Jean Tinguely, Roth, and Fluxus, among others, Spoerri engaged the object and chance in his work to confront historical and artistic time. Chance, in the historian Reinhart Koselleck's view, appears in modern history as *this* history's contretemps. Spoerri's Eat Art as it intersects with chance also constitutes a contretemps: Eat Art both slows down time to its point of stasis and accelerates it. Paradoxically, both Spoerri's food trap-paintings and banquets work as archaeological investigations of the meaning of the *contemporary* in history and, more specifically, in the history of art. Spoerri takes changes in time and by chance occurring in the world of food—that is, in culinary institutions, in gastronomic writing, in taste (personal, social, and cultural)—and interpolates them with art to investigate both the culinary and art (their institutions). Thereby he engages the notions of repetition and reproduction—both *multiplication* and invention—as these pertain particularly to the neo-avant-garde, to *his* contemporary art.

Accordingly, Spoerri's Eat Art was a crossroads for post-1945 European artistic production. Eat Art does not reject the legacy of the earlier avant-garde that it sets out to incorporate and digest. Eat Art sets itself up as a fragment—the waste—of a post–World War II world rapidly being devoured by capitalist consumer society and its tempos. Through its display of poverty and an unstoppable desire of production and consumption as one process, Eat Art's operations critique history-as-progress and suggest a way to think of art as occurring apart from a history founded on punctual breaks. Eat Art presents itself and the neo-avant-garde as a minor language within contemporaneous languages of art and culture. This language derails artistic historical classifications and stable orders (including the divisions between avant-garde and neo-avant-garde) as well as the economic ones presumed in capitalism (e.g., the stability imagined to exist in the logic of exchange value). It also undermines those stable notions of traditional, national, and subjective identity. In becoming minor, that is, in choosing to speak a minor language of dis/taste, Eat Art especially critiques the museum and transforms this institutional space of art (a space for visual consumption) into a temporary site of collective production and consumption of art. In the irreverent manner of Dada, Eat Art leaves its waste for the museum to exhibit, aestheticize, and turn into an original work.

This chapter situates Eat Art within the context of post-Duchampian approaches to the object, especially the context of European new realism. Spoerri both appropriated and displaced wide-ranging theories of culture such as Claude Lévi-Strauss's notions of *bricolage* and of the raw and the cooked; Gilles Deleuze and Félix Guattari's concepts of deterritorialization and minor literature; Michel Foucault's interpretation of "archaeology" (but also archaeology as in common parlance); and Georges Bataille's *informe* as disordering and impoverishing. These historical and theoretical reference-points are relevant, for they highlight the temporal features of Eat Art as well. A key role is also played by the artistic principle of multiplication, which in Eat Art links up with chance. The notion of multiplication changes during Spoerri's artistic career. One of its best expressions — as far as multiplication relates to time — is embodied by the food-multiples.

In my analysis of the food trap-paintings, and the role chance and temporality play in their conception, I focus more generally on Eat Art's archaeology, including the Restaurant Galleries. After the food-multiples, in which food-multiplication (or in Deleuze and Guattari's words, proliferation) finds yet other manifestations, and after Spoerri's Restaurant and Eat Art Gallery, I then take up Eat Art proper. However, since Eat Art defies a chronological reconstruction of its spiraling events, the next sections all attempt to break with any linear account.

Spoerri's Deterritorialized Territory: The Trap-Painting

The critic and artist Alain Jouffroy's comments about Spoerri's art in the 1960s serve as a foil for the present discussion of Spoerri's early Eat Art. Not only was Jouffroy among the first to write about Spoerri — together with the critic Pierre Restany — but he also interestingly introduced, at the time, the notion of poverty in relation to the trap-paintings. Furthermore, and most important, he associated Spoerri's early work with temporality through some notion of archaeology, as well as death. In addition, Jouffroy is one of the critics and friends with whom Spoerri still dialogues.

A Savage Diet

Upon seeing Spoerri's early trap-paintings in Paris, Jouffroy connected the disconcerting collages with the concept of a neo-avantgarde's *nourriture sauvage* (wild diet).[2] In the eighties, he remembered that the artist Friedrich Hundertwasser, upon his arrival in Paris, was living in the same hotel as Spoerri, in rue Mouffetard. Like Spoerri,

Tinguely, Filliou, and many other artists, Hundertwasser was poor in those years and occasionally ate stinging nettles of necessity. This "found food" became the material for a happening that Jouffroy and Jean-Jacques Lebel organized in 1960, wherein Hundertwasser prepared this wild plant for an eager audience.

By *nourriture sauvage* Jouffroy literally means the diet of wild leaves (and, metaphorically, of wild activities) on which these artists of the sixties and seventies survived. His notion, however, also invokes Lévi-Strauss's *Savage Mind* (*La pensée sauvage,* 1962), which Jouffroy uses in 1988 to think back to that earlier time. He intends to demystify and displace both Western art and its systems of knowledge by bringing home the wild and savage art. The concrete logic of the savage mind, which Lévi-Strauss illustrated through his concept of *bricolage* and which for Jouffroy translates the neo-avant-garde artists' wild diets, resists the naturalized and abstract cultural orders and discourses pervading Western industrial culture.[3] *Nourriture sauvage* debunks the classification systems and the distinctions between aesthetic and culinary taste in art. At the same time, the internal opposition between lavish (good) and poor taste is also questioned. Jouffroy's notion of *nourriture sauvage* brings to mind a primary, raw material. The wild diet that characterizes contemporary art at this time, however, is disconnected from the idea of naturalness. As is the case with *bricolage,* the wild diet deconstructs binary oppositions such as original versus derivative, high versus low, self versus other, including the divide between historical avant-garde and European modernism, or even avant-garde and neo-avant-garde.[4] By both concretely appropriating and referring to the pun in Lévi-Strauss's original title, *La pensée sauvage,* Jouffroy's idea of *nourriture sauvage* — a wild thought and a wild diet — is associable with a concreteness of materials and solutions, an otherness of making/thinking art that, as Lévi-Strauss pointed out, makes use of what is at hand. (The pun of the anthropologist's title is in the fact that, in French, "pensée" means both "thought" and "pansy," the flower, like Hundertwasser's stinging nettles.) These materials include not only those that are found but also those that come from the remnants of preceding systems. In the case of the avant-garde–neo-avant-garde relations, these remnants could belong to the historical avant-garde.[5] The delayed return and rearrangement of these elements (as mnemonic fragments) are shared by the concrete and wild diet of the neo-avant-garde, when one deals both

with objects and with food proper. Their return involves the metamorphosis of the scattered elements' function, their displacement into
a fully new context, and thus an asynchronous temporality. The basis
of the *nourriture sauvage* (as far as objects and food are concerned) is
in the scraps and remainders of industrial and consumer society that
interfere with the continuity of history. Hence *nourriture sauvage* calls
not for a return to nature or primitivism in art but for a concrete yet
reflective recourse to food as another discourse of taste. This other discourse "within" art — overtly purported by Eat Art — is the neo-avant-
garde's chance to find its point of underdevelopment (*Minor Literature*, 18), namely, a line of escape from the ill-fated teleological path
that has led and leads still any avant-garde into the museum. But,
through the wildness and poverty, to adopt Deleuze and Guattari's
terminology, "a line of flight" may be available even once Eat Art is
"trapped" in the museum. The artists who embraced *nourriture sauvage* — those artists who ate and used stinging nettles and so forth in
their art/life — adopted a strategy of devouring, that is, enacted a physical and temporal consumption of traces and cultural myths, against
the conservation and preservation of the same myths, including the
myth of self-identity, authorship, originality, heroic art.[6] In particular, Spoerri's neo-avant-garde Eat Art, for example, expressly sets out
to digest consumer society's own incessant digestion, almost as if in
a preemptive move.[7] For Jouffroy, Spoerri becomes, at this time, the
most coherent example of Lévi-Strauss's idea of concrete logic, which
Jouffroy reads as the new grounds for a contemporary art production
not yet imaginable, hence still fully outside the realm of "institutional"
contemporary art. Poverty and the stomach are the means through
which the neo-avant-garde derails Western consumer society and its
culture. Jouffroy's association of this art with a savage diet thus comments on the artistic context of the sixties, the artist's diet representing for him this new art's radical otherness from the traditional art
historical establishment, but also this new art's equally valid modes of
operation. The neo-avant-garde shows that these modes were already
at work in the classical avant-garde, although they were not overtly
emphasized. The neo-avant-garde's savage diet, as discussed by Jouffroy, expresses these concerns in a concrete language. The notion of
savage diet as *bricolage* offers an important introduction to how to
think about food in the neo-avant-garde: as the raw material of this
art and its philosophy and politics.

Looking and the Trap-Painting:
Time, Movement, and Stasis

Spoerri's Eat Art that—against his own insistence—I consider born with the early trap-paintings in 1960 is the most significant neo-avant-garde example of systematic engagement with post–World War II Western art from within the framework of the *Gastronoptikum*. Spoerri himself used this neologism. I read it as a gaze on art and the world that is displaced with respect to the eye. In the manner of Tristan Tzara's self-portrait, this gaze finds its eye in the stomach, or else the laws of the stomach are juxtaposed to those of optics. In 1967 Spoerri had titled *Gastronoptikum* a series of articles and stories about gastronomic curiosities he published in *Die Weltwoche*. Spoerri's idea was based in the eighteenth-century panopticon, the architecture of a total, all-encompassing view. Spoerri modified the panopticon, however, to become a *Bauchschau*—that is, a view from and of the stomach's labyrinths and instruments. Panopticism was the ground of collections of objects and curiosities worthy of being seen. Spoerri called his *Gastronoptikum* a collection of curiosities, which were specifically to be found in the familiar realms of cooking and the kitchen, and in collections of everyday tools (knives or egg peelers). Since the early sixties, these collections accompanied some of his exhibitions of trap-paintings (e.g., at the Galerie J). Spoerri applied the conception of the cabinet of curiosities (*Wunderkammer*) to the everyday activities of cooking and eating, which for him became experimental total laboratories of production and transformation, of art as much as of life. The project of the Spoerri Restaurant also pivots on this idea.[8]

When Jouffroy first saw Spoerri's trap-paintings, he believed that the "richness" of this art's poverty derived from the space in which Spoerri's simple boards (supports) were both made and exhibited. Spoerri's hotel room appeared constricted, with low ceilings that looked even lower because of the weight of all the trap-paintings hanging on the walls. In addition, these boards that filled the room had a double life: first, they were functional, serving as Spoerri's breakfast table; second, once they were hung on the walls, their mundane function changed radically. Most of all, they looked like petrifications, or, in Jouffroy's language, they were "landscapes of death."[9] According to this critic, Spoerri's trap-paintings literally turned extreme materiality into extreme spirituality. Literally, that is, because the artist turned these archaeological collages 90 degrees, namely, from the horizontal to the vertical plane. In my view, however, the turn does not erase the materiality of its base.

Jouffroy's first sighting of Spoerri's trap-paintings prompted him to comment that they conveyed a refreshing desire to forget art, "a kind of break with everything that presented itself as art at that time" ("Souvenirs sans douleur," 12). Accordingly, Spoerri's work appeared to demonstrate a will to leave behind art and pursue instead a kind of archaeology. This enigmatic, Saturnine tendency was new to the neo-avant-garde, Jouffroy writes, and did not seem to square with either contemporary art's formal tendencies (abstraction) or with its *informel* ones (including action painting). It also did not appear to suit the aesthetic of nouveau réalisme.[10] While Restany underscored the constructivist aspect of Spoerri's work, explicitly characterizing it as *bricolage,* Jouffroy situated Spoerri's trap-paintings also among the works of the nouveaux régardeurs, or the new observers.[11] Hence Spoerri's trap-paintings would demand a new gaze:

> For the first time one looks at things frontally, it is a way to face things, rather than dominate them. By hoisting these objects vertically one can discover a hidden meaning, or a lost one. Suddenly, everyday life becomes a form of objectivity that the instant alone cannot grasp.... [This is Spoerri's] change of optics which he then develops with his *optique moderne.* For me this is the beginning of the *revolution of the gaze*: no longer having to accept the everyday subjugation to utility as rule of perception. Instead, one must discover a new angle in relation to all things, a new manner of deciphering. To make objects for *reflection* rather than forgettable objects of consumption. ("Souvenirs sans douleur," 12; my emphasis)[12]

Looked at from this perspective, for Jouffroy, the "poor" tables express a metaphysical attitude toward the object and bear the character of lived experience. On this view the trap-paintings are metaphysical because they preserve what is perishable and thus convey the ongoing human struggle with time and death. The trap-paintings would offer disposable objects a chance to live on. Spoerri initially contested Jouffroy's stress on death and metaphysics. More recently, however, he has embraced the notion of death as relevant to his work.[13] Yet metaphysics does not seem to be part of Spoerri's archaeological investigations of the tensions between the living and the dead, art and death, human temporality and cosmic or natural history. The gap between these areas is instead Eat Art's location. This, I argue, is the Foucauldian

sense of "archaeology" that Eat Art unfolds: from the early trap-paintings, via the *Catalog Taboo* (*Katalog Tabu*) and *The Grocery Shop*
(*Krämerladen*), up to the banquets. Then one has to ask: what kind
of death do the trap-paintings capture? Or, rather, more generally: in
what relation does death stand with respect to consumption, specifically the consumption of food?[14] Moreover, what statement about art
and about its role in the contemporary world is made by the particular knot of time–consumption–death detected in the trap-paintings?
For trap-paintings are, undoubtedly, contemporary appropriations or
perhaps *expropriations* of the avant-garde's collages, of Dada readymades and of surrealist found objects.

In 1960, when he invented his trap-paintings, Spoerri considered
himself a collaborator of chance (*Handlanger des Zufalls*). He had
started making art precisely because he never thought of himself as
an artist but, rather, as *a metteur en scène des objets* (stage director of props). Through the trap-paintings he materially attempted to
unclothe objects of their fetishist aspect, whether the latter lies in their
artistic nature or in their commercial origins. According to Spoerri,
the dialectics between stasis and movement that grounds his trap-
paintings contributes to liberating the desire imprisoned by commodity fetishes, thus liberating the particular object into thing or, even
more generally, into movement itself. By trapping the banal, halting
the everyday, and especially putting on view the work of consumption
in the chance-instants of tables, objects, and food, Spoerri thought he
would thus whet the audience's desire for movement and life.

Spoerri's own view of the trap-painting as movement frozen is a
recurrent feature in his art, including Eat Art. Spoerri arrived in Paris
after a career first as a dancer and then as a stage manager. He never
entirely abandoned the ideas of working on movement and time, as
one does in dance, and of displaying situations, as one does in the
theater. The connections among objects (props), words, and actions
are already relevant in his early experiments with concrete poetry (in
the fifties) before becoming evident in Eat Art and the staged banquets
of the seventies and eighties. Spoerri drew on dance and the theater to
explore a dialectical look at art objects — the dialectics between motion
and stasis — and their relation to time and changing audiences.[15]

However, one needs to complicate the notion of simple, binary
oppositions to grasp their temporal element. For one thing, if the
archaeological element of the trap-painting — archaeology as Jouffroy

intends it — is paired with the dialectics between stasis and movement, then the trap-painting's affirmation of temporality counters any metaphysics. Spoerri's trap-paintings accelerate, through an archaeology of the contemporary, the time of consumption — putrefaction and disorder — which, for example, the Dada collages (and their poetics of disgust and indifference) had set forth. Furthermore, both Jouffroy and Spoerri mention petrification: Spoerri first refers to it in relation to pantomime; then, interestingly, petrification returns as *"Pompeification"* in direct reference to the fate of this ancient town. As Spoerri explains, the element of duration one finds in this settlement near Naples that was suddenly destroyed and petrified by volcanic lava (and is an important Italian archaeological site) lies in an imaginative construction of a geologic civilization that is at once found again and imagined anew from clues about human history. History must be excavated, extracted from natural history, from the halted flow of the lava that had descended uninterrupted from a raging volcano.[16] Archaeological artifacts never put an end to the telling of their stories, which — as fragmentary as they are — can always be actual and rethought, reconsidered with each new excavation, with each new set of historical, theoretical, or scientific insights. Spoerri's food trap-paintings as petrified landscapes of food make the same point with regard to contemporary (art) history.

In the trap-painting, life is caught as the process of being consumed by/in time and also as the outcome of food consumption, the result of a kind of productive material consumption that attempts to preserve life as it constantly remakes itself day after day. Food consumption, like the art it generates, is hence reiterated in time, over and over again, without ever provoking, however, the same experience or the same effects in the producers and the consumers of food, food that never shapes the same body the same way twice. In effect, the consumption of food at the source of the trap-painting produces the everyday as an infinite series of intense — both colorful and threatening — moments. The trap-paintings are threatening because of their immobility that, as Jouffroy remarked, is reminiscent of death. These are all originals that metamorphose in time eventually to their vanishing point (during and after their exhibition); they embody human time and its "important" passing, which Spoerri captures again and again. They are also almost automatic self-producing series, variants of the act of eating. The trap-paintings carry chance remainders of urban acts of consumption that might be worth a future archaeological excavation. Irony and paradox qualify Spoerri's idea of archaeology in the trap-paintings: archaeology is an ongoing process of incomplete excavation. As he suggests, this is the task of the neo-avant-garde.

According to Jouffroy, the trap-paintings' archaeological aspect breaks with art history. He sets these works apart from contemporary *art*'s projects, including the legacy of the avant-garde. But what if the trap-paintings' archaeological dimension highlighted a counterintuitive temporality *for* contemporary art and, in fact, involved most directly the avant-garde as it related to the sixties neo-avant-garde? The trap-painting's archaeology of everyday remainders presents an accelerated production, consumption, and again production: the production of a meal, its consumption, and this consumption's act of production of a temporal art (the trap-painting). The trap-painting then points to the fast modern tempos of life and art and displays the disorder of these tempos as if they were accelerated and condensed into an instant. The trap-paintings return over and over again, like everyday meals. The "present" is both there and immediately devoured. Not only do the trap-paintings' everyday objects transform at once contemporaneity into an already long-gone past, a residue of contemporary industrial societies (Western nations were still industrial in the sixties), they also condense the avant-garde's appropriations of everyday objects, in the temporality of consumption of the everyday. Spoerri makes this devouring of everyday objects and of the avant-garde explicit in his flea market trap-painting series. "The highlight of this series," he observes, "was the unwanted, chance and modern illustration of Lautréamont's famous phrase 'Beautiful like the encounter of a sewing machine and an umbrella on a surgery table.'" On a vendor's table, he finds "a Bauhaus-mirror, a baroque bed-head, a bicycle (the *Roue de bicyclette* by Marcel Duchamp), a chalk-nun, an old paper with Hitler's photos, a small painting with forget-me-not flowers (a painting within a painting) and much more." For Spoerri, "all this releases an astounding chain of associations" (*Anekdotomania*, 98; my translation). Comte de Lautréamont's notorious umbrella and sewing machine, as well as Duchamp's readymades (the bicycle tire and the urinal) appear in a found trap-painting from 1966. The forward-looking avant-garde has been devoured by and in *time*, and now in the trap-painting's landscapes of everyday ruins this avant-garde may be excavated from chance-instants of used objects found on tables and in flea markets.

The trap-painting presents itself as a tabula rasa, yet one that, paradoxically, always already bears the traces of experience. The tabula rasa was the avant-garde's principle for radical change, in constructivist terms—of art as construction rather than creation. Spoerri's trap-painting reappraises the tabula rasa principle (along with art as construction). Spoerri, however, now applies the principle to the *historical* avant-garde itself, which becomes the neo-avant-garde's *prehistory* as well as one of its possible futures. But the trap-painting is a particular kind of tabula rasa: the avant-garde's language figures paradoxically as a collage of avant-garde crumbs, leftovers of the neo-avant-garde's act of eating. For Spoerri and other participants in the project, the injunction "to eat art" makes the avant-garde lessons productive or, rather, makes the avant-garde proliferate as in an economy of used things refunctionalized, an inexhaustible economy of recycled leftovers.

While Spoerri acknowledges the ugliness and sadness that emanate from these waste landscapes, for him the trap-paintings are mostly about spurring the desire to move and thus the will to live: they do so by defying gravity.[17] Tzara, as seen, considered glue—*la colle*—the essence of the avant-garde collage. While Spoerri's early trap-paintings share the glue/collage with the avant-garde, his trapped objects appropriate the avant-garde to launch it into a different territory. The glue fixes these objects first, and then enables them to be suspended vertically. The act of suspension defies gravity and liberates these object-situations from having to occupy, necessarily, either the horizontal and contiguous space of objects or the vertical plane of art objects and perspectival view. The viewers see the effects of their consumption hanging vertically in front of their eyes, not beneath their gaze, as it happens with ordinary tables. The collage "takes off" from the walls of Spoerri's hotel room; in French "take off" translates literally as *dé-collage*. These boards of poverty rooted in the artist's *nourriture sauvage* transform into acts of reinterpretation of at least two crucial avant-garde principles and materials: (1) the glue and (2) the disparate objects of the collage.

In Deleuzian terms, Spoerri's neo-avant-garde trap-paintings are the point of underdevelopment within the avant-garde itself, a new point of flight. However, they are not punctual but a serialization of unique, unrepeatable moments (because of the key work of chance in them) captured as such only a posteriori.[18] In effect, the avant-garde is both present and outlived in the trap-paintings, which include their own neo-avant-garde *décollage,* an affirmative image ex-*negativo,* as it were, of the avant-garde.[19] Thanks to an archaeological gaze on the contemporary — archaeological also in the Foucauldian sense of investigation into modernity's discursive formations — the savage temporality and willed poverty of the trap-paintings erase and reshape themselves before they can ever be fixed or even thought.[20]

As works of chance, Spoerri's trap-paintings underscore that the movement at the dinner table is entropic and that each table's order will never be replicated. At the same time, the series of trap-paintings proliferates in multiple directions, resulting from collective banquets and individual meals. This becomes particularly evident in the Eat Art banquets. While people are eating and thus engaging in generating the trap-paintings that will later hang on the wall, other trap-paintings hang on the dining room walls, whether the walls of a gallery or that of Spoerri Restaurant. The trap-paintings thus break the unidirectional flow of time down to minimal unrepeatable units: the situations produced by the dirty cups and saucers, glasses, and silverware are different at each moment, hence in each trap-painting. These contaminations of objects, as Spoerri calls them, are proliferations of variations of variations produced in and by time, rather than instants of time that can be arranged historically, sequentially, or consequentially. Spoerri calls them contaminations because the trap-paintings emerge out of specific and uncontrollable contacts that ensue among heterogeneous objects. If the trap-painting's guiding principle is ultimately chance, then entropy — within one situation of objects and among trap-paintings in time — is their law. No logic of causality is applied here.

Jouffroy saw in the metaphysics of the trap-paintings a force to stimulate thinking. He contrasted reflection with consumption. Reflection blocks or halts the consumption of the trap-paintings, and of everyday objects, as forgettable commodities. In my view the trap-painting, however, enshrines a corporeal and memorable consumption. This does not necessarily disagree with Jouffroy's viewpoint. Consumption is not the antithesis of thinking. Rather, it means a reflective appropriation and inhabiting of the present. Spoerri's territory is produced through a series of acts of consumption that, once they are situated within the realm of the arts, are refunctionalized as the production of "serial originality," perhaps ironically. This production, however, inflates the original while making it possible. Consumption thus figures as an act of art-production and self-production and, as such, resists the everyday consumption typical of commodity fetishism and exchange value. At the same time the act devalues the museum's fetishism of originals that are locatable according to historical epochs or periods in an artist's life. Both the trap-painting and, later, the more ephemeral Eat Art present art — and its reproductive desire — as an attempt to counter the division between production and consumption. Thus Spoerri seeks to reappropriate a person's, a community's, a city's, and his guests' waste as art-product, and consumption as production itself. These never complete acts of *bricolage* — the work with leftover and found, consumed objects — confirm the subject's potential to overcome the alienation disguised in the novelty of the commodity fetish. In the trap-painting itself, consumption of and by time becomes a productive operation that questions consumerist forms of consumption and their economy of abjected waste.

Territorium: *From Personal Time to Collective Times*

Spoerri names the trap-painting his *Territorium*. This territory is a space that the subject occupies momentarily, a space seized away, albeit in passing, from the flow of time to catch time in its singular moments. Each singular moment becomes precious. In the trap-painting the subject observes itself as situated at different points in time. The objects, tools, or, simply, things are now glued onto an indistinct support that — through their presence — they refunctionalize into the base of a painting. They thus produce a different view (from a new angle) of the subject who involuntarily placed these things there and now finds or sees them as its own, a part of itself, formerly unnoticed. In Spoerri's words:

> My art, if you wish to call it art, was to have discovered my own territory [*Territorium*] in the objects that I had made. These objects are my territory; they are the fixations of my life. . . . These objects were no longer everyday objects. Rather, they were hanging on the wall; one could look at them and contemplate them. This was no longer a sordid territory, a poor student's hotel room, the room of someone who does not know who he is, and lives in a tiny seedy room or something. . . . I was rich because I could observe what

I had in front of me and that was me, well, at first . . . this is the reason why, at first, I did not get out of myself.[21]

The composition or, rather, in Spoerri's language, the situation of objects escapes will. Thus the trap-painting—through chance (*haz-ard*)—also produces an image of the self (the artist or diner who eats) as other than himself or herself.[22] In this otherness of the self Spoerri finds his mobile and changing spatial–temporal territory, made up of varying situations that become visible thanks to the principle of trapping time in chance situations. The unintended outcome of Spoerri's act of consumption in the meals has the power to set in motion interpretations, or rather vistas, of both the artist and the environment of objects in which he lives. These panoramas of the self in time do not depend on the artist's viewpoint. As Spoerri writes, he now can observe his territory as other, as art, as hanging on a wall.

Spoerri's intuition was to hoist these landscapes of remainders on the wall. The vertical trap-paintings first produced his personal *Territorium* and then inserted it into the world of art and the art market. Walter Benjamin had already remarked about how the disparate materials of Dada collages, caught within the frame of one painting hanging on the wall, embodied a different temporality than that of an ordinary painting. Spoerri's vertical food trap-paintings are not paintings, but they use paintings' exhibition value—as well as collage's exhibition value—to insert the temporality and mobility of the everyday into the temporality of art.[23]

The trap-painting, with its temporality of the present as always already archaeology, is grounded in historical collective time rather than in physiological notions of the body's deficiency as formulated by Dada. Temporality is specifically addressed in the trap-paintings composed with the leftover of *collective* meals such as those that ensued from the sixties banquets staged in Paris and Zurich. Here Spoerri cooked several meals that were consumed by invited guests (different menus for different dinners with different guests each time) for a few days. Subsequently, trap-paintings were exhibited in the same locales that had been transformed into restaurants for producing the art, and displaying the art as well. Art is the production of collective consumption. Not just one time but the disparate times of art's production and consumption as well as food production and consumption meet in the hybrid space of the Restaurant Galleries.

The Restaurant Galleries

Spoerri experimented with the Restaurant Gallery idea first at the Parisian Galerie J in 1963 (the gallery of the New Realists) and then at Bruno Bischofberger's City Galerie in Zurich in 1965. Both performances illustrate the multidimensionality of these Restaurant-actions. In particular, the meals prepared in these spaces juxtapose the synchronic and diachronic temporal axes through the concept of variation. By compressing in its own space–time, quite a few of Spoerri's experiments as he had practiced them through the years and by anticipating the future of Eat Art (the actual Spoerri Restaurant opened in 1968 and the Eat Art Gallery in 1970), the Restaurant Gallery offered a variation on Spoerri's artistic principles. On the occasion of the Gallery J exhibition Spoerri wrote:

> In the Restaurant of the Gallery J I could illustrate several of my previous ideas, not just individually, but combined: a) the tables in the restaurant became trap-paintings; b) as in my "grocery shop," regular foods (meals) are exhibited as artworks; c) the works of art are in transformation (and transient), just like all remainders, as shown by my trap-paintings in Schwarz's Gallery which were eaten by the rats; d) everyone could have produced at will his own trap-painting under my license; e) the sense of taste was directly involved, in addition to touch and sight, etc. (*Daniel Spoerri Presents Eat Art*, 46; my translation)

Spoerri transformed the Gallery J into a restaurant for eleven days. There he cooked a different meal with special menus for ten to twenty people each day, and at the end of each day he glued one trap-painting. During the eleven days the critics who, for Spoerri, have the function of *trait-d'union* between artists and public, took the role of waiters.[24] In addition, with this first theatrical Restaurant Gallery Spoerri began his practice of thematic meals pivoting on key questions. Among the menus he proposed to his guests were national/regional courses no longer widely common and hardly taken to represent a national or regional cuisine. For example, *testicules à la crème* were the centerpiece of his Franco-Niçois menu. Such a gesture questioned the meaning and boundaries of France's centralized culture and the place of regional cuisine within national gastronomy. Similarly, his Romanian menu revealed strong Eastern European influences that, according to Spoerri, had been assimilated into national Romanian cuisine. In short, Spoerri's menus insisted on the nonhomogeneity of national cuisines, a concept at the core of his *Gastronomic Journal* (*Gastronomisches Tagebuch*), annotated during his stay on the Greek island of Symi.[25]

At the Restaurant of the Gallery J one could also have a first taste of the *Menu Travesti* ("costumed" or "disguised" menu) in which the courses were doubly masked: the dessert came first and the appetizers last. Yet this was only apparently so: in fact, the dessert only looked like one; in reality, it was an appetizer masked as a dessert. With this gesture Spoerri first returned to the Futurists who also had jokingly reversed a meal's sequence of courses, and then he turned that very gesture upside down by inverting their inversion through a parodic mimetic costuming. Among the menus cooked and eaten in those days was a meal expressly focused on temporality. Spoerri called it the "prison meal." It was based in *simultaneity*: Spoerri copied his menu from prison inmates' diets and served this meal to his guests at the same time the prisoners were eating, thereby offering the diner the possibility of sharing the inmate's experience or, in other words, their "life-time."

An early version of the homonymous banquets (that returned in several variations, for example, in *Le Dîner de la Société Homonyme*) was already evident in the thematic meals at the Gallery J.[26] For example, Spoerri devoted one such banquet to Raymond Hains, another New Realist artist.[27] In this menu, the names of the dishes — after famous personalities such as Charlemagne and Napoleon — were accompanied by dishes named after avant-garde and neo-avant-garde artists. For example, among the classical (avant) cheeses figured Gala Claudel and, for dessert, éclairs from the bakery André Breton; among the neodishes were a "Potage lettriste" and "Coquilles Saint-Jacques au gratin, Mahé de la Villeglé" or "Pommes de terre en robe Deschampes." At the homonymous banquets, Spoerri parodied the historical practices of naming dishes after historical characters, actresses, or musicians often indeed forgotten in history (e.g., we don't recall that "peach Melba" was named after an actress esteemed by Auguste Escoffier). Spoerri multiplies this practice of naming by expanding it: he does not limit himself to naming all dishes and beverages in honor of some public figure; Spoerri also invites these individuals to taste "their" dishes, creating a doubling effect that displaces history from its fixed location. In the case of contemporary artists' names, one would physically incorporate the two avant-gardes, contemporary and modern (present and past) works. These early temporal motifs become crucial in the Eat Art happenings proper: the banquets, much reprised and expanded, comment over and over again on the cycles of return of the avant-garde as that body of art always in need to be taken in, digested, and reconstituted anew from its own ashes or leftovers.

To mark the Restaurant's official closing at Gallery J, Spoerri exhibited the trap-paintings—one for each night—at the end of the eleven days. The trap-paintings put an end to the living act of physical consumption; they literally stood there as the waste and memory of the cycle of nutrition at the root of all life. What is more, by hanging on the wall and testifying to the banquets and consumption passed, the exhibited trap-paintings—these instantaneous and transient works—were transformed into a kind of memento mori parallel to the diners' act of consumption. The guests had the opportunity to purchase their own table: as trap-painting, albeit at the high cost of the labor put into it (the production of food, the items on the table, and the hard work of gluing), roughly two thousand francs. Spoerri's "Certificate of Authenticity" (*Brevet de Garantie*) accompanied the tables. The certificate guaranteed that each table had been assembled according to the core principle of trap-painting, that is, *chance*. Above all, the certificate guaranteed the consumers' collaboration in the production of art, also an essential element of Spoerri's food works and his notion of the multiple. The certificate importantly added Spoerri's signature to a chance trap-painting while detaching the proper name from the actual producer of the trap-painting, the artist-maker. The consumers—diners—produced the composition (or contamination of objects). Spoerri signed the work of chance that put the objects in that composition according to the diners' random acts of consumption and interventions in space (the space of the table).

Spoerri had originally come up with the notion of certification in 1962 when asked by the Danish gallerist Addi Koepcke to participate in an exhibition in Copenhagen. Spoerri produced a certificate to allow *Koepcke* to glue trap-paintings, since the transportation of these artworks with crumbling leftovers was no easy task. Spoerri continued to use certificates on other occasions. For his retrospective at the Centre National d'Art Contemporain in Paris in 1972 he encouraged anyone to trap his or her own "chance situation of objects," which he would then certify with his name. The curators did not hesitate to show their fear of an inflation of "Spoerris." Still, the artist inspected ten works and signed five certificates for those that he judged were composed according to chance (and not the author's overcreative hand). Years later a collector who had just acquired a Spoerri at an auction threatened to sue the auction house upon discovering that the trap-painting just bought had been made by a twelve-year-old and his father: because a certificate of authenticity accompanied the work no lawsuit followed. On another occasion, Spoerri signed a blind certificate that he entrusted to Bischofberger who, in turn, asked Julian Schnabel to prepare a trap-painting and added Spoerri's certificate afterward. Spoerri thus certified at least one trap-painting (it was Schnabel's desk) without ever having seen it. (He saw it first at the Tinguely Museum in Basel in 2001.) These anecdotes point to Spoerri's games of alteration — if not quite subversion — of the art world's idioms of authenticity and originality where signed works should not proliferate. With Spoerri's certificates the proper name proliferates and produces in/authentic originals much as the trap-painting does in itself. The art market is challenged to mobilize quickly and respond to the multiplication of authorized copies (by anonymous or famous names) as well as crumbling, nontransportable, and hardly restorable food trap-paintings.

The early trap-paintings and gallery banquets already involved the viewers as producers who acted under the purview of time and chance. The Restaurant Galleries, which thus were collaborative actions, as to an extent were the trap-paintings, added to the simple trap-painting the element of taste, taste for both food and art. Finally, the Gallery J's exhibition of trap-paintings, following the restaurant activities, presented art as mnemonic trace. Contemporary art offered itself up as ready for immediate excavation: the trap-paintings were certainly contemporary, having been produced just a few days before their exhibition. Yet the landscapes of leftovers and waste demanded archaeological investigation, especially for viewers who saw the trap-paintings and had not participated in them. The trap-painting is a relic of contemporary society, Pompeiified in an instant, morphed into the *reliefs* (both the leavings of a meal in French and the bas- or haut-reliefs of art) of its own ancient past, ancient, that is, from the perspective of a future already here.

The performances after Paris, in New York (1964) and Zurich (1965), varied slightly. In New York the concept of the multiple, as derived from Spoerri's previous experiments with concrete poetry and his *Auto-Theater,* was more prominent than the Restaurant Galleries. The *29 Variations on a Meal: Eaten by,* as Spoerri called this action, featured well-known artists and performers (including Arman, Duchamp, Allan Kaprow, Michael Kirby, Roy Lichtenstein, Ben Patterson, and Andy Warhol). For this event that lasted four days and took place at the Allan Stone Gallery, Spoerri prepared thirty-one (rather than the anticipated twenty-nine) tables. Not all artists were invited on the same day. Spoerri arranged the tables identically and in the same colors (blue, red, and yellow). Each invited guest was to eat alone. The guest was free to decide when to end the meal, whereupon Spoerri glued the table and the remainders to trap that particular moment. The trap-painting was then authenticated by Spoerri's certificate. In this case, however, Spoerri added to the certificate the inscription "eaten by" followed by the diner's own signature. Thus the artists invited created a work of art that at same time was trapped

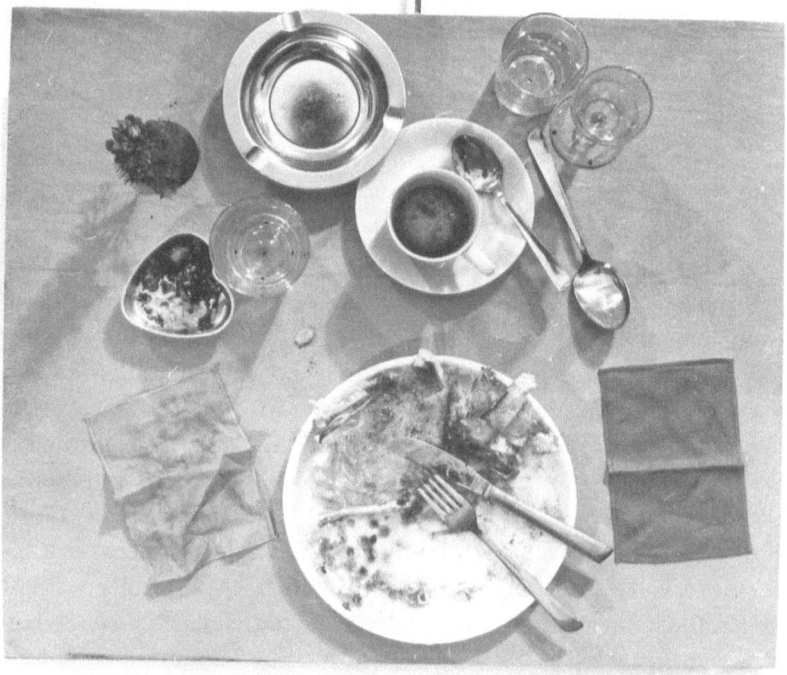

Daniel Spoerri, "Eaten by Duchamp. 31 Variations on a Meal," New York, 1964. Collection Armand P. Arman. Courtesy of Die Schweizerische Landesbibliothek, Archiv Daniel Spoerri. Copyright 2008 Artists Rights Society (ARS), New York / ProLitteris, Zurich.

by Spoerri's fixing of the artists' leftovers. Their signature is, yes, a guarantee, along with Spoerri's certificate, of the new trap-painting's exhibition value. Yet, as the *passive voice* of "eaten by" demonstrates, the big-name artist's signature is less crucial than the act of eating and the composition on/of the table by *chance*. One finds in these trap-paintings eaten by Duchamp, Arman, Warhol, and Kaprow, and so forth no typical "signature" features of these artists' work but only the plain traces of a meal organized formally by chance. If the trap-paintings alone thus proliferate and, with the aid of Spoerri's certificates of authenticity, Spoerri's signature also proliferates along with the trap-paintings "eaten by," then these other artists' signatures multiply as appendixes to Spoerri's own. But Spoerri's is itself—in his own words—an attendant to chance: "And I can afford to take pride in the accidental since I am only its conceited and at the same time modest 'attendant.' ... Attendant to the accidental—that could be my professional title. But I must admit that I am not the first. That's fine with me—I don't consider even originality as absolutely necessary."[28] Needless to say (and paradoxically) these signed trap-paintings were the most notorious and most sought-after by the public and galleries, which showed the fixity and stubbornness (but also endurance) of the art market, its tendency to revert to the same patterns of classification, naming, and thus value, at which the *29 Variations on a Meal* had ironically poked fun.

In Zurich, a year later, Spoerri varied the New York action. He asked his guests to bring their own table settings (plates and cutlery) from home. Here the action lasted only a few hours. Unlike at the Gallery J, the invitation cards specified that the trap-paintings—shown at the end of the day—were the *"pièces de resistance"* of these meals. With this specification Spoerri clearly declared that he was putting the trap-paintings up for consumption again while indicating that each one of them was still the distillate of that particular meal, a constitutive part in it. Through their shifting temporalities—between consumption and production—these collective actions physically contaminated the homogeneous empty time of the museum.[29] The immobile time of a linear art history was interrupted by the introduction in it of the messy processes and labor involved in collective production, by the disorder generated by consumption, and then by the visual consumption of art as exhibition of decaying organic remainders.

Trapping Time: Art = Rat

The trap-painting brings to its extreme Charles Baudelaire's defini-tion of the modern painter: the man who captures the Zeitgeist of a constantly passing — consuming and consumed — present, a man of his own time. Modernity in German is called the *neuste Zeit,* the newest time, a superlative that demands to be always at the top of one's own time, ready for an impending future that will soon be past. Yet in Spo-erri's personal and collective temporalities duration also matters. The duration of the trap-paintings is, however, traumatic. It entails the col-lapse of history into nature, which of course for Spoerri instigates, not unlike Benjamin, its dialectical reversal, an awakening to processes of reification. The trap-paintings dialectically point to these processes and to their interruption, their trapping.

The trap-paintings defy their preservation as originals both for their frailty and for their proliferation. One trap-painting highlights not only the complexity of temporality and chance but also collective agency and collaboration. Arturo Schwarz, the owner of a prominent avant-garde art gallery in Milan, was an early collector of Spoerri's trap-paintings, which he exhibited in the artist's first personal show in 1961. Spoerri had shown trap-paintings there before together with other artists at the 1960 Festival d'art d'avant-garde in Paris. As Spo-erri remembers in his *Anecdoted Topography of Chance* (1962), after his solo exhibition, Schwarz sent him a letter in which he sounded alarmed.[30] In the letter the collector asked Spoerri to replace the organic ingredients of his trap-paintings, such as bread, because rats had pene-trated the gallery's storage and had devoured the trap-paintings' lefto-vers. Spoerri declined Schwarz's request — and the offer of money for a restoration. In Spoerri's view, if the principle of the trap-painting is indeed chance, then it must surely apply to so-called finished works. The artwork is never complete when chance and time are taken into serious consideration because the artist's hand that does *not* paint and the rats become the agents, or at least each other's collaborators. Mod-ifications brought about by time, water, corrosion, dust, and so forth are the producers of the work.[31] Accordingly, Spoerri acknowledges in retrospect the rats of the Schwarz Gallery as artists and changes the title of one of the trap-paintings to *Les os du Szekely guljas, in col-laboration with the rats* (1960). Just a trace of the devoured bread is visible today, a mark of the trap-painting's nonidentity with itself in

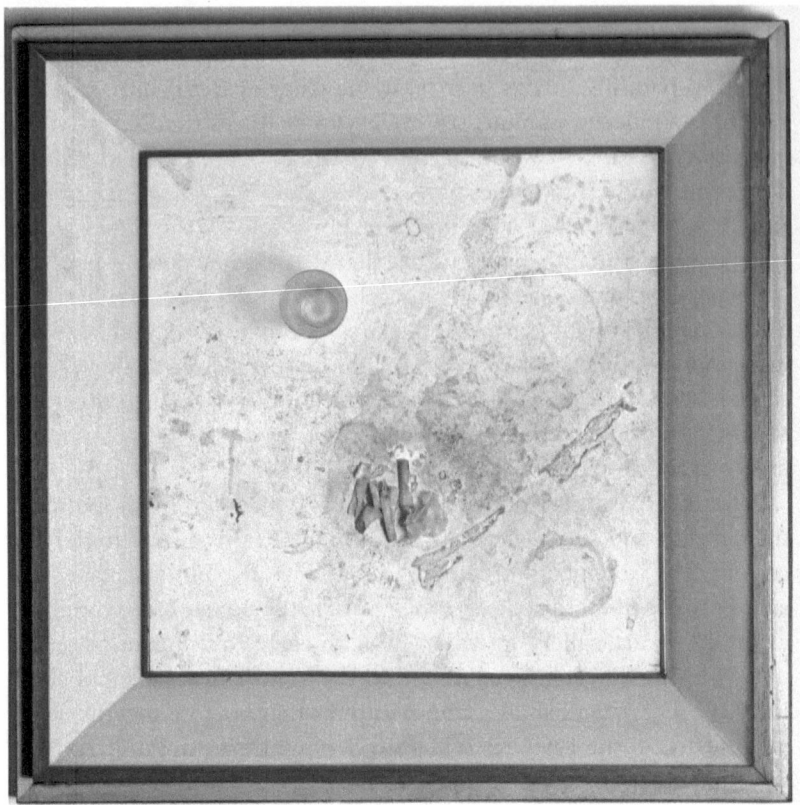

Daniel Spoerri, "Les Os du Szekely guljas, en collaboration avec les rats de la Galerie Schwarz," 1960. Private collection. Courtesy of Die Schweizerische Landesbibliothek, Archiv Daniel Spoerri. Copyright 2008 Artists Rights Society (ARS), New York / ProLitteris, Zurich.

time. (In this case he never changed the artwork's original date.) This act of chance and time-devouring repeated itself at the Bischofberger Gallery in Zurich. Spoerri labeled these trap-paintings, *En collaboration avec les rats de la galerie Bischofberger. 1966–1970.* This title explicitly declares the work to be an operation in and of time, a work in progress and in decay, or rather of progress as decay.

According to Spoerri's personal mythology, chance struck again to reveal — almost in surreal fashion — that collaboration *is* indeed the producer of Eat Art, from the food trap-paintings to the Eat Art multiples: the "found" anagram RAT = ART, ART = RAT underwrote Spoerri's approach to art and to rats, to production as active consumption.

Deleuzian Spoerri: Acts of Deterritorialization

The role played by time and chance in the trap-paintings is crucial to an understanding of Spoerri's Eat Art as well as their role in the relations between the avant-garde and neo-avant-garde. As mentioned, while the notion of *Territorium* and the trap-paintings appears to stress territoriality, "fixation," and immobility, in fact, *because* of time and chance, they point to their opposite, namely, movement (*décollage*: ungluing and taking off). Deleuze and Guattari's theoretical works *Anti-Oedipus* (1972) and *Kafka: Toward a Minor Literature* (1975) provide a theory of deterritorialization as a set of psychic and textual operations that resist the fixed and fixing paradigms of subject formation and culture formation typical of modern Western societies.[32] They criticize the common interpretations of the subject (and modernist texts) based in Sigmund Freud's oedipal construction and its triadic resolution of conflicts.[33] Instead, they posit a liberated subject centered on productive desiring machines or assemblages, as they aptly call them. Deleuze and Guattari, moreover, adopt terms, such as precisely *assemblage,* from the neo-avant-garde and explicitly turn to examples of contemporary art for their own theories. In talking about the assemblages, they stress that these desiring machines proliferate and produce both multiple lines of escape and multiple points of connection. They thus move away from territorialization, entrapment, absolute signification, and monodirectionality. Deleuze and Guattari explain thus that desire is "not a form, but a procedure, a process" (*Minor Literature,* 8).

Spoerri's assemblages practice deterritorialization through proliferation. They constantly shift between time's movement and arrest. At the same time, they find in chance the productive stimulation of desire, the motor that engenders a mobile, always protean, and changing territory. In particular, the trap-paintings' proliferation presents the viewer with the paradoxical notion of multiple trappings, multiple trapped meals. It is paradoxical because, through its multiplication, the principle of trapping turns into its opposite, that is, it provides lines of escape from artistic and temporal entrapments, as Spoerri indicates in the following statement:

> My trap paintings should create discomfort, because I hate stagnation. I hate fixation. I like the contrast provoked by fixating objects, to extract objects from the flow of constant changes and from their perennial possibilities

of movement; and this despite my love for change and movement. Movement will lead to stagnation. (*Theories and Documents,* 310; translation
slightly modified)

However, by the midsixties, Spoerri felt that the trap-painting had
indeed trapped him in a closed art world, so he tried to escape Paris.
In the summer of 1966 he left for the remote Greek island of Symi, a
few miles off the Turkish coast. This trip was not a form of fleeing or
departure but, rather, a fuller immersion in the temporality of the trap-
painting.[34] The first time Spoerri considered seriously the idea of opening a restaurant was indeed on Symi (while he had the idea of a gallery
in which to show Eat Art in New York, again "abroad"). In Spoerri's
own account, at the peak of his success he wanted to understand how
one arrives at the disorder of a table after a meal; thus, he decided he
needed to learn about cooking and all things culinary, including those
discourses of and around the kitchen such as gastrosophy and gastronomy.[35] Interestingly, he chose for this enterprise a faraway place,
far from Paris.

Spoerri does not discard the trap-painting concept; instead, it
returns in the banquets following Spoerri's year and a half stay on
the Greek island. Upon his return, the trap-painting's dynamic of stasis and movement took a turn. The poverty of the savage diet and
the productive "desert" that Spoerri experienced and experimented
with in Symi situated the trap-painting in a different temporal economy. For example, in the Spoerri Restaurant, one trap-painting hanging on the walls not only invoked movement by internal opposition
within the boundaries of the "painting" itself but also was situated
within a world of movement and multiple temporalities, namely, in
an actual restaurant where production and consumption coexist. Here
the trap-painting figures as neither end nor beginning. While an early
trap-painting (the product of previous meals) is hanging on the Spoerri
Restaurant walls, food is still being cooked in the kitchen. Simultaneously, anonymous guests mingling with friends and colleagues consume the food served: in short, in this locale, the past, the present, and
the future coexisted, or overlapped. As Deleuze and Guattari clarify,
escape is not fleeing, "a useless movement in space, a movement of
false liberty; but in contrast, flight is affirmed when it is a stationary
flight, a flight of intensity" (*Minor Literature,* 13). The stationary trap-
painting that already contained within itself the dialectic between

colle and *dé-collage* now gains in intensity because it is itself caught in its act of becoming, or in the "production of a continuum of intensities in a nonparallel and asymmetrical evolution" (13).

The restaurant idea did not emerge in Paris or one of the epicenters (with New York and Tokyo) of the neo-avant-garde. It was born out of the trap-painting's own *décollage*.[36] In Spoerri's work, food is explicitly a complex world of temporal and cultural relations, relations of production and consumption that pervade art as itself both a means of survival and a discursive realm. Thus Spoerri's food is *not* territoriality, as it is for Franz Kafka in Deleuze and Guattari's interpretation. Spoerri's gastrosophical and gastronomic project, as it is conceived on Symi, is rather a project of writing (*écriture*).

The textual element is essential to Spoerri's approach to food, cooking, cuisine, and gastronomy. For food to become part of a thinking process, writing is indispensable. Spoerri's writing—especially his *Gastronomic Journal*—is polyphonic and shifts between the present, his own and that of the Symi islanders, and a variety of pasts, not necessarily his own: the history of various recipes and foodstuffs as presented in the *Larousse Gastronomique* (which he cites often), in ancient Roman cookbooks, and in the local Greek traditions. Even if the framework is that of a journal, putatively personal, private, and written in the first person, food—as the fragmentation of self-identity as well as of history—compels the author to draw a more complex picture. In writing about food, food is born for Eat Art as deterritorialized, not unlike the way in which writing had also multiplied the notion of trap-painting in *The Anecdoted Topography of Chance*.

To adumbrate my argument—pursued elsewhere—about Spoerri's stay on Symi, his act of becoming Symian does not invoke the kind of primitivism adopted by so many modern artists.[37] His "primitivism" is attuned with Deleuze and Guattari's notion of "becoming animal." Spoerri's becoming Symian/Simian meant that he disentangled his artwork from the stability of artistic and cultural roots, from paradigms and fixed histories that, in his *Gastronomic Journal* (and his "Objects of Magic à la Noix"), are disclosed as useless or shameful constructs. From this site of self-abolition, Eat Art is born to interrogate taboos, boundaries, classificatory systems, and to order, in short, the organization of culture and art. Spoerri considers art's core to lie in a primal form of survival against fear and death, which food captures so well.

While cooking and eating his minimal but syncretic Simian food, Spoerri experiments with old and new recipes. However, to be faithful to its intrinsic gastronomic reason, the journal abandons any external, pregiven gastronomic dictum as "essential" guiding principle and allows itself to be woven by the intricate and unimagined networks of coincidences and circumstances that regulate the island's cycles of food production and consumption. This leads to positively remasticated uses of precisely those classical gastronomic texts informing this artist's culinary culture rather than to either their "ad hoc" assimilation or their complete dismissal: remembering recipes or rereading them from within the changed context demands a practical but especially imaginative readjustment. Then the journal does not deny or erase differences. Instead, these are immediately incorporated and reelaborated in the stories that arise with every adaptation of every recipe. The text constitutes the trace of the eater-artist's renegotiations of the space–time coordinates that inform his gastronomic experience. This also gradually constructs itself less around the eater as "autonomous subject" than around cooking and consuming as transformative moments between the subject and the subject's location in the in-between of cultures.

Spoerri's culinary encounter — before, during, and after Symi — is clearly both material and textual, the one because of the other. Spoerri's art making is closely linked not only to his theatrical perspective but also to his extremely reflective and conceptual view. One detects an Adornian antivisual liberation of sight from sight's own representational constraints — and of food from both its "natural" and industrial territoriality — which occur through Spoerri's recourse, in the Symi journal, to mobile texts and invented stories of powerful, everyday objects/fetishes (as in his "Objects of Magic à la Noix").[38] Here Spoerri investigates the roots and taboos of Western culinary traditions — and thus of cultural and economic systems of production and consumption — by experimenting with food's texts as much as with food. Modern humans now reproduce themselves through a remixing of the civilizational discourses that they have ingested, that have shaped them, and that they have forgotten or repressed. What is most significant is that Eat Art — from the trap-painting on — comes into being as neither a quest for an archaic origin nor a purely anthropological investigation of cultural difference. Rather, Eat Art engages the particular time-sensitive languages, or idioms, that construct our perceptions of the world.

Through deterritorialized food Spoerri brings to an extreme the work initiated in avant-garde ironic and concrete self-reflexive art, an art of production and construction, rather than of creation. The trap-painting and then Eat Art proper, namely, the food-multiples, the banquets, and the Spoerri Restaurant, remake themselves and history day after day. They appropriate the language of the avant-garde and test it against the contemporary consumption of art by time and the market. If Spoerri's trap-painting is a collage that takes off, then Duchamp's principles of indifference and chance are deterritorialized when offered to contemporary mouths that grind and chew them, and to stomachs that literally metabolize art and remake it through the body. Eat Art is the moment when the avant-garde and the neo-avant-garde give themselves up to their own temporary abolition as the ultimate act of production in the commodity age.[39] At the same time, Eat Art destabilizes the territorialized view of food's relation to national and individual identity as natural or necessary. No language is fixed forever in one idiom or grammar but is in fact made and remade "in the mouth," in acts that include writing, annotating, personalizing, and the sharing of recipes. The language of the avant-garde, including the neo-avant-garde and Eat Art itself, is received and transformed in the mouth, too, through always contemporary "utterances," voices and linguistic productions that belong to no one and to all at the same time, proliferations of proliferations that, in movement and time, are modifications without originals.

Deleuze and Guattari's ideas — deterritorialization, becoming animal, and the proliferating series — complement Foster's model of a parallactic reading of avant-garde–neo-avant-garde's relations.[40] One could, that is, reread Deleuze and Guattari's theorizations as proliferating parallactic visions. Foster focuses on constellations that shift "figuration" with respect to the eye of an observer who moves in time and thus changes point of view. He stresses the notion of a spatial–temporal disconnect between subject and object, a disconnect that illuminates the object in a different light. Foster's idea rewrites Benjamin's temporal concept of constellation to speak specifically of the neo-avant-garde in relation to the avant-garde. For their part Deleuze and Guattari often invoke neo-avant-garde practices — their contemporary art — through which they then re-view Kafka. They refer to Kafka's texts as *experimentation* (*Minor Literature,* 7) and, quoting Kafka's story "A Report to the Academy," they conclude that "a writer isn't a writer-man; he is a machine-man and an experimental man" (7). In reading this, who would not be tempted to think here of Tinguely's 1959 "Meta-Matic" painting and drawing machines?[41] Deleuze and Guattari also explicitly mention the Fluxus artist John Cage when looking at Kafka's "Description of a Struggle." They refer to Cage — another member of the neo-avant-garde — to make clear the operations of deterritorialization at work in Kafka's language and the liberating function of "unformed" sound. Cage's music — that is, his *4'33"* concert — becomes a way to refocus the canine concert with no music that takes place in Kafka's story (*Minor Literature*, 5). Deleuze and Guattari turn its "pure sonorous material," which returns in Cage as his unshaped music, into a crucial mechanism of Kafka's writing. Finally Richard Lindner, a contemporary artist who also contributed to Eat Art, is cited in *Anti-Oedipus* alongside several other neo-avant-garde artists, writers, and philosophers of modernity (including Henry Miller and Allen Ginsberg as well as the older philosophies of Marx and Nietzsche, and the modernist Bataille and Antonin Artaud, among others). And last but not least, the notion of flux, as it is taken up in the sixties by Fluxus via Bataille, is a starting point in *Anti-Oedipus* (*Minor Literature*, 6). One could argue, in line with Foster's idea of the parallax, that Deleuze and Guattari deterritorialize Kafka — modernism — from a territorialized framework. They *décollage* this writer's work away from historically bound frameworks and mobilize his texts by reading backward and forward at once, thereby rendering operative in Kafka's texts some of the mechanisms that emerge later, as if from a forgotten Kafkaesque world, in the neo-avant-garde. Hence Deleuze and Guattari reposition both the neo-avant-garde and Kafka's texts with respect to each other and to the present. This author's minor literature, from this perspective, also helps shed new light on the workings of contemporary society without having to be considered prophetic. Similarly, Foster speaks of the deferred action of the avant-garde that is comprehended anew in the neo-avant-garde of the sixties and seventies. Spoerri's work, which involves chance, temporality, and the materiality of food as well as food's complex intertextuality, operates along these same lines.

But can Spoerri's trap-painting, an early form of Eat Art, be read as the initial force of a productive, *sur*-individual and historically collective kind of remembering (*Erinnern*)? Can remembering, joined with the desiring machines of proliferation, halt the risk of indefinite multiplications (such as one finds with the capitalist movement and mobility of commodities)? And can remembering counter a fixed entrapping memory that characterizes the market of souvenirs? Without entering the specifics of Spoerri's biography, or Deleuze and Guattari's anti-oedipal schizo-investigations, one could situate Spoerri's actual deter-ritorialization, his nomadic spirit in terms of both residence and art, within the homelessness of many avant-garde artists both before and after the war: it suffices to state here that Spoerri lost his home and language in his childhood, because of his family's flight from Romania under Nazi occupation and resettlement in Switzerland (his mother's native country) after the father was murdered by the Nazis. For many artists, however, this was not the homelessness of someone forced into exile but the affirmative homelessness that descended from the over-whelming desire to keep desire on the move as productive energy and synergy with the real. At the end of the fifties, many artists went lit-erally hungry to live with art—as seen in the case of Hundertwasser who devised his nettle performances. Similarly, Gordon Matta-Clark opened his restaurant Food in 1971 in New York to support those less famous artists who were struggling to survive in the art world.[42]

For Spoerri homelessness had been real. After his arrival in Swit-zerland with his mother and siblings, he was cared for by his mother's brother, a professor of theology. Homelessness for Spoerri stemmed from a subterranean trauma of loss—the father's language and his own (Romanian) is not unlearned but repressed, as he explains in inter-views. But his memories of an authoritarian father also play down this loss and counteract it with his desire to dance, to be free, to be beyond the purview of the Father's Name: a single role, a location, a stable identity, or, as he writes in "Objects of Magic à la Noix" "the desire for instability and change" (*Mythological Travels*, 7). Thus he doesn't speak just one language but several, as if languages were all neces-sary but temporary homes. In Spoerri's case, it is the power of desire found in movement and change that generates his multifarious pro-ductions. Yet, because of the temporalities involved in his work with food, his deterritorializations and proliferations of food-multiples also anxiously remember. Remembering nonetheless is an unrestrained flow that rejects self-identity and instead grasps itself again in chance situations, chance territories, and broken languages. Thus remember-ing, in Spoerri's proliferating Eat Art, operates as the rumblings of the neo-avant-garde's digesting of the *Name* of the avant-garde (its own too!) and, not unlike Dada's call for indigestion and cannibalism, disturbs the triangulated (oedipal) economy of production, consumption, and evacuation typical of consumerism. Foster speaks of some postwar art, for example, art brut and Cobra, as both registering and disavowing the trauma of history (the war, the Holocaust, the atomic bomb). Through his nomadism, Spoerri—as some of his trap-paintings reveal—registers such trauma.[43] However, he does not disavow trauma and the relation of history with the avant-garde. Rather, he has both take flight into new forms of desire, after he entraps that history temporarily.

Multiplying Originals: Inflating the Art Market

In their attention to the ties between production and consumption, Spoerri's various food performances generated a peculiar kind of art object: the food-multiple. *The Grocery Shop* (*Der Krämerladen*), Spoerri's Restaurant, the banquets, the gastronomic texts, his Eat Art gallery, and his early writings—in particular his *Auto-Theater* (1959), the journal *material* (1957–59), and the *MAT Editions* (1959–65)—offer insights into his interest in food's complex relations to multiplication. Though the theatrical and poetic works had nothing explicitly to do with food, they were nevertheless informed by the idea that art—especially the notion of originality—is the outcome of a random collaboration between an object and its audience. Spoerri's and others' food-multiples, for example, the Eat Art objects exhibited in Spoerri's Eat Art Gallery and produced in numbered editions, carried over this idea. Here Spoerri appropriates more directly the chance collaboration he had already acknowledged with regard to the rats in Schwarz's gallery. Now the audiences take up the rats' role and constantly change the constellations of images through their "consumption" of art, as Karl Gerstner also put it: "The multiple consisted of an image resulting from thousands, in fact billions of images. And these combinations, which I called constellations, must be generated by consumers."[44]

Spoerri's notion of multiplication lies at the intersection of movement and time, an intersection that generates chance situations. The latter determine not just the trap-paintings but also and especially his food-multiples in which food cooks, spills, and boils out of anyone's control. In contrast to reproduction, multiplication involved, at least initially, mobile objects (kinetic art) that generated transformations in various ways: by themselves, namely, by way of the piece's structure; by gravity; by the aid of motors; and through the audience's intervention, the method used most often. Thus they produced multiplied originals or, as Spoerri called them, originals in series. They were "originals" because, like the trap-paintings, no composition left to chance and time (mostly expressed here through movement) could be repeated identically.

Multiplication meant constant variations of objects and images. Authenticity or originality was not self-sameness or identity for Spoerri: "For the animated, kinetic work, whether it is kinetic by itself or because of the spectator–collaborator's intervention, multiplication means to do justice to the infinite possibilities of transformation."[45] In this art, time is the dimension and principle that ensures the return of difference. Multiples question the uniqueness of the artwork itself and the "arbitrary" value ascribed to it by the art market, which Spoerri sets against the equally arbitrary exchange value ruling the commodity market. Yet the multiples do so through an inflation of originals in series.

Spoerri decided to sell the *MAT Edition*'s multiples as one would books, that is, at the cost of production, 200 francs per item. Likewise, in his *Grocery Shop* exhibit (*Krämerladen*, 1961), he sold regular cans of food at their current market value. In a move bearing affinities to conceptual art's operations, this exchange involving ready-made canned food — which all looked alike in the gallery but would all be different when cooked and eaten in various places and times — became a paradoxical means to let ideas circulate against the commodity fetish. The multiplied originals became Spoerri's means to inflate the market and the art market, too, which, as pointed out, he also did with his certificates of authenticity.

Food-Multiples

The Eat Art's project since the first trap-paintings is fused with the basic idea of multiplication. Ultimately, the main frame of reference for Spoerri's food-multiples, as also for his banquets, is the perennial return of difference — cultural, historical, and individual — that occurs consciously and unconsciously, individually and collectively, in culinary cultures and in food materials. Accordingly, one reason why Spoerri decided to open the Eat Art Gallery next to his Restaurant in Düsseldorf, in 1970, was the view that Eat Art was a way to expand the principle of his *MAT Editions*. The multiple would be greatly expanded through what Spoerri considered the most changeable, malleable material of all, namely, edible substances. Food, as he observes, is not only changeable because it perishes in time and because it transforms chemically at different temperatures but especially because it is a heterogeneous substance.

The food-multiples are less products (objects) than operations or processes of change. At the same time, the production of edible art (or food art more generally) is tantamount to producing social or public forms of consumption. The production of consumption—that is, the multiplying trap-paintings alongside the actual multiples—may be read through the lens of expenditure, in Bataille's sense.[46] In the art critic Yve-Alain Bois's interpretation: "Expenditure . . . is the regulation, through excess, of an initial disorder and such regulation is never successful because [it is] always insufficient" (*Formless*, 36). Following Bois's reading of expenditure, the trap-paintings—these disorderly chance situations of glued objects—proliferate, in the (failed) attempt to capture and regulate a disorder to which every new trap-painting only testifies further, like every new act of food consumption. This is like the proliferation of food-multiples, the materials of which are organic thus changing foodstuffs, either produced in series of originals, such as, for example, eggs, bread loaves, and chocolate bars, or simply taken as morphing materials: for instance, chocolate itself (which melts at different temperatures) and fat (like lard, butter, or margarine, which too are susceptible to temperature and easy to be manipulated).

On the one hand, the trap-paintings and the food-multiples focus on desire's erratic movement and transformation. In other words, these originals in series put on view one of the temporary forms desire takes on. While limited in their editions, food-multiples continuously change in time because of their organic substances. On the other hand, the same multiples exhibit the fact that desire eludes such forms and moves on at a rapid pace. Eat Art and the early food-multiples point, with a degree of awareness, to the return of desire (life) as difference(s), which then the multiples, as well as the staged banquets, capture only to immediately let go of, again and again. Unlike fashion, or the commodity fetish, the food fetish—as any kinetic work—disintegrates by itself or by way of its consumers' teeth: in short, it stages its own disappearance at a much faster rate of consumption than any other commodity. Commenting on the food-multiples, Roth, for example, stated that "letting go" of the form temporarily taken by desire meant that art would happen at the moment at which the process of decay (decomposition) of the foodstuffs in the multiplied objects was liberated from the artist's hands or "grasp." The artist's hands capture for a moment and then put on display only instances in the process of art's self-making, art that life produces in its own temporal consumption (decay).[47] The artist only puts his signature to this process. Hence, in the case of in/edible food-multiples, the artist does not sign a "completed" work.[48]

Food-multiples multiply—each in different ways and in their own time. While they thereby disperse or reproduce themselves in time as food does, they carve a space in which the other of art, or so-called life, becomes visible: this is a space for life's own temporal denouement. This life-space is carved out from within the art institution (or the artist's action as institutionally validated act of art making). Here art posits its other, which it needs and presupposes, and vice versa. Hence, in Filliou's words, "art is what makes life more interesting than art": the food-multiples expend themselves beyond their boundaries as either pure art or pure foodstuffs. Instead they mutually contaminate each other and disrupt a fixed dualism between the time of art and the times of life.

I would like to clarify that expenditure, especially as it concerns the work preceding Spoerri's banquets, does not have to involve display of excess (luxury in Bataille's words). Some of Spoerri's banquets (for instance, *The Last Supper* in 1970, a funereal banquet) do have an extravagant Daliesque "luxurious" trait. Yet Spoerri's expenditure is rather the *machinelike* desire that propels Spoerri's art. From the trap-painting through the entire culinary discourse (like the *Gastronomic Journal* on the island of Symi), through the food-multiples, and, finally, to the banquets, in each phase of his career, Spoerri embraced elaborations of artistic principles such as variation and multiplication inherent in the metamorphic material. Spoerri's multiplication of art, as the latter intersects with food, expends consumption—and desire—in ceaseless acts of displacement. This kind of desire constitutes the energy behind Spoerri's Eat Art project, including the meals he organized for the Swiss Pavilion at the Seville Exposition, in 1992, and for his Eat Art show at the Jeu de Paume in Paris, in 2002. In the entire Eat Art project (since 1960) expenditure does not coincide with the display of excess but with excess as temporal displacement and deferral.

As observed earlier, Spoerri's trap-paintings attempt to freeze or capture momentarily the state of disorder brought about by consumption. From this point of view, the fixation of disorder and entropic expenditure — disorder itself — are in a tension with one another in the trap-paintings. To use Bois's words, entropy is "the constant and irreversible degradation of energy in every system, a degradation that leads to a continually increasing state of disorder and of nondifferentiation within matter" (*Formless,* 34). Eat Art starts most literally — according to Spoerri's own recollections — as an investigation behind the scenes into what produces the irreversible temporality expressed in the disorder on the table, namely, the world of food, which he discovers to be as messy as it is systematic, as unpredictable and changing as it is reproducible. Eat Art (including its food-multiples and different meals) first isolates and then plays with instances of fixation and entropic expenditure. However, Spoerri never attempts to regulate these movements but rather underscores the movement (of life) that escapes such orders. Eat Art can position itself as "art" from within these orders, but only as an act of in-*forming* that remains constantly inconclusive, or rather *informe.*

The open instability that ensues from these movements, and which is the artistic principle of multiplication, reveals that food-multiples raise fundamental issues of heterogeneity and declassification. Heterogeneity lies in questioning and tensing the (temporal) boundaries of the edible/inedible. Declassification similarly points to the tensions and overlaps between art objects and food objects. It means to question the differences and analogies between art originals and food originals. Hence food-multiples — especially in Spoerri's early works — unsettle the principles behind clear-cut aesthetic distinctions, artistic and ethnographic categories, systems of order, and even art catalogs.

The Grocery Shop *and the* Catalog Taboo: *Bread, More or Less*

The critic Arthur Danto responds, indirectly, to Spoerri's provocative questions about the nature of art and its context, when elaborating on examples of postaesthetic art in the 1990s, in particular, on experiments of community-based art.[49] Spoerri asks: "Will a gallery in which vegetables are sold at market price not become definitively a grocery

shop? And a tomato, does it stop being a tomato just because someone declares it a work of art?" (*Anekdotomania,* 75; my translation).
Danto for his part considers a candy bar exhibited at the 1993 Culture
in Action event in Chicago. The underlying questions concerning this
work, titled "We Got It!" are about how the candy bar can become art,
at what point it does so, and whether this art expands beyond what
Danto calls an "art of their own," that is, an art the meaning of which
is limited to a single community. In Danto's opinion, in the latter case
one does not encounter art because art ought to speak to the imagination of many and different people, not just those belonging to one
community (although this would raise the issue of how to identify and
"close" the community in question).

Danto explains that this candy bar is in fact art (as is Warhol's
Brillo Boxes). It is art not because of

> the criteria by which candy bars themselves are graded into better or
> worse — by taste, size, nutritional considerations or whatever. "We Got It!"
> may fall short of these on all candy-bar criteria and still be art while *they*
> are merely candy bars. A candy bar that is a work of art need not be some
> especially good candy bar. It just has to be a candy bar produced with the
> intention that it be art. One can still eat it since its edibility is consistent with
> its being art. ("Museums and the Thirsting Millions," 184–85)

Quality, as determined by the criteria that determine an object's per-
tinence to a category (in the case of "We Got It!" the food's quality,
its taste) is not what matters, in Danto's view. Rather, what counts is
the performative function a thing or an action takes from within an
active discourse that, for "We Got It!" or in our case Spoerri's tomato,
is that of art in a "philosophical age" and a consumer age.[50] For Danto,
the presence (existence) of the museum allows this particular work to
extend the possibility of its aesthetic reception — as experience in a
postaesthetic age — beyond the confines of an "art of their own." Not
because "We Got It!" has to enter the museum or because it will enter
it but because it can be read through and against the history of art
and its institutions, namely, through the philosophical lens that reads
art today, alongside its other intentions of alternative artistic expression and despite those intentions or its location outside the museum.
Thus, as he writes,

> [the candy bar] belongs to everyone, as it should, being art. Indeed, it is fair
> to say that while the art world did not make the chocolate bar, they made it

possible for it [the candy bar] to be art when the confectioners made it under certain auspices, and at a certain moment in history—i.e., after the end of art, when in a sense everything is possible. . . . To someone who knows the art history of the candy, it is imaginable that they should be moved to think of all those men and women, far from the art world, thinking of what they [*sic*] gave meaning to their lives and deciding that they could make art out of that and at the same time the best candy in Chicago! ("Museums and the Thirsting Millions," 189)

Danto, while classifying the candy bar as art, does not exclude the possibility of overlaps of the meanings and functions, even tastes, and the history of production, of candy bars or other similar food. What about Spoerri? His Eat Art situates itself within postaesthetic art (the neo-avant-garde, or else, post-Duchampian art) and is in effect one of its initiators. Among the goals of Eat Art is the critical investigation of (post) aesthetic experience, of the meanings and limits of neo-avant-garde art, the actions and effects of which expressly situate themselves within the philosophical discourse of what may constitute art at different times. In this regard, the food-multiples engage art through the close otherness of the culinary discourse. While not raising the issue of quality (Eat Art is not about intrinsically "good" food), as Danto points out, Spoerri's work with food asks to what extent the value judgment one expresses instinctively upon tasting a tomato in fact compels the consumer to at least ponder how he or she approaches and values art. As he once put it in his *Auto-Theater*: if I find beer good when I drink it, can I find beer good when it is art? An extension of this would then be to ask: if I find an artwork "good," would I find it as good if I also had to eat it? What allows one to discriminate between one kind of good and the other? Such questions are at the core of Spoerri's *Grocery Shop*, which was established at Koepcke's gallery in Copenhagen in October 1961 alongside the *Catalog Taboo*, in fact a "work" that accompanied the show. This "catalog" was made of bread mixed in with garbage, which confused and disturbed the distinctions ordinarily drawn between the art objects on view and their "reproduction" in ordinary exhibition catalogs. Both *The Grocery Shop* and *Catalog Taboo* offer an early example of the neo-avant-garde's "philosophical" inquiries about art's ways to test the conceptual and physical relations between aesthetic and nonaesthetic experience, and their boundaries.

Spoerri speaks of the show at Koepcke's as taboo breaking: the quickly improvised grocery store ignored the institution of art's own

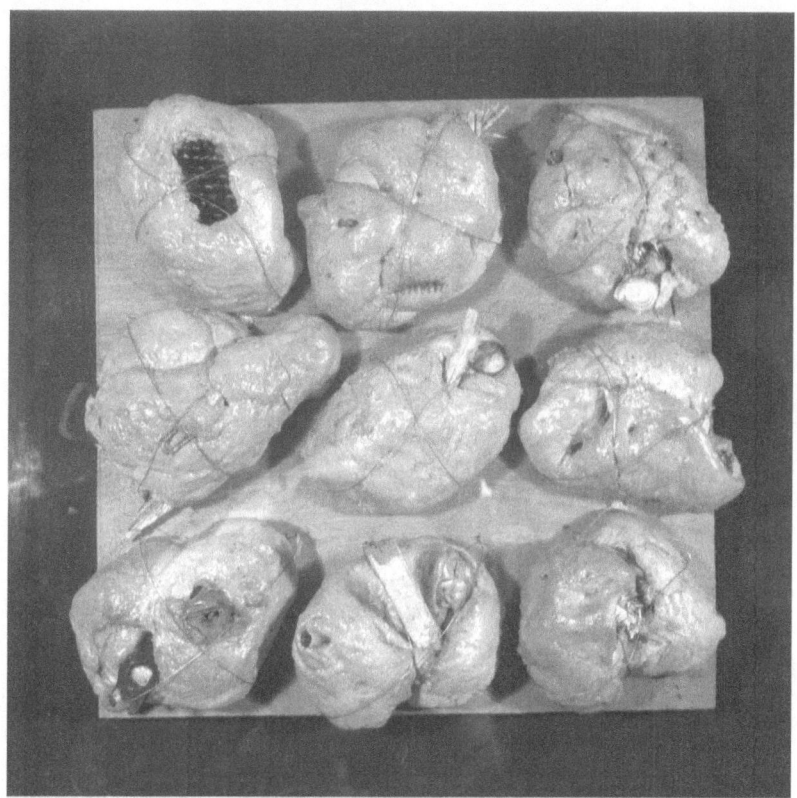

Daniel Spoerri, "Catalog Taboo," 1961. Museum of Modern Art Stiftung
Ludwig, Vienna (once Hahn Collection). Courtesy of Die Schweizerische
Landesbibliothek, Archiv Daniel Spoerri. Copyright 2008 Artists Rights
Society (ARS), New York / ProLitteris, Zurich.

market rules. *The Grocery Shop,* where he sold mostly canned food,
simply added itself to the gallery. It occupied parts of its space: one
would visit the gallery and take a look at "art" and, in an annexed
space, the visitor would also be able to buy groceries at regular market prices. Warhol's painted Campbell's soup cans were here literally
descended from the canvas and redistributed among the consumers.
Among Spoerri's questions to the consumer was whether he or she
would in fact engage in the purchase of art (canned foods) at the price
of regular groceries. The show violated the distinctions among different kinds of consumption: for example, optical and fetishist consumption (in the case of the art collector's desire), and a physical, digestive consumption of an art now explicitly juxtaposed with food and

presented as possibly edible. Indeed these cans of food could be opened and eaten in the private domestic space. Spoerri thus asked about the uses and effects that the consumption of art as food, and food as art, might bring to the ways of thinking art (ways that include naming and classifying art). (*The Grocery Shop* provokes skepticism about "cultivated" forms of consumption of and access to the domain and discourse of art, as opposed to popular forms of consumption — affective, experiential, and so forth. At the same time, Spoerri investigated the resistance of the everyday — of the lifeworld as it finds expression in the tomato — to its "aestheticized" or "fetishized" assimilation.)

The tomato, he suggests, may very well keep on tasting like one, despite having been declared an artwork. The spectator of art will be able to tell only by challenging the definition of art — the institutional space through which the artist's performative assertion is made even more plausible — and transforming himself or herself into an active consumer: an optical consumer initially but then eventually a buyer, a cook, and an eater. The visitor/consumer present at *The Grocery Shop* and the artist himself enter a silent dialogue, a dialogue through which different meanings of art are produced and art is conceived of differently, depending on each consumer's assumed position within the competing languages of art and the everyday. A consumer may also decide not to buy, an action that also expresses his or her position with regard to "art." The consumer who buys has ultimately the choice either to preserve the purchased food art rather than cook it and eat it, or to go ahead and physically digest it. In the process, the consumer perceives the intricacies of the overlap of languages involved in the production of art as well as life. The main difference between Duchamp's readymade and Spoerri's food cans is that now the dilemma about art or not art is the viewer/consumer's rather than the museum of modern art's (a museum, though, which is always already present).

Spoerri's *Grocery Shop* intended to set free foodstuffs in at least two ways. The exhibition presented Spoerri with the opportunity to free the food that in those days he was still gluing in his trap-paintings (*Anekdotomania*, 75). *The Grocery Shop* allowed him to recirculate foodstuffs as desire, in yet another form and context. Yet foodstuffs question their "commodity" status as paradoxical art by participating critically in ordinary market transactions at an art gallery. The readymade goods (cans of food, bottled drinks, packaged vegetables) here sold at market price in an art gallery contaminate the art world (with

Daniel Spoerri with Addi Koepcke, setting up the "Krämerladen" in Galerie Koepcke, Copenhagen, 1961. Courtesy of Die Schweizerische Landesbibliothek, Archiv Daniel Spoerri. Copyright 2008 Artists Rights Society (ARS), New York / ProLitteris, Zurich.

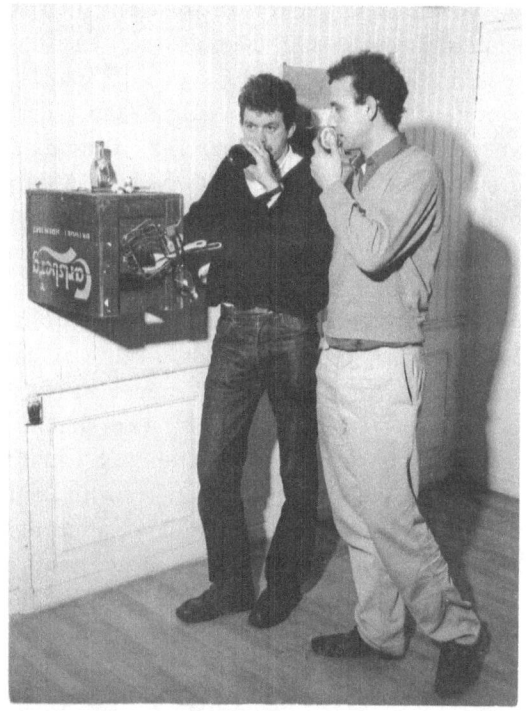

its exhibition values) — in which the trap-paintings also risked being trapped. They also contaminate the market of commodities (exchange value), in which they enter bearing the trace of the art world (i.e., an added value to the art world).

These common goods — which also serve use-value, for they can nourish their buyers if the latter opt to eat the food — are stamped *Attention, oeuvre d'art.* The stamps bear Spoerri's signature. These art-multiples, scattered randomly on a grocery table, and then among the buyers, become multivalent signs. The stamp, which may be read to mean "work of art: handle with care," could refer to how works of art themselves are packaged and marked when shipped from place to place on the way to various exhibitions. Thus the signature on the canned tomatoes or soups becomes the signature of the artist and locates the work in the world of art. But the stamp may ambiguously stand as a warning to the consumer, "beware, this is a work of art." One implication being: don't mistake this for food, because, in fact, you could! And if you do mistake it for food, perhaps rightly, what would the consequences of this confusion be? Could you—the consumer-diner—possibly be poisoned by (eating) art? Is this art safe as food, if this is art after all?

Attention, oeuvre d'art calls to the gallerist but even more to the viewer, buyer, and consumer to confront culinary taboos and artistic/ aesthetic anxieties, in the gallery shop. After purchasing the "food" in question, he or she now faces the dilemma whether to preserve it and thus handle it with care! (It is art! the stamp reminds him or her, also with its authorial signature) or not preserve it and not handle it with care. Or, perhaps, handling with care requires precisely that the food be prepared and eaten. Finally, a willful refusal to partake in Spoerri's subversive market would still signal the consumer's silent acceptance of the status quo (art is art, food is not sold in a gallery, and I don't buy it) and, perhaps, a silent rejection of Spoerri's alternative "open" proposal. It is open because it changes with each consumer's position.

Or, one could argue that looking at art at an exhibition makes the viewer into a passive consumer, an accomplice of the standing art market. But, were the consumers of art to become physical consumers of these early food art objects, they would be left with a shell of art—a used, opened can, stamped twice, once with whatever brand name and also with Spoerri's signature.[51] In this scenario, art would thus lie in an economically unaccountable—yet edible and nourishing—absent content (the polysemic statement *Attention, oeuvre d'art*). The content is always elsewhere, certainly beyond the stamp and the can, pure markers and themselves traces of absence. In *The Grocery Shop* and throughout the Eat Art project, the consumer is endowed with the possibility of reconstituting art, as one would powdered milk or soup, or simply to let it be, which also means, possibly, to let it expire and rot.

In *The Grocery Shop* the consumer must confront—and possibly infringe on—a cultural and aesthetic taboo, as the catalog's title indicates: *Catalog Taboo*. The consumer's presence in this hybrid space—which Spoerri reproduced later in his Restaurant Galleries—implicates him or her: he or she is immediately an operator of artistic definitions. Spoerri's market provokes anxiety through its unstable language and subverts the oedipalizing economy of consumer capitalism, which follows the triangulated rhythm of production, consumption, and discharge (dismissal, excretion). The buyer/consumer of art is torn between (at least) two forms of desire. He or she can either opt for desire's entrapment, namely, if he or she falls into or follows a fetishist economy, or he or she can liberate this desire. Liberation would occur here through incorporation (not against it). Incorporation may indeed counter a prepackaged memory, as it were. Here incorporation functions very much like Benjamin's own notion. As discussed, for Benjamin it is linked with processes of re-*member*-ing, namely, the bodily act of *er/innern*. From this perspective, the aforementioned tomato is the carrier of the taste of memory and the narrative flows that inform it, not in its singularity but in its multiplicability—the can of food, or the tomato in question, reconstitutes itself anew with each bite while the stamp remains to testify to the object's physical absence. It thus does not coincide with the object. This absence testifies to the presence of a renewable experience of consumption, not captured once and for all by the "one" original object or image, yet an experience that is never identical. Thus the stamp's role is both to point to the multiplication of the art/food and to the absence of any original. In contrast, fetishist desire produces the rigid souvenir as the disavowal of that absence or else, in Benjamin's terms, the mineralization of remembering and the reification of memory that is thus reduced to that particular object or image (*Reflections*, 134).[52]

The liberation of desire, the desire to consume the artwork and to incorporate the art experience(s) that ensue, may be problematic. Practices of desublimation are not intrinsically liberatory: consumerism can easily rechannel unstructured libidinal energy. Following Jean Baudrillard, the libidinal economy is already embedded in an economy less flexible than that of the commodity fetish, namely, the economy of sign-exchange value (*Art since 1900*, 437, 587). Signifiers efface objects and turn them into meanings prepackaged for exchange. Yet in Spoerri's *Grocery Shop* the act of remembering (as it springs also from the stamp) interferes with consumption and thus perhaps creates an opening in the consumption and reproduction of simulated experiences, even if remembering too occurs within the inescapable sign-exchange economy. The ready-made cans, in this sense, are multiples without an "original," but they are not simulacral "images," that is, representations that self-generate without having an external referent. Let me explain: the work is here multiplied, but the work is itself multiplication of spurious acts of remembering. These acts are spurred by the deliberate choice to eat, internalize physically, the food/art. The result: the exhibition of an absence, in short, the multiplication of the production of an absence and the proliferation of counter (bodily) memories. The multiplication of the work can thus resist the immediate fetishization of the art object, whether as original and authentic, or as sign — equally and identically exchangeable with other signs.

The second component of *The Grocery Shop* is its *Catalog Taboo,* which itself is a work of art in its own right. This catalog mixes the *sacred* daily bread with urban *waste*. It consists of eighty small bread rolls — food-multiples — mixed in with garbage: nails, glass debris, dust, and so forth. Spoerri does not highlight the sacred-versus-waste issue. He also does not devalue bread per se — which he nonetheless pollutes. Rather, he raises a question about the discursiveness of classifications. Intermixing soft and expanding matter (like dough) with given objects points to the porous boundaries between binary oppositions. The catalog of impure bread indeed demonstrates these boundaries' instability through its rolls' hybridity. The unanswerable questions the *Catalog Taboo* poses are: When does bread stop being edible or being sacred, of value, and turns into waste? And when does waste become edible, nourishing? Or when is it inedible but also sacred, that is, when does bread become an art object? Spoerri stated that bread — which he also used to make a shoe-bread-object and a typewriter-bread-object (part of his *Brotteigobjekte*) — used to be a metonymy for survival, for life in general, and also functioned as actual currency before becoming its metaphor (in English, for example, one uses the noun *dough* for money). Given this economic equivalence, Spoerri asks, why not use bread instead of money? Still, through dough's multiplied different shapes, through its physical, organic, almost boisterous and engulfing nature (to which other bread objects also testify), bread shows that it cannot "move" as easily as money. The market rejects it (it becomes waste), and it resists the market.

Consider, for example, a pair of old and worn women's shoes that Spoerri first kneaded together with bread dough and then baked (*Mettre les pieds dans le plat,* 1969). Bread is inside the shoes, in lieu of feet.[53] Dough incarnates physically the history, the work, the sweat of the person(s) who walked in these "misshaped" (*informe*/informal) shoes. A human trace themselves, the bread shoes also bear the weight of labor. If one works — and walks — for bread, bread captures labor as a meaningful act of cultural production, including the production and consumption of the bread of life and by extension life itself. Bread thus does not move with the apparent innocuous swiftness of money. In this artwork, bread also blocks the circulation of commodities, the new shoes shining in the shop windows (possibly eliciting desire with no strings attached).

From another perspective, shoes are not just typical fetishes. They have also become a contested "fetish" of much modernist and post-modernist art, from Vincent Van Gogh's *Pair of Boots* (1887) to René Magritte's *Le modèle rouge* (1935), from Dalí's *Objet Surrealiste à fonctionnement symbolique* (1932) to Meret Oppenheim's *Ma gouvernante* (1936). The theorist Fredric Jameson found in the painted and photographed shoes from Van Gogh to Warhol the transition from modernism to postmodernism.[54] Spoerri's material and affective approach to his bread shoes situates them within the modernist tradition. However, the erupting bread from within these shoes also engulfs this tradition with its abjected (inartistic and bodily) materials. The expansive bread dough encroaches and consumes precisely all those art shoes that Jameson and others (e.g., Martin Heidegger and Jacques Derrida) have taken into consideration and that, for the artist as well as the critic, can never be just shoes or just representations. Spoerri's shoes both consume these modernist icons and block the consumption of pure modernist art. In effect, Spoerri's bread explodes these shoes as artistic fetishes of modernist art. Bread brings up modernism's own internal difference: the neo-avant-garde bread dough rises to burst the fetish shoes of modernism and only collects its randomly scattered pieces.

Spoerri remarks that he views himself as an artist who, passing by after the explosion of a bomb that has shattered everything, gathers and puts together the remaindered fragments (*La messa in scena degli oggetti,* 35). A historical reference to a post-Holocaust and post–atomic bomb art, this statement also situates Eat Art from its inception in 1960 (with the trap-painting) within a neo-avant-garde that does not disavow the catastrophe of World War II in order to simply continue the tradition of the avant-garde without working through its history and historical breaks. Eat Art proposes that the neo-avant-garde artist be in fact an archaeologist of the avant-garde. As Spoerri's bread objects, in particular the shoes, the catalog of *The Grocery Shop* exhibition is the neo-avant-garde's dialogue with modernism, and so is the exhibition itself. The exhibition and its *Catalog Taboo* contain different and yet contiguous works of art (one not the reproduction of the other but an extension of art into another affine realm). While bread is a staple food in Western diets and has connotations of the sacred, it is also easily discarded when "old." Spoerri's bread multiples put on view the consumers' violation of *this* profane sacredness of bread. The violation occurs at and reflects the daily rhythms of industrial mass production and consumption: of new (bread) versus (old) bread. In this regard, the bread-waste agglomerates combine the high with the low in art, the inside and the outside of culture. With respect to the discourse of art, they provide an example of Spoerri's counteroptics or, in his words, a lesson in optics. The relation between sight and these loaves of bread was in effect also explicitly posited in *The Grocery Shop* exhibition.

Koepcke's gallery was tiny: it had only two rooms, which were used for Spoerri's exhibition. In the front room the market was staged; in the back room Spoerri showed trap-paintings made with the things left behind by his friend Filliou, who had just left Denmark.[55] Spoerri developed the idea of a negative optics at this time. Within the context of the market and the trap-paintings, he thus also exhibited blackened spectacles, with frames made of piercing and menacing nails, which then became part of a more extensive collection of glasses and optical equipment, called *Modern Optics* (1961–62). From the trap-paintings to Eat Art, but in particular since *The Grocery Shop,* Spoerri's project sketches a lesson in "negative" optics that entails the study of those senses other than sight (in particular, smell and taste) and their relevance for art. The *Catalog Taboo* has a role in Spoerri's negative optics: first, it negates visual representation — specifically, the representation of the in/edible objects on view and for sale in *The Grocery Shop*; second, it also breaks the consumers' view of the relations between bread and waste, edible/inedible, positive/negative, productive/unproductive, aesthetic taste/gastronomic taste, as well as the sacred and the profane, visible and invisible art.

Catalog Taboo infiltrates the interstices between distinctions by spreading itself eighty times through its eighty rolls. In this sense, Spoerri's recourse to waste (the abject) may be called *informe* (formless) following Bataille.[56] The latter defined the *informe* in an entry of the dictionary of anomalous definitions he published in his own (counter-)surrealist journal *Documents* (Bataille, 31). As Bois put it, Bataille's entry exemplifies what the entire project meant to accomplish, or, rather *not* to accomplish, in short what it did *not* intend to be: the dictionary did *not* aim to give the meaning but the *doings* of words. Accordingly, the adjective *informe* is used to indicate an action. Bois quotes Bataille:

> Thus he [Bataille] refuses to define *"informe"*: "It is not only an adjective having a given meaning, but a term that serves to bring down [*déclasser*] in the world." . . . It is not so much a stable motif to which we can refer, a symbolizable theme, a given quality, as it is a term allowing one to operate a declassification, in the double sense of lowering and of taxonomic disorder. Nothing in and of itself, the formless has only an operational existence: it is a performative, like obscene words, the violence of which derives less from semantics than from the very act of their delivery. . . . The formless is an operation. (*Formless*, 18)

The operation of the *informe* captures the uncontrollable growth of Spoerri's leftover. Waste is a function of excess out of which the heterogeneous rolls emerge. The *Catalog Taboo* mixes waste and bread into sacrilegious hybrid multiples: dough's transformation in the chemical process of baking, Spoerri asserts, cannot be fully controlled. Thus dough is both the creative agent of originals in series—each loaf collaged with garbage differing from every other—and the principle of an ever-changing ready-made.

Mary Douglas's perspective on dirt, which she defined as "matter out of place," could also be invoked to interpret Spoerri's *Catalog Taboo* and his *Bread-Dough Objects*.[57] For Douglas, dirt is matter that, eluding classification, is considered as a polluted/polluting substance. Julia Kristeva names this the abject, a term she interprets more psychoanalytically than Douglas and which refers to sociocultural practices of inclusion and exclusion, power in and by language, and modernist practices of writing. The abject, excluded from social structure, as well as from the subject, is what allows the social and the subject to be while the abject threatens both from their own margins. Spoerri's *Catalog Taboo* is a disturbing assemblage because its heterogeneity is one in which bread becomes waste and waste becomes bread. Not all of Spoerri's bread objects are inedible abject not-yet-objects: the rolls are in fact edible, and so is the food in the cans sold in *The Grocery Shop*. Thus they also defy their categorization as so-called abject art (art of the abject). Rather, as Spoerri noted years after the fact, they anticipated Eat Art. Spoerri writes in hindsight: "I could have not imagined, at that time, that these bread-rolls would be the unconscious forerunners of Eat Art" (*Anekdotomania*, 75). *Catalog*

Taboo shares with Bataille's *informe* the temporality as well as the spatiality of the operation of *displacing* matter. Dough is a material that changes in time and thus produces itself — and the objects to which it is applied — in constant acts of deferral/difference. *Catalog Taboo* puts on view the disorder or instability underlying classificatory systems, in this case those of artistic and comestible production and consumption. In a different manner and at a different level, the display of disorder is also the goal of *The Grocery Shop* exhibition.

Writing about Arman's accumulations, Umberto Eco addresses the notion of the catalog:

> The catalog, in order to be labeled as such, must be an *accumulation of difference in the light of a unifying motif, no matter how tiny.* . . . No catalog of the same exists. . . . Now, the majority of Arman's works unsettle the coherence of a theory of the catalog, as is clear when the artist boxes a plurality of identical objects, musical instruments, dolls, blotting pads, capsules, watches, phials, motorcycles, and other decanters. . . . Seemingly, Arman violates the rule of the catalog; in reality, he reaffirms it because these multiplied objects *are not the same object.* In the passionate yet very calculated game of these accumulations, every object distinguishes itself from other like objects, for a particular inclination, an imbalance, for a minor rotation. Each object thus takes on its own profile.[58]

According to Eco, Arman's accumulations disturb the received notion of catalog by confusing its parameters about the similar and the same. Accumulations thus work as mysterious catalogs of an uncanny sameness that, in fact, as Eco tells us, is grounded in difference. Spoerri's own catalog also plays with a seeming sameness (the identity of bread taken in the singular as "bread" and also as symbol) and difference (the implicit otherness of bread: the rolls are different, bread changes and becomes waste, and the plural significations that break the unity of the [Christian] symbolism). Spoerri's *Catalog Taboo* presents itself as an anticatalog, a literal mixing of the heterogenous element present in sameness. The heterogeneity in the catalog's operation emerges especially as temporal relation between bread and waste. While bread and garbage in the multiple are inconsistent in that they are made of different materials, waste (as in excrement) is a temporal state of (the wasted daily) bread. In this multiple, bread is bread and its waste: the *Catalog Taboo* juxtaposes two temporal moments and not just two classes of objects. The twofold temporality that this multiple catalog proposes again and again (eighty times) functions as a critique of historicism and of Spoerri's Eat Art's contemporary historical situation: the state of civilization in consumer Europe. It presents itself as the repressed evidence, that is, the expelled, the "corpse," and waste, of what Benjamin called the necessary barbarism of culture.[59]

In a conversation with Beuys, on the occasion of the latter's performance and exhibition of *Supreme Fried Fish-Bones* at the Eat Art Gallery (October 30, 1970), Spoerri asserted that the quantity of waste increases proportionally with the supposed degree of civilization (or of progress) of society. On the island of Symi, in contrast to France, nothing would go to waste because one could find some use in everything; every object could be reinvented without limitation. Thus where there is "abundance" there may be art, but also "absolute" waste; for Spoerri then it is key to bridge the gap between the two. The multiples take waste out of its location and (as in poorer societies) reduce waste both quantitatively and qualitatively into a material of art through their transformation of it—an act of augmentation and expansion of its meanings and functions. This is not simply utilitarian recycling but an expenditure of imaginative energy toward alternative production.

The willed poverty of Eat Art with which Spoerri experimented already at the time of *Catalog Taboo* sounds an alarm about the modalities of exclusion in archiving and cataloguing cultural history. It also proposes itself as an everyday infiltration into these procedures, as this history's taboo. Eat Art proposes that art be a series of operations of transformation never meant to produce art objects. The latter are too easily enveloped by the aura of exception, both artistic and historical, and such a production would reconfirm the cataloguing of history, rather than unsettle it.

Spoerri's Thematic Banquets and the Restaurant (1960–71)

The work with food that preceded Spoerri's opening of the Restaurant and the Eat Art Gallery culminated here, in these two locations. Here Spoerri both reassembled most of his artistic principles up to that point and experimented further with food in collaboration with other artists. For example, Spoerri himself explicitly connected multiplication with Eat Art at the opening of his Eat Art Gallery: "Today, after 10 years, we want to expand this idea [multiplication] to the most mutable existing thing, namely the edible. General questions of interest emerge: about eternal values, digestibility, art's transformations

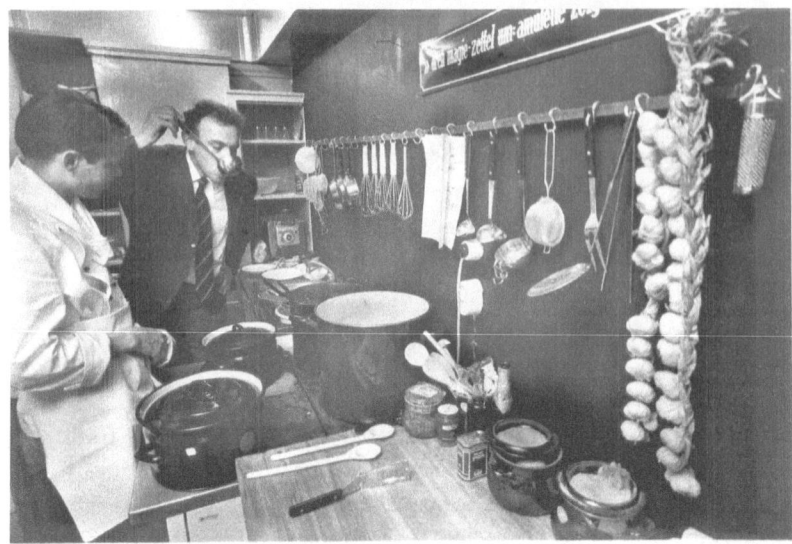

Daniel Spoerri in the kitchen of Spoerri Restaurant, Düsseldorf. Courtesy of Die Schweizerische Landesbibliothek, Archiv Daniel Spoerri. Copyright 2008 Artists Rights Society (ARS), New York / ProLitteris, Zurich.

and art as consumer's product."[60] Similarly, his Restaurant Galleries, where he staged his first banquets and exhibited the ensuing trap-paintings (the Galerie J, Bischofberger, and Allan Stone) are now assimilated into the Restaurant and Eat Art Gallery projects. Both are physical contiguous spaces (one on top of the other) and inter-changeable places: one could eat food art in the Gallery and one could take a look at trap-paintings, read palindromes or other personal cor-respondence, encyclopedias, and dictionaries while waiting for a meal or getting bored at some unwinding conversation at the table in the Restaurant (Stocker, 105).

Spoerri conceived of the Restaurant as another version of the *Gastronoptikum*; it was supposed to be a space for continuous multimedia happenings, that is, a prolonged series of actions inspired by life's activ-ities and carried out by artists and ordinary participants (cooks) alike. To show the intestinal and self-referential nature of Eat Art, Spoerri turned the Restaurant's space, its walls, its facade, its ambiance, into a *Wunderkammer*. Emmett Williams remembered the Restaurant as the meeting point for artists and friends, "a *milieu-collage* . . . an art-work itself in [a] constant process of renewal."[61] The Restaurant's external appearance confirmed Williams's impression. Spoerri covered its inte-rior with his letter-exchanges and other personal documents, while André Thomkins's palindromes decorated the building's facade. The palindromes formally addressed the mirroring of the art process and the eating process, occurring through chance. They could also be read as Eat Art's own communicating ends: the spiraling cycles of produc-tion and consumption of food, the tract connecting the mouth and the anus, with reading of the palindromes as the digestive process occur-ring in the space of the entrails. Indeed, the Restaurant was originally supposed to specialize in entrails. The impetus for this was not only to grant this bodily organ and regionally popular food a higher sta-tus in contemporary cuisine (thus restoring "popular cuisine" to the rank of "high cuisine") but especially to show how innards are the site of transformation, assimilation, and expulsion.[62] For Spoerri, as he made particularly clear in a project for a film directed by Tony Mor-gan (*Resurrection,* 1969), the digestive cycle can be taken for the para-digm of a spiraling temporality of reversibility, without coincidence, of the present and past: an irreversible reversibility. A temporal para-digm applicable to avant-garde–neo-avant-garde relations. This non-linear order constitutes the grounds of human reproduction as well as the cultural proliferation of human activity, as both difference (trans-formation) and return. This spiraling temporality—the Restaurant's agenda stressed—affects all forms of production and consumption, including artistic creation, which, in Spoerri's Eat Art does not have either a fixed point of origin or a sure end.

In the banquets staged at the Restaurant, Spoerri once again tested Western cultural taboos, specifically those concerning taste (aesthetic and gastronomic). His menus offered horsemeat, elephant meat, snake, ants, and so on. He also offered typical German fare, and the Restaurant was renowned for its steaks. Spoerri provided his guests with the opportunity to be daring or not (as in *The Grocery Shop*): they could taste one or other recipe and even mix all dishes together. These experiments were not simply Spoerri's occasion to investigate different cultural customs or to question Western tourists' taste for the exotic. They rather asked how people who exist in the same time—all at the same gathering, that is, participating in the same meal event—in fact live in multiple and different times. Spoerri had once annotated how geographic differences between the countryside and the city are expressed in country people's deeper connection with the land and space, and in the urban dweller's obsession with time. Most of the menus that Spoerri prepared for the Restaurant and for his banquets juxtaposed these multiple temporal coordinates of culture, as his *Catalog Taboo* had attempted already.

However, Eat Art emerged officially with the Eat Art Gallery, in 1970. And it was here that Spoerri's friends got truly involved, cooked in the Restaurant, and started producing in/edible multiples. Spoerri himself said more than once that the edible multiples had been inspired by Raymond Hains, a *décollagist* who had once used edible materials. As already mentioned, Spoerri had organized his first homonymous dinner in 1963, at the Galerie J, with Hains in mind (his homonymous was the brand name "Heinz"). In these banquets the brand names of food played the same role as the proper names of the guests, all more or less well-known and thus visible names. People's names change into brands, history into a labeling process that makes temporality into a digestible concept of organization of human collective experience.

Homage to Raymond Hains anticipated the cannibalistic features of other artist banquets, in which artists devoured other people's "named art" (by eating dishes named after them), other artists' art, or their own art. Among these banquets are, for example, the *Henkel Banquet, L'ultima cena* (both held in 1970), the subsequent *La faim du Cnac* (the title of which played with the phonetic identity between *faim* [hunger] and *fin* [end] and was organized for the closing of the Centre National d'Art Contemporain in 1976), and the action Spoerri staged for the burial of the idea of the trap-painting. The latter banquet became known as *Déjeuner sous l'herbe* (1983), a reversal of Edouard Manet's *Déjeuner sur l'herbe* (1863), in reference to the burial of his art, an actual meal first trapped and then laid in the ground. Yet according to participants, the most memorable action was explicitly devoted to cannibalism. It was Claude Lalanne and François Lalanne's *Dîner Cannibale*.

While the above meals were mostly about devouring artworks, the *Dîner Cannibale* was about eating the artist—François Lalanne's—own body (or rather eating the artist as art, art as an image, a cast, of the artist). For this meal, Lalanne made a cast of himself, which he then cut into pieces and used as molds for various dishes. The head, for example, was made of lamb tongue and rows of sausage (for the brain); champignons served as eyeballs, while their irises were made of truffles. The performance was reminiscent of the

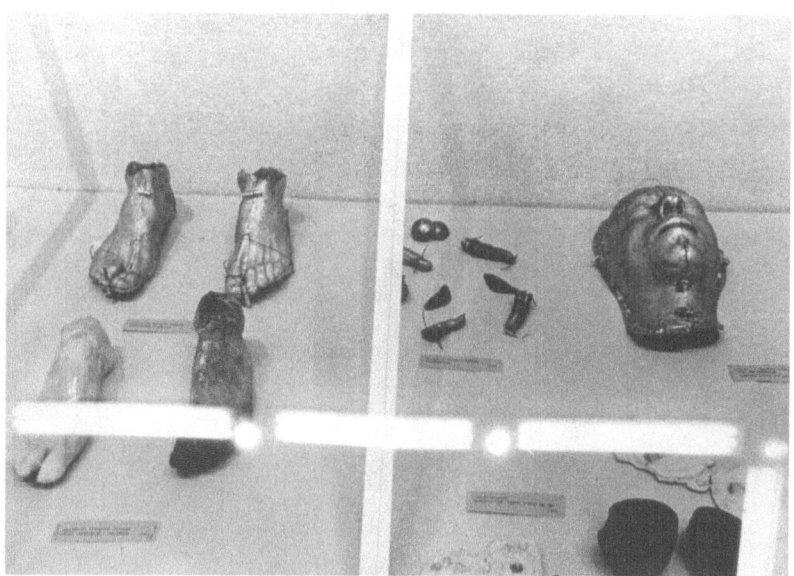

Daniel Spoerri, "Situation from Le Dîner Cannibale," Eat Art Gallery, 1970. Courtesy of Die Schweizerische Landesbibliothek, Archiv Daniel Spoerri. Copyright 2008 Artists Rights Society (ARS), New York / ProLitteris, Zurich.

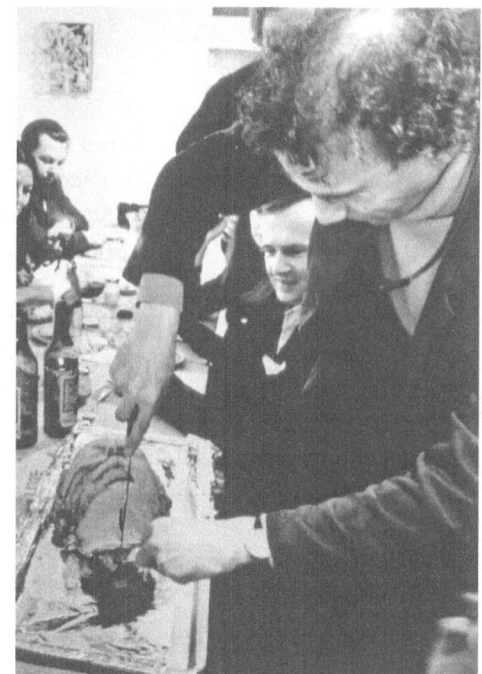

Daniel Spoerri cutting into a head at "Le Dîner Cannibale," 1970. Courtesy of Die Schweizerische Landesbibliothek, Archiv Daniel Spoerri. Copyright 2008 Artists Rights Society (ARS), New York / ProLitteris, Zurich.

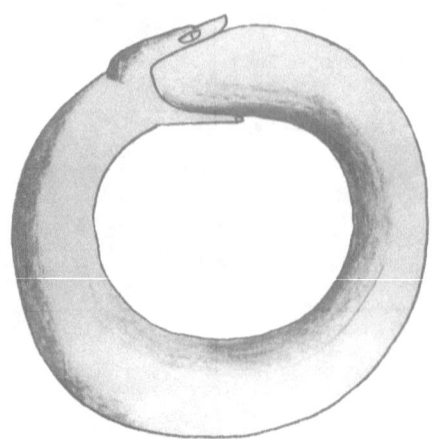

Daniel Spoerri presents Eat Art

Claude et François Lalanne
Le Dîner Cannibale

Daniel Spoerri, poster for "Le Dîner Cannibale," Eat Art Gallery, 1970. Courtesy of Die Schweizerische Landesbibliothek, Archiv Daniel Spoerri. Copyright 2008 Artists Rights Society (ARS), New York / ProLitteris, Zurich.

surrealist *Dîner sur la femme nue* held at the opening of the Exposition Internationale du Surrealisme in 1959, itself a "sensationalized" version of Meret Oppenheim's earlier *Spring Banquet.*[63] On those two occasions, a naked supine woman's body functioned as a tray filled with the most refined food — including Dalí's omnipresent lobsters. In his art-cannibalistic dinner Lalanne, by indirectly referencing these meals, and by substituting his own "contemporary" body to the eternal feminine's body of surrealism, literally gave the historical body of the avant-garde and its artists up for consumption.

Spoerri himself underscored that the *Dîner Cannibale,* while representing the summit and summary of the self-devouring serpent of art (literally printed on the exhibition's advertising poster), also points to the fact that art's cannibalism — as the principle of the neo-avant-garde — is ongoing: "Lalanne, your dinner was the final point of Eat Art, even though the latter will carry on. Even if we eat each other, the force of multiplication is such, that there will always be a pair of thighs left with which to continue Arman's accumulations."[64] Spoerri alludes

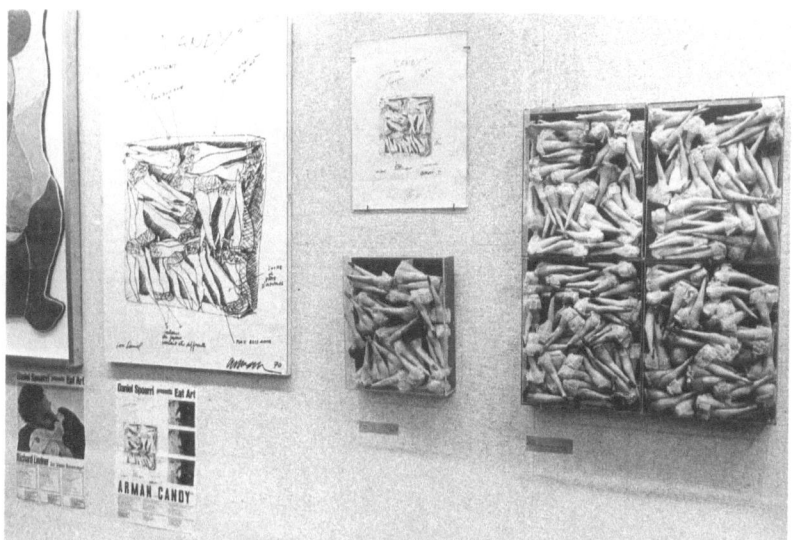

Arman, "Candy," Eat Art Gallery, 11 December 1970. Courtesy of Die Schweizerische Landesbibliothek, Archiv Daniel Spoerri. Copyright 2008 Artists Rights Society (ARS), New York/ProLitteris, Zurich.

to the accumulation that Arman prepared and exhibited at the Eat Art Gallery, an accumulation of women's legs produced in marzipan and which he interpreted as symbols of human reproduction. This kind of art-cannibalism took place both within and beyond the context of the Restaurant that Spoerri, not an entrepreneur after all, already abandoned in 1971, leaving it to his business partner Carlo Schröter.

As shown below, most Eat Art actions (banquets) bring into relief a temporal imaginary. Two sets of principles are important here: first, simultaneity and historical/artistic returns and, second, the construction in the present of an archaeological trace for the future.

The Neo-Avant-Garde's Devouring Serpent: Turns and Returns of the Avant-Garde

The homonymous banquets provide the base from which art-cannibalism — and the rewriting of art history — can be conceived for Spoerri. These happenings take the whole of cultural history as their purview, as seen in the homonymous meal *Hommage à Karl Marx*.

Spoerri organized this event at the Institute for the Arts (Kunsthochschule) in Cologne in 1978. He had been offered a post as profes-

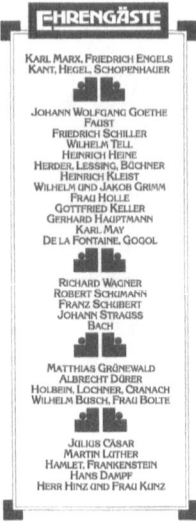 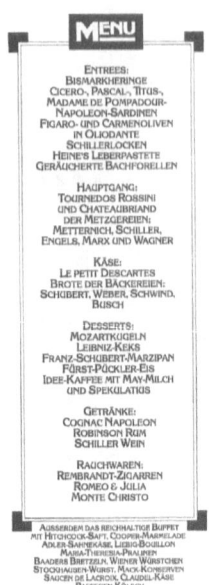

Daniel Spoerri, menu for the gala "Hommage à Karl Marx," Cologne, April 14, 1978. Courtesy of Die Schweizerische Landesbibliothek, Archiv Daniel Spoerri. Copyright 2008 Artists Rights Society (ARS), New York / ProLitteris, Zurich.

sor by the institute's rector, whose name was Dr. Karl Marx. To the banquet are invited people who happen to carry the same name as historical figures, just like the rector. Among the guests of honor are Marx, Engels, Kant, Hegel, and Schopenhauer. The long list also includes Goethe, Faust, Heine, Herder, Lessing, Kleist, Gogol, Dürer, Cranach, Martin Luther, Julius Caesar, Hamlet, and Frankenstein. The menu's typeface is Fin de Siècle and includes Bismarck herrings, Cicero-Pascal-Titus-Madame-de-Pompadour-Napoleon Sardines (all one dish), Heine's liver pastry, Tournedos Rossini; Chateaubriand coming from butchers named Metternich, Schiller, Engels, Marx, and Wagner; Mozart-balls as dessert, Schiller Wine, and Rembrandt Cigars.

The guests are selected at random (once their name is found to be apposite), thus guaranteeing a mixed audience. The diners do not know each other and might not share any cultural interest or background, other than their historical names also matching the dishes they eat, yet they will have to interact with one another. Thus, while history is reborn in this contemporary occasion, the guests will also make history again in unpredictable ways, by digesting first and then reincarnating the past. The names are the same, but are carried by different individuals at different times in history. Hence they physically embody historical *process* rather than progress. History moves in spirals, more akin to Spoerri's multiples. Because of the lack of the contemporary diners' gastronomic memory, the names and sometimes the dishes that accompany them turn into Dada linguistic (and etymological) games: the menu appears as a list of proper names, like a phone book. Now, once the menu and history are embodied and physically present *in* the present, a historically "inauthentic" memory returns, one that for its extemporaneous nature allows for fantastic reimagining. The menu that symmetrically accompanies the guest list is also a political statement: no class distinction, no difference between producers and consumers, and finally no separation between subject and object are visible here. Among other things, in this complex homonymous meal, history coincides with its rewriting in the present. Rewriting means here a random act of historical communication and consumption, and the present is disclosed to be, simultaneously, the present and the future of that past history.

Similarly, the actions involving art-cannibalism literally assign the task to remap the clean-cut times of art — and its historical reconstructions — to the mouth and the stomach. Most Eat Art meals contain one or the other aspect of Eat Art that came before: for example, on the Restaurant's walls hang the trap-paintings, and *Hommage à Karl Marx* is a more elaborate version of *Hommage à Raymond Hains*. Hence Eat Art cannibalizes itself. The focus on entrails underscores the deadly but regenerative aspect of art's cannibalism. As Spoerri declares in his analysis of the historical uses of entrails — also conducted by the hierophants of antiquity: "All the rituals of life and immortality include a preoccupation with the most perishable parts of the body, but the most indispensable to life" (*Mythological Travels,* 214).[65] Above all, Eat Art's actions compact art history again in a total simultaneous moment, a black hole. Although the black hole erases time as perceived in successive moments, it does not mean death without rebirth. Some banquets mark the "death" and burial of artistic moments, yet the return of the banquets themselves — for example, of the trap-painting after its burial celebrated in one such banquet — expresses the inherent relation between death and rebirth, like Spoerri and Morgan's film *Resurrection.*

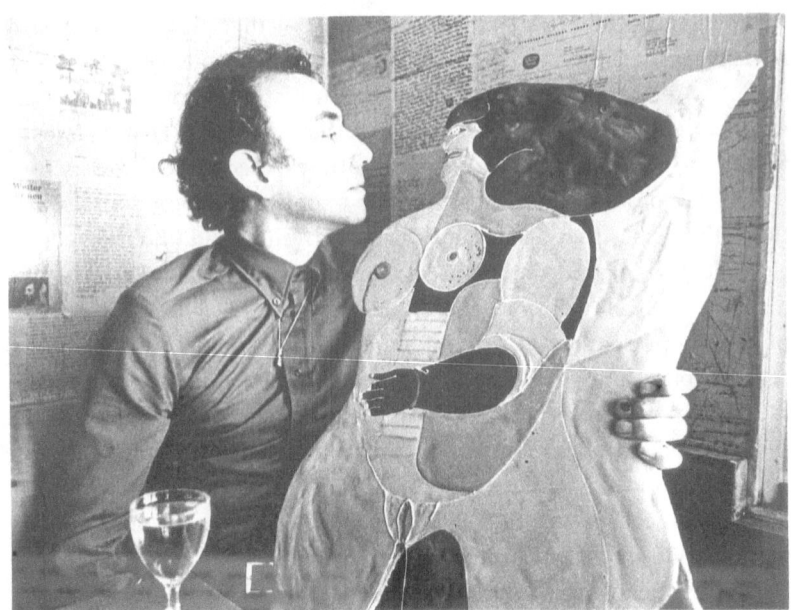

Daniel Spoerri with Richard Lindner's Der blaue Busenengel, Eat Art Gallery,
*1970. Courtesy of Die Schweizerische Landesbibliothek, Archiv Daniel Spoerri.
Copyright 2008 Artists Rights Society (ARS), New York / ProLitteris, Zurich.*

The *Henkel Banquet*'s menu of edible artworks pays tribute to
the conventions of art that demand a lasting trace of their immanent
presence. On this occasion (in 1970), the menu is the certificate of
authenticity that testifies that something indeed happened but is now
gone. The document is accordingly in the past tense. Space is provided for one's own name to be added to the certificate, which then
states: "So and so incorporated the following artists' works at the Eat
Art Banquet at the Henkel Regal Palace in Hoesel on October 29th
1970." A list of artists including Arman, Jasper Johns, Jim Dine, Roy
Lichtenstein, Soto, and Cy Twombly follows. The main course of this
meal, also known as "*Eat Art* Pop Art in the Cake," consisted of cakes
reproducing original art by the artists listed, some of whom were also
present among the 160 guests. As Spoerri explains, classical modern
art was represented by edible reproductions of Piet Mondrian and
Hans Arp, then "hard edge" art by those of Lindner and Morris. A
great number of cakes were inspired by Pop artists, among whom
were Claes Oldenburg, Robert Indiana, and Jim Dine. Finally, other
cakes reproduced Eat Art works (*Daniel Spoerri Presents Eat Art,*

GARANTIESCHEIN

[signature: Herr Daniel Spoerri]

hat am
29. Oktober 1970,
im Hause Henkel
in Hösel,
beim

EAT-ART-BANQUET

Werke
folgender Künstler
in sich
aufgenommen

Arman Beuys Brecht
Christo Dine
Fontana Filliou
Gerstner Graubner
Indiana Johns
Klapheck
Yves Klein Kricke
Lichtenstein Lindner
Mack de Maria
Manzoni Mondrian
Morgan Morris Louis
Oldenburg
Niki de Saint Phalle
Diter Rot Soto
Spoerri
Stella Thiebaud
Thomkins Twombly
Uecker Vasarely
Warhol
Weseler Wesselmann

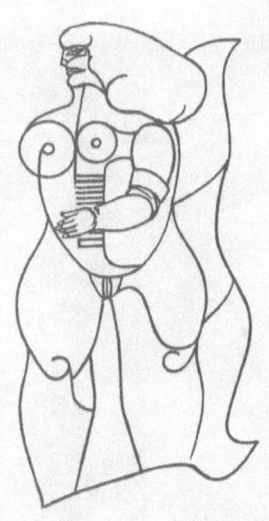

Richard Lindner »Der blaue Busenengel«

Daniel Spoerri, certificate of authenticity for guests participating in Henkel Banquet, *1970. Courtesy of Die Schweizerische Landesbibliothek, Archiv Daniel Spoerri. Lindner's* Der blaue Busenengel *was on the cover of the certificate. Copyright 2008 Artists Rights Society (ARS), New York / ProLitteris, Zurich.*

58). To stress the craftlike quality of this edible art, and to foster the renewal of the ancient and stubborn art of pastry, in conjunction with the reproductions typical of Pop Art, Spoerri collaborated closely with notorious bakers. As he had already underscored in the "Dissertation on Keftedes," at various points the culinary and the contemporary arts could find a point of contact through their reciprocal multiplication (*Mythological Travels,* 237).

At the *Henkel Banquet,* Eat Art was also cited in a silkscreen reproduction on a yellow tablecloth of four juxtaposed black-and-white photographs of a trap-painting from the meals held at the City Galerie (1965): depicting a trap-painting, this was an un/clean tablecloth on which a meal had already been eaten and/or not yet eaten. Of the twenty made, all signed and numbered by the artist, the invited guests stole ten: they thought it legitimate to have a souvenir. While stealing the tablecloths as souvenirs certainly contradicts Eat Art's principle of the ephemeral, the illegitimate act returns the essence of multiplication to the reproduction and transforms it into a kinetic object that is "moved" by the consumer. The tablecloth did not break with Eat Art's idea because it stood for yet another turn in and turning of Eat Art.

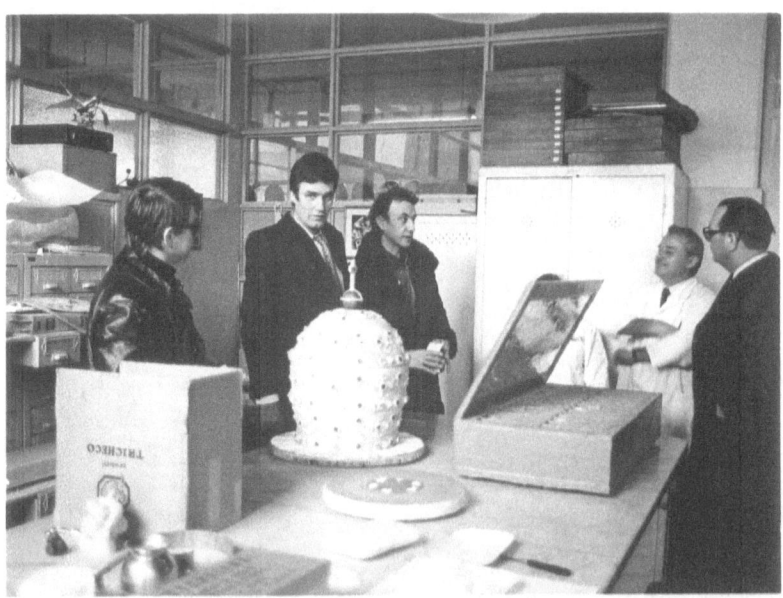

Daniel Spoerri, preparation of cakes for "L'Ultima Cena," Atelier Motta, Milan, 1970. Courtesy of Die Schweizerische Landesbibliothek, Archiv Daniel Spoerri. Copyright 2008 Artists Rights Society (ARS), New York / ProLitteris, Zurich.

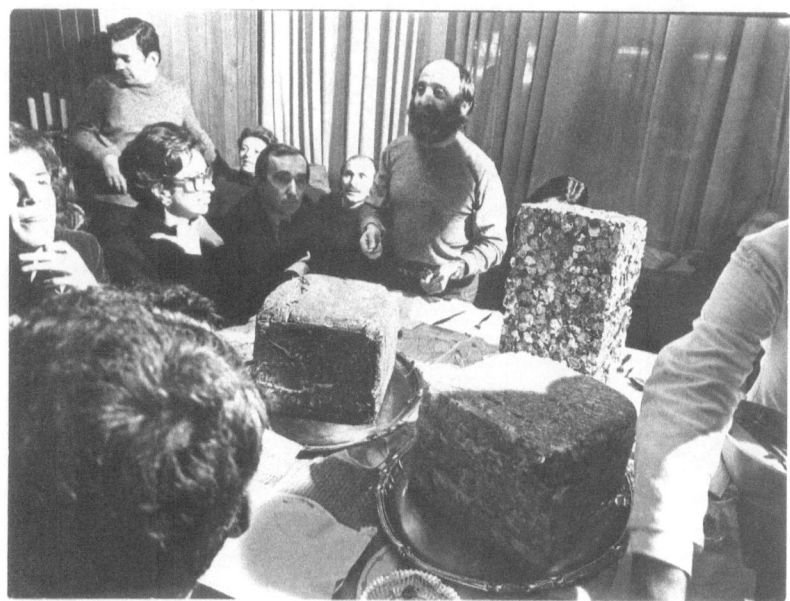

Daniel Spoerri, "Cesar's Table" at "L'Ultima Cena," Milan, 1970. Courtesy of Die Schweizerische Landesbibliothek, Archiv Daniel Spoerri. Copyright 2008 Artists Rights Society (ARS), New York / ProLitteris, Zurich.

The cloth put back on the table—that is, to its use-value—the artistic reproduction (also a staple principle of Pop Art, here reproduced and multiplied). The tablecloth thus repositioned horizontally the reproduced trap-painting, this time displacing its (this) aestheticized version—the silkscreen—from the walls onto the table.

If the *Henkel Banquet* celebrated the different returns of modern art and Eat Art itself, *L'ultima cena* (*The Last Supper*) in Milan, also staged ten years after the birth of new realism, in 1970, was the grandiose celebration of the movement's end. It concluded the series of actions and exhibitions staged by the artists all reunited here a last time. In this banquet held at the Restaurant Biffi in the city's central arcade, Spoerri cooked for each of the artist-participants one of their works, following their own artistic principles. So Arman was presented with accumulations of eel and lobster, Tinguely with an exploding cake in which air balloons were hidden, Jeanne-Claude and Christo with foods wrapped in aluminum foil, and César was offered for dessert a compression of liqueur candies. For Restany, the "pope-critic" of the movement, Spoerri had a tiara dessert made. The New

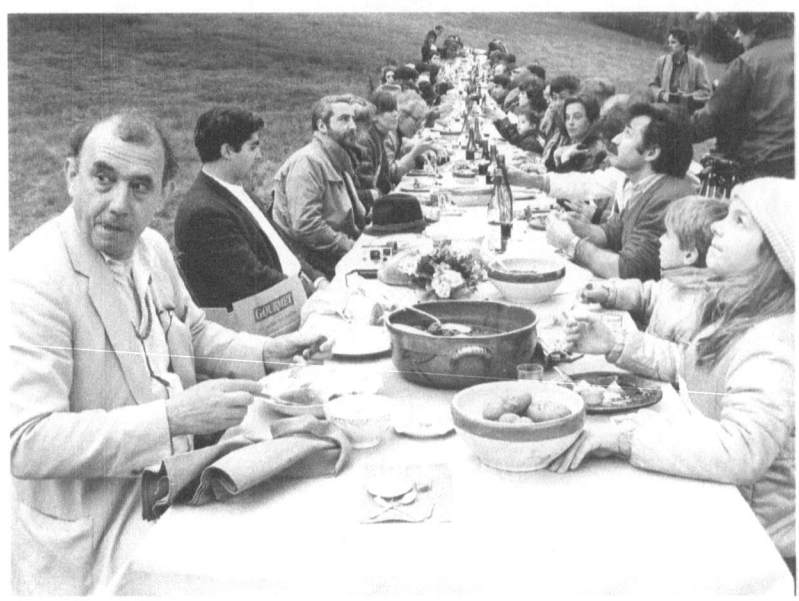

Daniel Spoerri, "Le déjeuner sous l'herbe ou enterrement du tableau-piège. Château du Montcel," Jouy-en-Josas, April 23, 1983. Courtesy of Die Schweizerische Landesbibliothek, Archiv Daniel Spoerri. Copyright 2008 Artists Rights Society (ARS), New York / ProLitteris, Zurich.

Realists ate themselves and each other. The artists fully incorporated, and embodied, or literally became one with their works in the act of destroying and digesting them. No trace of these works—and thus of Spoerri's own cooking art—remained, only the artists themselves in their unique individuality: the group is dissolved as such and the works transubstantiate into a short-lived materialist living presence.

Consider, in this light, that Spoerri's *Ultima cena* was ultimately a variation on Leonardo da Vinci's painting. The banquet brought the original back to life and set it in motion, duplicating it in its live-form in a location only a few steps away from where the original is on display. Multiple times (of history)—through Leonardo's work and Spoerri's but also those in between, including Warhol's own rendition—juxtapose, through repeated absences (the painting and its copies are not in the same space and time), without conflation. In this way *L'ultima cena* underscores the protean character of aesthetic traditions: First, with its return, the original *Last Supper* is not the last (not even in the Christian interpretation, for Christ rises from the dead);

second, Spoerri's variation on the timeless painting is edible and thus is time bound. Finally, the banquet was intended as a Dada act of autophagy, the artists' act of incorporation of neo-avant-garde art, a digestion ultimately completed in and by the stomach, as art's *technē* (*Kunst*). Spoerri's motto — in 1970 at his own retrospective in Amsterdam — was "When all arts perish, the noble cooking art will remain."

The stomach as time machine that produces never-ending endings is the conceptual operator behind Spoerri's *Déjeuner sous l'herbe* in 1983. On this occasion, Spoerri wanted to bury once and for all the trap-painting, which, in his view, had trapped him in the vicious digestive cycle of life and art. The happening took place in the park of the castle in Jouy-en-Josas where the Cartier Foundation had its headquarters. Several artists' and friends' installations, César's and Arman's, for example, "adorned" this site. Spoerri's theatrical lunch boasted a menu titled "Attrape-tripes: L'enterrement du tableau-piège" ("Trapping Tripe: The Burial of the Trap-painting"), which consisted of several dishes of entrails offered to 120 guests who brought with them their own plates and cutlery. The event's apogee was when the twenty tables on which the guests had eaten were buried in a forty-meter-long grave, in a row and in their condition of trap-paintings (the objects and remainders, however, were not glued). Enormous tractors had dug up the grave during the appetizers, but then everybody sat down to eat, including the tractor workers. In the same collective way, all the participants lowered the tables into the grave, and some, shovel in hand, ritualistically threw earth on them. The tractors then covered them completely, and Spoerri sowed there seeds of grass.

The temporal layering of this event is important. Indeed, this funeral was conceived with an eye to the future — but a future *archaeological excavation* of the trap-paintings/tables. Spoerri had already found an archaeologist who volunteered to excavate these grounds ten years after the event. (The excavation did not happen because the archaeologist in the meantime had quit his job and become a monk.) The funeral of a past idea — new realism dated from 1960 — in the present overlaps with the future excavation of this present as past. In this first planned excavation of contemporary art, the trap-painting renews some of its old meanings and functions. Three points are salient: first, the burial does not mean the trap-painting's end, for its return (from the grave, as for Spoerri entrails involve resurrection) is seen as immanent; second, remainders of *art* are here returned to be waste and refuse, ready to be "found" again (but differently); third, the banquet acts as the trap-painting of Manet's *Déjeuner sur l'herbe* (above the ground), which it turns upside down. Above the ground becomes under the ground, perhaps "underground." For new avant-garde or underground art to emerge, the trap-paintings of entrails need to be buried and found again, as repertories and ruins, fragments of themselves, a Pompeified present for the art of the future. This is an art that thus is not "free" of its legacy but is free to reconstruct it. At the same time, Spoerri's meal stages as living performance the new theatricality of Manet's own painting, in which the figure that looks at the viewer leaves the canvas in defiance of the viewer's voyeuristic gaze.

Finally, Spoerri himself revived the concept of trap-painting for the Swiss Pavilion at the Exposition in Sevilla in 1992. As Ewa Esterhazy notes, however, on this occasion another kind of reversal occurs: the trap-paintings are the results of other meals held *before* those taking place in the Pavilion. Spoerri writes that the food trap-paintings are now "memento mori altars, images of Vanitas," which again spur "our constant will to live, even in our mechanical . . . rationalistic consumer society." He adds that in Seville he has these "relics of lived survival" directly confront life as it is happening in a "total environment" (*Anekdotomania,* 232). In other words, the two times of "before" and "after" (life in motion and life petrified) now occupy the same time. While Spoerri quotes himself in a "retrospective" way, by reversing the order of exhibition and consumption of the trap-paintings and their actions, he also establishes a new temporality between life and death, life and art.

Conclusion

Spoerri returned most recently to Eat Art on several occasions, sometimes almost despite his own will (like at the Seville Expo in 1992), other times pleased to revive his banquets for new generations of artists, critics, and curious guests (e.g., at the retrospective of his banquets and the ensuing trap-paintings held at the Jeu de Paume between April 19 and June 2, 2002). Shows of the multiples, posters, and the few objects preserved have also taken place, either as part of general retrospectives of Spoerri's career (e.g., Tinguely Museum in Basel, in 2001, and in April 2007 at the center for contemporary art L. Pecci in Prato, Italy) or specifically devoted to Eat Art (such as in Munich at the Aktionsforum Praterinsel in 2001 and at the Parisian galerie fraîch'attitude in 2004). Is this return of Eat Art—especially the trap-paintings and the Restaurant Galleries (now staged in museums)—a final sellout of the neo-avant-garde, a cynical gesture on Spoerri's part to exploit the marketability of an idea (Eat Art) that remained at the margins of art (as willed poverty) in the seventies and now is raging?

Today in the context of transgenic food, mad cow disease, Slow food, ecological concerns, a diffusion of great varieties of cuisine, and immense poverty, Eat Art's resurrection—as restaged event (*premasticated* and *archicuit*, as Spoerri defines the meatball in his *Gastronomic Journal*), and as archaeological finding—does not glorify consumption and consumerism by turning them into spectacle. Its trap-paintings do not shock; they do not subvert the museum; yet they keep questioning its practices and values.[66] The return of banquets as art appears to be a conservative or resigned position, according to which art would be viewed as powerless and as slow paced as any everyday practice in the face of political and economic changes and challenges. Yet this return points to the limitations of the still-existing institutions and cultures of art that themselves are increasingly more steeped in consumerism. While the museum is eager to now appropriate this historical art and catch the audiences' attention, spectacularizing its eventlike nature, the new trap-paintings stemming in the old reheated (and reproposed) banquets inflate the concept of and the art original. Museums, galleries, collectors acquire originals that, as the Dadaists stated in their "Manifeste Cannibale," are like these artists' and their audience's (thus their own) excrement: products of consumption that return over and over again. The accompaniment of the certificate of authenticity only adds to this, guaranteeing an inflation of Spoerri's. True: the food trap-paintings are different at all times—they are products not only of consumption (self-corruption too) but also of chance and of entropy. Like actual cans of preserved food, their dates of expiration indicate a difference in quality. The older works decay, and the museums insist on preserving them. Are these food-multiples, posters, tablecloths, and trap-paintings, along with rehearsed banquets, avant-garde art or contemporary art, modern or postmodern art?

The old trap-paintings and food-multiples are hard to move—as are Spoerri's shoes contaminated with bread. The new trap-paintings indeed circulate at a faster speed (but their date is again an expiration date). They function like slightly varied (perhaps defective) acts of posthumous self-forgery, as in Wim Wenders's film *The American Friend*. There, the film's director, Nicholas Ray, plays the role of a master painter, presumed dead, who continues to paint and sell at auctions new works of his that are obviously believed to be exhumed posthumously. The exhumation, like that of the trap-paintings after their burial, has accrued these paintings' value so that now they go for high prices. Only few — craftsmen, with the piercing eyes and passion of long-gone detectives — detect differences in hues, because of newly produced colors. Spoerri's new/old trap-paintings could also function like authorial cinematic adaptations or remakes (Wenders's is an adaptation). However, the trap-paintings' adaptations are not in the author's hands, not in those of the culture/art industry, and not in the consumers'; rather, they are in the hands of chance and time: chance determines their contaminations of objects, and history — that of capitalist consumerism — manifests itself in the culture of objects, underscoring the fast-paced rather than the slow process that transforms the present into archaeology. These trap-paintings — an undecisively avant-garde, neo-avant-garde, and contemporary art — exhibit the archaeological status of the contemporary. Hence, while the numerous remakes sell, also inflating the market, the originals in the series leave room — again — for minute critical investigations into historical and cultural differences or heterogeneity, specifically as they relate, contrastively, to the homologizing global flow of commodities in and outside advanced capitalist societies. To adapt Weiss's words, Eat Art tempers actual modes of aesthetic appreciation through "a critique of utilization and destiny of aesthetic objects" (*Shattered Forms*, 3).

➎ *CONVIVIA* OF THE NEO-AVANT-GARDE

THIS FINAL CHAPTER considers two groupings of artists who worked with food. I first analyze neo-avant-garde collaborators in Spoerri's Eat Art project, namely, those artists who exhibited at Eat Art Gallery and, in certain cases, also cooked at his restaurant. I then address other contemporaneous artists who, although not directly in touch with Spoerri, worked with food as material and concept within their own art.

To read food works by those occasional Eat artists who showed at the Eat Art Gallery (Arman, César, and Joseph Beuys, among others) and by those individual artists who used food as Spoerri did (e.g., Piero Manzoni and Claes Oldenburg) may seem problematic. Yet even when collaborations between Spoerri and these other artists were fleeting and the ensuing food art was a momentary enterprise, the context was Eat Art or became Eat Art. The artists' "objects" on display at the Eat Art Gallery were in fact food-multiples, which multiplied both Eat Art (inflated it, proliferated it) and these individual artists' art. The food-multiples not only originated in these artists' individual artistic principles — as, for instance, accumulation or compression — but also gave an ironic touch to them and, consequently, to these artists' lifework.

In the case of sixties' artists such as Manzoni and Oldenburg who used food occasionally in their work without collaborating with Spoerri, this chapter focuses on those food works that, while embedded in philosophical or conceptual investigations differing from Spoerri's, still seemed to contribute to that notion of multiple and multiplication informing Eat Art. The readings that follow are limited to specific aspects of the art: I attempt to show how at the time of the neo-avant-garde some spoken or unspoken concerns about the historical situation of the avant-garde and postaesthetic art in general, before and after World War II, led to the use of food as material and concept through which to critique art production and consumption, and the institutions of art. Thus the analyses pursued confirm this book's overall thesis that by adopting metaphors of incorporation or, in the case of art objects (multiples) using food as material, the avant-garde (including the neo-avant-garde) promoted its own (and art's) instability. The avant-garde's instability highlights fractures and zones of potential change in the function of "official" art.

Friends & Co.: Exhibiting at the Eat Art Gallery

In 1970 "Eat Art" officially came into being when Spoerri opened his gallery after a sojourn in New York. He ascribes the anglophone name "Eat Art Gallery" to this trip. In New York Spoerri exhibited food-multiples by numerous artists. The most notorious was (and still is) Dieter Roth who had produced and continued to produce food-multiples also independently of the Eat Art project and who exhibited some of these in that venue, too, for example, his 1968 *Portrait of the Artist as Birdseed Bust (Portrait of the Artist as Vogelfutterbüste*; Roth identified this work by the acronym P.O.TH.A.A.VFB). Among those artists who showed edible multiples in the Eat Art Gallery, besides Roth, were Beuys, Arman, César, Robert Filliou, André Thomkins, Roy Lichtenstein, Richard Lindner, Ben Vautier, and George Brecht. Each produced multiple works of one hundred copies. César, for example, proposed a series of "sugar thumbs." Lindner baked a gigantic, edible Pop Art *The Blue Bosom Angel (Der Blaue Busenengel)*. Among the happenings, Vautier went on a "hunger strike": he sat in a box without food for twenty-four hours, and Beuys concocted an elaborate display of herring bones as "good" edible food, rather than garbage. The most memorable action, according to participants, was Claude Lalanne and François Lalanne's *Dîner Cannibale*.

Beuys and the couple Antoni Miralda and Dorothée Selz, like Roth, had consistently used food to make their art. Beuys focused on the energy quality of a few ingredients, such as fat and honey, and Miralda and Selz concentrated on shocking, artificial coloring. Unlike these artists quite accustomed to food as material, some of the featured artists, for example, Arman, César, and Lichtenstein, were not used to executing artworks with food. Yet they responded enthusiastically to Spoerri's suggestion that they contribute to the Eat Art Gallery. Those who agreed to collaborate with Spoerri thought that the material of food would match perfectly the principles that governed their regular artwork. For example, César saw sugar well suited for his expansions, ordinarily made of polyurethane. For Arman to be able to create food accumulations meant that his work with waste would come full circle. At the Eat Art Gallery the works exhibited were tested against the consumers' taste buds and by way of the stomach (at least some of them did), not just against the distant eyesight. Eat Art and the food-multiples viscerally take the notion of experience, especially art experience, which in the case of in/edible art, may be body changing (even threatening). Miralda and Selz remember how the visitors/consumers told them with excitement how, after eating their colorful food, they urinated in color. These artists' experiment/experience carried out almost literally Dada's provocations. For the postaesthetic experience to matter, the food artists stress, it has to involve the whole body, both that of the artist and that of the viewer/consumer. Eat Art not only operates as an action (like performance art or body art) but also exposes art and the artistic experience to physical transactions like the Futurists'. With Eat Art individuals take the risk to "incorporate" in/edible art physically as well as intellectually. Unlike Futurism, if individuals agree to engage art—and to do so they must go all the way and eat it—they also accept the eventuality of being poisoned and the possibility of finding in art an uncanny sensual dis/pleasure. They also risk remaining unmoved by the intake of food art.

Among the exhibitions at the Eat Art Gallery that took it upon themselves to investigate the "myths" of the edibility or digestibility of art were Beuys's *Supreme Fried Fish-Bones* (*1a gebratene Fischgräte*), which, like Filliou and Emmett Williams's *Spaghetti-Sandwich,* appeared to present art as an impoverished spectacle of life, as argued of Spoerri's own trap-paintings.[1]

Beuys's In/Edible Fish Bones

Many critics have engaged Beuys's use of foodstuffs and have elaborated on the shamanistic nature of his ritualistic actions. It is understood that Beuys appropriated ingredients such as fat, in both animal and vegetal forms, and honey, among others, to construct a symbolical language. For Beuys, this language would be based on the immediate reactions one has to certain foods or ingredients. Creativity is for

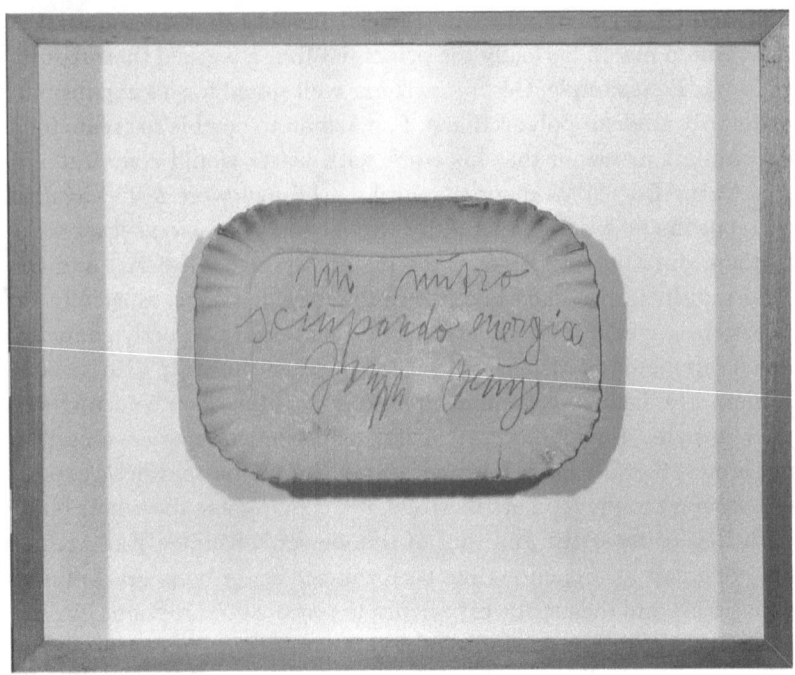

Joseph Beuys, Mi nutro sciupando energia. *Private collection, Milan. Copyright 2008 Artists Rights Society (ARS), New York/VG Bild-Kunst, Bonn.*

Beuys tantamount to energy flows in the process of life that these food-stuffs nourish, resurrect, and expend. For example, the work titled *I eat while expending energy (mi nutro sciupando energia)* under-scores the links between consumption and production, especially the fact that production corresponds to the process of thinking rather than to thought as a concrete "cold" (dead) object. Creativity — which for Beuys is a human faculty too often alienated and which also is the artistic impulse that has shaped history — is the energy expended first to move an unformed, live chaos into a shape and, second, to reener-gize form from "dead" fixity back to life.

To reenergize form Beuys often used honey, for example, in the action *How to Explain Pictures to a Dead Hare (wie man dem toten Hasen die Bilder erklärt,* 1965). On this occasion Beuys explained that "in putting honey on my head I am clearly doing something that has to do with thinking. Human ability is not to produce honey but to think, to produce ideas. In this way the deathlike character of thought becomes lifelike again. For honey is undoubtedly a living substance. Human thinking can be lively too."[2] He associated the edible materials' properties with art's healing and regenerating properties. Art is to be interpreted as the expanded field of creativity or, else, as the ability to shape one's own world with desire and imagination. The transformative qualities of Beuys's ingredients are transferred immediately to art's transformative potentials. Thus Beuys develops a utopian notion of expanded art that he calls "social sculpture" and that is eminently anthropological. In commenting on his work *Bathtub* (*"unbetitelt [Badewanne]*," 1960), Beuys elaborated on his concept of anthropological art in such a way that refers, albeit indirectly, to food and cooking. They are invoked here as an essential material and form of social sculpture for their qualities and capacities of creative transformation, energy transmission, shaping of bodies, and, thus, promotion of human growth, which for Beuys involves the crucial passage from matter to spirit:

> It is the transformation of substance that is my concern in art, rather than the traditional aesthetic understanding of beautiful appearances. *If creativity relates to the transformation, the change and the development of substance, then it can be applied to everything in the world. It is no longer restricted to art. . . . Then fat lies inside the tub, like the moulding or sculpting hand that lies behind everything in the world.* This is creativity in the anthropological sense, not restricted to artists. The relationship is with realities rather than artefacts.[3]

Beuys turned to food to express these ideas. For example, Beuys "melted" or cooked butter (or margarine) and worked with it in its multiple states, from hard to soft to liquid. When warm, fat expands and moves; when cold or frozen, it becomes hard, heavy, and nonmalleable. Energy is not only necessary to transform fat but also is the force that the artist uses to sculpt it. As Beuys reported of two of his most famous fat objects of the sixties, *Fat Corner (Fettecke,* 1960) and *Fat Chair (Fettstuhl,* 1964), fat in the former has hardened in the form of a quadrilateral, where fat on the chair "is not as geometrical as the fat corner, rather it preserves some chaotic character."[4] For its malleability fat becomes the material that best expressed the ideas of transformation from chaos to form, and vice versa, ideas that for Beuys exemplify processes of life, especially human social activity.

Human action can be organized according to the state of matter, that is, of fat.

Beuys was interested in the basics of life as the ground for art and society. Hence, in matters of food, Beuys focused on the nutritional, the archaic elements and functions of cooking as an act of transforming natural substances. The simple everyday gestures that go into daily cooking stand for the creative process in all humans.[5] These are actions such as cleaning or chopping vegetables that he performed, for example, for a TV documentary.[6] Thus cooking expands art or social sculpture, which subtracts itself from the freezing of ideas in artworks, ideas that are exhibited cold and appear "dead" in museums. He isolates everyday gestures from their usual context in his actions and reinvests them with highly symbolic meanings. Cooking or playing with food, both in daily uses and in performances, are one such continuous creative gesture of production of energy for life, a form of potentially "liberated" and liberating work, in his words, a simple springboard of creative energy.[7]

Beuys's view of art as social sculpture that would shape the future of humanity was holistic and total, an attempt to reshape humanity according to a view of creativity beyond the specialization of both the human faculties and the senses, the division of labor. Such total anthropological ideology stamps — problematically — Beuys's work.

As mentioned, honey, besides fat, plays an important role in Beuys's work. The connection between work and foodstuffs emerges most evidently in his 1977 *Honey-Pump in the Workplace* (*Honigpumpe am Arbeitsplatz*). As Tisdall notes, Beuys associates honey with the organization of bees' labor in which an end product of work, honey, is obtained through cooperation. Honey also appears as an epitome of the land of plenty — the land of milk and honey in both German and English — in addition to being a Christian symbol for resurrection. In the land of plenty, honey's association with work is either through the absence of work or through a reconceived notion of it whereby work becomes pleasure, the production of pleasure in a creative expenditure of energy. Beuys's *Honey-Pump* embodies such an idea. It is an enormous machine that works and reworks mountains of honey and margarine. This mechanical body of pumps and pipes all connected to produce a substance with only pleasurable connotations is a metaphor of a utopian social body. Beuys specifies: "With the honey pump I am expressing the principle of the F.I.U. [Free International University] that works in the blood circulation of society. . . . Feeling is in the heart and in the flow of honey that runs everywhere . . . the power of our will is represented by the chaotic energy of the dual engine which moves the blob of fat" (De Domizio Durini, 110).[8] As Ralph Beil put it, here "honey and fat become the sustaining *realia* of a multilayered model for the body, and vital flows of energy."[9]

Beuys's ritualistic actions recuperate some of the creative instances of life and of work that have disappeared from human life or, in the artist's view, that are in a crisis. Therefore Beuys embarks on the utopian project of emancipating humankind from its imprisoned status in contemporary civilization through these actions in which foodstuffs take a prominent regenerative role. His food materials attempt to heal the wound of the traumas that accompany human beings from their entry into the world. Although Beuys engages contemporary civilization and historical events, his view of trauma remains ontological: his approach to foodstuffs as the forces of art is symbolic–mythological.[10] Thus it is art's task to merge with science and nature to nourish, heal, and finally reconstitute a holistic organic human society from its wounds, its alienation, and its "deadly" aspects.

Beuys's approach to food differs from Spoerri's Eat Art project, if considered through this symbolic–mythological lens. For Beuys, food is one component, an energy source, in fabricating a new mythology for a different (healed) civilization. For Spoerri, eating — thus his stress on a possibly edible art — is appropriated for and within the avant-garde *discourse*. Eat Art confronts the writing of history (through the writing of art and of gastronomy) to test the grounds and meanings of the avant-garde in the present, even when his trap-paintings, journal, restaurants, and banquets appear not to relate to and comment on art. But, as Arthur Danto suggests about the candy bar "We Got It!" the phenomenological artistic instincts and creativity so prominent in Beuys's art are less at stake in Spoerri's food experiments than the discursive formations that generate forms of art as intricate as their readings.

Beuys presents himself as an artist-demiurge. For the art critic Achille Bonito Oliva, Beuys worked within the system of art, even if his production and his declarations often appear to be fully outside it and have been received as expressing a political program for the universal liberation of humankind. In Bonito Oliva's view, if one reads Beuys's work from within the discourse of art — as artistic intervention (not unlike Spoerri then)—then this allows a better grasp of Beuys's *totalitaristic* (not totalitarian) aesthetic. Yet the avant-garde is less at stake here. According to Bonito Oliva, Beuys shares with Friedrich Schiller's *On the Aesthetic Education of Man* (*Über die ästhetische Erziehung des Menschen in einer Reihe von Briefen,* 1794–95) the hope that "the arts can carry out a didactic role, a role of transformation" (quoted in De Domizio Durini, 85). Hence Beuys "puts art back in a position of centrality," what in a post-avant-garde world reveals, as Bonito Oliva states, "a type of ideology which stems in the Renaissance and is totalizing, an ideology that disregards history" (84). Bonito Oliva labels Beuys's social sculpture an ideological vice. It is a vice because it ignores history, in particular the history of alienation. Avant-garde art instead has shown and worked with alienation, especially its effects on language and the use of words. For Beuys, language remains a primary medium for his demiurgical, sculptural job, as he carries it out in his public lectures and addresses. The concept of performativity developed from Dada to Fluxus, however, radically differs from Beuys's ritualistic and symbolic performances that could be read as reinstating mythmaking, with personal yet universally conceived overtones.[11]

Unlike Spoerri's edible art in his banquets, Beuys's food art does not, in most cases, set forth its disappearance, thus engaging the commodity status of contemporary art. His food art does not leave behind traces of its consumption, perhaps with the exception of his *Supreme Fried Fish-Bones,* which also, however, display some totalitaristic aspect. In this action, the artist takes up Spoerri's original question of Eat Art, the issue of in/edibility. The performance staged by Beuys touched on myriad motifs, in addition to in/edibility that resonated with Western religious iconography and cultural symbols, such as fish, ashes, and Friday. He juxtaposed the received religious meanings to prosaic images, which, however, also come from the buried depths—the unconscious—of Western civilization's economic and political history. Yet the problem in Beuys's allegorical action is the loss of specific political content (as well as specific cultural critique) to its mythical quality. The Christian connotations and the meal's humble nature put forth an image of reconciliation and atonement as utopia, in other words, a humane future beyond history.

The performance unfolded in the following manner. Beuys bought twenty-five herrings on October 27, 1970, fried them, and ate some.

Most important, he also fried the fish bones that remained after his meal. On October 30, a Friday, he arrived at the Eat Art Gallery with two cardboard boxes filled with the fish bones that he hung — head pointed downward — on the walls, right below the ceiling. He wore a pair of pants on which he had sewn two dried fish (known by the name of "Chaplin"): one fish was pointed upward and the other downward, following the direction of blood circulation in the human body. They both suggested their return to life through the artist's blood while regenerating his life, which they would promote by offering themselves up as nourishment for his body. Beuys then covered his face with a mixture of ashes and coal. Ashes, coal and the fish, including the fish bones, which he also named "Friday-Objects," functioned like symbols.

The Chaplin fish may be a reference to the actor and director Charlie Chaplin. A scene from *The Gold Rush* comes to mind in which Chaplin, blinded by hunger, eats his own shoe with gusto. Poverty and hunger are the two main motifs of *Supreme Fried Fish-Bones,* which, however, are then also framed closely within Christian symbolism: the fish and ashes a reference to Jesus and his Resurrection. In the orthodox Catholic diet, one eats fish on Friday. *Karfreitag* or Holy Friday is the first day of the fast marking the long wait for Christ's Resurrection on Easter Sunday. Part of the Christian ritual also requires that one anoint one's own face with ashes.

More profane references are also present in the "Friday-Objects." As Beuys explains to Spoerri in a conversation about this performance, "Friday" was the name of Robinson Crusoe's servant-boy in Defoe's story.[12] Beuys possibly impersonates Friday (this is left open and could be problematic but also ironic) by painting his face with ashes, also in accordance with the above-mentioned Christian tradition. Friday and Christianity (through the in/edible fish bones) come together in this action — which took place on a Friday — in an open-ended way: the action may suggest a rebirth of Christianity through its appropriation (or expropriation if one wants to be critical) of the figure of the other, namely, Friday. A new, poor Christianity, redeemed from its history of violence, is resurrected as a phoenix from the ashes of a historical Christianity. Beuys is critical of the history of Christianity, for example, when he states: "Because the entire development which takes place through Christianity, the development in philosophy and science, is a reduction of life. Our concept of materialism refers to a dead materialism, to chemical analyses, to statistics: these are all life-less abstractions" (*Joseph Beuys in America,* 179).

While he associates Christianity with a kind of scientific material-ism, rather than his idea of spiritual creativity, and while the reference to materialist development is also a reference to capitalist society (and citing Robinson Crusoe may be one reason to make such a reference clear), he also envisions a reborn Christianity. In explaining how death in the contemporary world is associated with violence rather than with natural processes of rebirth, Beuys further elaborates that this is not merely an indication of political failure: "It is not just the bour-geoisie or the petit bourgeoisie which is the cause of our problem. . . . The cause is far deeper and has something to do with Christianity. This doesn't mean that Christianity is a failure, but simply that it was only a preliminary step, albeit an important one, and that Christian-ity—i.e. socialism—can only begin now, by thinking about death in positive terms" (180). Beuys redeems Christianity, in a simplistic con-densation of Christianity with socialism, from its own history. Simi-larly, Beuys wrongfully appropriates—colonizes perhaps—Friday, the "black" slave, by impersonating him and reducing him to a new icon of a socialist Christ. It is true, however, that no single reading is ever sufficient or complete, and one may also stress the ironic dimension of the action in which Beuys is also condemning the association between capitalism, colonization, slavery, and Christianity.

Beuys continued his performance by hanging on his body three tape recorders that he marked with his name and a cross. The tape record-ers, also bearing an oil stain, were known to the connoisseur of Beuys's work from yet another performance, also held in 1970, titled *Celtic.* All these paraphernalia became signs of Beuys's personal and mythi-cal "identity." They helped bring his persona directly into the action, and through it the action would expand beyond its time and space. In the specific case of *Supreme Fried Fish-Bones,* this is evinced from one remark made by Beuys. He explains that the recorded and played-back noise was a trace of the space and time in which the action itself had been conceived and initially staged, the kitchen where he fried the fish bones and ate them in the company of his family. The tape record-ers inserted a residue of the food world outside the exhibition space, a space–time that Beuys deemed necessary to include in this and, like-wise, in every exhibition. For Beuys, the recorded noise was a signifi-cant part of the action in question, which should never be separated from its genealogy. In this respect every action strives to some completeness while presenting itself always as just a fragment of a total, absolute creative space that can never be fully "contained," only suggested metonymically.

With the tape-recorded noise in the background, Beuys started to make his fish bone multiples: he cut the oily paper in which the fish bones had been wrapped into regular-size sheets, signed the sheets, and stamped them. The paper sheets thus stamped were the certificates that accompanied the work *Supreme Fried Fish-Bones*. One multiple consisted of a small wooden box containing the fish bone and this certificate. The action finally concluded when Beuys, after picking up the same walking cane he had used in *Celtic,* leaned on it, with his left hand under his chin, and remained standing in this position for three hours, facing the audience who were coming and going.[13]

In *Catalog Taboo* Spoerri had offered a taboo-breaking catalog, a new artistic operation that undid categorizations, including the difference between presentation and representation, between art and its catalog, and, by extension, the classification of art as expression of life rather than of art as a way of life. In accord with this vision of art and life, Beuys presented his series of fish bone multiples as edible. The fish bone is the negative of the fish: the fish is commonly represented in art as an image of death and resurrection. In the Gospels one reads of Christ's miracle of the *multiplication* of fish and bread. Beuys presents the audience with the fish bones — the image *ex negativo* of Christ's multiplication — as encapsulating a nourishing, positive energy for life, which through Beuys's miraculous action reproduces itself in the guise of the edible multiple. Beuys multiplies fish bones, instead of fish, and juxtaposes the symbolic element in classical art with the poverty of Eat Art that challenges the boundaries of the inedible. Looked at from this perspective, Beuys reinterprets the narrative of Christianity through a creative materiality (spiritual in his ideology) that expands the body of Christ's "edibility."

Beuys's fish bones are the outcome of a series of apocryphal actions that ultimately construct art as a process endowed with the magical culinary power to transform disparate natural sources and ingredients (i.e., the waste forgotten and discarded by the commonly used language and the cultural systems in place) into new images, a different system of thought. *Catalog Taboo* confronts us with its silent and simple multiplication, the mechanism through which art makes itself into an operation and involves different practices of looking and "capturing" the real. In contrast, Beuys's action poses the fish bone — and the making of it into a multiple — as a quasi-religious artistic miracle. Beuys makes himself retrace and relive Western civilization's itinerary, from Christ's death and rebirth through Beuys's own empathetic identification with the black slave and colonialized subject (on whose shoulders capitalism has built itself) to expiate the traumatic energy of history and redress it in the utopian moment of break that his messianic action announces. The overall symbolic framework overshoots the simplicity of the fish bone as multiple that otherwise would be more attuned with Eat Art's operational tactics of quiet disturbance — disordering — of cultural myths. Eat Art drags these myths down, in Georges Bataille's sense of "lowering," or deterritorializes them, in Gilles Deleuze and Félix Guattari's language.

Despite its mystifying aspects, a few critical instances in this performance break the highly symbolic setup. First, Beuys ascribes a nomadic character to this performance, which took place in Spoerri's locale on Düsseldorf's *Burgplatz* — the Fortress Square of this German city. His leaning on the cane, in wait, is the nomadic feature that marks both the beggar-slave and the prophet that Beuys, the artist-demiurge, embodies in his performance, as he explains to Spoerri. The presence of these characters on this Düsseldorf square questions, in his view, the Fortress's rule and its apparently stable history.[14] As is the case with his malleable materials that redress flows of energy, the nomad character challenges the power and strength of German history, and generates, in his opinion, new currents for thinking and writing history. Second, and more important, the fish bone presented here as edible, when most Westerners consider it to be inedible, is a challenge to the visitor's accustomed taste, in that he or she must acknowledge that the distinction between good and bad needs to be made over and over again, and is not determined once and for all by religious, ethical, or aesthetic parameters. In Spoerri's words, the constant redefinitions of the boundaries between good and bad, an issue at the core of nutrition, which stands as the epitome of one or the other culture, is the task of "evolution."[15]

Third, Beuys contributes to the work of revaluation (*Verwertung*) of garbage and questions of value in general also pursued by Spoerri and other New Realists. In his conversation with Spoerri, Beuys stresses two points about such revaluation and his fish bone multiples

(*Fischgräte,* 54) First, Beuys stresses simplicity, but also production. As Beuys tells Spoerri, garbage is produced; it is the outcome of selection, separation, and expulsion — like digestion — which also characterizes artistic or creative production (*Ausscheidung*). Second, he underscores that a work of art, which undergoes selection and separation from the physiological and cultural processes of production, is a document that like garbage attests to its history. Thus Beuys wanted to show the production of his multiple, the labor and the cost expended in imagining a project and then realizing it, in short, the making of art into a social action: "The costs, pure work, wages, art and culture and work: all of this steps in with any preparation: buy, clean, cook" (*Fischgräte,* 44). These three moments (buy, clean, cook) focus Beuys's performance around shared concerns with Eat Art and New Realism, concerns that then interfere with the artist's mythopoesis and his phenomenology.

The critic Benjamin H. D. Buchloh situates Beuys's work within the national context of German art and culture in the second postwar period, by analyzing Beuys's specifically German works such as *Auschwitz-Demonstration* (1964). In doing so, Buchloh can argue that, despite the artist's "definition of the performative as therapeutic and exorcistic," Beuys is one of the few German artists of his time to engage historical memory and counter the memory crisis (the repression of the Nazi past) in his country (*Art since 1900,* 483). The *Auschwitz-Demonstration* is a group of vitrines (glass cases) in which various "heterogeneous" elements are assembled that for the most part do not bear any immediate relation to Auschwitz. Among the objects showcased are sausages and sausage rings as well as Christian symbols alongside objects that may suggest mockery. In particular, there is "a cookie lying like a Eucharist next to a Christ figure on a dinner plate" (484). Brought together under one rubric as the work's title suggests, the objects constructed a unifying historical context, which Beuys then extended to encompass the present condition of human work and degradation of intellectual creativity under capitalism. This connection between the Nazi past and the present is reminiscent of the Frankfurt school's critique of the culture industry. Yet Beuys performs this critique by having recourse to supposedly universal symbols, beyond history. Similar to the ambivalence of Christian symbols in his fish bone performance, the objects don't allow the historical critique to become historically specific, to sharpen its focus around Germans' forgetting and avoidance of working-through after Auschwitz (analyzed by Theodor Adorno). Instead, Beuys's universal symbols highlight less the impossibility of representation of forgetting than the general anthropological, and in his case mythopoeic, ability to resurrect, cathartically, humanity. As Buchloh concludes, "Beuys attempts to synthesize two mutually exclusive epistemes aesthetically: to emphasize the object's investment, if not with cathartic ritual, then at least with a mnemonic dimension, and simultaneously to foreground the object's condition as pure matter and process according to his obsession with proto- and pseudoscientific positivism" (485).

Beuys's food shows that the historical mnemonic trace is mostly absent (in *Fischgräte*, the reference to colonialism and "Friday"—itself problematic in its empathetic appropriation—is confused, not just ironically, with the reference to Christianity). In general, only a few times does canonical German food (sauerkraut and potatoes) appear, and when it does it is never from a clear-cut critical or mnemonic perspective. When an approach to food as cultural–historical discourse emerges, it is a critique aimed at reconstituting a new language beyond history, even when using history's residues. In this regard, Beuys's vitrine or his performances are not like Walter Benjamin's constellations in which dialectical images ensue or Spoerri's contaminated situations of objects, which, both, produce a new temporality. This is Benjamin's now-time from which one can reread and rewrite historical accounts. Dada antidiets had dispersed gastronomical grammars and liberated ingredients; in contrast, Beuys appropriates these scattered foodstuffs but, through his antidiets, his miracle of multiplication of the negative fish still reconstitutes them as universal and mythological clusters of therapeutic energy.

Richness in Scarcity, Poetry in Poverty:
The Spaghetti-Sandwich *and* 24-Hour Fast

If Beuys builds a mythological narrative around the poor but nourishing fish bone multiple, other artists, like Filliou and Williams, share their art's poverty, and the poverty in their life, with their audience. Poverty, in this context, means leaving behind high professionalism and a culture of one-dimensional specialists. Through poverty Filliou embraces what, in 1962, he called the revolt of mediocrity, a concept similar to Beuys's "expanded art": "A refusal to be colonized culturally by a self-styled race of specialists in painting, sculpture, poetry, music, etc. . . . This is what *La Révolte des Médiocres* is all about. With wonderful results in modern art, so far. Tomorrow could everybody revolt? How? Investigate" (quoted in *My Life in Flux,* 35). While Beuys seemed to propose solutions, Filliou and Williams conceive of a poor mediocre art as an investigation into new, undefined possibilities of creativity and unaesthetic judgment. Filliou, for example, marked his works with a stamp that offered him three possibilities among which to choose: "Bien Fait, Mal Fait, Pas Fait" (Well Done, Badly Done, Not Done). After stamping the work, he would check one of three. The "Badly Done" was the most stimulating of the possibilities; the work's imperfections and even perhaps amateurish traits remove it from the world of serial and perfect commodities, and avoid a designer's style.[16] The politics of culture Filliou labeled the revolt of the mediocre — which Herbert Marcuse invoked in his more overtly political critique of capitalist organization in *One-Dimensional Man: Studies in the Ideology of Advanced Industrial Society* (1964) and which he theorized as "The Great Refusal" — is detectable in the coproduction of Williams and Filliou's *Spaghetti-Sandwich.*[17] This 1963 coinvention was proposed as a multiple at the Eat Art Gallery in 1971. The visitors were called on to eat the two artists' in/edible (mediocre or *mal fait*) food on which they had fed and that at the same time fed their art. The *Spaghetti-Sandwich* in this regard bore a resemblance to Friedrich Hundertwasser's nettle soup.

As Williams recollects, the origins of the *Spaghetti-Sandwich* went back to a "bleak period," when both Filliou and he often went hungry and yet were happy. At this time, to be artists, they took up various small jobs, attended art openings "where the drinks flowed freely and the *canapés* were *gratuits,*" or simply accepted all the help they could get from friends. Their life was not specialized, not one-dimensional. Out of this "happy" dispersion of creative energy — in flux — came the *Spaghetti-Sandwich.* Filliou described it as the most humane and dignified food to a *Paris-Match* journalist: "You can talk about art, music and poetry all you want, but remember, with *The Spaghetti-Sandwich* you can feed an entire army. And the astronauts. The cosmonauts as well!" (*My Life in Flux,* 128). Quite opposite to Futurism's antipasta invectives, this is a cacophonic sandwich, a simple poetic game: who would ever squeeze together spaghetti and bread in a sandwich? It is culinary anathema! The *Spaghetti-Sandwich* is

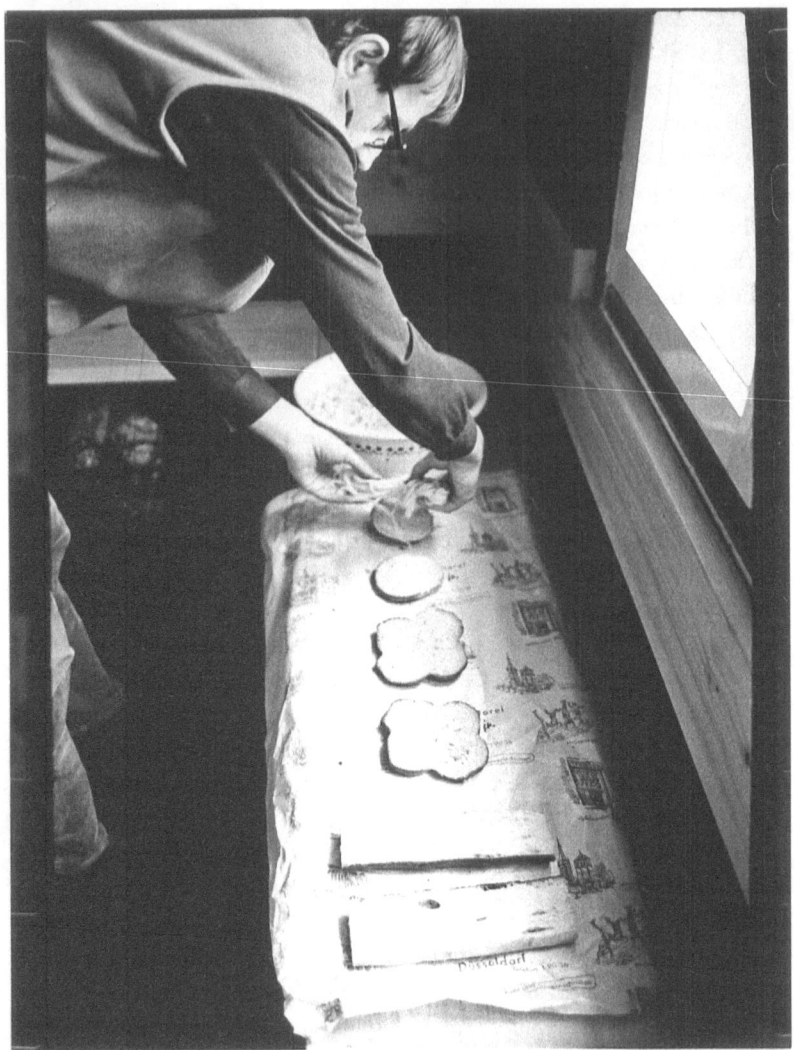

Emmett Williams and Robert Filliou, Spaghetti Sandwich—Co-invention,
*Eat Art Gallery, 1971. Courtesy of Emmett Williams and Die Schweizerische
Landesbibliothek, Archiv Daniel Spoerri. Copyright Emmett Williams.*

purposefully disrespectful or ignorant of eating habits, of the laws
of a balanced nutrition, and of bourgeois taste. However, it generates a brief poetic instant, the impetuousness of an artistic creativity found in everyday ingredients that come together in unorthodox
and *informe* agglomerates of dubious "good" taste, but considerable

energy. The alliteration of the two words (spaghetti and sandwich) in this one-line composition echoes the tautological food that adds carbohydrates to carbohydrates, spaghetti to bread in a sandwich that is yet another catalog of similitude, rather than sameness. The coinvention *Spaghetti-Sandwich* was a happening. It was food for art as social energy rather than an art object/food commodity. Perhaps it also reappropriates the content, matter, and alienation of advertising: the sandwich-men. Williams, in his autobiography, offers a genesis of the happening. As a token of gratitude toward some friends who had lent him their tiny flat while they were abroad, Williams

> cooked up an enormous batch of the spaghetti sauce for which I am famous, and put it in the refrigerator as a surprise for Sharon and Erik [Dietmann] upon their return. Unfortunately for Sharon and Erik, Robert and I decided to sample the sauce. It was very good, even cold. We spread it on bread, and ate it in this fashion several times, and even invited some of our friends to do the same, until there was very little sauce left for Sharon and Erik. But no matter, *The Spaghetti Sandwich* was born. I think that this background material is sufficient to convince the historians of art of the truth of the co-inventors' declaration, silk-screened on linen napkins for the Eat-Art "revival" edition of the *Spaghetti Sandwich* in 1971, that it was indeed "born from necessity and consumed forthwith" eight years earlier. (*My Life in Flux*, 128)

This sandwiched spaghetti space of convergence embodied the "leftover spaces and temporal structures that have remained mysteriously outside an ever-increasing process of commodification" while this space of improvised poor commensality and coinventions was also a nonform of cultural experience and a form of countercultural experience (*Art since 1900,* 461). The *Spaghetti-Sandwich* squares with Fluxus's association with the "low" arts of popular culture—the two-word poem is after all an instantaneous gag. And this art differs from the iconic status of American food in Pop Art.[18] The *Spaghetti-Sandwich* exists in the "action"—the event—of collaboration, the so-called coinvention, which emerges in the joy taken in the unexpected production and consumption of this poor but excessive food. The *Spaghetti-Sandwich*—which is devoured voraciously in good company—constitutes an instant of experience that carves itself out from within the state of "poverty of experience" in a consumer society already diagnosed, for example, by Benjamin in the thirties.

Vautier's performance *24-Hour Fast* (1970) also addressed "poverty" and a reaction to it. Vautier locked himself up in a box without

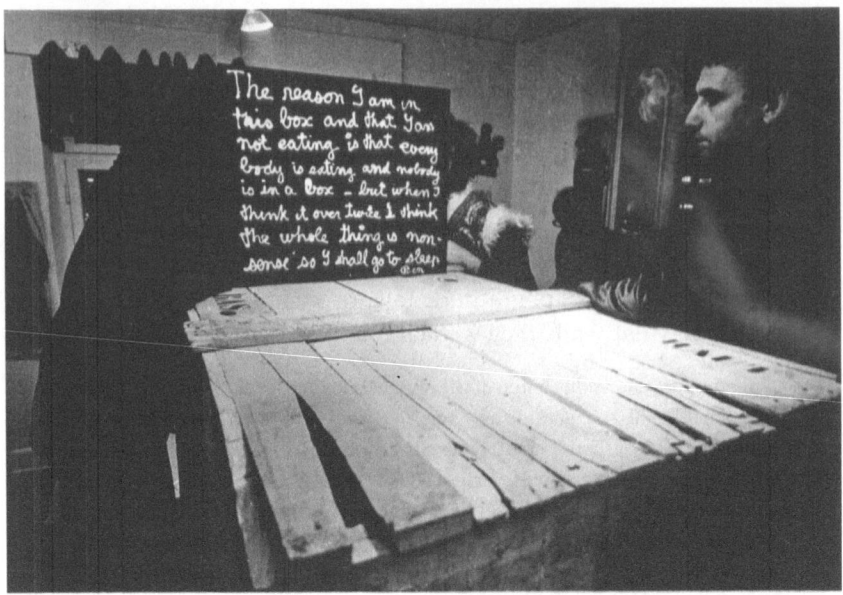

Ben Vautier, Ben on Hunger Strike for Twenty-Four Hours, *Eat Art Gallery, 1970. Courtesy of Die Schweizerische Landesbibliothek, Archiv Daniel Spoerri. Copyright Artists Rights Society (ARS), New York.*

food and presented the absence of the artist and of his art — which was on view at the Hans Mayer-Denis Renée gallery next door in an exhibition of print artists — as the only viable form of edible art, art that in the end makes itself invisible. Ben, the name by which he is best known, forced the viewer into an act of fasting when he pointed to his invisible presence (his erasure) within the gallery. The erasure occurred through the medium of writing that in the gallery substituted itself as a trace for the artist's and the visitor's act(s) of consumption. A blackboard announcing his absence in his own handwriting stood on top of the box that contained him. At the same time, in the gallery next door where his work was on display, another blackboard announced that his absence there was due to his absent-presence at the Eat Art Gallery. Like writing itself, the box is another container of absence, or a deferral, in this case, of the "Eat" artist who in fact is fasting and not producing, or rather producing an action that consists in abstention. Ben takes on the position of Kafka's hunger artist who exhibits his own vanishing and gradual invisibility and whose absence is finally realized in writing — the story we read. In Ben's case, Eat artists are those artists who subtract their production from the industrious production and performance principles of advanced industrial society and pro- voke hunger in their viewer, for example, an appetite for an experience that is not yet available or that has already been erased and that needs (re)imagining.[19] In short, Ben's *24-Hour Fast* "resuscitated and articu- lated the individual subject's limited capacity to recognize the collec- tively prevailing conditions of 'experience'" (*Art since 1900*, 461).

Nauseating Fetishes: Arman's Candy *Accumulation, Roth's Chocolate, and César's* Sugar Thumb

When Arman, César, and even Lichtenstein produced edible accumu- lations, sculptures, and pop-icons for the Eat Art Gallery, these fol- lowed the general artistic principles regulating their production. So, in the case of Arman's food accumulations it may be instructive to read the presence of food precisely through Arman's principle of accumu- lation and to see how accumulation and food intersect. Eat Art and accumulation come together, and the question is, what are the effects of such juxtaposition? Taking Arman as an example (but it could be César's compressions),[20] accumulation repeats itself throughout his work, a repeated series of acts of accumulation that are all different with respect to their objects, but also continuous as gestures.

Let us then examine *Candy*, Arman's accumulation of "Barbie dolls' legs" made of marzipan and, as usual, amassed in a Plexiglas box. *Candy* is the official title: it takes an English proper name and a common name at once and thus renames the Barbie doll. These legs titillate the consumer's fetishistic and childlike desire and are even more provoking because of their explicit edibility. They excite the anx- ious desire of incorporation of the doll's legs as the fetish that momen- tarily erases sexual difference and fills up the anguish about "lack" and "void" (castration anxiety). From another perspective, the fetishistic edible legs of dolls as commodities for sale and ready to be consumed could perhaps also be a reference to Arman's 1960 exhibition *Le Plein* (*Full Up*). But there is an obvious difference: the former accumula- tion entails an element of desire and pleasure (albeit one imbricated with anxiety); the latter, on the contrary, displays repulsive and nau- seous excess. *Le Plein* responded to Yves Klein's exhibition titled *Le Vide* (1957, 1958), both performances taking place in the same gallery (Iris Clert) in Paris: "For two days, Arman and Martial Raysse piled, accumulated, heaped up bandy-legged furniture . . . chairs, tables, bidets, old bicycles. . . . The passers-by could see a spectacular mass of garbage in a 3.5 meter-high shop-window."[21] The visitor to the gallery could enter the latter only from a side entrance: the heaps of garbage blocked the main entrance or main access to this accumulation. In addition, the art collector was left with nothing but detritus to buy. Tellingly, the invitation to the exhibition was a sardine tin filled with garbage and also containing a text by Pierre Restany announcing the event. The art critic Francoise Choay wrote in the December 1960 issue of *Art International*: "There is nothing left to buy in this gigantic heap that is truly a gesture, an event that will return to nothingness without letting any collector profit from it. . . . This is a dissertation, grounded in humanism, on a certain state of decomposition (ours)" (quoted in *Arman,* 195). And the decomposition is shared by the marzipan legs accumulated in a Plexiglas box: these legs — as the shop window and gallery full of garbage — indeed also bar access to their consumption by the mouth. *Candy* bars the desire the sugar legs arouse, which is caught in a limbo of frustrated expectation, by rendering their (tactile as well as oral) consumption impossible. The consumer is left with a watering mouth and unable to touch or eat the object. The inaccessible fetish or the substitute counterfetish — the sugary legs in *Candy* and waste in the gallery Clert — leave the fetishistic consumer (or collector) exposed to his or her own "void," or lack. The consumer is forced into the position of anxious voyeur: he becomes a viewer left to confront his own fetishistic gaze, a gaze that traps him. This is a viewer who is unable to give way to his desire to consume and, thus, in the process, unable to destroy — or disavow — difference. In the case of the art consumer of marzipan Barbie legs, difference may be both sexual and the difference that supposedly distinguishes the love for art from the desire to possess commodities and eat food. This viewer faces a glass that returns to him his own voyeurism. But what about the women consumers or viewers — how can they relate to these dolls' legs, to these metonymies of metonymies of themselves, that is, women's legs replicated as Barbie's legs replicated as almond-paste doll's legs? The desire to devour the alienated body, to incorporate it and make it one's own, is again blocked. Women viewers are excluded three times by this language of desire, hence by the sugary legs: they have not "cooked" the legs, they cannot eat the legs, and the legs are not theirs. The pleasure of eating, as well as the pleasure of their own other sexuality, is *not* here (to be found between *those* legs, which Spoerri identifies as the site of reproduction). However, the almond legs promote and stimulate — again, through their sweet and kitschy edibility — woman's desire to devour and repossess differently these reproduced parts of her self, a desire that remains dissatisfied in *Candy*. The legs, however, confront her with the *possibility* that she could make herself into *her own* cake, to become the artist-maker of herself.[22] In facing Arman's sweet replicas of women's legs behind Plexiglas, a woman viewer acknowledges the sugarcoated sadism present in art, the sadism that turns women into "beautiful" — tasty — fetishes offered up for public consumption.[23] In *Candy* this feminine is less eternal than perishable, less beautiful than nauseating in the excessive and uncanny accumulation of a sweetness that is in fact left to first disturb and then rot.[24]

While evidently different in nature and kind, Arman's *Candy* doll-legs — with their references to castration anxiety, fetishism, and the threatening aspects of desire exploited by consumer culture — may be this artist's rewriting of the fragmented and open dolls' bodies by a German artist on the margins of surrealism, Hans Bellmer. As Hal Foster remarks, Bellmer's dolls — all individual variants of fragmented female bodies — speak to a *subject* that in viewing them faces his sadistic and masochistic desire, desire that entails its own dissolution, now projected onto the dolls (*Compulsive Beauty*, 109). After the mass annihilations of World War II and in the society of mass production, Arman's accumulations of in/edible (comestible but inaccessible) dolls' legs expose especially the subject's wish and fear of disintegration as fully administered and mastered by consumer-society. This is a society that reproduces, fetishistically, such misogynistic wishes as integral to the condition of failed collective subjecthood, as Buchloh puts it.

More generally, Arman's *Candy* explores the notion of excess: adding sugar to the sugary image of the doll, *Candy* turns into kitsch and parodies the doll's "ritualistic" function of domestication. "Candy" accumulates the excess of the doll's reinstatement of the laws of sexual and social reproduction, of the values of the traditional and patriarchal family structure. Excess exposes the ideology of reproduction, for *Candy* is only made of legs that, as Spoerri put it to Arman, point to the greatest multiplication that exists, human multiplication in birth. In Spoerri's words: "The greatest accumulation of beings: and it all happens between women's legs!" (*Daniel Spoerri Presents Eat Art,* 86). In an earlier version of this statement, Spoerri underscored the threat concealed in human multiplication but made visible in Arman's accumulations of legs: "Arman, my rabbit, it is right between the legs that the greatest accumulation is produced, which will make the world explode. Let us hope we will be able to laugh" (*Wenn alle Künste,* 36). The multiplication of accumulated legs, reproduced here with edible materials, raised the dilemma of the ratio between human reproduction and food production (resources), to which Spoerri alludes in the quote. The friendly address, "rabbit," points to the fast multiplication rate of humans, who sexually seem to behave like rabbits. Ultimately, Spoerri implies, human reproduction, which alone guarantees human existence, paradoxically, may come to threaten human existence. (Overpopulation, as overproduction, was a concern strongly debated in the sixties and seventies.)[25]

The 1970 *Candy* may also be compared with Dieter Roth's own doll drowned in chocolate (untitled, *Doll,* 1969).[26] In Roth's sculpture, a doll is submerged in a cylinder filled with chocolate with only the doll's legs spared. Here chocolate exceeds the boundaries of its own sweetness, thus also invading the territory of commodified sentimentality. In other words, the chocolate's sweetness suffocates the sweetness of the doll, domesticity, and family values. As with other ingredients used by Roth, such as yogurt and sour milk, but also cheese, for example, in his notorious *Staple Cheese (A Race)* (1970), food is exhibited as a live substance mutating in time. It "eats" up its own contexts, territories, and cultural meanings to which it has been traditionally confined. In Los Angeles, for instance, Roth had exhibited thirty-seven suitcases filled with cheese that in the month of May started to "run," producing an unbearable stench and larvae in great quantities. The U.S. health authorities threatened to shut down the exhibition, but the gallerist was successful in preventing it.[27] In the case of chocolate, which became for Roth a central material, he counters chocolate's cultural and commercial meanings by way of association or of excess, not without a childlike gaze. For example, chocolate is confused with excrement, yet it also has strong positive connotations. It can stand for spontaneous delight, a game, or an ironic statement. More often, it becomes a threatening flow of boiling lava — an oppressive mass — that suffocates with its own bittersweetness. Then chocolate immobilizes and gobbles up toys, knickknacks, garden gnomes, and souvenirs.[28]

Dieter Roth, Untitled
(Doll in Chocolate),
1969 (Ohne Titel,
Puppe in Schokolade).
Courtesy of the Dieter
Roth Foundation,
Hamburg. Copyright
Dirk Dobke.

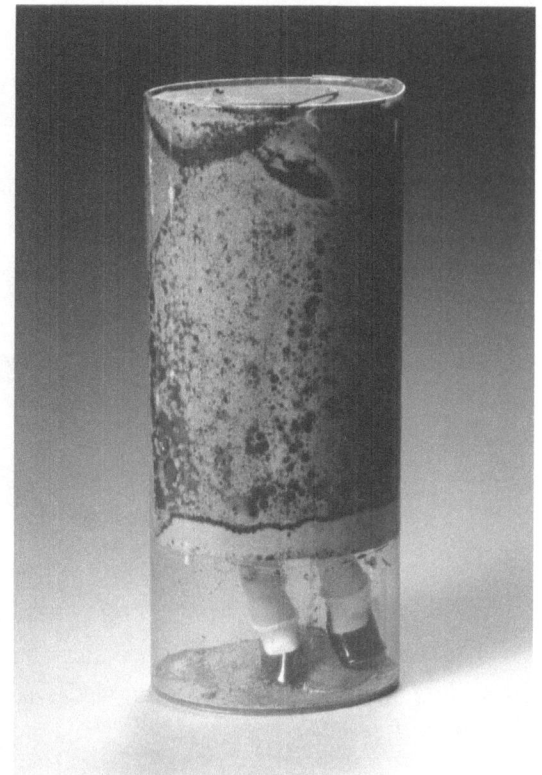

The ambivalent aspect and function of chocolate as art—*its pharma-kon*-like qualities—are highlighted in Spoerri's own homage to Roth: among Spoerri's *Bread-Dough Objects* (used for the opening exhibition of the Eat Art Gallery) is a *Small Oven* (1970) flooded by an uncontrollable rising of bread dough, as if it were flowing from every opening of the stove and from every pot on top of it. Roth too had proposed a *Stove (Herd)* in 1969 from which chocolate spilled over. Unlike Spoerri's, this was not in miniature format and reminded one of Roth's actual stove that he used for his chocolate productions.[29] Roth contributed all his chocolate sculptures until that time to the Eat Art Gallery, in addition to his *Spice Windows (Gewürzfenster,* 1970), and the *Rabbit Dropping Rabbit (Karnickelköttelkarnickel)* made for Spoerri's gallery in 1971. *Spice Windows* focused on smell and through it on this sense's mnemonic qualities, memories that were freed and mixed in the exhibition room by visitors willing to open the upper

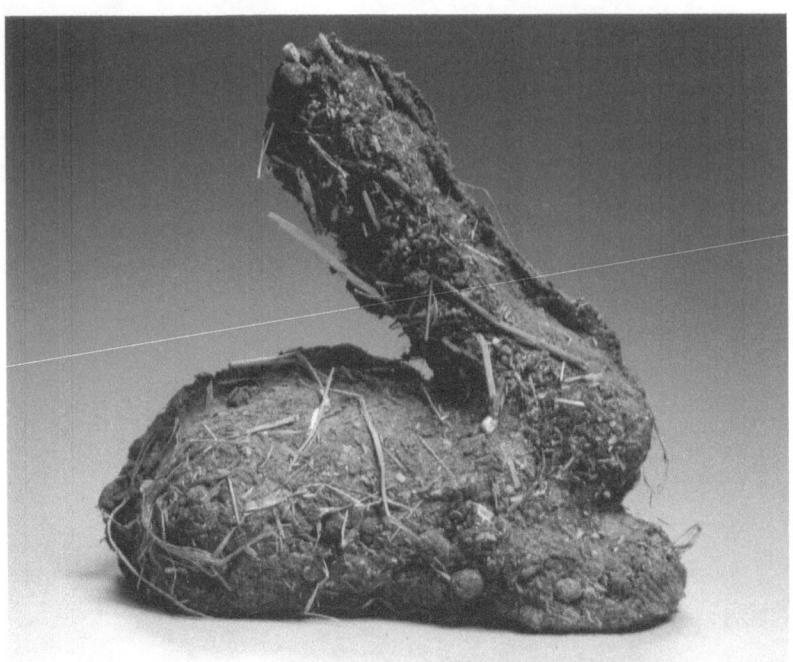

Dieter Roth, Karnickelköttelkarnickel, *1972. Courtesy of the Dieter Roth Foundation, Hamburg. Copyright Dirk Dobke.*

surface of the window frames or, more simply, smelling the fragrances that escaped their encasing anyway. The *Rabbit Dropping Rabbit* was more attuned with the excremental nature that Roth ascribed to chocolate, a scatological attribute that for Roth also related to the cycles of life and death. Dirk Dobke describes *Rabbit Dropping Rabbit*:

> He [Roth] had the mould, which is vaguely reminiscent of the forms for chocolate Easter bunnies, tightly packed with rabbit ordure by the Basle sculptor Walter Moser and left to dry. Each of the total 210 copies had a label based on a drawing attached at the bottom, which was signed and numbered by Roth. The "Karnickelköttelkarnickel" was and remains the only multiple in which Roth took excrement, as the concluding stage of the organic process of disintegration, as his artistic material. (*Books and Multiples,* 16)

If Roth used other foodstuffs like yogurt to show the process of disintegration, he adopted chocolate to comment on natural processes of decomposition, as in the case of his bird-food sculptures, which he meant to be exposed to all weather conditions. Additionally, through chocolate's association with excrement, he suggested the regenerative powers of the putrid and dung (as in the rotting cheese). Spoerri himself explains this when engaging yet another of Roth's works on view at the Eat Art Gallery, the *Garden Gnome as Squirrel Feed Sculpture (Gartenzwerg als Einhörnchenfutterplastik,* 1969), which itself is a less literary and more "cultural" version of Roth's ironic P.O.TH.A.A.VFB (1968).

The *Garden Gnome* is fully immersed in a dark brown substance — chocolate, although this is not immediately obvious — which makes it difficult to identify the gnome as anything at all, were it not for the tip of the gnome's recognizable red hat. While the garden

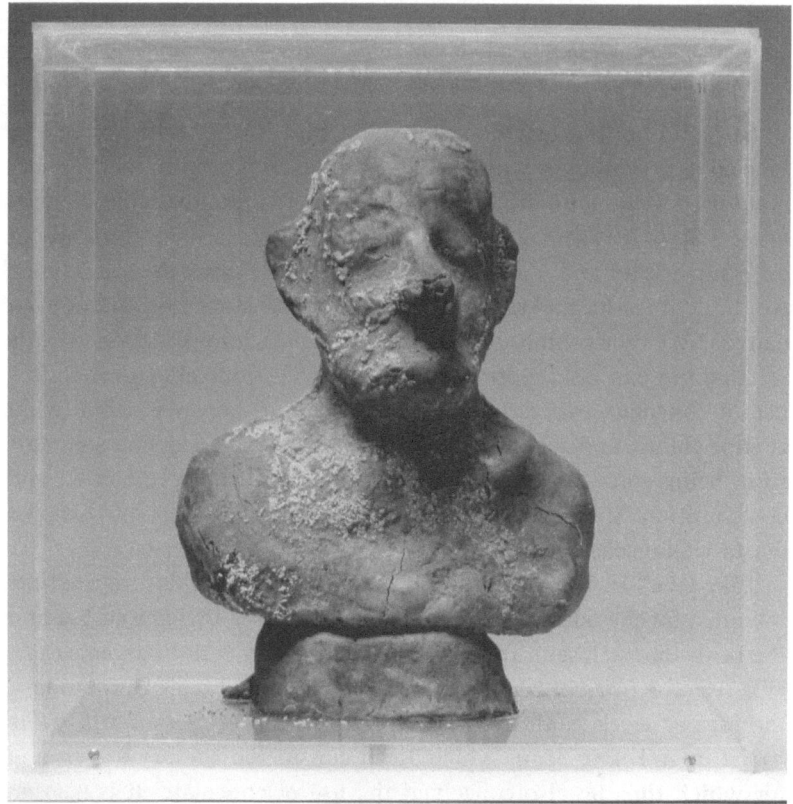

Dieter Roth, P.O.TH.A.A.VFB (Portrait of the Artist as Birdseed Bust), *1970. Courtesy of Dieter Roth Foundation, Hamburg. Copyright Dirk Dobke.*

gnome thus submerged in what appears to be its own excrement functions as a sarcastic indictment of German petit bourgeois customs (the
spiessig way to keep house, car, and garden), Spoerri also offers a more
specific and a more existential interpretation of this work. He focused
more on his conception of institutional critique of art and his ideas
about the regeneration of the life cycle through eating and discarding,
which Spoerri and Tony Morgan had illustrated in their short film
Resurrection. Hence Spoerri explains that for Roth,

> chocolate is tantamount to excrement, excrement to fertilizer . . . and so
> on until an entire cycle is formed: from fertilizer the grass grows, and ani-
> mals eat grass and we eat animals, don't we? And again we produce excre-
> ment. . . . And garden gnomes are tantamount to humans, ridiculous little
> humans who are there and move on and about, right? And these are cast in
> chocolate and they drown in their own excrement, to put it brutally. And
> then they are offered to the birds as food, so that again they transform into
> nourishment and fertilizer, into something positive. (*Anekdotomania,* 198;
> my translation)

Responding to a teacher's statement that Roth's gnome could be
viewed as a symbol of waste in the societies of plenty, in which chocolate used to be a luxury good and now is readily available, Spoerri
asks: why is it that if we see art made of chocolate we think about
art's superfluity and about waste, but we don't think the same when
we think of traditional materials of art, such as stone or chalk or even
canvas? We don't think that art is waste when it makes use of textile
for making canvases instead of clothing. He concludes that Roth's
use of chocolate makes us question what and how we define what
is superfluous and what not and to what extent we define some art
from being considered waste but not other forms of production and
consumption. Spoerri here incorporates Roth's waste-art into his own
waste-weltanschauung.

Like P.O.TH.A.A.VFB, the *Garden Gnome* is a sculpture-multiple
intended for the outdoors and for its consumption by the weather and
the birds that will set it free from its kitschy and petit bourgeois cage.
Whereas the *Garden Gnome* indicts a certain bourgeois Germanness,
the former work is an ironic take on James Joyce's *Portrait of the
Artist as a Young Man,* which Roth considered literary kitsch and
for which thus he also conceived the use of chocolate. It is also an
ironic comment about the art of self-portraiture. Roth had recourse to
foodstuffs — for example, chocolate — to portray himself. Not only did

the use of chocolate in both his *Self-Portrait* and *Self-Towers* (*Selbst-turme,* also displayed at the Eat Art Gallery) show the young man as an old man, but this decaying material, supposedly imperishable art, now serves the artist to accelerate the process of aging, anticipating the death of life rather than eternalizing life and with it the subject of art: the artist. This is carnivalesque (grotesque) narcissism, both the artist's and art's.

This kind of reflexive sarcasm appears often in Roth's work, espe-cially as it relates to literature: Roth was fond of books, and he devoted much of his career to expanding the medium of print, printmaking, and bookbinding. In other instances, Roth had turned printed materials or literary works he disliked into sausages, such as Günter Grass's *Dog Years* (*Hundejahre,* 1963), Martin Walser's *Halftime* (*Halbzeit,* 1960), tabloids and magazines (*The Daily Mirrors, Der Spiegel*). On these occasions, Roth reprocessed physically the contents of these texts into something apparently digestible but, in fact, indigestible because ined-ible. Roth simply substituted books made into pulp for the pork, then spiced and prepared the sausages according to recipes (*Roth Time,* 75). The first literature sausage he ever made was a gift for Spoerri in 1961, while Hegel's *Complete Works in 20 Volumes* concluded the series in 1974: twenty sausages were hung in two rows on a wooden frame as in a slaughterhouse (74). The literature sausages ironically and para-doxically purified — rescued — the eyes (that read books and look at art) by turning them into base organs, connecting them ultimately to the mouth (that takes in and tastes) via the intestines (which also make up the skin of the sausage) (*Scheisse: neue Gedichte von Dieter Rot,* 1966; see *Roth Time,* 97). As Dobke remarks, first quoting Roth and then interpreting him, seeing was the original sin, but ultimately it was also the act of forgiveness of seeing: "The fact that in his view seeing and representing are basically speaking criminal activities reveals him as an iconoclast in the original sense of the word, as a rebel against the cult of images. . . . With the telling difference, however that in his opinion in order to destroy images it is necessary to create new ones, because as he sees it language is also an image" (*Multiples + Books,* 138).

Food-multiples, such as Roth's chocolate works and Arman's *Candy,* intensify playfully some of these artists' art, which they now offer up for a seemingly immediate but at second glance mediated and self-reflexive form of consumption. In Arman's case the edible yet inaccessible accumulations—preserved in Plexiglas—accentuate the effects of all his preceding inedible accumulations to which they add themselves and which maintain both elements of evanescence and futility. Most evidently, the edible multiples by Arman, Roth, and César, while different, were all intended to investigate Spoerri's injunction to eat art, to engage the contemporary postaesthetic situation of neo-avant-garde art's production and consumption.

Like Arman and Roth, for example, César proposed for the Eat Art Gallery sugar-thumbs and compressions of candies, both reproducing his bronze sculptures in edible form, thereby ironizing on the artist's role while distributing artistic energy. Unlike Arman's work, protected by Plexiglas, César's thumbs could be eaten and, in fact, were offered to the public to suck on. The narcissistic pre-oedipal desire to suck one's thumb, added to the presence of the thumb itself—usually considered the attribute that turned humans into *homo faber,* that is, into the quintessential artist—may point in César's work to a different interpretation of "narcissism."[30] The sweet narcissism for which the edible thumb could stand reflects the image of a human-made art and, in addition, an art made in the image of these artists' own art, as much in the case of César as in that of Arman. Arman, César, Lichtenstein, and other occasional contributors to the project of Eat Art "narcissistically" reproduced *their own* artworks as edible, which in the end they (not just the audiences) had to digest. Furthermore, because most of these multiples were made for the Gallery after Spoerri's *Last Supper* in Milan (1970), their narcissistic reproductions also reproduced Spoerri's own imagined edible versions of each artist's artistic principle that Spoerri had already proposed at that crucial dinner. In short, César's edible thumb is a metonymy of a narcissistic art that, while reproducing itself over and over again (the thumb was reproduced in different sizes and materials in time) at the same time is nonegotistical and not self-monumentalizing. Rather, César's edible thumb reproposes art as the renewable and constantly renewed desire for art making as essential to human beings and human societies. To explain his *art vivant*—which César pursued also through his early happenings with expansions in polyurethane—César was quoted as saying: "As there are people who have a green thumb and are able to make plants grow, so I have a sense for matter, I love cardboard, Plexiglas, iron, crystal. When I start kneading dough, I make love with it."[31]

A certain ironic play on narcissism, not unlike Roth's, is also evinced from César's recurrent self-portraits of which, in 1973, he offered multiples in bread dough that had been baked by the most Parisian of all French bakers, Poîlane. At the opening of the exhibition Tête à Têtes at the Gallery Creuzeveault, his bread-head was sliced and distributed, multiplied as the "body of Christ." However, instead of Christ's body this one was a model of a deformed edible head, partly actor's mask, partly emperor's effigies — César posing as the homonymous Roman emperor — partly a malleable mirror image in between the temporary and the grotesque. In effect, the bread-head is just one of the multiple heads that César had initially cast in polyvinyl and then reworked for this show, distorting and extending their facial features into a vast panorama of deformed physiognomies (some of these he then casts in bronze). In these images self and other merge into indistinguishable new and hybrid morphologies, as if each gave birth to the other, without the need for any "real" original face. César added to these heads other materials from textile to found objects that he fixed in wax or resin to stress their lack of homogeneity. In the case of those bread-heads not for consumption, César manipulated the bread's thin surface, emptied of its soft dough (and thus resting on emptiness, as it were), and consolidated it with fiberglass, transforming bread into a durable substance bearing traits of a possibly imminent disintegration or of an archaeological artifact.

Among César's formative experiences for his early iron sculptures was a trip to Pompei, after which he sculpted his *Nu assis Pompei* (*Sitting Naked Body Pompei,* 1954.) In Pompei he saw how sculptures of the people who died during the eruption of the volcano were made out of the empty holes in which the bodies had originally left an imprint. Sculptures of once-existing bodies were made out of emptiness and rose like ghosts centuries after their burial. These figures, perhaps the antecedent to his self-portraits, were the material product of an absence. The bread-head (to be eaten) stresses the absence out of which the presence of sculpture or art (and of the self) emerges. In 1957 César underscores this paradoxical materiality in the dialectics between absence and presence, between otherness and identity:

> I start from an idea that is in me, from nothing and I set out on an adventure until the moment when I find myself face to face with a thing that is foreign to me. This is why it is reality, reality that is detached from me, that exists in its own material, in its own content, in its own space. . . . A kind of internal pressure is in it and on the verge of explosion. I have the impression that it is someone else who is demanding to exist, to be whoever s/he wants to be. . . . A work can always become something else. (quoted in *César,* 199)

The proliferation of reality as both the product of a self-adventure and the auto-generative impulse of matter inform the creative narcissism of César's *Pouces (Thumbs)* and self-portraits. The spontaneous encounter between the artist and the uncontrollable rising of matter—like Spoerri's *Bread-Dough Objects*—is most evident in the artificial mousse expansions that César created in the sixties and presented to the audience as happenings (e.g, at the Galerie Mathias Fels, in 1967). César, himself like a magic cook, pours the liquid polyurethane from heavy bins on the ground with a few gestures: in less than a minute this industrial substance, soft as whipping cream, first becomes alive, like lava descending from a volcano to finally solidify into a chance shape. Industry transforms into nature—a cataclysmic force—through a few gestures of the hand, a hand that in this case allows matter to paradoxically form itself into *informe* in/edible substance. César sliced this in/edible meringue and offered it to the public, expanding it publicly. As he often remarked, César viewed his various sculpting (or nonsculpting) acts as analogous to experimental baking and cooking: "It is as when I cook, I choose, mix, take away, put back in, season etc." (*César,* 243). According to him the *coulades* were the result of the "collaboration" among air, time, matter, and the artist-cook.

César's narcissistic instances are better interpreted through the lens of Marcuse's revision of Freud's take on it. As Freud stated, Marcuse argues, sublimation starts with a reactivation of narcissistic libido "which somehow overflows and extends to objects. The hypothesis all but revolutionizes the idea of sublimation: it hints at a non-repressive mode of sublimation which results from an extension rather than from a constraining deflection of the libido."[32] In this regard, Marcuse writes that the narcissistic experience of the world annihilates the principle of performance if one regards such experience as imbued with *eros* (eroticism). Eros redirects the Nirvana principle from its association with death to the redemption of life. Thus the opposition between subject and object is negated, and existence is understood as the satisfaction that unites humankind and nature without the violence of conquest. This libido can change into the desire for new modes of being or, better, new modes of production to which, I would add, edible art alludes. This is evident especially in César's *Sugar Thumb,* for example, the artist's finger proffered to the consumer who sucks on it, thereby sucking its creativity and energy. Spoerri remarks how happy César was during his experimentations with sugar as an artistic medium, remembering that during his work César would repeatedly exclaim: "This is the language of matter!" Accordingly, César's *Sugar Thumb,* alongside his narcissistic play with masks and bread, could well illustrate Marcuse's words: "Beyond any immature auto-eroticism, narcissism reveals a profound affinity with reality that may generate a comprehensive, existential order," thus integrating the narcissistic I with the world. This, for Marcuse, is an act of resistance against a world order based on libidinal repression, resistance exercised by both Narcissus and the poet-artist Orpheus (*Eros and Civilization,* 191). He writes: "This Refusal aims at reuniting with what has been separated. Orpheus is the archetype of the poet as liberator and creator. . . . In his person, art, freedom and culture are eternally reunited" (192). From within this framework, the *Sugar Thumb* offered as sacrificial art and protocannibalistic gesture is an act of liberation of art from its constraints and its return to the extended capacity to mould and move about in the world of *homo ludens — homo faber,* to adopt Restany on César.

Besides Spoerri's friends and artists who contributed occasional edible art multiples to the Eat Art Gallery, there are several other artists who also used food systematically in their art. In some of these food works that were not showcased at Spoerri's gallery, food appears as the works' immanent necessity and internal language. Manzoni devoted considerable attention to bread and eggs, but could never contribute to Eat Art, because of his premature death. In the attempt to underline that food-multiples are processes of thinking as much as operations of art production and consumption, I shall limit the discussion of his and a few other selected works to the food-multiples that test the boundaries of the neo-avant-garde's own proposal of antidiets based in the in/edibility of art—the instability of art's principles—in the age of commodification.[33]

The Neo-Avant-Garde's Side Dishes

Fluxus Food and Its Secrets

In the sixties, prior to the establishment of Spoerri's restaurant and gallery, several artists had used food as a material. These include the initial forms of body art, from Viennese Actionism (especially Otto Muehl's performances filmed by Kurt Krens) to the early feminist performances (e.g., Carolee Schneemann's *Meat Joy* in 1964). Among the artists who also included food, food objects, and food-multiples in their works and whose investigations were closer to Spoerri's own inquiry into the institutionalization of art and commodification were happening artists such as Oldenburg, but also the affiliates of Fluxus, that is, the international group founded by George Maciunas in 1961. Spoerri was acquainted with Fluxus and partly affiliated with it. Among the very first collections of an individual artist's scores published in 1963 by Maciunas were Spoerri and François Dufrêne's *L'optique moderne (Modern Optics)*. Spoerri participated in some other Fluxus events and so did Filliou and Williams, Vautier, Brecht, and Beuys, who also took part in Eat Art. Fluxus declared that everything is art or deserving to be called art, and its members organized numerous eclectic activities, festivals, music, and theatrical events.[34] Through simple performative acts of language — declarations — they created new fields and ideas "for" the experience of art. They found and carved these out of the experience of the everyday: for example, they declared silence to be music (John Cage) or cooking to be a concert (Alison Knowles). Like the poets of the Beat Generation, they decided that artists, indeed not unlike collectives of poets, could work outside the traditional art venues, meeting in garages, lofts, the streets, or coffeehouses, where their cheap artworks would consist of actions and readily available materials (Hendricks, quoted in *Fluxus Codex*, 22). They gradually came to produce, under the entrepreneurial spirit of Maciunas, editions of cheap commodities, invented by anyone who desired to contribute ideas that would be "realized" and varied sometimes indefinitely by Fluxus, that is, the "brand" name of a collective production. The intention was a playful and political attempt at democratization, at the extension of art to everyone (or the elimination of bourgeois art or art as institution). However, the centralization of production and final control of the product operated mostly by Maciunas in one way or another partly contradicted that political intention, although it did not stop artists from collaborating.[35] (So it is that, for example, some works by Vautier, Brecht, or Williams, all Fluxus artists, are not counted among their Fluxus oeuvre either because they were not intentionally declared as such when conceived or because a correspondence or relation with Maciunas is absent.)

In the present section I focus on a few Fluxus works that made reference to eating, cooking, or food in general to assess whether, at the time of the neo-avant-garde, the *culinary* discourse returned to highlight this art's engagement with temporality. Fluxus intensely occupied itself with food that offered the possibilities of indefinite and collective variations and interpretations of recipes or celebratory banquets (for Christmas, the New Year, art openings, etc.). Food in this regard became one of the terrains for implementing the collective ethos of Fluxus: everyone could contribute their proposals (as they were called) for meals or drinks: "You may participate by contributing either a food or drink of your own invention, or make something up from the list below (except what is marked with *, since these will already be made up) . . . Write George Maciunas, POB 180, Canal St. Sta. New York 10013)" (*Fluxus Codex,* 67).

Not unlike some of the Futurist banquets, several Fluxus food events confused gustatory expectations and perceptions. For example, Fluxus organized monomeals, either all based in the same colors (a white meal, a red meal) or in the same "ingredient" (as in the "Potatomeal" or in the "Fishmeal").[36] The "Fishmeal" included clear fish carbonated drink, fish Jell-O, fish bread (from fish bone flour), fish pudding, fish ice cream, fish salad, fish pastry, fish candy. The Futurists, however, were interested in the shaping and development of an "ideological" man. Fluxus food aimed not only, like the Futurists, to dissipate aesthetic categories within cooking but also to liberate experiential confusions and disorganization of the senses. Most Fluxus experiments also involved archiving everyday habits. The subversion of the gastronomic grammar by Fluxus was similar to Dada's stress on "indigestion," excremental flows, and *dégôut,* as the name "Fluxus" also indicates and as it was stated expressly in the movement's manifesto in 1963: "3. *Med.* To cause a discharge from, as in purging. // flux (flŭks), *n.* [OF., fr. L. *fluxus,* fr. *fluere, fluxum,* to flow. See FLUENT; cf. FLUSH, n. (of cards).] 1. *Med.* a A flowing or fluid discharge from the bowels or other part: esp. an excessive and morbid discharge: as, the body *flux,* or dysentery. b The matter thus discharged" (reproduced in *Fluxus Codex,* 24).

In the case of Fluxus, the grammatical subversion of gastronomy occurred through the disorderly in(di)gestion of loose ingredients, for example, through a gastronomically arbitrary approach to the set language of food. For example, Vautier came up with his *Flux Mystery Food* (1963) that became part of his actual diet. In the scholar Hannah Higgins's words:

He purchased unlabeled cans [sic] of identical size in the grocery store and ate whatever was inside them — whether lychee nuts (as at the first performance) or salmon, canned sausages or sauerkraut; in 1966–67 he launched a variation on this theme, having Maciunas relabel each can as "Flux Mystery Food." In these Fluxus food works the food appears the same or very similar, thus relegating differentiation by sight to the periphery of the eating experience. . . . Other Fluxus food work has emphasized the ritual of eating, associations between food and non-food, and the obsessive measuring and counting of foods characteristic of a society preoccupied with personal hygiene and self control.[37]

Boundaries between the edible and inedible were also tested through the differences in taste among those substances that *look* similar, thus again underscoring the relevance of the "nonaesthetic" approach to food. Among these dishes testing the limits of art as provocation in and against life's habits — including the habituation to provocation itself — were Knowles's 1969 *Shit Porridge* prepared for that New Year's banquet. One could not identify the actual ingredients and be sure that it was not made of excrement. The only way to find out this

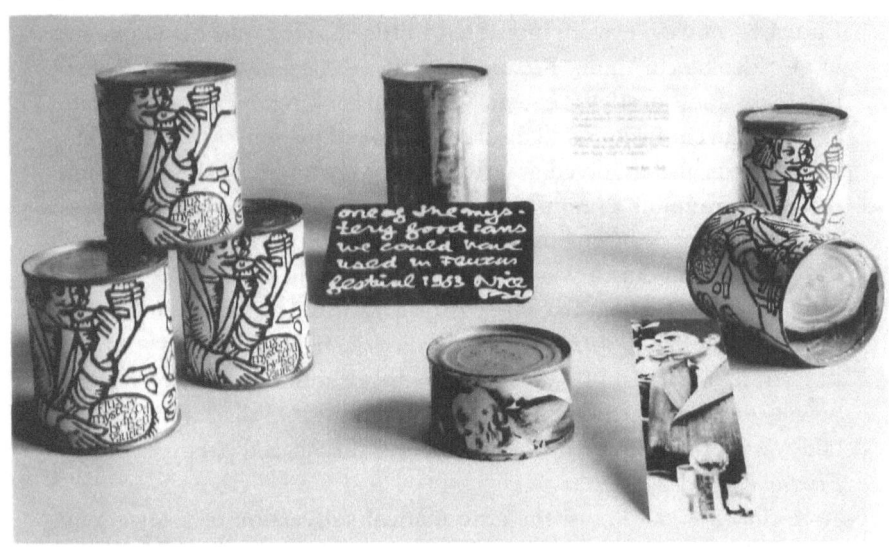

Ben Vautier, Flux Mystery Food. *Two Fluxus packagings and an original unlabeled can from the Fluxus Festival in Nice in 1963; a Vautier label from 1963; and a plaque made by the artist in 1984. Photograph by Brad Iverson. Courtesy of The Gilbert and Lila Silverman Fluxus Collection, Detroit. Copyright 2008 Artists Rights Society (ARS), New York/ADAGP, Paris.*

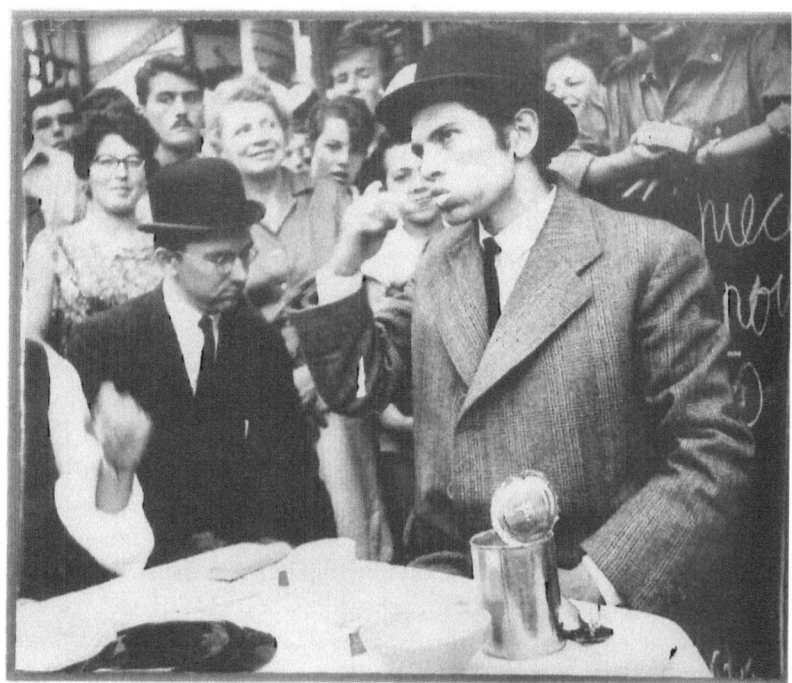

Ben Vautier brushing his teeth after eating Flux Mystery Food. George Maciunas looks on, during Festival d'Art Total et du Comportement, Nice, July 1963. This photograph was cropped and used for the label of smaller cans of Flux Mystery Food. Courtesy of The Gilbert and Lila Silverman Fluxus Collection, Detroit. Copyright 2008 Artists Rights Society (ARS), New York/ ADAGP, Paris.

porridge's in/edibility was to risk tasting it. It was in fact made of beans, a favorite ingredient in Knowles's Fluxus diet of musical and other scores, for example, her 1963 multiples, *Bean Rolls,* which she called canned books.[38]

In general, as Higgins remarks, "much Fluxus work rejects the representational approach to art. Instead it is generally presentational or reality based. Even a Fluxus artist choosing a representational mode . . . uses it at cross-purposes to conventional representation, to undermine the tenets of Western illusionism and to push representation itself toward the primary mode of experience" (49). Higgins stresses the sensory basis of the experience of smelling or tasting that, importantly, is disclosed to be profoundly social: sharing the unusual and surprising experience of tasting these unexpected food-stuffs becomes the centerpiece for the social relations — the conversations — that mostly pivot around the food itself (46). Spoerri's banquets also exhibited some of these elements. However, throughout his Eat Art "project," he explored more systematically the ins and outs of the historical and cultural (temporal) relations between culinary discourse and artistic discourse, including the history of both. His focus on the temporal relations between the experience of "difference" and tradition, in art as much as in the everyday, is more central to Eat Art. Among the Fluxus artists who indeed elaborated on the "times" of eating is Knowles.

Throughout the sixties, Knowles proposed recipes and their instantaneous execution as musical scores, for example, in *Make a Salad* and *Make a Soup* (both happenings that took place in 1962). In the original execution of the former score, at the Institute of Contemporary Art in London, Knowles drew attention away from the performance's more obvious visual aspects by highlighting the sounds of the labor-intensive actions of slicing, chopping, and cutting to "make" a salad. The critic Julia Robinson explains that the Fluxus scores "operated as templates, open to expansion in the arena of realization. Elements of chance were incorporated in the temporal framework so that each performance of a single score might differ greatly, far beyond the expectations of the composer" (98). Each time the performance would contain new chance factors and thus produce different experiences and sounds. In addition, Knowles's work — as Cage's — literally heightened sound and thus hearing in those experiences that are usually already claimed by other senses. Hence Knowles's *Make a Salad* accentuated the rhythmic and the temporal structure. It also focused on the value and quality of labor against the aesthetics of purely visual representation, or against the aestheticization of the end product. At the same time, the sound of labor (rather than the sound of music) may infiltrate taste by overextending itself through mnemonic associations to the consumer's act of eating a salad.[39] Furthermore, hearing does not contribute to a fluid total and atemporal sensation (or synesthesia) but rather a temporal interference of discontinuous beats.[40]

As reported by Higgins, various Fluxus events involved measuring and counting, hence a form of archiving and cataloging of the everyday. This well describes Knowles's *Identical Lunch* (1967–73), which consisted of the same lunch consumed everyday at the same time and location for a number of years. Knowles's *Identical Lunch* score, as described by Robinson, "evolved from her daily meal at Riss Restaurant in Chelsea, a diner not far from her home in those years. The score demanded wheat toast, butter, tuna fish, lettuce, and soup or buttermilk to be assembled and consumed in any manner the performer wished. The *Identical Lunch* was famously taken up, over a period of years, by many of Knowles's artist-friends" (101). While Spoerri's trap-paintings underscored the differences among the chance situations of objects created by repeated acts of consumption, Knowles's *Identical Lunch* stressed the habitual act. The artist's life and that of her friends and collaborators become the live containers, or the catalog according to Eco, that morph with the accumulation of assimilated like-foodstuffs, an accumulation that is not transparent and visible. The *Identical Lunch* thus ironically underscores the variations that in fact are always part and parcel of what appears to be identical, how a supposedly unvaried meal based in the same ingredients gives rise to multiple combinations. (Maciunas suggested that the meal combined all ingredients in a blender, rendering it thus homogeneous). The changes can be perceived only through continuity. By following the process, day after day — through external variations of time, the social space, and the physical configuration of the other container/context of the artists' bodies and the diner-restaurant — can change be perceived. Art here is a performative gesture beyond any object and even any actual action. In contrast, Spoerri's Eat Art, including his trap-paintings and multiples, offers the spectator a site of confrontation with the consumption/erasure of the art object — that is, with the production of its absence. Thus Eat Art is the action of displaying art's awareness about its move beyond visibility or full presence and full absence, in front of the practitioners as well as the consumers.

The difference between Eat Art's and Fluxus's conceptual and sensorial approaches to food is that Eat Art produces an artistic void (art's absence as its presence) while offering or producing art in the process of its consumption. Eat Art is the erosion of art that, while being consumed or decaying (in the case of Roth's multiples, for example), produces remainders of itself, other forms of production that are all artistic actions. In the case of Eat Art, the focus is on manipulating the gastronomic discursive field per se — its mechanisms both of transformation and of gastronomy's "strong" acculturation and domestication processes. The recipe approach to art, in this case, involves less the expansion of art's experience beyond the purview of what pertains to the art object than Eat Art's self-reflective, genealogical, or archaeological impulse with regard to avant-garde art: its provenance, its itinerary, its present. Thus typical avant-garde elements such as provocation and scandal, even spectacle, are crucial in Eat Art to the extent that they question the formation of cultural parameters, categorization of different forms, and cultural values. However, they are even more crucial because they specifically investigate and challenge the practices of the art market and art institutions without ever totally leaving them behind or working outside the artworld. (The trap-paintings are paintings after all, and the banquets the motor that generates them.) Eat Art in this regard is not operating outside or beyond the art institutions, as some critics have implied when referring to Spoerri's *Gastronomic Journal* or when describing the Restaurant. Instead, I argue, Spoerri's actions constructed an outside that they situated within the artistic enterprise of the neo-avant-garde. To return once again to Deleuze and Guattari, this outside may coincide with Eat Art's operation of becoming minor, that is, of creating a minority status — a deterritorializing effect — within the neo-avant-garde. Eat Art investigates more specifically than Fluxus (and the movement's meals and food) how — in a time when anything could potentially be art — a postaesthetic yet memorable experience and understanding of *art* can be generated with the experience of food.

Food, as let loose from its coherent body of writing and of everyday practices, becomes in neo-avant-garde art the mnemonic corpus that constitutes an internal alterity of art: its other taste (or distaste), its other language of desire (or death drive), its Dionysian abyss, the other of the other of art. If the other of art is life — thus food — food in art is, for the neo-avant-garde, the other of food in life as well as the other of artistic food. In this regard, the neo-avant-garde's investment in food materials, in the production of semantically unstable in/edible multiples, and, more generally, in cultural gastronomic and physically digestive practices does not coincide with enjoyable food and, by extension, with art that is easy to digest. Adorno, among others, used the term *culinary* as a derogatory qualifier to distinguish commercial art — that is, the culture industry — from inedible (in his view) modernist art. From this viewpoint, one could paradoxically state that Eat Art's antidiet makes the neo-avant-garde into a *non*-culinary art, if culinary not only is interpreted from a gastronomic perspective but also is taken in Adorno's sense. The neo-avant-garde's in/edibility is aimed at the art field. Eat Art does not intervene in the culinary discourse to have a direct impact on the latter. Rather, it questions the boundaries between the two in its use of the language of production and consumption. In the remaining section I analyze the food works by Manzoni, who was active before Eat Art.

Bread, Eggs, and More Eggs: Piero Manzoni

Manzoni's conceptual approach to life but especially to art situates this artist's work with and around food, in certain occasions, at the opposite end of the Fluxus food performances. Manzoni made use of food, specifically of bread and eggs, in art objects, multiples, and performances. These foodstuffs helped him elaborate on the equation between the work of art and the work performed by the human body, that is, the *artist*'s body, which was his central concern. In particular, his infamous cans of *Artist's Shit* (*Merda d'artista,* 1961) made in Italy half-ironically and half-seriously centered art on the artist's bodily activities. The body, in this case the mouth–stomach tract, is the artist's most intimate, unique, and at the same time shareable means of (art) production.

In the same years as Spoerri developed his *Grocery Shop,* the series of trap-paintings known as *Variations on a Meal: Eaten by* and the Restaurant Galleries, Manzoni staged his food performances. Among them figure, for example, *Consumazione dell'arte, dinamica del pubblico, divorare l'arte* (*Consumption of Art, Audience's Dynamics, Devouring Art,* 1960). He also exhibited his *Achrome* collages, frames filled with uncoloured — white — objects distributed in grids, among which bread rolls in kaolin. Yet Manzoni did not contribute to Eat Art, in part because of his untimely death, at the age of twenty-nine in 1963, well before Spoerri opened his restaurant (1968) and gallery (1970). Spoerri, who had met Manzoni, acknowledged this artist's feat, his *Artist's Shit,* in the series of objects that he himself created in Symi and that accompanied his *Gastronomic Journal:* "Objects of Magic à la Noix." There Spoerri wrote, in Dada fashion, that his admiration for Manzoni concretized in his favorite curse "de los diablos de los mierdas de los cojones de los artistas di Manzoni, which I wrote as an epitaph in a booklet dedicated to him after his death" (*Mythologi-cal Travels*, 29). Later, in 1970, Spoerri also crafted the *Hommage à la merda d'artista di Piero Manzoni* in chocolate and sugar.

Manzoni anticipated some of Spoerri's interests. For example, Manzoni's food works are concerned with art's temporality, art's com-modification, and the desire to demystify the artist's cult. This cult, in the fifties, had first surrounded Jackson Pollock and, later, had been exploited by Georges Mathieu. Manzoni was irreverent toward such personalities. Unlike Spoerri's Eat Art, however, Manzoni's events focused especially on the body. The body served him as the ground for his metaphysical/ontological as well as critical approach to art. Man-zoni's numerous events in the early sixties — most of which involved also the bodies of other people, his so-called living sculptures — are an *embodied* form of conceptual art, in other words, an art of con-sciousness that takes shape in and through living matter. For Man-zoni, the body is a radically new canvas, where the subject, both as human being and as artwork, undergoes metamorphosis. Unlike for other performance artists, for example, Wolf Vostell, however, both

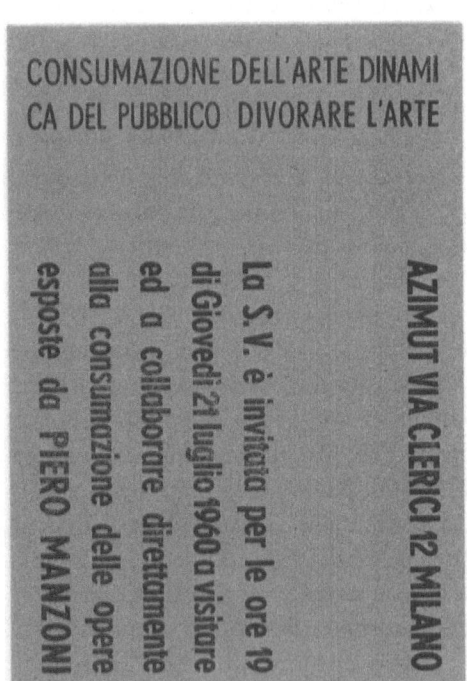

CONSUMAZIONE DELL'ARTE DINAMI
CA DEL PUBBLICO DIVORARE L'ARTE

esposte da PIERO MANZONI
alla consumazione delle opere
ed a collaborare direttamente
di Giovedi 21 luglio 1960 a visitare
La S.V. è invitata per le ore 19
AZIMUT VIA CLERICI 12 MILANO

Piero Manzoni, invitation to Consumazione dell'arte, dinamica del pubblico, divorare l'arte, *July 21, 1960. Manzoni offered 150 hard-boiled eggs with his fingerprint to the audience. Courtesy of Piero Manzoni Archive, Milan. Copyright 2008 Artists Rights Society (ARS), New York/ SIAE, Rome.*

Piero Manzoni boils and fingerprints eggs for the short film Uova *produced by Studio Filmgiornale Sedi di Milano, 1960. Photographs by Giuseppe Bellone; film by Giampaolo Macentelli. Courtesy of Piero Manzoni Archive, Milan. Copyright 2008 Artists Rights Society (ARS), New York/SIAE, Rome.*

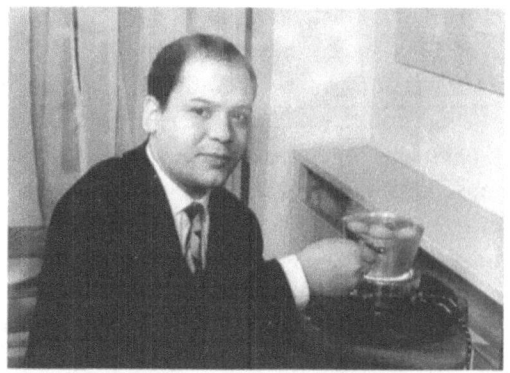

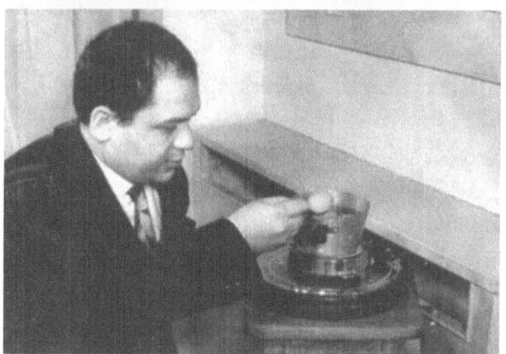

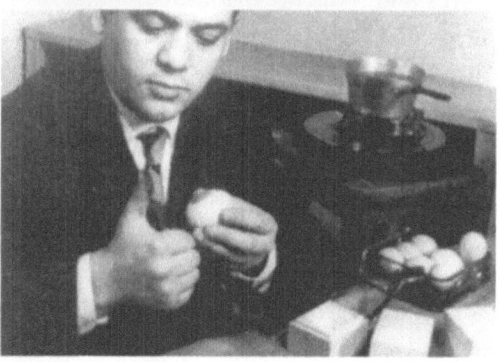

the space of the gallery and the artist are decisive factors in defining what work or action is ultimately art, and not vice versa. Marcel Duchamp looms large in Manzoni's case. Yet the latter's accent on process, the important role the body in art takes for Manzoni, hence the displacement of art from the isolated readymade object onto the ready-*making* and consuming of art, expanded the field of Duchamp's object. (The itinerary moves from the urinal to the cans of *Artist's Shit*.) While the can seems to present the artwork as complete, an end product, in fact the substance hidden inside the can is subject to the effects of time, which expose it as both unstable product and a product that can be opened and thus changed. Duchamp's urinal once in the museum is not used or transformed. *Artist's Shit* keeps transforming, even if invisibly. Once trapped (canned?) in the museum it also cannot be restored — its decay interrupted — lest it be fully destroyed as complete work. Restoration of its substance would demand opening the can, thus exposing its secret. (Spoerri once stated that he indeed irreverently opened a can and was still unsure what the contents of the can really were.)

Manzoni's ironic gestures against the establishment of art, art collecting, and the traditional forms of art exhibitions (which he shared with most other artists in the sixties, from Klein to Allan Kaprow) were also the expression of another, different, artistic impulse. Manzoni was on a quest for a "true" art, as he repeated often in his theoretical texts, an art that is, or else an art the meaning of which might be its sole existence, the pure event. Manzoni believed that the contemporary artist's mission was to investigate, from the now of consumer society, art's power "of bringing to light the preconscious universal myths and reducing them to an image."[41] For Manzoni, an authentic art, which must be separated from the "extraneous facts and pointless gestures that contaminate the usual art of our time," allows the viewer and the artist to understand one's own time only if it goes back to the universal roots of humanity, to what he names the "creative" unconscious. To make art, for Manzoni, is a phenomenological process of shedding style, getting rid of subjective conditioning, in short, a process of elimination through which one "must reach individual mythology at the point where it coincides with universal mythology" (69). Art's main task, as he writes, is to look for the "primordial mythologemes (where individual and universal myths correspond)" (70). In this respect, Manzoni's food art — aside from his *Artist's Shit* — gains a cultural–symbolical as well as a psychological dimension that distances it both from Dada's irreverence toward art and philosophy (irreverence that, however, is also part of Manzoni's actions, yet not its sole element) and from Spoerri's Eat Art. The latter concentrates more on the cultural history and prehistory of the neo-avant-garde than on art's archetypes.

Manzoni's spiritual/universalizing approach to food is present in his *Achrome,* especially his 1962 bread rolls. The artist used *rosette,* a common kind of Italian bread in the shape of a rose. The rolls are hollow inside and with a crisp crust on the outside. The roselike shape allows the bread to break easily between the fingers. The critic Jan Thompson states:

> These particular *Achrome* brought to the surface his [Manzoni's] fascination with pneumatics as a spiritual exercise (the breaking of bread in the Christian Mass) and with pneumatology, a concern for the nature of spiritual beings. Indeed, Manzoni's works in general, and the *Achrome* in particular, are rooted in a specifically metaphysical vision of corporeality, one that starts by acknowledging a special mutuality between substances and light — between something that endures, in other words, and something that is always changing. (quoted in *Manzoni,* 42)

In addition to pneumatology — the breathing and spiritual side of this bread — the rosette in kaolin resemble impossible archaeological artifacts from a long-lost time: impossible because bread is perishable and would not survive time. The familiar bread returns defamiliarized through a temporality that disrupts its quotidian consumption and literally transforms the everyday food into an almost illegible and unknown "Rosetta stone."

Manzoni's art is a gesture of being that, as the Italian critic Gianni Celant writes, defies interpretation, especially the blank *Achrome* because, as tautologies, they always return one to their physical materials. Yet, as Thompson puts it, their multiple variations transform them "into a transcendent unity through the reduction of chromatic difference to a nominal zero-point" (*Manzoni,* 43). The *Achrome* — the in/edible rosette — highlights an optical ambiguity that Thompson ascribes to a point of intersection between thought and substance. In Bois's terms, the ambiguity is a contrast or an unresolved dialectic: "These collages of rows of bread rolls stacked in grid fashion, or of pebbles, produce a strange combination, half macabre, half silly, of abstraction (monochrome) and readymade" (*Art since 1900,* 414).

This optical ambiguity is a common feature of all of Manzoni's art, which always involves a play between visibility and invisibility. The whiteness of the *Achrome* produces an optical sensation of blurring positive and negative light, as if they were simultaneously themselves and a mold of themselves. The frustration of visibility is a strategy against the spectacularization of art, as in the case of Ben's *Flux Mystery Food*. But it also is, for Manzoni, a way to joke about the mysterious, transubstantiating potential of an art turned into food.

Manzoni's approach to eggs then is ambiguous and ironic at once: eggs can be viewed as perfectly edible *Achrome* (after all, they are all white, and they are serial, like rosette or pebbles), and they are mystical objects of becoming. They prove his belief in the act of creation—artistic creation—as demanding in the present a constant act of consumption. Eggs imply the ongoing cultural and organic cycle of reprocessing and consuming. Yet they are abstract, either pagan or Christian symbols of regeneration and birth. In Manzoni's performance, the sacrilegious and the sacred coexist in an artistic performative act: the artist's gesture of offering this symbol (and multiple at once)—the egg—as his (fingerprinted) primary material to an audience. Consuming the eggs and fingerprinting the eggs merge with the ritual of the Communion. The latter is indeed the priest's performative gesture of "naming" and thus transforming bread and wine into Christ's body. In Manzoni's performance, the audience's faith in art, rather than God, may allow the miracle of art to occur. This would be the miracle of a reversed transubstantiation: the egg as sacred object now transforms into an object of profane culture, that is, a hard-boiled egg that is eaten and consumed. First the artist boils the egg—thus transferring the egg from nature to culture; second, art takes place as a secondary transformation, namely, through the act of eating the cultural object. The time of the artwork in the performance is the time in which the original cultural transformation—the transformation of nature (raw food) into culture or cooked food—is made to occur again, through the consumer's body. Art is a second-degree transformation that involves an act of physical (and cultural) incorporation—and again transformation—of cultural symbols, such as the egg. For Manzoni, the egg stands for a becoming alive. It implies a radical transformation of this object/substance into something other than what it is. The egg becomes the artist's presentation of the unstable space–time of art as becoming and as in becoming (other). Hence Manzoni's "egg-art" is the best example of an art that intends to have its foundations in becoming as essence of life. In short, the egg is art because it is a product of life and of life's creative potentials. It is also life because the egg reproduces life, but in another form.

Manzoni marks his egg-art with a criminal fingerprint. It is criminal because the fingerprint is the personal signature of a living artist who expropriates the object first of its nature (pure white eggs) and subsequently of culture (as hard-boiled eggs) and from this robbery makes its own "stolen" creation. In this regard, art is also stealing away time from life, boxing this time (the fingerprinted egg lies in a wooden box), although not for long. The egg is still subject to organic life's laws: it decays in time. Hence, paradoxically, only through imme-diate consumption does this art survive — defeating decay — at the cost of becoming invisible.[42] Manzoni's fingerprinted egg stands for the noncoincidence between life and art, a noncoincidence of the order of similitude rather than representation, as illustrated by Foucault on the painter René Magritte.[43] One finds it in the differance (Derrida) that the egg's becoming also implies and which is well portrayed in Mag-ritte's *Clairvoyance* (1936).[44]

The picture portrays a painter who is looking at an egg on a table. However, instead of depicting the egg, he is painting a dove. The painting thereby questions temporality: does art come after life? And if it does, is then representation never representation but indeed a new presentation altogether? Or does art come before life? In this case, the dove in the painting is at the origins of the egg on the table: accordingly

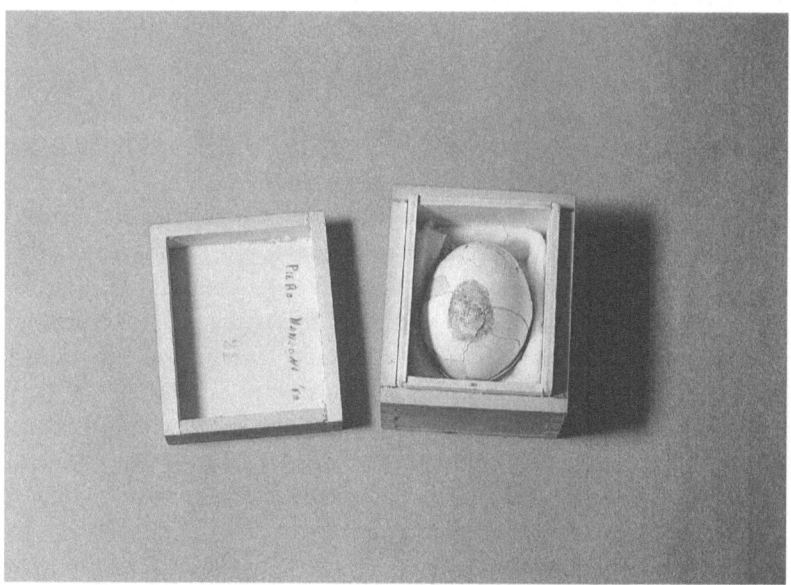

Piero Manzoni, Egg Sculpture #21 *(Egg in wooden box), 1960. Courtesy of Piero Manzoni Archive, Milan. Copyright 2008 Artists Rights Society (ARS), New York/SIAE, Rome.*

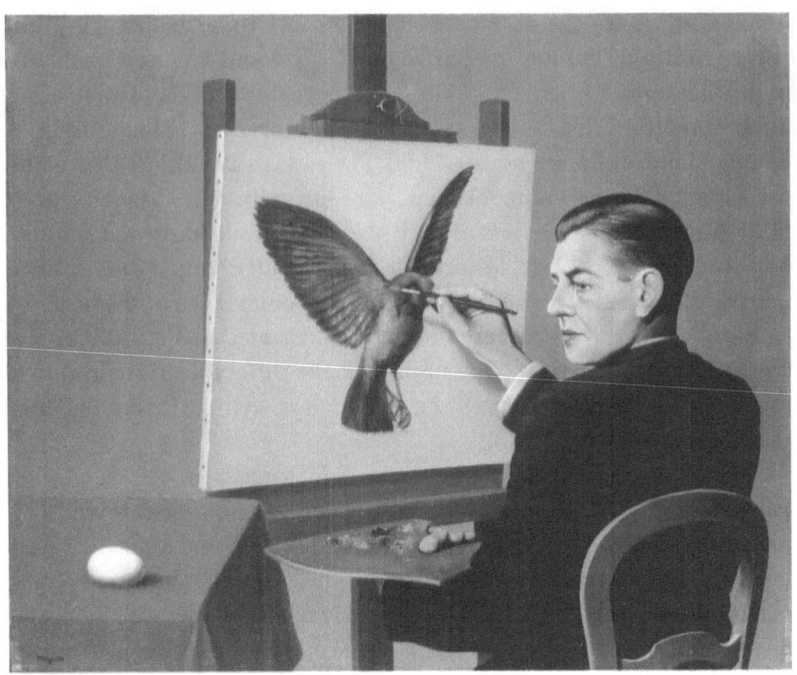

René Magritte, La clairvoyance, *1936. Private collection. Photograph by C. Herscovici/Art Resource, New York. Copyright 2008 C. Herscovici, Brussels / Artists Rights Society (ARS), New York.*

art would generate a different form, a different life, one that would be informed most literally by art. The painter in Magritte's picture is definitely looking at the egg on the table as he paints: the time elapsed between the act of looking at the object and its representation is sufficient to alter the fragile reality—that is, the egg—as well as its impossible copy. The time of art and the time of life are the time of becoming, a time that does not allow for reproduction of the identical but, rather, in Celant's words, the "expression of sameness in different ways" (25). The temporal question is ultimately suspended because in Magritte's picture the painting painter, his act of dove painting, and the (painted) egg on the (painted) table all figure at once in the same spatiotemporal frame (the frame of Magritte's painting).

Manzoni's own words in *Free Dimension* (1960) could be used to comment on the emphasis in *Clairvoyance* on the trappings of representation and on the neo-avant-garde's distance from such issues: "Allusion, expression and representation are non-existent problems today . . . whether or not one is dealing with the representation of objects, facts, ideas or dynamic or inert phenomena." With reference to the *Achrome,* Celant adds that these unusual collages are in fact an "attempt at autonomous existence" (*Manzoni,* 24, 25). Magritte's own game of the chicken (the dove) and the egg, instead, seemed to see no escape from the dilemmas of representation, only a straightforward confrontation with it.

Other artists of the sixties addressed more indirectly food in art. For instance, Oldenburg opened *Store* in 1961 to exhibit and to sell his reproduced, fake gigantic foodstuffs as soft and mobile sculpture. In this ironic and playful gesture, Oldenburg used food to comment on the out-of-control, all-encompassing nature of consumer culture.[45]

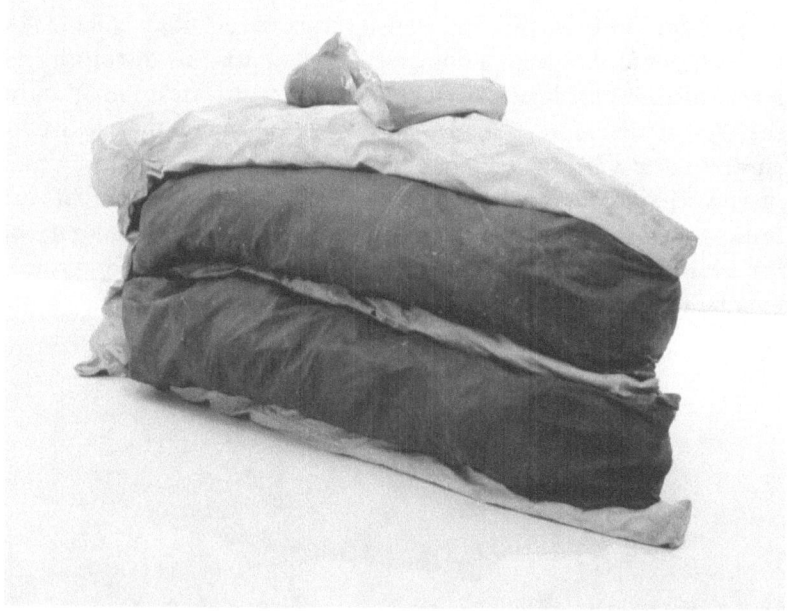

Claes Oldenburg, Floor Cake *(Giant Piece of Cake), 1962. Synthetic polymer paint and latex on canvas filled with foam rubber and cardboard boxes, 58 3/8 inches x 9 feet 6 1/4 inches x 58 3/8 inches. Gift of Philip Johnson. Courtesy of The Museum of Modern Art, New York, New York. Digital image copyright The Museum of Modern Art. Licensed by SCALA/Art Resource, New York.*

Spoerri's interest in producing food that is called art and becomes art, and thus producing art that is potentially edible, raises slightly different questions about art than Oldenburg's soft sculptures, and than other fake food art — for example, the many pictorial references to food one finds in Pop Art, from Warhol, via Rosenquist, to Wayne Thiebaud and Erró's more critical *Foodscape*.

As shown in this book, Eat Art asks what kind of art can exist after the avant-garde, namely, after the emergence of the event and eventually the disappearance of the object, eroded by the commodity. Furthermore, engaged obliquely and critically, the gastronomic field becomes the interface for dealing with questions of cultural memory: in the case of the neo-avant-garde, of activations of avant-garde residues, of returns and transformations of paradigms of production and consumption in art.

To conclude, the Eat Art's interventions in contemporary art hypothesize: if instead of making art to be preserved and exhibited, artists made art to eat, art that transforms in the act of assimilation or through physical abjection (indigestion) what art — art discourse and infrastructures, art history — would one live with? Most importantly, the introduction of "real" food as art becomes a way for the neo-avant-garde to deal with the temporality of contemporary art. In the case of Spoerri and his friends, to "practice" art then means to situate art in time, namely, to practice an art that works through the legacy of the avant-garde, including the immediacy of the contemporary neo-avant-garde.

CONCLUSION

In/Edible Art: What Remains?

THIS BOOK has traced the aesthetic interrelations between the classical movements of the avant-garde at the beginning of the twentieth century and the neo-avant-garde between the sixties and eighties. It has examined how critical attention to the presence of food in the avant-garde (first in metaphoric form and later in material form) helps redefine the neo-avant-garde according to a temporality of returns that does not preclude aesthetic change.

The avant-garde links food not only to the temporal process of the production and consumption of art but also, metaphorically, to spiraling temporalities in history. The analyses of food reveal how the avant-garde positioned itself within a history of returning cultural practices of incorporation. While keeping gastronomy, gastrosophy, and food-as-practice in mind, this book has focused on why and how incorporative and digestive functions, as well as (anti)dietary systems, are present in nonrepresentational ways in the self-reflexive, abstract yet material, and critical works examined. The main objective was to show how a series of concrete and figurative invocations of the gastrosophic centrally mediated and displaced various temporal and conceptual concerns in avant-garde studies. Within the avant-garde, gastrosophic discourse functions as "metadiscourse," that is, as aesthetic reflections of the avant-garde's own temporalities. This leaves open the question of what critical reflections about art's temporality and what temporalities contemporary food art — increasingly pervasive today — is trying to make.

In the chapters on Eat Art, particularly in the analyses of Spoerri's institutional critique and other food artists' engagements in the sixties and seventies, I elaborated on the return of concepts such as inedibility through the lens of theoretical works that were important not only to the critics of the period (and of today) but also to the artists at that time, from Georges Bataille to Claude Lévi-Strauss, from anthropological and semiotic notions of pollution and the abject to the proliferation of desire and Gilles Deleuze and Félix Guattari's concepts of the "minor" and impoverishment. I hope that the book has clarified that the avant-garde's mimetic impulses with regard to indigestibility and in/edibility—as in certain absurdist Dada poems and in Walter Benjamin's performative texts about eating—are better understood as rhetorical strategies imbued with semiotic skepticism. I referred, in particular, to the physical digestive system in these works as a linguistic apparatus whose modes of functioning and malfunctioning are grounded—pace these avant-garde practitioners—in continuous acts of transformation, destruction, and reassemblage. These acts constitute the body itself as a site of reception, metamorphosis, and construction. Such "works" ceaselessly produce a renewed and renewable subject whose renewal includes aging and decay. Yet they do not take raw material (nature) or some Hegelian Spirit (totality) as a point of either departure or arrival for the work of production itself. For Benjamin, mimesis means "nonsensory" (nonsensual) similarity. Children's play—a child who impersonates a mountain, a river, a star—is perhaps the clearest example, and language the supreme manifestation, of the mimetic faculty, its last "negative" repository.

By examining incorporation (e.g., Benjamin) and indigestion (e.g., Dada) rather than assimilation or digestion, the book argues that the avant-garde questioned the hierarchies of the body's senses. An aesthetic that privileges sight (along with hearing/sound) over physical taste (and smell) is critiqued—along with, therein, the Western history of post-Kantian aesthetics with its claim to disinterested judgment. The avant-garde, including Benjamin, emphasizes a spontaneous attentiveness to the body that is generated by and focused on incorporation, a rejoinder to both Kantian contemplation and, to some extent, Theodor Adorno's reiteration of art's autonomy. This does not diminish, however, the important institutional critique of the neo-avant-garde, which has revealed itself as more than a renewed attempt at bridging art and life so called.

My analyses of the avant-garde's works also have shown that the incorporative body is not just a simple matter of sensory perception or cognition, for the latter are endowed with mnemonic layers of cultural and subjective history, that is, multiple temporalities. The incorporative body is also the site of confrontation, the laboratory for interrogating and testing the conventional relations between subject and object, self and other, and thus the very language of aesthetic experience and the form of the *one* presupposed aesthetic object. Where we find incorporation, indigestion or, in short, antidiets we find that aesthetics enters a crisis of communication of the aesthetic experience, or the rediscovery of the latter as embedded in the production of linguistic crises. (One need only think of René Magritte's paintings.) It could be said that the avant-garde's reference to incorporation, indigestion, and scattered food fits in the theoretical tradition of negative aesthetics from Friedrich Nietzsche to Adorno (i.e., the trajectory of negative aesthetics proposed by Gianni Vattimo). Through incorporation, indigestion, and the questioning of putatively organic and unproblematic relations among the world, the object, and the subject, between nature and art, an internal dialectic persists in this art, despite its entropic and proliferating tendencies. This dialectic, however, is deprived of any Hegelian resolution: the sublation of art in philosophy or, in Kantian terms, the subsumption of the anxiety about loss and fear into the redemptive sublime or the spectacle is suspended, interrupted, or at least scrutinized for traces or wounds.

But in our times of extreme spectacularization both inside and outside the museum (museums themselves have become spectacles in their designs, in their competitions with each other, and in the art they exhibit), the questions that arise are, what antidiets does contemporary art propose, if any at all? Is the in/edibility of art and life still an issue or, through a decisive move of art into the field of discursivity and sociability—into the horizontal axis of expanded interdisciplinary fields, from ethnography to science—is art today perhaps proposing food as immediate experience, the representable presence, the graspable site for "good living"? Is such food art problematically utopian? The next few pages generate more such questions rather than answers. Moreover, the vast number of works and performances with and around food that have accelerated since the eighties makes it nearly impossible to find representative examples. Yet some of these works offer possible ways to think about modalities in which food appears in a world of varied and dispersed artworks today, a world where systematization and projectuality are insufficient for interpretation. To put some of these questions in the form of concerns, then, I seek in the remaining pages to briefly investigate first whether food in art and art in food engages in institutional critique. (The institution is to be considered, especially after the neo-avant-garde, more than just the spaces of art: it is the expanded discursive field including the various forms of publicity around art, alongside notions of the subject.)[1] Second, I consider how food art today relates to "its communities," and, third, whether food today is a way to archive (for the purpose of rescuing) forms of identity or communication that are evanescent. In sum, I ask, what kind of mnemonic and future-oriented panoramas does food bring to the fore? In addressing these issues, albeit in cursory form, I consider Ben Kinmont, Rirkrit Tiravanija, Janine Antoni, and Jana Sterbak.

Communities and/as Institutional Critique: Kinmont and Tiravanija

During the show *Casual Ceremony* at White Columns in New York (1991), Kinmont exhibited paper plates, which he used as invitation cards for gallery visitors: he invited anyone to pick up a plate and call him on the phone to arrange a breakfast with him at his home. Of the 468 plates taken, thirty-two people took up the invitation and had waffles with him. With this performance Kinmont pursued the possibility that a gallery can be a "situation of trust" to see whether this institutional space, more intimate than the museum (a corporation), would generate the desire for another intimate relation, friendship between a host and a guest.[2] He was not interested — unlike artists in the seventies — to "bring life into the gallery" and to engage the history of the avant-garde (which was "good" and "fine" as *history* in his words); rather, he wished to use the gallery to move "art" outside the gallery into the private space of the artist's home. Kinmont is not the first to operate along these lines. In the 1960s Spoerri had opened his room in the Chelsea Hotel to visitors and simply exhibited this space. Most of Spoerri's Eat Art — in his own Restaurant or in other Restaurant Galleries — still tested and questioned the definitions and boundaries of art through some confrontation with or juxtaposition of public spaces (even in New York, his room was a transient hotel space, a bed occupied only temporarily by an artist). Fluxus art such as Ben Vautier's *Mystery Food* or Alison Knowles's *Make a Salad* engage the institutional spaces (the discourses of and around art) in the all-too-present absence of that very space that has historically conferred identity to art. In Kinmont's *Waffles for an Opening* the debates and deliberations about the artistic quality (or lack thereof) of the work itself move to the domestic sphere. Here the artist is prepared to open his home and himself to a debate with the public. The public, however, is a "guest" whom the artist honors and serves, with whom he also shares the meal, and whom, through his gesture of gift giving, he also holds temporarily captive. As the artist notes, more often than not he and his guests would talk about the project. The hope, it seems, is that a face-to-face conversation between the artist and his public about the meaning of art will ensue, perhaps a discussion about the elements of the project itself: is Kinmont's art only in the invitation plates/cards on display in the gallery, or only in the breakfasts, or both and more? Thus the conversations that take place "at home" (his home) shape ideas of art through direct dialogue and, perhaps similarly, also all those conversations that have *not* taken place in his home but surely in other spaces, beyond the artist's ears, thus still shaping the imaginations and expectations of various publics.

In the private conversation punctuated by the conviviality and hospitality of sharing food there is the promise of a mutual exchange of ideas, which could perhaps pass up the institutional strictures of defining and negotiating "art." In such artwork/performance there seems to be a willful forgetting of, for example, the power dynamics already existing between the roles inhabited by the artist-host and the public-guest, in hopes that a new art may emerge from these apparently hybrid domestic– public spaces. *Waffles for an Opening* breaks with notions of the private as "ownership" (of space, time, relations, etc.) through hospitality, conviviality, and the gift. Still, it does not take into account the "representative" function of the artist/art as already situated in publicity, the effects of which this project does not seem to be concerned with. Art remains here as an open yet temporary invitation to a private artist-home, a station that brings people together and then disperses them in hopes of finding, studying, and perhaps forming other communities, other models of living well (as Tiravanija would have it, niches of sociability in a world where interactivity seems to be mediatic). The artist, who in this case also plays the role of a casual native informant — despite his insistence that the conversations not be recorded — does not engage the already mediatic/mediated space of the home and the conversations, whether with or without the recorder, with or without the memento of the plates signed by both "guests" and "host" ("Untitled Artists' Projects," 136).

The doubly oral aspect of the project (food and conversations) is emphasized by the artist's decision not to hold on to the coauthored invitation plates/cards, which, in this case, not unlike the certificates of authenticity or invitations to Spoerri's banquets, are dispersed with and among his guests for use or as souvenirs. There is a sense of extreme generosity and play in the artist's willingness to give up the Name-of-the-Artist by signing it on a plate for a guest, like an autograph, and thus by turning himself, the artist, into an actor or a sportsman, just another "star." (Though Kinmont emphasizes these are not "heavy-duty" performances.) This is a reflection on the image of the artist in contemporary society. Other artists such as Manzoni (who signed his name on living people and declared them works of art, thus ironically questioning both the figure and the artist's actions) and Spoerri (who signed "certificates" or "eaten-by" trap-paintings) were less interested in forming a community than in exposing the dynamics of art as institution. In contrast, Kinmont's distribution of his plates as mementos of temporary communicative communities proves the artificiality of these short-lived art "worlds." It does so because the act of sharing foods and words, an act supposedly taking place among equals and, accordingly, offering a momentary utopia (or illusion) of an egalitarian democracy, dissipates quickly, for the artist does not keep (for himself, as it were) a memento from his visitor. Indeed, the plate with both signatures is carried away by the latter. This may be read as the renunciation of the temptation on the part of the artist to abuse the moment of community by resisting its transformation into a museum artifact. Yet precisely the acknowledgment of such a possibility, on top of the circulation of the gift in one direction only — from artist to public — betrays the pervasiveness of "art as institution," which Kinmont's work does not, ultimately, engage critically. Hence this utopian instance of gifting underscores the artificial institution of private versus public.

In a similar vein, another of Kinmont's projects is both intriguing and disquieting. It pivots around "leftovers," the in/visible or marginal spaces in art (and performance as well) that Spoerri's trap-paintings or *Bread-Dough Objects* had already used. Yet again Kinmont's focus is on his own experience of the domestic realm, this time the homes of anonymous, ordinary people. Here he provides the public with domestic service that then translates as "artistic gift." The action is called *I will wash your dirty dishes* (Munich, 1994), and it continues — in reverse, as it were — the invitation-breakfast-plate project just discussed. Both projects touch on distribution, of the idea and work of the artist.

I will wash your dirty dishes arose from within the context of a curatorial project about communication in public spaces. (Hence the framework "communication" and "public" was given, with the implications that these curatorial choices have in terms of stimulating but also defining artistic tendencies, which means institutional frameworks for reading and interacting with art). Kinmont opted to transfer communication from the public to the private. As an ethnographer, he *picked* demographically different neighborhoods in the city: "So they are different spaces in terms of economics but also in terms of functions, what happens in those spaces" ("Untitled Artists' Projects," 138). He would sign people up for the project, then give them a card as a reminder of his appointment to wash their dishes. A contract (waiver) would be signed to allow the artist to photograph and record the event, the spaces and so forth, and to let the public/participants choose whether they wished to remain anonymous in the products to be later exhibited. The contract also allowed them to decide whether they would like to know about future exhibitions of the project. This work is a sort of documentary — a kind of ethnographic endeavour. The choice of doing the dishes is another way to work with food — that is, through the conviviality that allows (supposedly) for free-flowing conversations — but, this time, from a less ceremonial perspective. Walking into and working in private homes — just as individuals had entered his private home — is meant to redistribute "trust" (137). The artist who in this instance only serves (works for) people he does not know (he does not always eat with the family or individuals in question, though this also occasionally occurred) not only studies these groups anthropologically but also does the dishes "as a catalyst to get into their home and talk about these issues of art and life" (137). The ethnographic study, which presumably is part of the project's final objective, especially the conversations about art and life catalyzed by the artist's action, is based in *seeing*: "The leftovers of food, you are seeing the residue, you are seeing what people didn't want to eat, you are seeing what type of eaters they are, what they use to eat with" (137).

The artist's project that is oriented by the question of communication does tackle more specific aspects of art related to "work" (labor),

art's rhythms or temporalities, the contrast between the durable object
or memento and the ephemeral action of washing dishes — ephemeral
for the artist who, in his words, enters these homes as a welcome ghost
and is there only once and never more. The project also offers reflections about art and the gendered private sphere, the double burden
of women as domestic workers inside and outside the home. As Kinmont put it: "What does it mean to be a man doing dishes as art? What
does it mean to be a man and doing food as art?" (139). Here the private sphere becomes more meaningful, and Kinmont's action seems to
resonate with feminist concerns. Yet the numerous critical aspects on
which the project touches and that again are supposedly brought into
relief by the conversations between hosts and guest (in this case the
artist is the guest/servant) do not coalesce. Attempts at understanding
and proposing art as unpaid work and service to communities — communities that are thus involved with art and its effects — are certainly
significant. But they also need to be elaborated and questioned critically, as do the communities thereby "constructed."

Kinmont keeps archives of those projects that then enter the gallery. There he "tries to describe truthfully what happened. . . . I'm also
trying to allow someone else to experience what happened" (142). His
goal is to think of an art that, based in experience, may provoke forms
of understanding about its location in and relations with other everyday practices, whether of work or leisure (washing dishes or sharing a
breakfast). He considers his ethnographic interventions and archives
of memory of these happenings — exhibited in the separate space of
the gallery — to be instances of sudden and brief estrangement from
normalcy (albeit through normalcy, that is, through typical activities
of the private sphere). Estrangement forces one to rethink one's activity or rather experience of that activity: in short, Kinmont proposes a
mutual — and interactive — raising of consciousness.

Yet some questions haunt this artist's enterprise. For instance,
how do his art projects help rethink work (domestic labor, immigrant
labor)? How would or could a ghost–artist–worker interfere with typically low-paid domestic work? How does a semiprivate conversation
that is archived as hypothetical and parenthetical event open possibilities for grassroots art, a kind of art that confronts the "discourse" of
art? Problems arise, in my view, mostly because this food art's premise
and goal are to form alternative — even if transient — communities that
then are carved from an idealized (natural, as it were) domestic realm.

They are alternative with respect to the anonymous contacts established in an increasingly globalized world of commerce. A didacticism is evident here that is based in the belief in the egalitarian spaces for conversation that art supposedly offers. Arguably, the hope is that small instances of art will counter the flaws and lacks of real-existing democracy by providing temporary relief and home remedies for and from democracy's (and capital's) internal contradictions.

Some ethnographic art of the nineties — which, like Kinmont's art, is based in fieldwork, the reconsideration of the archive, and the notion of reportage — while partaking of the discursivity of the field of art and of questions about subjectivity and otherness, however, risks losing sight of its institutional role. This art, too, may involuntarily reaffirm the authority of the artist/ethnographer rather than question its own marketable or symbolic authority. In Kinmont's case, the relinquishing of a temporal perspective — a historical critical appropriation of the preceding neo-avant-garde on some of these issues — may transform his art into ludic or private experiments that lose their critical input and artistic legibility.

Tiravanija's work is in some regards as utopian and therefore as problematic as Kinmont's. Tiravanija engages, however, with the architectural space of the museum or gallery rather than with these purely as "institution," unlike many artists who preceded him. His subdued offering of food along with the artist sitting at a table at which the gallery visitor is also invited for a chat at openings again proposes art as a momentary gift. While nowadays such offerings may be familiar also through the experience of online chat rooms, thanks to the materiality of food the contact between the artist and the recipient/visitor is meant to be physical, sensual, as "close" and authentic as possible. In fact, it counters the abstractness and invisibility or anonymity of the electronic medium. It is significant that these exchanges happen in semi-official exhibition spaces or, in Tiravanija's words, in "non-spaces" (*Eating Culture*, 154). In using this term, he has in mind a 1989 show in New York during which he exhibited pots of an unmistakably aromatic curry in an entryway, an in-between space: the performance took place neither in the gallery nor in the street but, so to speak, between a door and a window (154). On most occasions Tiravanija uses institutional spaces for his cooking and eating performances, sometimes the gallery space normally devoted to exhibiting art, other times back rooms of various sorts. For the show *Back Stage,* which opened at the Kunstverein in Hamburg, he staged a soup kitchen in the museum's loading dock. (The action was inspired by Jan Schütte's film *Dragon Chow,* a film from the 1980s about the life and struggles of two immigrants to Germany who try to run their own restaurant in Hamburg despite insurmountable difficulties. In the end, one of them is deported, and the enterprise fails—or so we are left to think.) Tiravanija offered his German "soup" in the space where the art pieces for the museum's exhibitions are physically moved, lifted, and touched by behind-the-scenes workers, often immigrants to Germany. To make and offer a German soup in an official German space while holding the "main event" backstage, as it were, questioned notions of belonging or assimilation, whether with regard to (German) citizenship and nationality or to the "art" in question, that is, a spontaneous and essential art of life equal to the art of giving. Tiravanija asks: What does it mean for this art to be served to Germans in the loading docks of an important German institution? (Tiravanija's food works are mostly site specific; they change with the contexts to which they refer and in which they intervene, both socially and artistically.)

For Tiravanija, it is important that the viewers be actor-participants who contribute to the art-making process by transferring one of their everyday acts—eating, helping to set the table—into the museum. The everyday becomes both an essential constituent of the authenticity of art (the possibility of experiencing life as it is) and an instance not easily locatable as either art or everyday life but suspended between the two, that is, between the entrance into the gallery and the exit onto the street. On this threshold the public may see art as precisely that instant of suspension that allows art and the everyday to overlap and, in the overlap, to be estranged from each other. Tiravanija states: "If you make life into art, then what would be more meaningful is just to have your life rather than to force it into something. So it is not just serving food. Food is kind of the frame and what happens within that frame is something else. . . . on the one hand, it's quite a rupture to see food being served in a gallery, but on the other hand it is an activity that everyone does, it's something everyone can enter into after that initial point" (156). Tiravanija's performances thus are less about food—and food as material—than occasions to rethink the sites and positionalities of artists and public, of galleries and kitchens, and of producers and consumers. He disturbs the homogeneity of these sites and identities in much the same way as some of the neo-avant-garde artists examined in this book. Yet his focus is identity and sociability and how art can recontextualize or find situations in which social dynamics can come to conflate, positively, with artistic reflection. Consider Tiravanija's contribution to *Viennese Stories* at the Vienna Secession in 1993. On that occasion he had found out that two cooks in the café at the Secession were from Thailand — like himself (although he was raised in Argentina and now lives in New York City) — but cooked Austrian food with the exception of one day a week when they could add to the menu a Thai dish. He befriended the cooks, shopped with them, and chose the dish to add to the menu. The whole procedure was finally recorded. The video was then put on display in the Secession café. "It was like you might be any place and look up and see this thing that doesn't quite belong there. . . . And then you might just kind of slowly focus on it at some point and realize what it is that's happening in it" (160). Of course it is not only the video that does not belong in the café but also the cooks who are normally hidden in the kitchen — backstage. By suddenly standing in the dining hall (albeit on a screen), they expose national and cultural contradictions and beliefs about the authenticity of people and of art, about the identity of artists and consumers. Displacements are the site of Tiravanija's food art: the displacements of artistic sites of productions, of national identities, of the locations and consumption of art. At what point if at all art happens in these actions is irrelevant to Tiravanija, who leaves it for his audience to decide and to see in these events "encounters," conversations, art or, eventually, nothing at all. For him, art is an act of becoming conscious, bringing oneself to a level of consciousness about art's possibility (160).

Tiravanija offers more than food as art and art as food, and his art is not about generating authentic communities in and through discussion, as for Kinmont. However, in the need to be truthful to the chance situations found, he too speaks of the "real relationship" people establish when they sit down at the table to eat. Of his use of documentary videos, he states: "I wanted to make video function in a natural way." He does hope that different, more aware, and perhaps even happy forms of sociability may arise from this kind of "food art." He shares a belief in the rise of spontaneous awareness through direct experience with at least some of the neo-avant-garde artists examined. However, he also tends to tinge this art with an optimism that may obscure the subtle moments of institutional critique that are indeed present, such as through the architectural nonspaces in which his food events take place. Furthermore, the political risk of this food art is perhaps its mobility: Tiravanija travels the world to offer his company and his food to a great variety of publics. This mobile food art can be confused with a global flow of free-floating "good intentions," with facile and familiar slogans about superficial forms of multiculturalism, and thus it can be flattened into a particular sort of "cosmopolitanism" in which exchange and communication about "good living" erase the politics of difference, especially in liberal capitalist democracies. Again, one reason for this risk may lie precisely in the lack of a conscious confrontation with the neo-avant-garde's reflections about art — especially those these artists entertained through the use of food — its pitfalls, failures, and forgotten dreams.

Subjects and Archives: Antoni and Sterbak

There are other artists, in particular Antoni and Sterbak, whose work with eating and food materials ought to be considered here, though only briefly and alas reductively. Antoni and Sterbak are important because they engage and appropriate art and issues of previous decades that came to be dismissed as old-fashioned already in the eighties. Antoni engages quite explicitly with minimalism that she critically incorporates and questions from a feminist perspective, and Sterbak cites feminist performance art (e.g., Carolee Schneemann's *Meat Joy* and Yoko Ono's *Cut Piece,* both from 1964, and Valie Export's provocative *Tapp und Tastkino* from 1968) while literally refashioning it toward critical reflections about women and industry, both the meat industry and the fashion industry.[3] The engagement with the aestheticization and fetishization of women and their bodies, after the critiques of these in the 1960s, is taken up in both artists' works through references to consumerism. Antoni's famous two pieces — *Chocolate Gnaw* and *Lard Gnaw* (both 1992) — bring back into her interpretation of minimalism the question of industry and consumption, especially those of cosmetics and sweets. Not only did she gnaw at two enormous cubes, one of lard and one of chocolate, spit the torn and chewed pieces out, but most importantly she used the indigestible remainders to produce in one case lipsticks and, in the other, chocolate hearts. The deformation of the industrial "essential" cube of minimalism, appositely put on a small pedestal for display, first produces a lava of running *informe* lard that the base cannot contain any longer. Second, it is transformed into a commercial item, a commodity aimed to shape — according to the mass canons of beauty — those dangerously unshaped bodies of women, especially women "eaters." This is a comment about subjectivity as much as about the reshaping of art and artistic resistance into fashionable commodities. A sense of nausea and a desire for destruction, however, pervade this act of consumption and hinder any act or medium of aestheticization.

Sterbak used raw meat — the meat of steaks — as material for fashionable dresses that she has exhibited in various venues since 1987 (since *Vanitas: Flesh Dress for an Albino Anorectic*). On the occasion of an opening in Montreal a model wore a bloody fifty-pound dress.[4] The contrast between this peculiar fashion model, dripping blood, carrying a weight that pulls her down, exposing as it were this second naked flesh (flesh rather than just skin) to the gaze of the viewers in the museum is an indictment of the fashion industry's multiple erasures: the erasure of "work," the labor and sweat on the part of the models themselves; the engineering first and exploitation then of temporary (anorexic) beauties, impersonal (albino, transparent) prototypes in flesh and blood to be chewed up and spit out by the market. The work makes visible the devouring desires of a misogynistic and carnivorous culture that associates women's bodies to "good meat" while it hypocritically prefers to cover them up with the refined skins of dead animals. Later the dried-up meat dresses, hung on display-dummies, both hide and reveal this hypocrisy, for they are easily mistaken for leather with no traces of blood or death. Cured and preserved as they are with salt, these dresses point precisely to the preservation of beauty — in art as in fashion — as the preservation of death. If the raw meat on the live woman's body was also briefly brought to life, now it is killed again and reduced to a layer of skin/leather that forgets the blood involved in killing. In an indirect way this work may also indict a society in which slaughtering animals — and feeding off the dead carcasses we kill — is removed from sight and thus made bearable and sin free.

In sum, while it is difficult to systematize and presumptuous to find clear paths for reading the many encounters between food and contemporary art, food is taken as an immediate "tool" for imagining art as a site of sociability and communicative action. But the artistic enterprise is limited when it seeks to substitute itself for the publicities and communities it intends to shape. This art, with its utopian aroma of possibility, often forgets to think temporally/historically and thus to counter consumption, the consumption of art itself as a consumerist–touristic culture of art sampling. It also risks essentializing "eating" and "food" as immediate experience.

Yet there are moments in this novel food art and in comparable projects in which art's locations in relation to consumption and identity formation are critically considered. It is, accordingly, important to distinguish between the different negative, critical moments and various affirmative ones within contemporary art. In this we can identify, perhaps, the positive energies that tend toward a thinking of alternative futures while working through, or at least keeping at bay, the false appropriations of precisely those values — individual freedom, private well-being, and so forth — that capitalism claims as its own quintessential by-products.

ACKNOWLEDGMENTS

Many institutions and people contributed to the making of this book. Certain chapters were originally conceived for my thesis at the University of Chicago, and I owe a first debt to my adviser, Katie Trumpener, who always went out of her way to assist and encourage me.

I am also indebted to those individuals who offered ideas and comments about the avant-garde and "eating" through their own stimulating publications and through constructive criticism about this book at its different stages. I am grateful to Allen S. Weiss, Priscilla Parkhurst Ferguson, Beatrice Hanssen, Gerhard Richter, Gary Smith, and Hal Foster for their challenging texts, and I extend thanks to Anke Pinkert, Laura Lomas, Cathy Steblyk, Jeff Hardwick, Daniel Purdy, and Ted Norton, among others, for their insights. Two anonymous readers offered helpful critiques of the manuscript. Erika Wolf, Silvia Lopez, Nicholas Rennie, Carsten Strathausen, Aaron Levy, and Jean-Michel Rabaté provided me the opportunity to present my work in public venues. I wish to thank Raleigh Whitinger and Rodney Symington at *Seminar: A Journal of Germanic Studies* where I published an early version of chapter 2 of this book. Elisabeth Hartung invited me to contribute an essay on Daniel Spoerri for the catalog on Eat Art published for the exhibition at Aktionsforum Praterinsel in Munich. For their support, I thank Andrea Kleinhuber, Adam Brunner, Laura Westlund, and Richard Morrison at the University of Minnesota Press.

A great number of individuals helped me locate invaluable materials. First and foremost is Daniel Spoerri, who has been not only approachable but especially friendly. I will always remember our informal conversations about his work and much more in different venues, including a typical Bavarian restaurant in Munich in 2001. I thank the curator of the Spoerri retrospective at Museum Jean Tinguely in Basel; the artist Pavel Schmidt, who introduced me to the techniques of restoration of Spoerri's trap-paintings; and Katrin Zurbruegg at this museum's press office. While in Basel, I was a guest of the Zuelliger family, to whom I owe my gratitude.

Other important institutions and people were instrumental for the writing of this book: Jolanda Bucher and Monika Bohnenblust at the Daniel Spoerri Archives of the Swiss National Library in Bern; Henry Vauth at the library of the Kunstsammlung in Düsseldorf, and Stephan von Wiese at Düsseldorf Kunstmuseum; in Paris the team at Light Cone, the staff of the INA, and Françoise Bonnefoy at the Jeu de Paume. My warmest thanks go to Ewa Esterhazy for making available to me her important dissertation on Spoerri. My research abroad occurred with the support of a Pennsylvania State University summer grant (RGSO). I thank Laura Knoppers, former director of the Institute for the Arts and Humanities at PSU, for helping make my semester at the Institute rewarding. Daniel Mack at PSU Pattee Library was extremely helpful, as always, as was my research assistant, Sally Whitley.

Parts of this book were written while I was at Cornell University with a DAAD summer grant: I am grateful to Peter U. Hohendahl and the other participants for a pleasant and engaging workshop on the Frankfurt school. I express my gratitude to Nadia Urbinati, Marina Calloni, and Cesare Pianciola for their time and suggestions in matters of critical theory. When writing this book in Italy, I benefited immensely from the social and artistic environment to which I was introduced by Guido Curto, director of Accademia di Belle Arti in Turin, and by Rocco Moliterni at the newspaper *La Stampa*. Had it not been for Rocco I would not have become acquainted with Guido Spaini, who was instrumental in locating important Futurist menus. With his help I made contact with a private collector who provided me with images of two such menus from his collection and one work by Joseph Beuys. *Grazie,* Michele!

For the procurement of images and relative reproduction rights I extend my thanks to, besides the aforementioned individuals, Ryan Jensen and John Benicewicz at Art Resource in New York, Cristin O'Keefe Aptowicz (ARS, New York), Anne Sanouillet, Emmett Williams (who was exceptionally forthcoming), Jon Hendricks, Dirk Dobke (from Dieter Roth Estate, Basel), Rosalia Pasqualino di Marineo

(Archivio Opera Piero Manzoni, Milan), and Timothy Shipe (International Dada Archive, Iowa City), who was particularly friendly and always ready to lend a hand.

On a personal note: my sincere thanks to all those who provided emotional support during the past years. I express my gratitude to Gautam Ghosh, my husband, whose constructive comments, close reading, and emotional support are evident in every word of this book — and elsewhere. Thanks to my other family members, especially my parents, who have inspired me with conversations, ideas, and by simply being there. During my research in Germany my dear friend Wally Feld and her husband, Micha, made me feel at home on every visit, as has Irmtraut Voss in Berlin and Andreas Leusink. Liza, Joan, Roselyn, and Marta and Tom kept my spirits high in difficult times, as have many other dear friends.

This book is dedicated to Emilio Kumar, my son.

NOTES

Introduction

1. On the issue of the culinary as a "field"—drawing on which I pursue the idea of the antidiet field, and so forth—see Priscilla Parkhurst Ferguson, "A Cultural Field in the Making: Gastronomy in Nineteenth Century France," in *French Food: On the Table, on the Page, and in French Culture,* ed. Lawrence R. Schehr and Allan S. Weiss (New York: Routledge, 2001), 5–50.

2. Franz Kafka, *The Complete Stories,* ed. Nahum N. Glazer (New York: Schocken Books, 1971).

3. Kafka speaks of his need to write. Writing is a need as much as a desire. The two are not separable in Kafka's story, which then brings to the fore the complications that arise in distinguishing one from the other, as is evident when dealing with food, too.

4. Both Stephane Mallarmé (see his text "The Pipe") and Marcel Proust were obviously major forerunners of Benjamin's intoxication poetics, but Benjamin is closer to the surrealists, for through his profane illumination he attempts to leave behind the subjectivity of experience found in the other authors. Benjamin's choice of incorporation of "food"—which he associates also with the "everyday" magical act of reading—is telling. Eating in Benjamin's case is considered more often than not as a public moment, or, if not shared by an immediate collectivity, eating occurs either in the open or as the memory of a ritual, perhaps on the verge of being forgotten.

5. See Richard Wolin, "Benjamin, Adorno, Surrealism," in *The Semblance of Subjectivity: Essays in Adorno's Aesthetic Theory,* ed. Tom Huhn and Lambert Zuidervaart (Cambridge, Mass.: MIT Press, 1997), 93–122.

6. Georges Didi-Huberman, "L'histoire de l'art à rebrousse-poile: Temps de l'image et 'travail au seins des choses' selon Walter Benjamin," *Les Cahiers du Musée National d'Art Moderne* 72 (Summer 2000): 92–117.

7. Benjamin does not so sharply distinguish between attentiveness and distraction as illustrated by Jonathan Crary. An analysis of incorporation shows how *Zerstreuung*—the scattering of perception outside any synthesis—is inherent in a process of destruction or in *Zerstörung,* which is necessary for modern experience.

276 NOTES TO INTRODUCTION NOTES TO INTRODUCTION

For Benjamin, the subject of incorporation consumes self-identity in interplay with an open body, a body of fragmented perception that can then be "coagulated" again toward action. Destruction and distraction are indispensable to a bodily presence of mind leading up to action. See Jonathan Crary, *Techniques of the Observer* (Cambridge, Mass.: MIT Press, 1999), 50–51.

8. See Walter Benjamin, "Breakfast Room," in *Selected Writings*, ed. Michael Jennings (Cambridge, Mass.: Harvard University Press, 1999), 1: 444–45.

9. See Crary's *Techniques of the Observer* and also Helmut Lethen, *Verhaltenslehren der Kälte: Lebensversuche zwischen den Kriegen* (Frankfurt am Main: Suhrkamp, 1994).

10. For an analysis, within the German context, of the oral anxieties hidden in the proliferation of "words" of food, see Thomas Kleinspehn, "Sprechen — Schauen — Essen," in *Kulturthema Essen: Ansichten und Problemfelder*, ed. Alois Wierlacher, Gerhard Neumann, and Hans Jürgen Teutenberg (Berlin: Akademie Verlag, 1993), 257–68.

11. Priscilla Parkhurst Ferguson, *Accounting for Taste: The Triumph of French Cuisine*, (Chicago: University of Chicago Press, 2006), 3.

12. On the cosmological nature of ancient dietetics, see Dietrich von Engelhardt, "Hunger und Appetit: Essen und Trinken im System der Diätetik — Kulturhistorische Perspektiven," in *Kulturthema Essen*, 137–50.

13. Massimo Montanari, *La fame e l'abbondanza: Storia dell'alimentazione in Europa* (Rome: Laterza, 1993), 121.

14. Apropos the constant quest for simplicity, see Stephen Mennell, *All Manners of Food: Eating and Taste in England and France from the Middle Ages to the Present* (Urbana: University of Illinois Press, 1996), 165. Mennell reads in particular Auguste Escoffier's "revolution" as part of the complex process of "the civilizing of taste," which he opposes to the vagaries of fashion. While I find the term *civilizing* problematic, I agree with Mennell that the "succession of dominant styles in French professional cookery" has less to do with fashion and revolution — in the historical sense — than with renewal. The avant-garde antidiets configure the avant-garde less as revolutions against the past — although these are the proclamations of the manifestos — than as "instances" of renewal, which, however, do not aim at development.

15. Roland Barthes, "Reading Brillat Savarin," in *Rustle of Language* (Berkeley: University of California Press, 1989), 250–70.

16. The debate around synesthesia as the term defining the phenomenon of sensorial associations, especially between sight and hearing, intersects with developments in such new scientific disciplines as brain physiology around the mid-nineteenth century. For discussion of this and of the impact that such research and debate has had on the arts, see Pascal Rousseau, "Confusion des sens: Le débat évolutionniste sur la synesthésie dans les débuts de l'abstraction en France," *Les Cahiers du Musée National d'Art Moderne* 74 (Winter 2000–1): 433.

17. Philip Hyman, "Culina Mutata: Carême and l'*ancienne* Cuisine," in *French Food*, 80–81.

18. Gilles Deleuze and Félix Guattari, *Anti-Oedipus: Capitalism and Schizophrenia* (New York: Viking, 1977), 31. See also Allen S. Weiss, *Perverse Desire and the Ambiguous Icon* (Albany: State University of New York Press, 1994), 67. There are strong resonances between Hal Foster's examination of Max Ernst's parodic, hyperbolic constructed machines and my theorizing about Dada's "indigestion" and its mimetic — performative — character. For an early version of chapter 2 of this book, see "Dada-Diets: Dysfunctional Physiologies of Devouring," *seminar* 37, no. 1 (2001): 1–20, which first appeared in my dissertation (2000). More recently, Foster tackled Dada's parodic mimesis in terms of "hypertrophy" in "A Bashed Ego: Max Ernst in Cologne," in *The Dada Seminars*, ed. Leah Dickerman with Matthew S. Witkowsky (Washington, D.C.: National Gallery of Art, 2005), 127–47.

19. Barthes spoke of food grammars in his text on semiology. See Roland Barthes, *Elements of Semiology* (New York: Hill and Wang, 1968).

20. For an analysis of the avant-garde as postaesthetic and as "event" but not as postartistic (as in poietic), see Krzysztof Ziarek, *The Historicity of Experience: Modernity, the Avant-Garde, and the Event* (Evanston, Ill.: Northwestern University Press, 2001). See also his essay "The Work of Art in the Age of Electronic Mutability," in *Walter Benjamin and Art*, ed. Andrew Benjamin (London: Continuum, 2005), 209–25, especially 212.

21. Richard Sheppard bases his reading of modernism — and of Dada as the modernist movement that purged itself most thoroughly of nineteenth-century values — on these movements and on the internal contradictions, ambivalences, or fissures of authors and artists. While modernism was pulled both away and in by the bourgeois values that modernity threw into a deep crisis, a crisis that modernism still attempted to solve, postmodernist art rehearses a crisis that is not felt apocalyptically. See Sheppard, *Modernism — Dada — Postmodernism* (Evanston, Ill.: Northwestern University Press, 2000), especially chapter 1 (11–30) and chapter 13 (356–57).

22. Theodor W. Adorno, *Aesthetic Theory* (Minneapolis: University of Minnesota Press, 1997), 49.

23. Theodor W. Adorno, "Art and the Arts," in *Can One Live after Auschwitz: A Philosophical Reader,* ed. Rolf Tiedemann (Stanford, Calif.: Stanford University Press, 2003), 375; my emphasis. On the critique of art as culinary, see *Can One Live,* 371. See also his concept that, in eroding art, modern art is a false destruction of it. Here too, again, Adorno has recourse to the trope of devouring. The arts "eat away at one another," thereby exhibiting more and more the need for art in the post-Holocaust era of the culture industry (387). Its self-imposed abrogation is the measure of art's renewed/renewable existence as nourishing. In particular, Adorno considers the nonidentity of art, by which he means mostly modernist art. Modernist art does not dissolve its boundary with empirical reality but works to keep the tension with it as the nonidentical within itself, which is revealed by the "affixed debris [that] cleaves visible scars in the work's meaning." See *Aesthetic Theory,* 155. All English translations have been checked against the German original and bear the same connotations.

24. He explicitly condemns Benjamin's ambivalence about the aura in his art-work essay, in which, for Adorno, the writer relegates to the past the distance found in the aura. Here he writes that "aesthetic comportment must not grasp at the object, not devour it" (*Aesthetic Theory*, 310). When Benjamin deliberately approaches eating and devouring, his theory of incorporation always involves a confrontation with otherness. Adorno obviously did not support the desublimation into the life praxis invoked by the avant-garde. Instead he praised high modernism.

25. Fernande Olivier, *Picasso and His Friends*, trans. Jane Miller (New York: Appleton-Century, 1965), 97; my emphasis.

26. Allen S. Weiss, *Feast and Folly* (Albany: State Univeristy of New York Press, 2002), 24.

27. Hal Foster, "A Bashed Ego: Max Ernst in Cologne," in Dickerman, *Dada Seminars*.

28. In Burke's view the sublime is the privation of the privation that death would be. As a suspension of that final privation of life, Burke's sublime thus has a temporal dimension, according to Lyotard. The delight taken in meals — meals that suspend the course of life toward death and temporarily grant life victory over time — is on this view associated with the sublime, too.

29. Guillaume Apollinaire, *Apollinaire: Critique d'art* (Paris: Gallimard, 1993), 36.

30. See convolute N, in Walter Benjamin, *Arcades Project*, trans. Howard Eiland and Kevin McLaughlin (Cambridge, Mass.: Belknap Press of Harvard University Press, 1999). See especially N2a, 3 (462), N3, 1 (463), N3a, 3 (464).

31. Both Foster (*The Return of the Real* [Cambridge, Mass.: MIT Press, 1996]) and Lyotard ("Rewriting Modernity," in Lyotard, *The Inhuman: Reflections on Time* [Cambridge: Polity, 1991], 24–35) each in different ways tackle respectively the problems of writing about the avant-garde and its history (or histories) and about modernity. Their suggestions about how to write these histories is reminiscent of Benjamin's antihistoricist approach, at least, to art history. Both Foster and Lyotard refer to Freud, the former to the notion of *Nachträglichkeit* (deferred action) and the latter to the concept of analysis as "working through." Lyotard also uses Kant's idea of the sublime, which he temporalizes through the adoption of Burke's theory of the sublime ("The Sublime Is Now," in *Inhuman*). Both Foster and Lyotard conclude that "punctual" approaches to the history of the avant-garde and of modernity (Lyotard) are flawed, as are chronological — linear — accounts. The analysis of the countersublime antidiets of the avant-garde and neo-avant-garde, I argue, shows resistance to such accounts as already embedded in the works themselves. For Foster, see *Return of the Real*.

32. Quoted in Fabrizio Desideri, "The Mimetic Bond," in *Walter Benjamin and Art*, ed. Andrew Benjamin (New York: Continuum, 2005), 108–20.

33. *Dada au grand air* (*Der Sängerkrieg in Tirol*), p. 1, in Michel Sanouillet, ed., *Dada: Réimpression intégrale et dossier critique de la revue publiée de 1917 à 1922 par Tristan Tzara*, 2 vols. (Nice: Centre du XXe siècle, 1976–83), 1: 119; herafter cited as *Réimpression*.

34. This recipe is in *Dada 8*, otherwise known as *Dada au grand air* (or *Der Sängerkrieg in Tirol*) (discussed in chapter 2). Peter Bürger mentions the recipe character of Dada's instructions in poetics in relation to this avant-garde attempt to break down the separation between producer and consumer. He does not elaborate, however. See Peter Bürger, *Theory of the Avant-Garde* (Minneapolis: University of Minnesota Press, 1989), 53.

35. Georges Braque, *Tout l'oeuvre peint de Braque: 1908–1929* (Paris: Flammarion 1973), 13; my translation.

36. This is Renato Poggioli's position in his work *The Theory of the Avant-Garde* (New York: Harper and Row, 1971).

37. In particular, one could cite here the critical works of Yve Alain Bois and Rosalind Krauss on the impact of *informe* on art (not *informel* art), and Weiss and his mentioned close readings of Artaud and art brut, in addition to his analyses of French thought of the 1960s (Lyotard and Deleuze). See also Foster's work, in which the *informe* is brought to bear on an analysis of recent "abject" art.

38. Foster, commenting on Freud's almost contemporaneous essays (1919), argues for a strong presence of the death drive in this movement. See Hal Foster, *Compulsive Beauty* (Cambridge, Mass.: MIT Press, 1993), 11–12.

39. Timothy Shipe comments: "The two numbers of Picabia's *Cannibale*, while closer than *Proverbe* to the expected format of a literary review, are virtual compendia of Dada techniques. There are parodies of literary news and gossip. . . ." The magazine was published in two issues in 1920. See Timothy Shipe, "Dada Periodicals at Iowa," http://www.lib.uiowa.edu/spec-coll/Bai/shipe.htm, originally in *Books at Iowa* 46 (April 1987): n.p. Note the use of the term *cannibalism* by both Dada and the Brazilian members (the writer and intellectual Oswald de Andrade and the painter Tarsila do Amaral) of the avant-garde movement Antropofagia. It was formed in the late 1920s in Brazil, but already in 1922 Amaral had her studio in Montmartre, in Paris. She introduced de Andrade to Blaise Cendrars, Jean Cocteau, and other avant-garde figures who frequented her atelier. Her painting *Antropofagia* (1929) echoes themes she already touched on in *A Negra* (1923) and *Abaporu* (1928). The bibliography on Antropofagia is extensive. Recently there was a crucial exhibition in Sao Paolo for which a comprehensive catalog was published. See *Brasil 1920–1950: De la Antropofagia a Brasilia* (Valencia: IVAM Centre Julio Gonzalez, 2001). On the crossings and differences between the European avant-garde — for example, Dada's references to cannibalism — and the Brazilian avant-garde, see K. David Jackson, "Three Glad Races: Primitivism and Ethnicity in Brazilian Modernist Literature," *Modernism/Modernity* 1, no. 2 (1994): 89–112. Although the use of Picabia's term *cannibal* has been critiqued as not being political, Dada, like Antropofagia, attacks other avant-garde movements, including cubism and expressionism. Yet the cannibal may be read from within the Dadaist absolute metaphorics of consumption.

40. On the ambivalent positions of F. T. Marinetti's aesthetic, at times still informed by symbolism, at times anticipating surrealism, at times invoking genital sexuality, at times an expanded eroticism, see Luciano De Maria, introduction to

F. T. Marinetti, *Teoria e invenzione futurista* (Milan: Arnoldo Mondadori, 1968), lxiii.

41. Translation found in *Futurist Manifestos*, ed. Umbro Apollonió, trans. Robert Brain, R. W. Flint, J. C. Higgitt, and Caroline Tisdall (London: Tate Publishing, 2009), 20–21.

42. See Allen S. Weiss, "Drunken Space," in *Feast and Folly*, 17–37 and above.

43. The bibliography on scatological rites and history is vast, from John Gregory Bourke's classic *Scatologic Rites of All Nations* (1891) to Dominique Laporte's *History of Shit*. On pathological forms of eating as they relate to art and pathology in art, see Allen S. Weiss, *Shattered Forms: Art Brut, Phantasms, Modernism* (Albany: State University of New York Press, 1992) and Weiss, *The Aesthetics of Excess* (Albany: State University of New York, 1989). On abject art, see Foster, *Return of the Real.*

44. Among the prolific food artists whose work I do not discuss in full is Dieter Roth. He could be cited as a histrionic producer of food and degradable multiples, as well as of "useless" recycling machines, in which waste goes in and poisonous juice comes out. He was also an archivist of scrap and discarded fragments of all sorts. Both he and his friend Spoerri, in this regard, dissolve the "monument" — the *Bau* — still present in Merz's architecture of counterinteriors, and fetishistic grottos. See Leah Dickerman, "Merz and Memory: On Kurt Schwitters," in *Dada Seminars*, 103–26. Various retrospectives devoted to Roth have recently taken place.

45. Quoted in *Les Cahiers du Musée National d'Art Moderne* 74 (Winter 2000–1): 3, from Jorge Luis Borges and Adolfo Bioy Casares, "Un art abstrait," in *Chroniques de Bustos Domecq* (Paris: Denoël, 1970), n.p.; my translation.

1. Futurist Banquets

1. Paolo Sorcinelli, *Gli Italiani e il cibo: Appetiti, digiuni, rinunce dalla realtà contadina alla società del benessere* (Bologna: Cooperativa Libraria Universitaria Editrice, 1995), 96.

2. *Accounting for Taste*, 39.

3. Note that Parkhurst Ferguson speaks of this contradiction as typical of the *modern* cookbooks. See what she writes of La Varenne in *Accounting for Taste,* 39.

4. The Italian version of the cookbook to which I refer is now out of print. See *La cucina futurista*, ed. Filippo Tommaso Marinetti and Fillìa (Milan: Longanesi, 1986). The English translation used here is *The Futurist Cookbook*, ed. Lesley Chamberlain, trans. Suzanne Brill (San Francisco: Bedford Arts, 1989).

5. Claudia Salaris details the relations between Marinetti and fascism in *Marinetti: Arte e vita Futurista* (Rome: Editori Riuniti, 1997). On the banquet organized on September 20, 1928, to remind Mussolini that Marinetti came before him, see, in particular, 244, 246, 247; for the years closer to the time of the Futurist culinary revolution, see 279, 281; on the reception of his radio war aeropoems in 1941, see 285.

NOTES TO CHAPTER I 281

6. On Italianism, see Emilio Gentile, "The Conquest of Modernity: From Modernist Nationalism to Fascism," *Modernism/Modernity* 1, no. 3 (1994): 55–58. According to Gentile, fascism is a modernist avant-garde that attempted to negotiate the relationship between an emergent mass culture and modernity by politicizing aesthetics. In the process, however, the political gradually took the place of the sacred. The myth of a new civilization borne out of the creation of a new spiritual unity in mass society brought with itself an apparatus of rites like those of religion. Italianism was this modern religion.

7. Text reprinted in *Oeuvres en prose* (Paris: Gallimard, 1977), 1: 401; my translation.

8. "Le Gastro-Astronomisme ou la cuisine nouvelle," *Paris-Journal*, May 21, 1912; reprinted in *Oeuvres en prose*, 1: 378–404.

9. Note that in describing the restaurant, the stress is laid on the fact that it is *Italian* aluminum that is used for its decoration (70).

10. See F. T. Marinetti, *Teoria e invenzione Futurista*, ed. Luciano De Maria (Milan: Mondadori, 1968). See also Claudia Salaris, *Filippo Tommaso Marinetti* (Florence: La Nuova Italia, 1988), 189. On the dissolution of the lyric "I" and its relation to the synthetic qualities of life that art must capture, see Marinetti's manifesto "Destruction of Syntax" (1913).

11. Banquets of this genre had taken place in the past, for example, in Trieste in 1910, when a meal was served that started with coffee and ended with the appetizer. See Salaris, 291.

12. See Walter Benjamin, "The Work of Art in the Age of Mechanical Reproduction," in *Illuminations: Essays and Reflections*, ed. Hannah Arendt, trans. Harry Zohn (New York: Schocken Books, 1968), 242.

13. See Bruno Girveau, "La comédie alimentaire," in *À table au XIX siècle* (Paris: Flammarion, 2001), 20–39.

14. Apollonió, *Futurist Manifestos*, 171.

15. Michel Onfray, *Le ventre des philosophes: Critique de le raison diététique* (Paris: Grasset, 1989), 171.

16. See the stress laid by Marinetti on the meaning of "analogy," in "Destruction of Syntax" (Apollonió, *Futurist Manifestos*, 95–106).

17. The Futurists' hatred for the museum—as typical Italian religion of the past, enslaving the innovative artist or poet—returns in many early manifestos. It suffices to mention here the 1909 manifesto that launched Futurism as a movement and the "Futurist Painting: Technical Manifesto" (published in *Poesia* on April 11, 1910) as two examples. In the former, Marinetti writes: "We mean to free her [Italy] from the numberless museums that cover her like so many graveyards. Museums: cemeteries! . . . [. . .] Museums: public dormitories where one lies forever beside hated or unknown beings. Museums: absurd abattoirs of painters and sculptors ferociously slaughtering each other with color-blows and line-blows, the length of the fought-over walls!" (in Apollonió, *Futurist Manifestos*, 22).

18. See "Futurist Painting: Technical Manifesto," 27–31.

19. See Andrew Hewitt's interpretation, in his *Fascist Modernism: Aesthetics,*

Politics, and the Avant-Garde (Stanford, Calif.: Stanford University Press, 1993), especially 106–16. My only point of disagreement is his interpretation of Marinetti's nationalism.

20. Filling a void clearly refers to the despicable function of pasta. Accordingly, the rejection of pasta is the rejection of a false feeling of eternal satisfaction, the promise of metaphysical presence. In contrast, noise and perfumes stand on the side of the present, rather than presence. The aerobanquets in particular seem to "accelerate the temporality of modernity to the point where no moment of presence can be posited" (Hewitt, 109). In addition, the temporality of presence staged at the aerobanquets is not simply the here and now. As Hewitt explains, and as the banquets demonstrate, the temporality of deferral celebrates in the banquets the emotions "for the moment of its disappearance" (108–9).

21. The artists' production of fetishes offers a countermodel to the capitalist conception of commodity fetishism. On commodity fetishism in Marinetti, see Hewitt, especially "The Politics of the Manifest" and "Avant-Garde and Technology," in *Fascist Modernism.*

22. Cinzia Sartini-Blum, *The Other Modernism: F. T. Marinetti's Futurist Fiction of Power* (Berkeley: University of California Press, 2005), 45.

23. For insightful feminist work on second-wave Futurism, see Barbara Spackman, *Fascist Virilities: Rhetoric, Ideology, and Social Fantasy in Italy* (Minneapolis: University of Minnesota Press, 1996); Sartini-Blum, *Other Modernism*; and Graziella Parati, "Speaking through Her Body," in *Public History, Private Stories: Italian Women's Autobiography* (Minneapolis: University of Minnesota Press, 1996).

24. F. T. Marinetti, *Selected Writings,* ed. R. W. Flint (New York: Farrar, Straus and Giroux, 1971), 43.

25. With a few exceptions, less in art history than in cultural analyses or history. In Italy, see the work of De Maria, Salaris, Gentile, Giovanni Lista; in the English-speaking world, see Spackman, Sartini-Blum, and Hewitt, among a few others.

2. Antimeals of Antiart

1. I refer to *Réimpression*; see also *Dada* 1–7, International Dada Archive, Digital Dada Library Collection, University of Iowa, http://sdrc.lib.uiowa.edu/dada/collection.html (accessed October 8, 2009).

2. For example, Dickerman, analyzing Kurt Schwitters's grotto and grotesque architecture *Merzbau*, discovers a bodily dimension that brings about a mnemonic instance in Dada, often suppressed in the analyses of the movement so focused on its nihilistic aspects. The body and sexuality, repressed in bourgeois society, appear in *Merzbau* that, in Dickerman's words, proposes "a kind of visceral unconscious — of things being digested and circulating within the depths. Its absorptive structure doubles the act of psychic repression, or of forgetting, with the physical submergence of stuff." See Dickerman, *Dada Seminars,* 117–18.

3. I am not claiming an immediate link between Dada and these texts. These texts and practices contribute to ideas of modernity within which the Dada artists

and poets situate their work. In fact, Dada attacks the naturalization of the links between cause and effect, in particular the correspondences between language and reality. For an account of the origins of nutritional science in the science of work, see Anson Rabinbach, *The Human Motor: Energy, Fatigue, and the Origins of Modernity* (Berkeley: University of California Press, 1990). The major nutritionist during the Weimar years (and in the years preceding the Weimar Republic) was Max Rubner. He was also the author of an important pamphlet, published in 1929 by the Ministry of Agriculture in a series devoted to the diffusion of nutritional questions among the lay people. See Max Rubner, *Deutschlands Volksernährung: Zeitgemässe Betrachtungen* (Berlin: Springer, 1930).

4. See also Foster, "Bashed Ego," 133. Foster speaks of the rhetorical mimetic strategies of Dada in terms of hypertrophy. This mimetic strategy, Foster explains, is a kind of exacerbation, "whereby an excessive identification renders the given conditions absurd or at least insecure" (133).

5. Cited in Weiss, *Feast and Folly*, 67. On pathology, Artaud, and Daniel Paul Schreber in relation to modernism, see Weiss, "Other as Muse" and "Psychopompomania" in *Aesthetics of Excess*, 96–144.

6. On the perturbing encounters between pathology and art, especially since modernism, see Weiss's work, in particular "Écrits Bruts: The Other Scene of Writing," in *Shattered Forms*, on "glossolalia": "Glossolalia—which entails the enunciation of the pure signifier, the refusal of meaning, and the reduction of speech to the pure voice, of language to the body—manifests that foregrounding of the signifier that now seems to be a central tenet of modernism" (81).

7. See Sheppard on Futurism and Dada, in *Modernism—Dada—Postmodernism*.

8. Richard Huelsenbeck, ed., *Eine Literarische Dokumentation* (Reinbek bei Hamburg: Rowohl Taschenbuch Verlag, 1964), 47, 48.

9. To best understand these dilemmas, consider, for example, Julie Elias's *Das Neue Kochbuch* (*The New Cookbook*, 1925) and Cornelia Kopp's *Backe nach Grundrezepten* (*Bake with Basic Recipes*, 1933). The latter, a specialized book on baking, was published after her 1933 innovative cookbook specifically targeted at beginners. Assuming an insufficient tradition of motherly experience, Kopp encourages readers to learn useful and innovative scientific techniques that a cook must know to be successful. A body of more than five hundred carefully selected black-and-white photographs illustrates precise directions through the various stages of baking. Detailed and numbered captions are juxtaposed to the photos. The book also contains graphs that illustrate the text's structure and show, in a quite complicated way, how each subsection relates to the others. For an interesting contemporaneous article on rationalization in the kitchen, see also Grete Lihotzky, "Rationalization in the Household," in *The Weimar Republic Sourcebook*, ed. Anton Kaes Martin Jay and Edward Dimendberg (Berkeley: University of California Press, 1994). For an analysis of the above-mentioned cookbooks, see Cecilia Novero, "Stories of Food: German Nutritional Texts and Cookbooks between the Wars," *Journal of Popular Culture* 34, no. 3 (2000): 163–81.

10. In 1921 Arp and Ernst spent a summer in the Tyrol with Eluard and Tzara. Here they put together *Dada au grand air,* number 8 of the *Revue Dada,* published in Paris in 1921. The date of September 16, 1886, printed on the cover was Arp's birthday.

11. The texts are all in French except for this sentence, which is in German.

12. *Dada au grand air (Der Sängerkrieg in Tirol),* p. 1 *(Réimpression,* 1: 119); my translation.

13. See Walter Serner, *Letzte Lockerung: Ein Handbrevier für Hochstapler und solche die es werden wollen,* ed. Thomas Milch (Munich: Deutscher Taschenbuch Verlag, 1984). There in section 12 Serner writes: "Silk stockings are priceless. A vice queen IS an armchair. World views are word mixtures. A dog IS a hammock. *L'art est mort.* Viva Dada!" See translation as "The Last Loosening Manifesto," in *Blago Bung Blago Bung Rosso Fataka: First Texts of German Dada,* ed. Malcom Green (London: Atlas, 1995), 160. Serner's words are the conclusion of his manifesto. See, especially, ibid., sec. 6, 155. The manifesto was also published both in French and in German — the latter was its original language — in *Dada 5,* May 1919. In French "word mixtures" translates as "salad." See also *Réimpression,* 1: 88–90 (for the German text) and 2: 202–5 (for the French).

14. The term *salad* or *salad mix* returns often in Dada. On the connections between the reference to salad, schizophrenia, and its appropriation by Dada, see Foster, "Bashed Ego," 135. Ernst uses *salade de mer,* which, in Foster's interpretation, evokes both *mère* (mother) and *merde* (shit). The two together — in the elaborate caption of a drawing, titled and presenting a "Self-Constructed Small Machine" (1919–20) — mock the palingenetic births of Futurism, conflating the sexual and the scatological. The self-construction is dysfunctional and a fantasy of regression.

15. See *Concise Oxford Dictionary,* adapted by F. G. Fowler and H. W. Fowler, 4th ed. (Oxford: Clarendon), 1951.

16. In this regard, see Tzara's "Seven Dada Manifestoes," in *The Dada Painters and Poets,* ed. Robert Motherwell (Cambridge, Mass.: Belknap Press of Harvard University Press, 1989). Cf. also Ribemont-Dessaignes's "To the public," in Motherwell, 109. In addition, note, for example, how Hans Richter emphasizes the organic material nature of the new art as well as its everyday character: "Let us compose from good digestible salad train tickets and from the most instantaneous of all reflexes a melody with the occasional beat of all chances of soul-crossings. / Please, do you want happiness? / Voilà, this time however really without stealing it from someone? Take this mix (Salad, Train, Reflex — you know!!!)" (quoted in *Literarische Dokumentation,* 234). Furthermore, forerunners such as Erik Satie and Arthur Cravan clearly conflate life and art. Cravan recommends a diet of pills, laxatives, and sex. Satie's "Day of a Musician" includes a "white diet," containing a detailed list of all-white foods (quoted in Motherwell, 10–12). The link between the musician and the diet is not explained, and if, on the one hand, the diet may produce the musician, on the other hand, music seems to fit in the diet as just another of its ingredients. Significantly, music combined with salad will return with Alison

Knowles's "Make a Salad" (see chapter 5). Other Fluxus artists will propose white meals, black meals, and other colored food (see Jon Hendricks, ed., *Fluxus Codex* [Detroit: Gilbert and Lila Silverman Fluxus Collection, 1995], 67).

17. On cannibalism in Dada, see Picabia's "Manifeste Cannibale Dada" (1920), reproduced in *Literarische Dokumentation*, 44. As always, the Dada artists show that cannibalism is, metaphorically, a practice of capitalist society; as such, the Dada artists also appropriate it for themselves to expose consumer society. *Cannibale* was also the title of a magazine of which only two issues were ever published, on April 25 and May 25, 1920. See *Réimpression*, 2: 128, as well as Georges Hugnet, *Dictionnaire du Dadaisme, 1916–1922* (Paris: Simoen, 1976). See also Shipe, "Dada Periodicals at Iowa," http://www.lib.uiowa.edu/spec-coll/Bai/Shipe. htm (accessed October 10, 2009) (from *Books at Iowa* 46 [April 1987]). For the appropriation of cannibalism as detoxication, in other words, as a necessary ritual of purification from capitalist cannibalism, see Theo van Doesburg, "Was Ist Dada?" in *Literarische Dokumentation*, 47. Finally, Sheppard connects the destruction brought about by World War I — the worst aspects of human nature — with cannibalism. Hence Hausmann expressed his sense of human bestiality, between 1918 and 1923, in the "image of a gaping mouth filled with carnivorous teeth" (*Modernism — Dada — Postmodernism*, 180).

18. See especially Picabia's "manifeste cannibale dada," originally published in *Dadaphone 7*, 3 (*Réimpression*, 1: 113). Picabia uses scatology to mock nationalist sentiments. See also Tzara's "manifeste de monsieur antipyrine," quoted in Riha, 31, and note 16. Tzara stresses the peculiar quality of the beautiful Dadaist excrement and thus its distinction from, as well as its affinity with, that of the bourgeois. The scatological references also return in Tzara's "Chronique Zurich" where he writes, "Shit was born for the first time [in] Zurich in cheese" (*Dada 4–5*, p. 11 [*Réimpression*, 1: 74]). The indirect reference to the birth of Dada as shit (as cheese) echoes the birth of Dada as disgust and the end of the 1918 manifesto where Dada is "simple Life." The beautiful excrement appears in *Dada au grand air* (*Réimpression*, 1: 120, 122) where one reads: "The region of Tirol is beautiful in the snow, it is nothing but the Dadaists' excrement." Finally, excrement appears often as insult or in Tzara's texts as diarrhea. The paradoxical nature of the beautiful excrement results from recuperating the distinction operated by the excretory apparatus rather than the distinction operated through taste. Hence Dada privileges physiology over the spirit. See also Julia Kristeva, *Powers of Horror: An Essay in Abjection* (New York: Columbia University Press, 1982); and Kelly Oliver, "Nourishing the Speaking Subject," in *Cooking, Eating, Thinking: Transformative Philosophies of Food*, ed. Deane W. Curtin and Lisa M. Heldke (Bloomington: Indiana University Press, 1992). On how excrement is transformed into a magical good object, see also Allen S. Weiss, "Sign of the Scorpion," in *Aesthetics of Excess*, especially the passage on Luis Buñuel's "L'age d'or" (166–67).

19. "The Galérie Dada was a small and cluttered kitchen of literary conventions." For the definition of Galérie Dada as "kitchen," see Richard Huelsenbeck, "En Avant Dada: The History of Dadaism (1920)," in Motherwell, 33.

20. On the hidden materiality of words that are created between the stomach and the mouth, see also "Monsieur Aa l'antiphilosophe" (*Dada au grand air* [*Réimpression,* 1: 120]). "It was indeed not without intentions that Monsieur Aa had discovered the joyous complicity of the stomach. The inventory of his cerebral storage has been going on since his adolescence, zero is the result: pure and simple. . . . As the last hour of everyday life approaches I have felt for a long time the indisposition fixed by the anonymous collectivity in a word, and the sentimental signification that it conceals, earth and odors under the nest and eggs. Words become inimical conclusions, uttered at once. They take a life that acts directly in the cellule and the speculation of blood." The text claims it is vulgar to provide words endowed with values.

21. This is the topic of Doesburg's manifesto "Was Ist Dada?" See *Literarische Dokumentation,* 46.

22. On the pathological elements and perversions of surrealism, see Foster, *Compulsive Beauty,* and Weiss, "Sign of the Scorpion."

23. Serner, *Letzte Lockerung.*

24. See Jean Cocteau, *Dada 4–5* (*Réimpression,* 1: 76); Picabia, "Salive américaine," *Dada 3* (*Réimpression,* 1: 58); Tzara, "Vélodrome aux oignons," *Dadaphone 7* (*Réimpression,* 1: 112); Ribemont-Dessaignes, "Artichauts," *Dadaphone 7* (*Réimpression,* 1: 112) and his "Artichauts nouveaux," in *Le coeur à barbe* (April 1922) (*Réimpression,* 2: 177); Vincent Huidobro, "Vol-au-vent," in *Le coeur à barbe* (April 1922) (*Réimpression,* 2: 176).

25. Serner views hypocritical embarrassment as the essence of style and poetry, a way to "clap a redeeming heaven over this chaos of filth and enigma! To perfume and order this pile of human excrement! Thanks a lot! . . . Is there a more idiotic picture than an (ugh!) ingenious stylizing mind playing the coquette with itself during this activity? . . . O, that frightfully cheerful embarassment that ends with a bow before one's own self! THAT's the reason (on account of this stylized curvature) why philosophies and novels are sweated out of peoples's pores, pictures are daubed, sculptures hewn, symphonies groaned out and religions founded" (quoted in Green, 156).

26. Serner publishes a poem in French in *Le coeur à barbe* in which he takes up the physiological origin of poetry and "in-distinction" between eating food or writing and reading literature. He is disgusted by the critics whom he depicts as hypocritical *rastas* affected by digestive disorders in his manifesto. Rastas are the models for contemporary artists, they are con-artists (also in *Réimpression,* 2: 179). Ribemont-Dessaignes also writes a poem, "Trombone a coulisse" (sliding trombone), where the senses and the objects sensually perceived are confused and relate to each other in oxymoronic ways: the poet has an ocarina in his stomach and nourishes "his" poet "with the feet of a woman pianist, whose teeth are even and odd" (171). The poet's trombone and his body are not distinct, the object is anthropomorphized, and its physiology is not functional but depicted in a confused, antihierarchical, and flat way. Huelsenbeck's own poems in the collection "Fantastic Prayers," published in 1920, have recourse to food and putrefaction quite

often and quite suddenly. These images always evoke death as the final and only victorious player in the game of life (*Literarische Dokumentation,* 204, 207, 209). See, in translation, "Plane," "Rivers," "The Philosopher, Improvisation, Meistersinger, Death," "May Night Blissful Rhythms, Death," "Claperston Dies of Fish Poisoning," "Evening Approaches the Lambs Return Home," "The Onion Baker: Invitation" (in Green).

27. As a perfect example of a recipe without food, consider Serner's section 9 of his *Last Loosening Manifesto* where he describes poetry thus: "A young lad finds himself in a jam. Recipe: ask him whom he dreams of and you can tell him with whom he has not yet slept." See Green, 158.

28. See Weiss on Schwitters's "Ursonata" (primal sonata). In contrast to the child's entry into the symbolic world of language, this work represents "an antirepresentational, iconoclastic art which forces upon the spectator the recognition of the very materiality, the body, of the artwork." See Weiss, "Other as Muse," 101.

29. Sheppard argues that this notion of indistinction may be read less nihilistically than it sounds: "The Dada frame of mind involves the ability to live openendedly but with integrity amid a mess of confusion, indeterminacy, paradoxes, and constant change." See *Modernism — Dada — Postmodernism,* 188.

30. See, especially, sec. 5 in Green, 155.

31. Lack of distinction marks various forms of disgust in Tzara's manifesto: "Disgust with all the catalogued categories . . . , disgust with the divorce of good and evil, the beautiful and the ugly. . . . Disgust finally with the Jesuitical dialectic which can explain everything and fill people's minds with oblique and obtuse ideas without any physiological basis or ethnic roots, all this by blinding artifice and ignoble charlatan's promises" (Motherwell, 250).

32. Aron writes: "Artistic initiation: the apprentice learns to make plans, to sculpt the basic object; the master creates the shapes, he adorns them according to his fancy, he illumines them with enticing colors. Patisserie . . . serves as culinary archetype: the confection fulfilled, brought to perfection, through the manner of its presentation, ideally a dish which takes its form from the construction itself." See Jean Paul Aron, *The Art of Eating in France: Manners and Menus in the Nineteenth Century,* trans. Nina Roote (London: Owen, 1975), 123.

33. Nietzsche writes in *Ecce Homo*: "The German spirit is an indigestion: it does not finish with anything." The German spirit has its origin in "distressed intestines"; it is the product of a stomach that not only has ingested too much but has also eaten poorly, without choosing, "tasting," and without selecting according to one's own bodily needs. Dada's criticism starts from this observation by Nietzsche, takes it as fact, as it were, and then sets out to provoke an even stronger constipation or indigestion in the bourgeois stomach, which is always concerned with keeping up, at least ideally, the most functional circulation. See Friedrich Nietzsche, *The Genealogy of Morals and Ecce Homo,* ed. Walter Kaufman (New York: Vintage Books, 1989), 238.

34. For how in accounts of pathologies logorrhea is associated with diarrhea, see Weiss's insightful analyses of Schreber in "The Other as Muse": "Since all of

Schreber's physical and mental processes — defecation as well as speech — are controlled by 'divine miracles,' his diarrhea is no less significant than his logorrhea: both aim at the destruction of his rationality" (102).

35. Friedrich Nietzsche, "On Truth and Lie in an Extra-Moral Sense," *The Portable Nietzsche,* ed. Walter Kaufman (New York: Viking, 1982), 1.

36. "Américaine" also has a realistic overtone and may metonymically stand for America. In effect, one may read saliva to relate, for instance, to the act of chewing gum that at the time was becoming both popular and a symbol of Americanization (see Ernst Lorsy, "The Hour of Chewing Gum," in *Weimar Republic Sourcebook,* 662). According to this journalist, chewing gum is the cheapest way to Americanize oneself. The article also quotes the major advertising slogans for chewing gum, such as it "aids digestion," "preserves your teeth," "perfumes your breath." The machinelike movements of the stomach are also consonant with rationalized work and high technology as indeed associated with the image/myth of America in these years. Furthermore, Stefan Zweig reads Americanization as a process of leveling out of differences, just like Picabia's description of the stomach, at once mechanical and foggy. See Stefan Zweig, "Monotonization of the World," in *Weimar Republic Sourcebook,* 399.

37. The qualifier "American" in the poem's title — like Tzara's "American costumes" mentioned elsewhere — is a reference to modern civilization, for example, Taylorism and the conveyor belt, too, as "imported" from the United States. American saliva is thus poetry as mass produced.

38. On another important aspect of Dada's resistance to binary thinking, namely, androgyny, see Hanne Bergius, *Das Lachen Dadas: Die Berliner Dadaisten und ihre Aktionen* (Giessen: Anabas, 1989); Amelia Jones, *Postmodernism and the Engendering of Marcel Duchamp* (Cambridge: Cambridge University Press, 1994); and Maud Lavin, *Cut with a Kitchen Knife: The Weimar Photomontages of Hannah Höch* (New Haven, Conn.: Yale University Press, 1993). See also Sheppard, 418n83.

39. After the Dadaist verbal descriptions and metaphors for the inseparable construct of art and life, the surrealist painters will incorporate food in their works and will transform art into an edible product. For example, Dalí represents Gala with a steak on her shoulders. Dalí develops in detail an aesthetics of edibles and excrement. In this regard, see Dalí's own writings and Ignacio Gomez de Liano, *Dalí* (New York: Rizzoli, 1984).

40. The manifesto was read by Breton on March 27, 1920.

41. See Doesburg: "In the Dadaists' opinion, human beings are inclined, due to their fetishistic instincts, to let themselves be blinded by specific characteristic billboards. . . . Dada does not want to proselyte. Dada has had enough experience to know that one can win over the masses by means of a big 'nothing,' if one knows how to influence their atavistic instincts with persuasive ads. Dada considers every dogma, every formula, like a nail, with which one tries to hold together a rotten sinking ship (our Western culture)" (*Literarische Dokumentation,* 46). The issue of *Suggestion* (in German) is of crucial relevance for Serner's conceptualization of the

con-artist and, more generally, the modern artist. See Alfons Backes-Haase, *"Über topographische Anatomie, psychischen Luftwechsel und Verwandtes": Walter Serner—Autor der "Letzten Lockerung"* (Bielefeld: Aisthesis Verlag, 1989), 101–6. The poet Francesco Meriano invokes the example of Leopardi and demands in *Dada 1*: "Move away, Leopardi, your breath stinks of extract of tomato concentrate" (*Réimpression,* 1: 10).

42. Walter Benjamin, *Reflections: Essays, Aphorisms, Autobiographical Writings,* ed. Peter Demetz, trans. Edmund Jephcott (New York: Schocken Books, 1986), 184.

43. I borrow the notion of the "within" from Andreas Huyssen, *After the Great Divide: Modernism, Mass Culture, Postmodernism* (Bloomington: Indiana University Press, 1986).

3. Walter Benjamin's Gastro-Constellations

1. Gerhard Richter, introduction to *Walter Benjamin and the Corpus of Autobiography* (Detroit: Wayne State University Press), 20, 36.

2. Rainer Nägele, Beatrice Hanssen, and Rebecca Comay have recently noted and discussed "incorporation" in Benjamin. See especially Hanssen on Benjamin's *Raubengel* and on Karl Kraus in her *Walter Benjamin's Other History: Of Stones, Animals, Human Beings, and Angels* (Berkeley: University of California Press, 2000), 114–27.

3. The stories in the chapter "Eating" ("Food" in the collected works in English) were published individually first and then all together in the *Frankfurter Zeitung* in 1930. It is now in *Gesammelte Schriften,* ed. Rolf Tiedemann and Hermann Schweppenhäuser (Frankfurt: Suhrkamp Verlag), 4: 374–81 (hereafter cited as *GS*); trans. in Benjamin, *Selected Writings,* 2: 358–64.

4. On surrealism and the avant-garde's impact on Benjamin, see Joseph Fürnkas, *Surrealismus als Erkenntnis* (Stuttgart: Metzler, 1988).

5. Saturn—as divine cannibalism, or profane time—becomes important because, identified originally with the Greek god of time Chronos, he is presented allegorically at one time as the son who emasculated his father (Uranus) and as the devourer of his own children. He is both the reaper of death (human time) and the profane god of the earth and fertility (nature's generations). From Mount Olympus, he was exiled to the earth, *Latium,* where Janus welcomed him and renamed him Saturn. He gave the name to the Roman carnival, Saturnalia.

6. On the marvelous in surrealism, see Foster, *Compulsive Beauty,* 19–23.

7. André Breton, "Second Manifesto of Surrealism," in *Manifestoes of Surrealism* (Ann Arbor: University of Michigan Press, 1972), 152.

8. André Breton, "First Manifesto of Surrealism," in *Manifestoes of Surrealism,* 16.

9. On allegory as multilayered text, see Lavin, 24.

10. *Arcades Project,* 389 (K 1, 4).

11. Breton uses the term "negation of negation," in reference to G. W. F. Hegel's and Karl Marx's dialectics. Breton insists on dialectical materialism to counter

both "realism" (which for him stems in vulgar naturalism) and reflection theories popular with the Communist Party in the 1930s. See "Second Manifesto," 140.

12. *Arcades Project,* 470, N 7, 6. Benjamin writes: "It is important for the materialist historian, in the most rigorous way possible, to differentiate the construction of a historical state of affairs from what one customarily calls its 'reconstruction.' The 'reconstruction' in empathy is one-dimensional. 'Construction' presupposes destruction."

13. Although there are no direct connections between Georges Bataille's *informe* and Benjamin's *Einverleibung* (incorporation and, as it has been often translated, absorption), I believe that Bataille's approach to his term of choice is analogous to Benjamin's own at least insofar as both appear in their works as *operations.* They do not share, however, the same "effects" on the works ensuing from such operations and on the subjects of these operations. See Georges Bataille, *Visions of Excess: Selected Writings, 1927–1939,* ed. and trans. Allan Stoekl (Minneapolis: University of Minnesota Press, 1994), 31.

14. Marxism also becomes for Benjamin a strategic discipline. Likewise, revolutionary discipline is the corrective for intoxication, as he writes in the surrealism essay. See Benjamin, as quoted in Richard Wolin, *Walter Benjamin: An Aesthetic of Redemption* (Berkeley: University of California Press, 1994), 116, and Wolin's interpretation thereafter, 116–17.

15. See *Techniques of the Observer,* 50–51.

16. See Miriam Hansen, "Benjamin and the Cinema: Not a One-Way Street," in *Benjamin's Ghosts: Interventions in Contemporary Literary and Cultural Theory,* ed. Gerhard Richter (Stanford, Calif.: Stanford University Press, 2002), 41–73. In this essay, Hansen reads Benjamin's reference to yoga meditation as an early example of bodily innervation. She argues, however, that Benjamin never dissociates this "creaturely" aspect of humans from a technological component that ultimately always is a bodily predisposition to interplay with technology. I argue that in Benjamin's texts incorporation is the "primitive" form of interplay. For Hansen, yoga translates into the contemporary medium of film, of which it may be considered the origin.

17. See Breton's "First Manifesto," 14–16.

18. Benjamin often speaks of Paul Klee's and his voracious angel (one example is in his essay on Kraus), praises Dada photomontage, in particular John Heartfield's, and those works, paintings included which, as he remarks, convert social emotion — political energy — into visual images. On Heartfield, see Benjamin, "Letter from Paris (2)," in *Selected Writings,* 3: 242. This conversion deforms nature rather than being inspired by it (3: 242). Describing Klee's and Loos's work in "Experience and Poverty," he writes specifically that "they turn . . . to the naked man of the contemporary world who lies screaming like a newborn babe in the dirty diapers of the present" (2: 733). These words could well refer to Hannah Höch's photomontages, for example, *Kinder (Children)* of 1925, in which a monstrously deformed face of a child screaming, less in agony than sardonically, looks straight in the onlooker's eye, and *Cut with a Kitchen Knife Dada through the Last Weimar*

Beer Belly Cultural Epoch of Germany (1919–20). On Höch, see Sophie Bernard, "Höch," in *Dada,* ed. Laurent Le Bon (Paris: Centre Pompidou Editions, 2005), 494. See also Lavin, 23–24.

19. Processes of internal mirroring interested Benjamin as techniques of dialectical encounters. See his mention of reflecting — inverted — mirrors, for example, in the *Elective Affinities,* when describing sobriety, and in *The Arcades Project,* in reference to the avant-garde (Picabia, ibid., 837, E°, 56) and Paris or the "city of mirrors" (ibid., 877, c°, 1 and c°, 2).

20. See *GS,* 6: 921; my translation. The interpretation of how humans eat and grow is repeated almost identically in Benjamin's "Reading Novels."

21. On language as divine gift, see Marleen Stoessel, *Aura: Das vergessene Menschliche: Zu Sprache und Erfahrung bei Walter Benjamin* (Munich: Carl Hanser Verlag, 1983). In "To the Planetarium" (*Selected Writings,* 2: 487) he writes, "Men [human beings] as a species completed their development thousands of years ago; but mankind [humanity] as a species is just beginning his."

22. See Benjamin, "False Criticism," in *Selected Writings, 2*: 405. See also "Reflections on the New Generation" (2: 401–2).

23. See "Surrealism," in *Selected Writings, 2*: 207.

24. *Arcades Project,* 473, N 9, 4. The way in which phenomena are rescued, Benjamin adds, is "through the exhibition of the fissure within them" (ibid.).

25. The other four groups of sauces enumerated by Carême are béchamel (white), brown (demi-glace) or espagnole, hollandaise (butter), tomato (red). This classification appears to draw on spatial parameters either as a metaphoric traveling through foreign regions (Spain, Holland, the Mediterranean for the tomatoes) or as a traveling through art. In the latter case, colors (white, red, etc.) are the defining feature. Benjamin too speaks of food through the framework of both traveling and art.

26. Benjamin writes of colors in relation to taste. Like taste, colors are to be received by the body and cannot be "produced. Yet colors — as belonging to nature — can be actively received, as nature does in cooking, when in children's books, toys (soap-bubbles, the magic lantern etc.) and play, they speak." See "The World of Children's Books" (1926), where he also quotes his own description of the *Suprême* (*Selected Writings,* 1: 443).

27. See how Sergei Eisenstein defined his "montage of attractions" in *Walter Benjamin and Art,* 8.

28. On the grid, see Rosalind Krauss, *The Optical Unconscious* (Cambridge, Mass.: MIT Press, 1994), 12, 14.

29. Remember, for example, Max Ernst's use of figures, numbers, and animals in his *frottages.* These ciphers of Ernst's pictures bear the quality of mysterious chance encounters — not unlike superimposed images in a film.

30. In an early version of "Reading Novels," Benjamin writes a "Gastronomic Classification of Prose," which is part of his micro theory of the novel, rather than a theory of gastronomy: "Gastronomic classification of prose: the popular way to tell stories — a whole canon of proceedings — is to prose that which the daily fare is

to cooking. In this regard one must consider how many important raw materials, primary substances of experience (*Erlebens*) are non-enjoyable in their raw status and gain their nutritional value, which implies the invigoration of a person, when received not in order to live them out, but rather to listen to them" (*Selected Writings*, 2: 729).

31. *Arcades Project*, 416, M 1, 2. Mothers — such as in "Pranzo Caprese" — recur in Benjamin's texts, from his early philosophical fragments, via his essay on the Elective Affinities, to his *Denkbilder,* including "Eating," and *Berlin Childhood.*

32. See Foster, *Compulsive Beauty,* especially chap. 2.

33. See Benjamin's own critique of surrealism and interpretation in "Madame Ariane — Second Courtyard on the Left," in *One-Way Street.* Benjamin speaks of reading as laying hands on the present as a moment of danger. Unlike interpretation, active reading has the power to provoke "a precise awareness of the moment," which is indispensable for revolutionary politics as demanding the use of body in time and the use of time.

34. Prostitutes and thresholds appear connected in several pictures by Eugene Atget.

35. In their own critique of the instrumentalization of reason, Adorno and Max Horkheimer tell the story of Odysseus's confrontation with Polyphemus, the one-eyed giant who captures him. Odysseus notably defies Polyphemus by lying about his "name," telling the giant that he is *no-body.* Odysseus escapes thanks to this act of cunning. However, one implication is that the defeat of myth also involved the "sacrifice" of the body. In his essay on Kafka, Benjamin mentions Odysseus's cunning and posits this figure on the threshold between myth and fairy tale. In "Eating/Food," it seems that Benjamin goes farther to examine the costs of a kind of knowledge grounded in the sacrifice of the body.

36. On the notion of aesthetic as "another kind of knowledge," see Giorgio Agamben, "Gusto," in *Enciclopedia Einaudi,* ed. Ruggiero Romano, 16 vols. (Turin: Einaudi, 1977–84), 6: 1019–38. Agamben writes that the problem of taste has presented itself as that of "other knowledge" (knowledge that cannot account for its own knowing but that is able to enjoy the act of knowing; . . .) and of "other pleasure" (pleasure that knows and judges). The aesthetic problems about knowledge and its relation to pleasure are the objects of Benjamin's philosophy of incorporation.

37. As Benjamin points out in the *Arcades Project,* the word *experience* entails the idea of passage and crossroads. "*Erfahren*" means to come from a distance and to travel a distance. It embodies the intertwining of space and time and the subject's rootedness in the two dimensions at once. This concept returns in the term *Schwelle* (threshold). The word also stresses metamorphosis. Benjamin writes in the *Arcades Project*: "A *Schwelle* 'threshold' is a zone. Transformation, passage, wave and action are in the word '*schwellen,*' and etymology ought not to overlook these senses. . . . We have grown very poor in threshold experiences" (494, O2a,1).

38. In his "Ibizan Sequence," there is a short chapter titled "Downhill." There Benjamin writes of the body, its "states" of being — exhaustion in climbing a mountain and back — in relation to the perception of truth. See especially 2: 593.

39. Sigrid Weigel, *Body- and Image-Space: Re-reading Walter Benjamin* (New York: Routledge, 1996).

40. Kristeva, *Powers of Horror,* 78. She refers to Mary Douglas, *Purity and Danger: An Analysis of the Concepts of Pollution and Taboo* (New York: Routledge, 1966). For Douglas, pollution is a threat to the symbolic order because it inhibits the prohibitions (taboos) and exclusions (abjection) that create the internal and external boundaries constituting both the speaking subject and the structured society. As such, rituals work out from the symbolic realm the traces of an archaic fear of a lost identity and the invasion of the other.

41. On the influence of Asja Lacis on Benjamin's revision of notions of communism, see his letter to Gerhard Scholem, "Capri, September 16, 1924," in *The Correspondence of Walter Benjamin, 1910–1940,* ed. Gershom Scholem and Theodor W. Adorno, trans. M. R. Jacobson and E. M. Jacobson (Chicago: University of Chicago Press, 1994), 246–51, especially 248.

42. If one were to use Bataille's expression — of which Benjamin's seems indirectly to remind us — one could speak of expenditure or excess.

43. In "Notes (IV)" Benjamin writes: "To have presence of mind means to let oneself go at the moment of danger." See *Selected Writings,* 2: 687.

44. The Kafka essay was published in 1934, after "Eating/Food." On fairy tales, see both this essay and Benjamin on Leskov. For Benjamin, Kafka writes "fairy tales for dialecticians" (*Selected Writings,* 2: 799) or, rather, dialectical fairy tales in which, as he saw it, there is a *liberating magic* (*Selected Writings,* 3: 157). Leaning on Johann Jakob Bachofen, Benjamin argues that the anterior times — or base prehistorical times — found in Kafka's stories are dominated by forces "justifiably regarded as belonging to our world as well" (*Selected Writings,* 2: 807). "Animal becoming" (Deleuze) is never individual; it is an ancestral world that has been forgotten. In turn, the forgotten is this ancestral world to which belong the totemic animals, our estranged other. In the modern world, the body is this internalized other animal. For Benjamin, the profane and base world after the Fall does not admit purity but only possibilities of purification. Immersion in this dangerous voluptuousness is the only dialectical way out. As Kafka's cough speaks from within his body, in Benjamin's description, Benjamin's other voice emerges through the subject's immersion — defilement and purification, embracement and struggle — in an unpredictable encounter with deeply mythical and modern food. "Pranzo Caprese," "Fresh Figs," and also "Café Crême" are examples of these temporal journeys or dialectical fairy tales.

45. Benjamin explicitly connects criticism and dreams in "The Task of the Critic" (see *Selected Writings,* 2: 548). For his part, Dalí proposes his paranoiac-critical method in which images are produced as form of hallucinatory criticism. See especially "New Generational Considerations Regarding the Mechanism of the Paranoiac Phenomenon from the Surrealist Point of View," originally published in *Minotaure* 1 (June 1933).

46. The relations between destruction and justice are retraceable in Benjamin's studies of Kraus, both his essay and an earlier fragment on him, published as addendum to *One-Way Street.* In the former, Benjamin, speaking of Kraus as

Unmensch (the Inhuman translated here with monster) writes: "And therefore the monster [*Unmensch*] stands among us as the messenger of a more real humanism." Benjamin opposes the destructive, more human monster to the "creative" artist, or he contrasts the organic with construction. Speaking of Paul Karl Wilhelm Scheerbart's characters, he states that their feature is "their penchant for the randomly constructive, namely in contrast to the organic." Thus they "reject human likeness." This destructiveness connects language with his notion of Judaic justice, as Hanssen explains. Quotation — as used by Kraus — brings about "violently" the power of names, and this is the principle of justice. See Hanssen, *Walter Benjamin's Other History*, 124–26.

47. See "On Some Motifs in Baudelaire." In this essay Benjamin speaks of memory as conservative faculty. See *Illuminations*, 155–200. See also Breton, "First Manifesto," 11.

48. Benjamin often works around unorthodox etymologies or philosophical assonances. This could be in the wake of Ferdinand de Saussure's own investigations in this realm, investigations that also echo with Freud's. See Renato Barilli on Saussure's paragrams — which Benjamin uses in his intoxication reports — and how Saussure's micro rhetoric "provides contemporary poetry with new ground for experimenting." See Renato Barilli, *Rhetoric*, trans. Giuliana Menozzi (Minneapolis: University of Minnesota Press, 1989), 109–10.

49. Barthes's anatomy of reading in *The Pleasure of the Text* (New York: Hill and Wang, 1975) is similar to Benjamin's incorporative blissful notion of reading.

50. He writes of cannibalism as assimilation. However, he stresses the violence of incorporation. In addition, he explains that the endurance of Kraus's convictions is "persistence in a role, in its stereotypes, its cues," while impersonating the parts that "let him taste blood" (see *Selected Writings*, 2: 450).

51. Benjamin elaborates on his theory of the novel in his essay on Leskov. He owes some of these ideas to Lukacs. Yet he distances himself from the latter in the implications he draws from these ideas.

52. Benjamin initially uses the term "expressionless," which translates in later essays with the term "sobriety," or, at least, the two terms are juxtaposed. Sobriety is a concept Benjamin appropriates from Friedrich Hölderlin. The expressionless is a category pertaining to language. As such, it is closer to the realm of decision than to the passive realm of silence. Hence the connection between Hölderlin's caesura and Benjamin's expressionless.

53. See Charles Baudelaire, "Painter of Modern Life," in *Baudelaire: Selected Writings on Art and Artists*, trans. P. E. Charvet (Harmondsworth, U.K.: Penguin Books, 1972), 392.

54. Interestingly, the child's games of the imagination echo Benjamin's own remembrances in "Berlin Childhood around 1900" (see especially "Boys' Books," in *Selected Writings*, 3: 356).

55. For this reference to Proust and mirrors, see *GS*, vol. 4, 1: 358. On the mirrors of Paris and their effects, see *Arcades Project*, see convolute R, 537–42, in

particular, the beginning of R 1 on the flaneur and R 1, 3, 537, mentioned above. See also in the same book, 877 (c°, 2).

56. "The transformation of a shattering experience into habit — that is the essence of play. For play and nothing else is the mother of every habit. Eating, sleeping, getting dressed, washing have to be instilled into the struggling little brat in a playful way, following the rhythm of nursery rhymes" ("Toys and Play" [1928], in *Selected Writings*, 2: 120).

57. The traveler, like Benjamin himself in his food stories, is the subject of experience. In these texts the flaneur, who perceives the familiar as distant, or the *Reisende*, who travels through distance, experiences both himself and the world as if he were remembering. See *GS*, 6: 203. Proximity is produced by remembering, too. Remembering involves all the senses. One is closer to things when they can come close to one's own body. The traveler discovers the truth of things when he travels through them, which for Benjamin means to morph into a remembered image of oneself.

58. See Julia Kristeva, *Proust and the Sense of Time* (New York: Columbia University Press, 1993).

59. See *Arcades Project*, 547, S2a, 1.

60. Barthes, *Pleasure of the Text*, 40–41.

61. This is Benjamin's use of paragram, which, as Barilli explains, is a new word obtained "through the partial application of verbal elements from another word" (*Rhetoric*, 109).

62. See on words as names in children's games, "Brezel, Feder, Pause, Klage, Firlefanz," in *Denkbilder, GS*, 6.1: 432–33.

63. Benjamin explains succinctly the word *rebus* and its use in the nineteenth century, in "The World of Children's Books" (*Selected Writings*, 1: 437): "The rebus (a word that, curiously, was formerly traced back to *rêver* instead of *res*) has the most distinguished origins: it descends directly from the hieroglyphics of the Renaissance." Thus the two distinct etymologies of the word, dream and thing, already point to the tensions within allegory that Benjamin exacerbates in his own rebus texts. Yet the hieroglyphics — as mysterious code, almost undecipherable — transform the rebus into a language of nature. The reference also indicates that this language is "reified" or petrified in the rebus.

64. Let me note that Breton refers to Hamsun's fits of hunger as stimulating the imagination and creation. He also mentions Giorgio de Chirico's paintings as produced amid migraines, colics, and so forth. See "First Manifesto," 22–23.

65. See Salvador Dalí, *The Collected Writings of Salvador Dalí*, ed. and trans. Haim Finkelstein (Cambridge: Cambridge University Press, 1998). In "Conquest of the Irrational" (1935), Finkelstein explains, the painter "defined the paranoiac-critical activity in terms of the formation of a systematic delirium and the interpretative act that brings it to light and as a means of revealing the hidden obsessive character of the object under consideration" (*Collected Writings*, 216).

66. Benjamin refers to Breton's "Second Manifesto." See "Paris Diary," in *Selected Writings*, 2: 350.

67. *One-Way Street* is devoted to Lacis precisely in these terms: "This street is named / Asja Lacis Street / after her who / as an engineer / cut it through the author" (*Selected Writings*, 1: 444).

68. "Nowhere does the hearth seem to glow with such splendor as here. But radiance is captured in all the wood that the peasant carves and paints. And when varnished, it is fire frozen in all colors" (*Selected Writings*, 2: 33).

69. "One is tempted to say that minutes are a cheap liquor of which they [the Russians] can never get enough, that they are tipsy with time" (*Selected Writings*, 2: 31).

70. In the *Arcades Project*, Benjamin quotes Breton on Mayakovsky in *Minotaure*, five years after the poet's suicide (see 745, d 2, 1).

71. The poem has been translated with great variations into English. I use more than one translation. See *Mayakovsky and His Poetry*, ed. and trans. Herbert Marshall (London: Pilot, 1945), 34. For an analysis of the poem, see Cyrill Stieger, *Majakovskijs "Oblako v štanach": Versuch einer sprachorientierten Interpretation* (Bern: Peter Lang, 1980).

72. For this translation of the "Prologue," I relied on http://mayakovsky.com/cloud1-en.htm.

73. See Mikhail Bakhtin, *Rabelais and His World* (Cambridge, Mass.: MIT Press, 1968).

74. On Russian Futurism's carnivalesque, see Silvija Jestrovic, "Theatricality as Estrangement of Art and Life in the Russian Avant-Garde," *SubStance* 31, nos. 2–3 (2002): 52.

75. Homi Bhabha uses the term "contra-modern," a space within the modern that does not coincide with it, alongside the notions borrowed from Barthes of "non-sentence," "writing aloud," and "reading a posteriori." See Homi Bhabha, *The Location of Culture* (New York: Routledge, 1994), 183.

76. Dialectics at a standstill is for Benjamin "that in which the Then and Now come together into a constellation like a flash of lightning." Note that Benjamin's metaphor of constellation includes the possibility of a "flash" of historical insight that could only "enter into legibility at a specific time," and thus a critique of historicism. This critique is grounded in "the retrieval of the unfulfilled potential of the past," a retrieval that, however, always occurs belatedly. "Borscht"—in all its facets—is the constellation of then and Now, of the ancestral soup that turns around and becomes the red soup of the Soviet state, in which peasantry and urbanism are mixed. Micrology can be seen as strictly connected with the highest life of the works of art, in Benjamin's phrase, and thus in the dialectical transmigration—from decay to emergence—of the truth-content. The truth-content moves from an art form to another, from one life to another, which demands the consumption of the former. Benjamin refers to the concept of the life of artworks, which is at the core of his essay on Goethe's *Elective Affinities*, in the *Arcades Project*, 461, N1a, 4. He further elaborates on the need to pursue truth-content through micrology, or an operation of cutting—the work of critique—that coincides specifically with montage. See *Arcades Project*, 461, N2, 6.

77. Kenneth F. Kiple and Kriemhild Coneè Ornelas, eds., *Cambridge World History of Food* (Cambridge: Cambridge University Press, 2000), 2: 1730–31.

78. Alan Davidson, ed., *The Oxford Companion to Food* (Oxford: Oxford University Press, 1999), 70; my emphasis.

79. Benjamin explains his notion of practice: "To weary the master to the point of exhaustion through diligence and hard work, so that at long last his body and each of his limbs can act in accordance with their own rationality: this is what is called 'practice.' It is a form of posthypnotic suggestion that starts to work from within the body, as it were, at the moment the will abdicates its power once and for all in favor of the organs — the hand, for instance" ("Spain, 1932," in *Selected Writings*, 2: 643).

80. On the end of private life Benjamin writes: "Bolshevism has abolished private life. . . . Apartments that earlier accommodated single families in their five to eight rooms now often lodge eight. . . . Their dwelling place is the office, the club, the street. . . . For this reason, there is no 'homeyness'" (*Selected Writings*, 2: 30–31).

81. On progress as the first step, or the first revolutionary measure taken against the stagnating status quo, see *Arcades Project*, 474, N 10, 2.

82. See Benjamin's essay on Leskov, "The Storyteller," in *Illuminations*, 83–109. These are the grounds of "Mulberry Omelet," with which Benjamin concludes "Eating/Food."

83. On Cézanne, see Benjamin, "Moscow Diary," in *GS*, 6: 325. Crary connects Freud, Henri Bergson, and Cézanne on perception. See Jonathan Crary, *Suspensions of Perception: Attention, Spectacle, and Modern Culture* (Cambridge, Mass.: MIT Press, 1999), 336–37.

84. In the essay on surrealism, Benjamin proclaims, as later in the *Arcades Project*, too, that "the trick by which this world of things is mastered — it is more proper to speak of a trick than a method — consists in the substitution of a political for a historical view of the past." Later he adds: "The collective is a body too. And the *physis* that is being organized for it in technology can, through all its political and factual reality, be produced only in that image space to which profane illumination initiates us" (*Selected Writings*, 2: 217). On actuality (*Aktualität*) in Benjamin, see Weigel, especially 4, 14.

4. Daniel Spoerri's *Gastronoptikum*

1. Eat Art has received renewed attention of late. Spoerri's banquets were restaged in April 2002 at the Jeu de Paume in Paris.

2. See Alain Jouffroy and Patrick Beurard, "Daniel Spoerri: Souvenirs sans douleurs," *Opus International*, no. 110 (September–October 1988): 13.

3. Claude Lévi-Strauss, *The Savage Mind* (Chicago: University of Chicago Press, 1966). On *bricolage*, see especially 16–17, 19–20. On the linguistic and temporal deferral and difference that inform *bricolage*, also mentioned by Jacques Derrida, see *Savage Mind*, 21. On the temporality of *bricolage*, read the following: "Now, the characteristic feature of mythical thought, as of 'bricolage' on the

practical plane, is that it builds up structured sets, not directly with other struc-tured sets [i.e., language] but by using the remains and debris of events" (21–22). Although Lévi-Strauss's *bricolage* presupposes the notion of a generalized struc-ture of thinking, the particularity of it, extrapolated from such context, may in-terestingly be paired with Deleuze and Guattari's notion of minor literature, a literature that—through the intensities and fragments, the silences and leftovers ignored within a major language—in fact deterritorializes the major language. In this sense, minor literature is a collective machine of expression. See Gilles Deleuze and Félix Guattari, *Kafka: Toward a Minor Literature* (Minneapolis: University of Minnesota Press, 1986), especially 18–19.

4. Hal Foster, *Recodings: Art, Spectacle, Cultural Politics* (New York: New Press, 1985), 202.

5. On the periodization of the neo-avant-garde in an early phase from the post-war years to the mid- and late 1950s, and a self-reflexive second phase in the 1960s and 1970s, see Foster, *Return of the Real*, 24–25.

6. Foster highlights the possibly erroneous confusion of the mythical sys-tem—the second-degree language of myth described by Barthes—and Lévi-Strauss's description of the linguistic operations of *bricolage* as mythical thought. Clearly, while the myths described by Barthes are "abstractions" that naturalize the sign-system, Foster points out, for Lévi-Strauss *bricolage* is an intellectually concrete and each time particular mode of approaching a question. Thus it defeats universalisms and the abstract logic necessary for Barthes's myths to work. See Foster, *Recodings*, 201.

7. The notion of devouring devouring (which Spoerri, like Benjamin, also finds in the conflation of Cronos [Saturn] with Chronos [Time] and in a cannibalistic natural time [exploited by capitalism fetishistically]) could well suit Adorno's no-tion of mimesis, or preemptive reification.

8. At the Gallery J in Paris, Spoerri exhibited 723 kitchen gadgets mounted on ten wood supports. For a brief discussion of Spoerri's articles in *Gastronopti-kum* (now collected at the Archive Spoerri in Bern), see Christian Besson, "Daniel Spoerri Gastrosophe," in *Restaurant Spoerri* (Paris: Galerie Nationale du Jeu de Paume, 2002), 9.

9. Spoerri borrows the term *petrification* from his pantomime teacher, De-croux, who compared pantomime with petrification. For Spoerri, the trap-paint-ing traps a chance-instant of time and the disorder time creates on a table: the disorder of order that one notices only when time and movement are frozen, as in pantomime.

10. For a quick introduction to the movement known as *informel*, see David Hopkins, *After Modern Art: 1945–2000* (Oxford: Oxford University Press, 2000), 17–19. For a different interpretation of *art informel* and its critique, see Yves Alain Bois and Rosalind Krauss, *Formless: A User's Guide* (New York: Zone Books, 1999), 138–46. For Jouffroy, Spoerri's Saturnine vision was also atypical within nouveau réalisme, a loose formation of artists including Spoerri. According to

Restany, the official and founder critic of new realism, the movement had a strong, solar approach to the real. Restany was the critical voice of the group from its inception on October 27, 1960. See Kristine Stiles and Peter Selz, eds., *Theories and Documents of Contemporary Art: A Sourcebook of Artists' Writings* (Berkeley: University of California Press, 1996), 284.

11. The reference is to the contemporaneous *Ecole du Régard,* associated with Alain Robbe-Grillet's nouveau roman and his collaborations with the filmmaker Alain Resnais. In these years the films of the French nouvelle vague were shown. Among the directors or auteurs figured were Resnais, Eric Rohmer, Jean-Luc Godard, Claude Chabrol, Roger Vadim, Louis Malle, Jacques Rivette, and François Truffaut. The auteurs' critical views about the specificity of film as medium were published in the film magazine *Cahiers du Cinéma.* Accordingly, the cinema does not need to recur to symbols, metaphors, allusions because the cinema "shows" reality (Giovanna Grignaffini, ed., *La pelle e l'anima: Intorno alla nouvelle vague* [Florence: La Casa Usher, 1984], xxix).

12. See also François Dagognet, "Pourquoi l'objet, mais surtout pourquoi l'objet usé, délabré?" *Opus International* 110 (September–October 1988): 57.

13. The motif of death is present throughout Spoerri's career; note in particular his *Dorotheanum,* also known as "The Non-Profit Institute for Suicide" (1964). On this occasion, the audience was invited to make use of the instruments on display to self-inflict death, if they so wished. (Spoerri notes that nobody took advantage of this opportunity.) The viewers were asked to participate in this exhibition, as it were, by fast-forwarding time's consumption of life and by intervening in such an act of consumption. Especially Spoerri's *natures mortes,* which in his definition were assisted trap-paintings in the style of Duchamp's assisted readymades, presented death physically. They exhibited mounted bones and actual corpses of cats, birds, and other animals. Finally, Spoerri produced a series of photographs portraying victims of a violent death. This series was the "deadly" version of the previous, innocuous *Détrompe-l'oeils.*

14. In *Daniel Spoerri: Catalogue anecdoté de seize oeuvres de l'artiste de 1960 à 1964* (Geneva: Galerie Bonnier, 1981), Spoerri writes: "These objects, these landscapes of death, death's palace" (2).

15. Spoerri prefers to underscore the connections between his concrete poetry — the invention of words and stream of thoughts from sheer variations of letter combinations — and Eat Art, than those between Eat Art and dance, for example. This is so because Spoerri does not consider his work prior to Symi (even when it includes the Restaurant Galleries) part of the Eat Art project proper. His position is arguable, although ascribing most of the principles he explored to Eat Art also runs the risk of oversystematizing his work, a criticism to which this chapter is subject.

16. Daniel Spoerri, *Anekdotomania: Daniel Spoerri über Daniel Spoerri* (Basel: Museum Jean Tinguely and Hatje Cantz Verlag, 2001), 239.

17. These landscapes of death are here read as liminal sites where the subject

confronts death as necessary limit. From Bataille's perspective, death is always connected with life and its exuberance through orgasm, the "little death" of the subject at the core of life.

18. I use the term *punctual* to mean an event that manifests itself as instant rupture and is presumed to be perceived as such at the instant of its appearance. Foster opposes the punctual to the *nachträglich,* or the deferred action, a series of relays through which only one comes to identify historical ruptures or moments. See Foster, *Return of the Real.*

19. *Décollage* was a practice developed in the early 1950s by Raymond Hains and Jacques de la Villeglé (the latter stopped collaborating with the former already in 1954). The *décollagistes* did not make their own art; rather, they put on view the anonymous but public gesture of tearing, a gesture interpreted as resisting commercial or political advertisement. These artists captured a gesture of defacing that is spontaneous. Their work differed from both abstraction and *informel,* and also from the cubist collage and the readymade. While Schwitters (Merz) composed his collages with urban waste (at times fabricated waste) and Duchamp selected one manufactured object — through the principle of indifference — the *décollagistes* relied on the spontaneity of an anonymous gesture against a public object, against public display. See *1960: Les nouveaux réalistes* (Paris: Musée d'Art Moderne de la Ville de Paris, 1986), 56. See also Arturo Schwarz, "De la poétique Duchampienne à celle du nouveau réalisme," in *Le nouveau réalisme: Conférence et colloques* (Paris: Galerie Nationale du Jeu de Paume, 1998), 33. Wolf Vostell was a major proponent of the European happening and Fluxus. He was the German theoretician of *décollage,* which for him became a total principle of art and life, as is apparent in his 1963 manifesto. Here *décollage* encompasses activities such as digesting, defecating, feeling pain, collapsing alongside living, analyzing, and being *décollaged.* See the catalog of the exhibition curated by Ulrich Fickel, *Vostell: Leben = Kunst = Leben* (Gera: Kunstgalerie Gera, 1993–94), 13.

20. The term "willed poverty" comes from Deleuze and Guattari (*Minor Literature,* 18-19): they illustrate the two ways in which the German language is "rendered" minor by Jewish writers, such as Max Brod and Kafka. While Brod "artificially enrich[es] this German, to swell it up" and in so doing attempts to reterritorialize it symbolically, Kafka goes the other way: "He will opt for the German language of Prague as it is and in its very poverty." I argue that this is the kind of willed poverty and deterritorialization practiced in the language of the avant-garde as it informs Spoerri's "trap-paintings" and, later, his banquets. On poverty and deterritorialization of language, see also Deleuze and Guattari on Godard (23).

21. See *Catalogue anecdoté,* 11.

22. Branden Joseph demonstrates that the neo-avant-garde differs from the avant-garde because it posits difference — or nonidentity — positively. For Joseph, the neo-avant-garde opens up new possibilities for art after the avant-garde because it rejects the punctual dimension of shock. In contrast, neo-avant-garde art favors a temporality of perpetual becoming — of what is always in the making,

rather than the aesthetics of the made. Within this Bergsonian time—as duration—shared in particular by Cage and Robert Rauschenberg, Joseph identifies a concept of difference as affirmation or one of "affirming difference" that dissolves the absolute negation of the historical avant-garde and the autonomy of modernist "painting." Rauschenberg's collage—not unlike Spoerri's trap-paintings, albeit in different ways—allows for "the possibility (or impossibility) of an integral, experiential relationship to history and memory in the era of burgeoning late-twentieth century capitalism" (Branden W. Joseph, *Random Order: Robert Rauschenberg and the Neo-Avant-Garde* [Cambridge, Mass.: MIT Press, 2003], 131).

23. The collage had been widely accepted as art by 1960: for example, a major retrospective had already been devoted to Schwitters in Hannover in 1956.

24. Spoerri states: "Art is what artists make. If artists cook, then the critics must bring the artist's products closer to the public" (quoted in Ewa Esterhazy, *Das gastronomische Theater des Daniel Spoerri* [Vienna: University of Vienna, 1997], 94).

25. For a discussion of Spoerri's journal, see Cecilia Novero, "Daniel Spoerri's 'Invention of Tradition': Symi and Eat Art," in *Daniel Spoerri Presents Eat Art*, catalog (in German) of the exhibition at Aktionsforum Praterinsel curated by Elizabeth Hartung (Munich, 2001), 64–75. See also the English translation of the journal *The Mythological Travels of a modern Sir John Mandeville, being an account of the Magic, Meatballs, and other Monkey Business Peculiar to the Sojourn of Daniel Spoerri upon the Isle of Symi, together with divers speculations thereon*, translation and introduction by Emmett Williams (New York: Something Else, 1970).

26. There is a historical tradition of homonyms in gastronomy. To name dishes after famous characters became a typical practice in the nineteenth century. Carême, but especially Escoffier, cooked special dishes for important historical figures or named dishes after them. For more details on this history and its relation to Spoerri, see Esterhazy, 135.

27. On Raymond Hains, see *1960 Les Nouveaux Réalistes* (Paris: Musée d'Art Moderne de la Ville de Paris, 1986), 232–34.

28. Daniel Spoerri, "Zu den Fallenbildern" (December 1960), *zero 3* (1961), quoted in *Theories and Documents of Contemporary Art*, 310; translation slightly modified.

29. The phrase, which comes from Benjamin, was appropriated most famously by Benedict Anderson. For a good illustration of its meanings, see Gautam Ghosh, introduction to "Partition, Unification, Nation: Imagined Moral Communities in Modernity," special issue, *Social Analysis* 42, no. 1 (1998): 3–15.

30. The first edition of the book came out in 1962, for a Spoerri exhibition at the Galerie Lawrence in Paris. His friends edited the volume separately and at different times and constantly added new comments, discrepant observations, drawings, and so forth.

31. *Petit Lexique, sentimental autour de Daniel Spoerri*, ed. André Kamber, Hans Saner, Jean Paul Ameline (Solothurn: Musée des Beaux-Arts, 1990), 83.

32. My references to Deleuze and Guattari's principle of deterritorialization and to minor literature are not always consistent with the complexity of their theoretical system. I adopt the terms to point out that Spoerri's approach to food/eating means, on the one hand, a confrontation with the major discourses of modernism and gastronomy from the position of both neo-avant-garde's minority and especially of Eat Art as the neo-avant-garde's own minority, in the 1960s and 1970s. On the other hand, the trap-paintings function, in the realm of art, very much like "writing" for Derrida, or as deconstructed *bricolage*. They question territoriality without ever overcoming it: hence their frequent reterritorialization. Most importantly, my own "indisciplined" (Foster) or heterogeneous assemblage of theoretical models, which may sound incompatible (such as Bataille, Lévi-Strauss, Barthes, Derrida, and Deleuze and Guattari), is itself intended to uproot the readings of food in art and literature. So, for instance, Derrida's notion of *différance* helps me bring back the temporality of relays and deferral that is crucial for examining the avant-garde and neo-avant-garde and that risks being elided in the theories of flight (and on flight) proposed by Deleuze and Guattari. These theoreticians were contemporaries of Spoerri, and he, an avid reader, was and is abreast of most cultural theoretical discourses.

33. The family's triadic structure — also at the grounds of capitalism — is the most evident social form of oedipalization. Here the child's desires shift from the mother's pre-oedipal realm to the symbolic paternal function, where they stabilize. Deleuze and Guattari elaborate their notion of schizophrenia against oedipalization in *Anti-Oedipus: Capitalism and Schizophrenia* (Minneapolis: University of Minnesota Press, 1990), but they also elaborate more briefly the same motif in their analysis of Kafka's anti-oedipal letter to the father in *Minor Literature*.

34. Spoerri speaks of a "before" and "after" Symi and of a break; thus here he would reject my reading.

35. Quoted in *Du*, special issue, *Le musée vecu de Daniel Spoerri* 1 (January 1989): 58.

36. The notion of taking off — as it related to the page — was not just Spoerri's. Williams embraces his own form of deterritorialization of genres and language. With regard to his "Alphabet Symphony" (1962), Williams writes that he calls this work a symphony, "although it is a poem, of course. A poem that *gets off* the page." See Emmett Williams, *My Life in Flux — and Vice Versa* (London: Thames and Hudson, 1992), 59.

37. Spoerri comments in the *Gastronomic Journal* on the different etymologies of "Symi" and "Simian." However, the homophony and the misunderstanding it provokes, added to the fact that in this book he underscores etymology as a Dada enterprise altogether, concedes a humorous appropriation of the word games between the two.

38. On the relation between the ethnosyncretic objects (1986) and the "Objects of Magic à la Noix," see Hans Saner, "Zur politischen Dimension von Daniel Spoerris Objektkunst," *Daniel Spoerri: Werke 1960–2001* (Bielefeld: Kerber Verlag, 2001), 14–15.

39. The Destruction in Art Symposium was organized in London by the German-born Jewish immigrant Gustav Metzger already in 1961. Many Fluxus artists partook in it. Fluxus artists carried out destructive performances often on musical instruments. Among such events, Nam June Paik's *One for Violin Solo,* in which a violin was slammed down on the floor, best illustrates Deleuze and Guattari's concept of abolition in Kafka. They speak of "a deterritorialized musical sound, a cry that escapes signification, composition, sound, words, a sonority that ruptures in order to break away from a chain that is still too signifying. . . . Thus, in the *Trial,* the monotone cry of a warder who is being punished 'did not seem to come from a human being, but from a martyred instrument'" (*Minor Literature,* 6). The year 1961 is also the year of Jean Tinguely's *Homage to New York,* in which an assemblage of auto-destructive machines put itself to death by fire. Finally, César had produced his first scandalous cars' compressions in 1960. Piero Manzoni—who used his body, and others', to produce immaterial art objects, such as his *Artist's Breath,* filled ninety cans of *Merda d'Artista* (*Artist's Shit*) in 1961. Later, in 1966, John Latham, an assemblage artist based in London, organized a meeting with his students from St Martin's School of Art in London to chew up—for real—Clement Greenberg's book *Art and Culture.* Here an iconic figure of art criticism, who upheld the aesthetic of high modernism and the autonomy of art, was literally made to mix and transform—to be contaminated—with the *Fluxus* of an artist's body, as well as with Greenberg's readers' bodies (namely, the students in question). Spoerri's trap-paintings and then, more evidently, his Eat Art banquets—especially *L'ultima cena* (1970)—eat the avant-garde less with an iconoclastic impulse than from within the paradigms of multiplication and proliferation.

40. Foster defines the parallax as "the apparent displacement of an object due to the actual movement of its observer." This is important mostly because this notion shifts "the terms of these definitions [of the past, he means] away from a logic of avant-gardist transgression toward a model of deconstructive (dis)placement, which is far more appropriate to contemporary practices" (*Return of the Real,* xii).

41. These machines or sculptures that themselves paint (thus meta-matic) demonstrated Tinguely's critical position with regard to abstract lyrical painting (abstract expressionism). At the exhibition of Meta (July 1, 1959, in Paris) a competition for the best meta-matic drawing was announced. Tzara viewed in this experiment the final consecration of Dada and the end of painting. Duchamp, who was in Paris for the presentation of Robert Lebel's book devoted to himself, collaborated on a drawing with Meta-matic number 8. Some observers noted that in 1915, a donkey known as Lolo (alias Boronali, an excessivist painter) had already painted *Sunset on the Adriatic Sea* by immersing its tail in several pots of colors. Yet what one witnesses with Tinguely is not the metamorphosis of man into animal but that from the animal as pure "intensity," as pure desire, into the proliferation of machines. This metamorphosis also constitutes the Deleuzian idea of assemblages. As Deleuze and Guattari note, Kafka also gradually moves from his animal stories of deterritorialization (from animal becoming) to stories involving things and

objects (also writing machines), which first act and then in the novels dismantle themselves. See *Minor Literature*, 43–52.

42. On Food, the restaurant established by Gordon Matta-Clark, see the catalog of the exhibition Food, ed. Klaus Bussmann and Markus Müller (New York: White Columns, 1999), especially 16–17.

43. See Foster's comments in the roundtable discussion "Art of Mid-Century," in *Art since 1900: Modernism, Antimodernism, Postmodernism*, ed. Hal Foster, Rosalind Krauss, Yve-Alain Bois, and Benjamin H. D. Buchloh (New York: Thames and Hudson, 2004), 322.

44. *Sammlung Karl Gerstner* (Bremen: Neues Museum Weserburg, 1991), 15.

45. *Cnacharchives: Daniel Spoerri* (Paris: Centre National d'Art Contemporain, 1972), 76. Spoerri defined quite rigorously the notion of the multiple, which was to be made in accordance with the certificate of authenticity. The multiple could be reproduced and changed by someone other than the artist, but he or she was bound by the idea in question. On this Spoerri disagreed with George Maciunas. See *Petit Lexique*, 50, 51. On Spoerri's idea of the multiple, see also Dieter Roth in Daniel Spoerri, *An Anecdoted Topography of Chance*, ed., trans., and annotated by Robert Filliou, Emmett Williams, Dieter Roth, and Roland Topor (London: Atlas, 1995), 70. Here Roth defines the multiples and the principle of multiplication as based in transformation and movement. Thus Roth distinguishes it from other kinds of so-called multiplication, which instead are forms of reproductions of the same. Roth produced an amazing quantity of food-multiples, some of which he also exhibited at the Eat Art Gallery.

46. See Georges Bataille, "The Notion of Expenditure," in *Visions of Excess: Selected Writings,* ed. Allan Stoekl (Minneapolis: University of Minnesota Press, 1985), 116–29. See, especially, the following remarks: "Now it is necessary to reserve the use of the word *expenditure* for the designation of these unproductive forms, and not for the designation of all the modes of consumption that serve as means to the end of production. Even though it is always possible to set the various forms of expenditure in opposition to each other, they constitute a group characterized by the fact that in each case the accent is placed on a *loss* that must be as great as possible in order for that activity to take on its true meaning" (118).

47. For thorough analyses of Roth's work, see *Dieter Roth: Books and Multiples,* ed. Dirk Dobke (London: Edition Hansjörg Mayer, 2004). On "Multiples," see 15–18. See also *Sammlung Karl Gerstner,* 38.

48. I define in/edible those multiples that are either made with edible ingredients but are not necessarily eaten or edible, or made with edible ingredients and are indeed eaten. In certain cases, edibility remains as an undecided/undecidable quality of the food-multiples. A work that *is* also food and thus operates like a dish is never fully complete as a work of art, until it leaves the artist's and the exhibition's space–time, that is, the art world.

49. See Arthur Danto, "Museums and the Thirsting Millions," in *After the End of Art: Contemporary Art and the Plea of History* (Princeton, N.J.: Princeton University Press, 1997), 175–90.

50. I use the term "philosophical age" to mean the period of aesthetic

investigations first, since Kant, and second, since postaesthetic art, the latter related to the avant-garde and "post-Duchampian" art.

51. Marcel Broodthaers was a great master of assemblages, installations, and photographs with shells (egg shells and mussels), which he used in numerous works. Broodthaers, like Spoerri (and in a different way like Hans Haacke), investigated art through language: the language of art forms, language in general, and the language of the institution (museums especially). Through his use of mussels in particular (the national dish in Belgium), he visualizes, without representing, the condition of reification and emptying out of art (and of the conditions for the subject's presence) in consumer society. For good insights into this artist, see *October* 42, *Marcel Broodthaers: Writings, Interviews, Photographs* (Autumn 1987). See also the catalog *Marcel Broodthaers* (Minneapolis: Walker Art Center, 1989).

52. See chapter titled "Shellfish and Oyster stalls," in "Marseilles," in Benjamin, *Reflections*, 134–35. Benjamin opposes oysters to seashells frozen into kitschy souvenirs. He illustrates how the desire to be enmeshed with these "quivering creatures," the oysters, changes — on the other side of the quay — into the "mountain range of 'souvenirs,' the mineral hereafter of seashells." This hereafter does not erase the quivering creatures, which are buried in the souvenirs (memory) and threaten to become alive, liberating, according to Benjamin, the desire trapped in the commodity fetish.

53. See *Daniel Spoerri: La messa in scena degli oggetti*, ed. Sandro Parmiggiani (Milan: Skira, 2004), 25–26. Spoerri made several bread objects with shoes, and used shoes in other works unrelated to Eat Art.

54. See Fredric Jameson, *Postmodernism, or, The Cultural Logic of Late Capitalism* (Durham, N.C.: Duke University Press, 1991), 6-16. On Van Gogh's "original" shoes, see Jacques Derrida, "Restitutions of the Truth in Pointing," in *A Derrida Reader: Between the Blinds*, ed. Peggy Kamuf (New York: Columbia University Press, 1991), 279–309. This is a dialogue on Van Gogh's shoes among Heidegger, Meyer Schapiro, and other voices. "Pointing" refers to the French "pointure," the meanings of which are given in the epigraph to Derrida's text.

55. It is unclear, from Spoerri's accounts, whether Filliou was forced to leave Copenhagen because of a missing residence permit or whether he simply decided to return to Paris and live there with his Danish wife. The suddenness of his departure suggests, in Spoerri's version of the story, that he had to leave. Or, at least, that he had no money to "move," thus leaving behind parts of his house furniture and possessions, which Spoerri then traps and exhibits at Koepcke's.

56. The *informe* is not to be confused with *informel, tachisme,* and abstract expressionism. Spoerri, like most nouveaux réalistes, reacted against *informel* art (in Tapié's interpretation). See Spoerri's own statement in *La messa in scena degli oggetti*, 27.

57. Mary Douglas, *Purity and Danger: An Analysis of the Concepts of Pollution and Taboo* (London: Routledge and Kegan Paul, 1966).

58. Umberto Eco, "Sur Arman," in *Arman* (Paris: Galerie Nationale du Jeu de Paume, 1998), 12–13; my translation.

59. Walter Benjamin, "Theses on the Philosophy of History," in *Illuminations,*

256. Benjamin's exact phrase is "There is no document of civilization which is not at the same time a document of barbarism."

60. Betty Stocker, "Eat Art Multiples," in *Daniel Spoerri Presents Eat Art,* ed. Elisabeth Hartung (Nuremberg: Verlag für moderne Kunst, 2001), 109. Previously quoted in *Du,* 58.

61. Heidi E. Violand-Hobi, *Daniel Spoerri* (Munich: Prestel, 1998), 58.

62. At the origins of the restaurant in Düsseldorf was another project. Spoerri had wanted to open a restaurant in Omaha, Nebraska, and devote it entirely to tripe. He and his collaborator wanted to call it "Guts Buckets." Spoerri failed to find funding, and the project failed. The idea of a restaurant had occupied Spoerri's mind since 1962. Stocker remarks that Spoerri took note of this idea in an unpublished text thus dated. See "Eat Art Multiples," 105. See also my comments on Tony Morgan's and Spoerri's film *Resurrection* — focused on the digestive tract — in *Daniel Spoerri Presents Eat-Art,* 72–73.

63. Ralf Beil, *Künstlerküche: Lebensmittel als Kunstmaterial von Schiele bis Jason Rhoades* (Cologne: Dumont, 2002), 193–94.

64. Quoted in *Wenn alle Künste untergehen die edle Kochkunst bleibt bestehen* (Amsterdam, 1971), 37. Many other "cannibalistic events" took place after this. For example, within the context of the Great Eat Art Festival in 1980 in Chalon sur Saone, several of the previous banquets were organized again, in addition to a few new ones. Another example was *Das Langschweinessen oder Die essbaren menschlichen Formen,* a banquet that also was part of the Grand Eat Art Festival. In this banquet, Spoerri played with a presupposed human atavistic pleasure in tasting human meat, a pleasure that, as Spoerri notes, transpires in all those edible miniature forms present in every culture, from Mexico to England. In his interpretation of cannibalism, Spoerri sounds both Freudian and materialist, à la Marvin Harris. Yet Spoerri underscores "desire" and "pleasure" rather than "need." He mentions that in the languages of primitive people the phrase "long pig" (*Langschwein*) is thought to mean human beings as favorite food, hence the title of Spoerri's banquet.

65. Entrails are Spoerri's favorite dish. Not only has he gathered recipes of innards to go into in his cookery books collection that Roland Topor illustrated (each volume is devoted to bodily parts that one can eat, heart, feet, brains, etc.), but also Spoerri's original project for the Restaurant was to focus only on tripes. The tripes return finally in the "Attrape tripes" in 1980.

66. For an insightful analysis of the museum today, see Allen S. Weiss, "Outside In: On the Problem of Demarginalization," in *Shattered Forms,* 1–59.

5. *Convivia* of the Neo-Avant-Garde

1. As pointed out in chapter 4, the term "willed poverty" derives from Deleuze and Guattari and their essay on minor literature. See *Minor Literature,* 18–19.

2. Quoted in Lucrezia De Domizio Durini, *Joseph Beuys: The Art of Cooking — La Cucina di Beuys* (Florence: Charta, 1999), 100.

3. Caroline Tisdall, *Joseph Beuys* (London: Thames and Hudson, 1979), 14; my emphasis. See also Tisdall, *Joseph Beuys: We Go This Way* (London: Violette Editions, 1998).

4. Hiltrud Oman, *Joseph Beuys: Die Kunst auf dem Weg zum Leben* (Munich: Wilhelm Heyne Verlag, 1998), 74.

5. See Elisabeth Hartung, "Comida, arte y comunicacion: La comida como nuevo modelo de recepcion artistica," in *Comer o no comer* (Salamanca: Centro de Arte de Salamanca, 2002), 75–83.

6. *Joseph Beuys: Jeder Mensch ist ein Künstler* (1979), film directed by Werner Krüger in 1979, distributed by Artemedia, Cologne, 1985 (60 minutes, color, sound); cited in *Joseph Beuys: Films et vidéos*, ed. Fabrice Hergott (Paris: Centre Georges Pompidou, 1994), 67.

7. Carin Kuoni, ed., *Energy Plan for the Western Man: Joseph Beuys in America* (New York: Four Walls Eight Windows, 1990), 32.

8. In his document "Foundation for the Rebirth of Agriculture: Presentation of the F.I.U. in Italy," Beuys illustrates his project for this university, a "phenomenologically open and tolerant alternative which principally sees a creative being in every man. . . . This is confirmed by the fact that concepts change each time that they are freed from their ideological wrapping and one gets to their phenomenological nucleus. Such a broadened concept of art is something very different from the traditional bourgeois concept. In fact, the latter is applied in the so-called 'artbusinesses' — primarily museums, galleries, and the art markets — and shapes the methodological activity of critics, art historians and, in a complementary fashion, the art education taught in schools. It appears evident to me that it is impossible to develop within these institutions an anthropological concept of art which relates to all men" (De Domizio Durini, 61). See also *Joseph Beuys: Par la présente, je n'appartiens plus à l'art* (Paris: L'arche, 1988), 30, 47, 50, 92.

9. Ralph Beil, *Künstlerküche: Lebensmittel als Kunstmaterial von Schiele bis Jason Rhoades* (Munich: Dumont, 2002), 214. Beil examines in detail Beuys's actions and work in relation to his use of food materials.

10. On the regression away from creativity of civilization and its move toward a focus on death, see his interview with Achille Bonito Oliva, in *Energy Plan for the Western Man*, 173–75.

11. On this difference, see *Art since 1900*, 482–83.

12. See Joseph Beuys, *1a gebratene Fischgräte* (Berlin: Edition Hundertmark, 1972), 26.

13. For a thorough description of this action, see Uwe M. Schneede, *Joseph Beuys: Die Aktionen* (Stuttgart: Gert Hatje Publishers, 1994).

14. "The situation on this Fortress square: it won't remain the same, so stiff, so hard, as it is now, don't you think? This is the reason for this nomadism, the nomadic habit in standing and . . . well, ultimately, one could say the nomadic character of sounds, it is that simple" (quoted in Schneede, 301; my translation).

15. Spoerri states: "As far as nutrition is concerned, two problems arise

immediately: what can I eat? And what can I not eat? What hurts me? And what does not? Here lies the distinction between good and bad, if you will. Here, with eating, one begins to distinguish between good and bad, in its smallest core. . . . If one were to say, what hurts me . . . now you have just exhibited what one does not consider edible, thus what is bad, garbage, which people throw out, but just a moment ago you said: 'I live on this garbage, my wife eats the meat, for instance. To make such a distinction, to decide over and over again what good and what bad is, is, well this is the task of . . . evolution'" (quoted in Beuys, *1a gebratene Fischgräte*, 37; my translation).

16. In this, Filliou may be compared also to Roth and his vast work, including his furniture pieces, but also his endless experimentations with printing and pressing an almost infinite variety of found materials, including food. The *bricoleur* in the two artists compels both to become designers.

17. In the introduction to *One-Dimensional Man: Studies in the Ideology of Advanced Industrial Society* (Boston: Beacon, 1964), Marcuse wrote: "Our society distinguishes itself by conquering the centrifugal social forces with Technology rather than Terror on the dual basis of an overwhelming efficiency and an increasing standard of living. To investigate the roots of these developments and examine their historical alternatives is part of the aim of a critical theory of contemporary society, a theory which analyzes society in the light of its used and unused or abused capabilities for improving the human condition" (x).

18. At most, it is reminiscent of some of James Rosenquist's paintings, in which America ambivalently presents itself as sugarcoated consumer world, offering its myths up for consumption. See, for example, *President Elect, 1960* ¼ where a woman's hands are caught in the act of breaking a slice of cake and, perhaps, offering it to the eager consumer of icons as of commodities, but especially the bleaker — and importantly later — *F 111* (1965) in which some of the spaghetti cans one found in other paintings by Rosenquist are here splattered into a messy mush next to a jet fighter and an atomic explosion.

19. Ben takes up and goes beyond Kafka's early-twentieth-century "Hunger Artist" who stages his vanishing for hungry viewers in an animal cage in a zoo. Ben starts where Kafka's hunger artist ends, with invisibility.

20. César compressed industrial products into "colorful" forms made of industrial scrap. He also used actual commodities, still in use, such as cars to make his compressions.

21. *Arman: Collected Works, 1958–64* (La Jolla, Calif.: La Jolla Museum of Contemporary Art, 1974), 194.

22. This was precisely the main character's route in Margaret Atwood's novel *The Edible Woman* (1968).

23. Arman at the end of the 1950s had recourse to artful destruction of objects, especially violins, which he smashed, sliced, or burnt. Arman once reflected: "A violin has a perfect form that nobody has been able to improve since the 18th century . . . almost feminine, it reminds me of those beautiful Cycladic idols." Arman calls the works that ensue from these aggressive gestures of destruction *colères* or,

roughly, tantrums. See Jan van der Marck, "Logician of Form/Magician of Gesture," in *Arman*, n.p., fn. 8.

24. On uncanny and the maternal in surrealism, see Foster, *Compulsive Beauty*, 202.

25. For example, human reproduction and its predicament (overpopulation, the third world, etc.) became the topic of a sarcastic short novel by Günter Grass published in 1980. Here he takes the occasion to ironize on the first world's preoccupations about the third world's overpopulation, a fear and preoccupation that justified — hypocritically — developmental interventions and standardization of cultural and economic standards. See Günter Grass, *Headbirths, or the Germans Are Dying Out* (San Diego: Harcourt Brace Jovanovich, 1990).

26. In an e-mail exchange (October 2009), Dirk Dobke wrote to me that some collectors exhibited the "Doll" with its legs up, either out of ignorance or because the top lid was missing, and perhaps to insist on its static condition ("aus statischen Gründen"). As he comments: "That the legs protrude up there, as if in desperation, is not bad." However, as Dobke added, "there is a normal position" for the exhibition; this is in his opinion "legs down," with the top part infused with chocolate.

27. See *Dieter Roth: Books + Multiples* (London: Edition Hansjörg Mayer, 2004), 17.

28. See *Roth Time: A Dieter Roth Retrospective,* ed. Theodora Vischer and Bernadette Walter, text by Dirk Dobke and B. Walter (New York: Museum of Modern Art/Lars Mueller Publishers, 2004), 116. The reader interested in Roth finds a good starting point for the study of his oeuvre in the above-cited catalog and in *Dieter Roth: Books + Multiples.* Most interesting, in addition to Roth's work with chocolate and spices that he presented at the Eat Art gallery, is his work with cheese.

29. During the exhibition held at the MoMA and P.S. 1 in New York, in 2004, Roth's kitchen/atelier — including his oven — was reconstructed so as to offer the visitor an idea of the procedures used by this artist in making his eclectic art, procedures that were as important for the works as the works themselves. See *Roth Time.*

30. On Narcissus, see Herbert Marcuse, *Eros and Civilisation: A Philosophical Inquiry into Freud* (New York: Beacon, 1966); *Eros e civiltà* (Turin: Einaudi, 1968), 190–91; my translation.

31. Quoted in *César,* ed. Daniel Abadie (Paris: Editions du Jeu de Paume and Gallimard, 1997), 228; my translation.

32. See Marcuse, *Eros and Civilization,* 169–70.

33. On globalization and art, see the collection of essays *Estetiche della globalizzazione,* ed. Achille Bonito Oliva and Anna Maria Nassisi (Rome: manifestolibri, 2000), especially Nassisi's contribution, "Postmodernism and Globalization: The Myth of Narcissus as Representation of Contemporary Cultural Identity," 119–36.

34. On Fluxus in general, see *Fluxus Codex,* 25. Precisely the filtering control Maciunas exercised over the definition (thus the boundaries) of Fluxus defeated

in part some of the strong collectivist features at the basis of this group of artists. On Maciunas's control and modifications of the "collaborative" works, see *Fluxus Codex*, 27, 38.

35. See Hendricks's explanation of how the archivists of Fluxus had to go about the classification of Fluxus objects and performances in *Fluxus Codex*, 25.

36. These meals resonate with Satie's "white meal" (see chapter 2).

37. Hannah Higgins, *Fluxus Experience* (Berkeley: University of California Press, 2002), 47. It is unlikely that food cans can be bought unlabeled, not even displaying the food they contained. It is more likely that the labels were simply torn out after the cans were purchased, as a picture of Vautier during the Festival d'Art Total et du Comportement held in Nice in 1963 shows. Maciunas, in his description, speaks of ready-made cans. As other photos indicate, subsequently the cans used were all relabeled in the same way, "Flux Mystery Food by Ben Vautier," making it impossible to recognize what they contained. So Ben writes: "In Nice, the contents of one of the boxes of cans at *The Provence* were lychees. They looked very curious" (*Fluxus Codex*, 507). The photo reprinted on this page and here shows an older unlabeled can and the later relabeled cans. Both presentations of the cans are called "packagings," suggesting an alteration of the "bought" or ready-made cans. Packaging was in the hands of Maciunas most of the times.

38. Julia Robinson, "The Sculpture of Indeterminacy: Alison Knowles's Beans and Variations," *Art Journal* 63, no. 4 (2004): 96–115. Robinson describes the *Bean Rolls* thus: "The work consisted of a found tea tin containing fourteen tiny paper scrolls with text describing all manner of details about beans—including people named Bean, proverbs and stories about beans, bean recipes and ads for L.L.Bean—accompanied by real (dried) beans. . . . Knowles was presenting the "Bean Rolls" as something to be read and experienced" (103). The encyclopedic nature of the word "bean" captured by the *Bean Rolls* returns, albeit differently, in Spoerri's Fluxus Project—that, however, remained unachieved as it had been originally conceived—which he called his "Eggcyclopedia," an open work made of all words and objects containing the term "Ei" (egg) in German.

39. Unfortunately, I could not verify anywhere whether Knowles's performance *Make a Salad* ever involved the consumption of food by the audience, the workers involved, the artist herself, in either the private or the public space.

40. Robinson, in "Sculpture of Indeterminacy," illustrates Knowles's revival of *Make a Salad* in 2003 as part of the touring exhibition Work Ethic in Baltimore (1). She explains that the main difference between the 1962 event and the most recent version of it was its musical frame. In Robinson's opinion, by framing her everyday music within a conventional musical setting, understood by all as "classical" music (Mozart), both the musical elements of her own score and the disruptive elements in it came to light, without "sounding" purely destructive. In my view, Knowles's choice seems to imply that temporal difference is made more visible through its immersion in the dominant paradigms of culture, that is, the culture of the spectacle and aestheticization of the everyday in which we are immersed. The past (of Fluxus in this case) returns in the present as this present's otherness, an otherness

carved in the now rather than as an antecedent. The latter would be a historical piece that cannot be read or experienced any longer. Instead the "new" one is integral (yet not assimilated) to the present by pointing to itself in new ways – and certainly not as shocking surprise. The question remains whether by framing the score within classical music, in fact, the piece loses its abrasiveness.

41. Manzoni, quoted in "Prolegomena for an Artistic Activity," in *Piero Manzoni*, ed. Germano Celant (London: Serpentine Gallery 1998), 68.

42. See Giorgio Agamben's quote from *Stanze* in *Manzoni*: "Art 'has no other option but to become invisible: we who with part of our being partake of invisibility have at least a small share in it and we can increase our holding of invisibility during our sojourn on earth'" (276).

43. Michel Foucault, *Ceci n'est pas une pipe* (Montpelier: Scholies Fata Morgana, 1973).

44. Much classical and modern art has taken eggs as its subject and medium. Most recently an Italian chef, Carlo Cracco, has published a book devoted to the egg in which he surveys philosophical, musical, artistic, and mathematical (geometric) theories and histories. See *The Squaring of the Egg* (Casalnoceto: Editoriale Fernando Folini, 2004). See also "An Interview with Carlo Cracco: The Squaring of the Egg," http://venturabroadcast.com/index.php?page=vb01-2_en.

45. Because of their engagement with the temporality of sculpture and with the introduction of mobility in sculpture, Oldenburg's mock food-icons approach the in/edible Eat Art multiples. These soft food sculptures, however, are no different than other soft sculptures, for example, his soft *snickers*. Indeed, Oldenburg's art is a general comment about consumption as consumerism, the encroach of consumption on consumerism, at large (see *Art since 1900*, 454–55).

Conclusion

1. For a good definition of publicity in the avant-garde–neo-avant-garde world, see Frazer Ward, "The Haunted Museum: Institutional Critique and Publicity" *October* 73 (Summer 1995): 71–89. There he writes: "Publicity is referred to in this context as the medium, not only for art, but for all those practices of intervention in economies of cultural production and reception that go to realize conceptions of the public sphere. Publicity in this sense includes not only the familiar forms of corporate advertising and state propaganda, but such apparently diverse cultural practices as, for example, museum exhibitions; conceptually based art, to the extent that it interrogates the institutional construction of subjects; academic journals and trade union publications, to the extent that they constitute reading publics, and political demonstrations, [etc.]" (72). What these have in common is their potential to give rise to debates and opinions.

2. For this (p. 164) and other quotations from Kinmont and Tiravanija, see Laura Trippi, "Untitled Artists' Projects by Janine Antoni, Ben Kinmont, Rirkrit Tiravanija," in *Eating Culture*, ed. Ron Scapp and Brian Seitz (Albany: State University of New York Press, 1998), 132–60.

3. Antoni also clearly refers to Joseph Beuys's *Mouth Sculptures*. However,

while Beuys, in these pieces, focused on impressing (*Hineindrücken*) and shaping matter — fat — with his teeth, Antoni disintegrates and deforms her initially sculpted cubes. For Beuys's *Mouth Sculptures,* see Eva Hubert, *Joseph Beuys: Hauptstrom und Fettraum* (Darmstadt: Verlag Jürgen Häusser, 1993), 24.

4. Monika Wagner, *Das Material der Kunst: Eine andere Geschichte der Moderne* (Munich: Verlag Beck, 2001), 232.

INDEX

CECILIA NOVERO is lecturer of German and European studies at the University of Otago in New Zealand.